UNSHACKLING AMERICA

ALSO BY WILLARD STERNE RANDALL

Ethan Allen: His Life and Times

Alexander Hamilton: A Life

Thomas Jefferson: A Life

Benedict Arnold: Patriot and Traitor

A Little Revenge: Benjamin Franklin and His Son

Building Six: Tragedy at Bridesburg (with Stephen D. Solomon)

Founding City (with David R. Boldt)

Thomas Chittenden's Town (with Nancy Nahra)

American Lives (with Nancy Nahra)

Forgotten Americans (with Nancy Nahra)

UNSHACKLING
AMERICA

HOW THE WAR OF 1812 TRULY ENDED
THE AMERICAN REVOLUTION

WILLARD STERNE RANDALL

ST. MARTIN'S PRESS   NEW YORK

www.stmartins.com

Designed by Kelly S. Too

Library of Congress Cataloging-in-Publication Data

Names: Randall, Willard Sterne, author.
Title: Unshackling America : how the War of 1812 truly ended the American Revolution /
    Willard Sterne Randall.
Description: First edition. | New York : St. Martin's Press, 2017.
Identifiers: LCCN 2017004246| ISBN 9781250111838 (hardback) | ISBN 9781250111845 (e-book)
Subjects: LCSH: United States—History—War of 1812—Causes. | United States—History—
    Revolution, 1775–1783. | United States—History—1783–1815. | Free trade—Political aspects—
    United States—History. | Free trade—Political aspects—Great Britain—History. | United
    States—Foreign economic relations—Great Britain. | Great Britain—Foreign economic
    relations—United States. | Merchant marine—United States—History. | International
    trade—History. | World politics—To 1900. | BISAC: HISTORY / United States / Revolutionary
    Period (1775–1800). | HISTORY / Revolutionary.
Classification: LCC E354 .R36 2017 | DDC 973.5/2—dc23
LC record available at https://lccn.loc.gov/2017004246

Our books may be purchased in bulk for promotional, educational, or business use. Please
contact your local bookseller or the Macmillan Corporate and Premium Sales Department at
1-800-221-7945, extension 5442, or by e-mail at MacmillanSpecialMarkets@macmillan.com.

First Edition: June 2017

10 9 8 7 6 5 4 3 2 1

Dedicated to the memory
of my brother
James Fairbanks Randall
United States Merchant Marine Academy
Class of 1978

CONTENTS

The people of America had been educated in an habitual affection for England as their mother country, and while they thought her a kind and tender parent . . . no affection could be more sincere. . . . But when Americans discovered that the mother country was willing, like Lady Macbeth, to "dash their brains out," it is no wonder if their filial affections ceased, and were changed into indignation and horror.

John Adams to Henry Niles, February 13, 1818

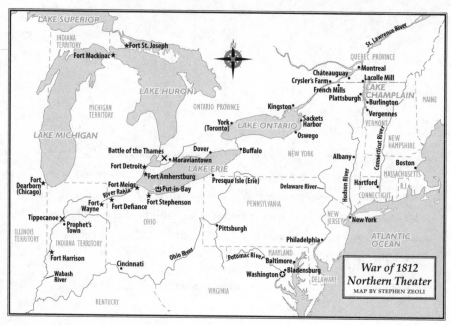

LAKE SUPERIOR

INDIANA
TERRITORY

★ Fort St. Joseph

Fort Mackinac ★

LAKE HURON

MICHIGAN
TERRITORY

LAKE MICHIGAN

ONTARIO PROVINCE

St. Lawrence River

QUEBEC PROVINCE

Châteauguay
Crysler's Farm •
French Mills
Kingston •

Montreal •
Lacolle Mill •

LAKE
CHAMPLAIN

Plattsburgh

Sackets
Harbor

York
(Toronto) •

LAKE ONTARIO

Oswego •

Burlington •

Vergennes •

VERMONT

MAINE

NEW
HAMPSHIRE

Battle of the Thames
Fort Detroit ★
× Moraviantown
★ Fort Amherstburg
Fort Meigs ★
River Raisin
Fort Defiance ★
Fort Stephenson

Dover •

Buffalo •

Presque Isle (Erie) •

NEW YORK

Albany •

Connecticut River

Hudson River

Boston •

MASSACHUSETTS

Hartford •

CONNECTICUT

R.I.

Fort
Dearborn
(Chicago)

Fort
Wayne ★

Put-in-Bay

OHIO

Delaware River •

PENNSYLVANIA

NEW
JERSEY

• New York

ATLANTIC
OCEAN

Tippecanoe ×
• Prophet's
Town

ILLINOIS
TERRITORY

INDIANA TERRITORY

• Fort Harrison

Wabash
River

Cincinnati •

Ohio River

Pittsburgh •

Philadelphia •

KENTUCKY

VIRGINIA

Potomac River

Washington ⊕

Baltimore •
Bladensburg •

MARYLAND

DELAWARE

War of 1812
Northern Theater
MAP BY STEPHEN ZEOLI

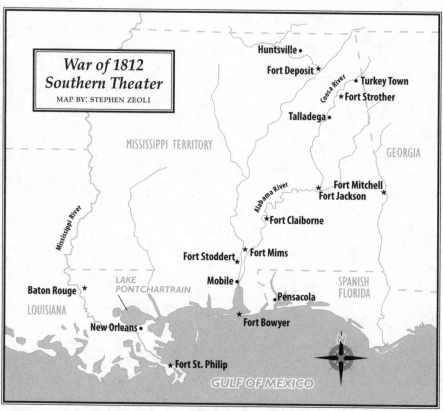

War of 1812
Southern Theater
MAP BY: STEPHEN ZEOLI

Huntsville •
Fort Deposit ★

Coosa River

• Turkey Town
★ Fort Strother

Talladega •

MISSISSIPPI TERRITORY

GEORGIA

Alabama River

Fort Mitchell ★
Fort Jackson ★

★ Fort Claiborne

Mississippi River

Fort Stoddert ★

★ Fort Mims

Baton Rouge ★

LAKE
PONTCHARTRAIN

Mobile •

• Pensacola

SPANISH
FLORIDA

LOUISIANA

New Orleans •

★ Fort Bowyer

★ Fort St. Philip

GULF OF MEXICO

UNSHACKLING AMERICA

"A Glow of Patriotic Fire"

On April 25, 1806, three British men-of-war, *Leander, Cambrian* and *Driver*, were patrolling the entrance to New York harbor. All day, the sixty-gun frigate *Leander* had stopped every American ship, first lobbing a cannonball across its bow, the signal to heave to, be boarded and be searched for deserters from the Royal Navy and contraband from Britain's enemy, France. Toward evening, the Delaware coastal schooner *Richard*, hauling produce to market, was only a quarter mile offshore. Two eighteen-pound cannonballs suddenly erupted from *Leander*, one cutting across *Richard's* bow, the other arcing overhead. Immediately *Richard* hove to, waiting for the British boarding party. But then a third projectile, skipping along the surface, crashed through the schooner's taff rail, driving a large splinter through the neck of the helmsman John Pierce, decapitating him.

Pierce's brother somehow managed to steer the schooner to the city docks in lower Manhattan. As he carried his brother's headless body through the streets, an angry crowd gathered. They had watched helplessly as British boarding parties, in an illegal peacetime blockade, seized American vessels before sailing them off to Halifax to be condemned by a British Admiralty court and auctioned off, the proceeds divided among *Leander's* captain and crew. A crowd of volunteers commandeered two

British pilot vessels anchored at the wharf, overtook three British supply boats and forced them back to port, unloading their cargoes into carts for distribution among the city's poorhouses.

In front of the Tontine Coffee House, New York's incipient stock exchange, Pierce's corpse remained on display during days of rioting. Britain's consul-general hid in his house as a mob hurled stones through his windows. At Hardy's waterfront tavern, merchants blamed President Thomas Jefferson for failing to resist years of British interference with America's commerce. Like many Americans, they also blamed Jefferson for refusing to maintain a proper navy to protect America's burgeoning maritime trade. Irate citizens also organized a city militia.[1] The city's Common Council ordered Pierce's burial at public expense and, as American ships in the harbor flew their flags at half mast, as a body led thousands to the interment to honor the seaman whose death had brought to a head years of fruitless protests against Britain's attempts to stifle American trade.

When an express rider reached Washington City with Mayor DeWitt Clinton's dispatches, Jefferson ordered the *Leander* and her sister ships to "immediately & without any delay depart from the harbours & waters of the U.S." Even though the United States had won the Revolutionary War a generation earlier, Jefferson could do nothing now beyond issuing an empty decree that all British ships must leave American waters. After a hastily summoned New York grand jury indicted *Leander*'s captain, Henry Whitby for murder, Jefferson decreed that if Whitby were ever found again in American territory, he was to be arrested and returned to New York to face the charge. If British ships ignored Jefferson's executive order and continued to come into American waters, Americans were forbidden to pilot them into ports, sell them provisions or provide them with fresh water or "supplies of any kind." Jefferson called the stationing of British warships off Sandy Hook "an atrocious violation of our territorial rights."[2]

Jefferson must have known it was impossible to enforce his executive order. He had drastically downsized the navy, ordering its half dozen frigates into dry dock and replacing them with what naval officers called a "mosquito navy" of shallow-draft, poorly armed gunboats useful only close to shore.

Like fellow veterans of the Tripoli Wars, Navy commodore William

Bainbridge fumed at this latest affront. "How long must we bear these violations of our National honor, property, and loss of our fellow Citizens," he wrote to Captain Edward Preble. "O Lord! Grant us a more honorable Peace or a sanguinary war!"[3]

All along the Atlantic seaboard, as news spread of the latest British provocation, newspaper editors trumpeted calls for war. DeWitt Clinton later wrote, "I well remember the sensation excited by the murder of Pierce. It was a glow of patriotic fire that pervaded the whole community . . . from Georgia to Maine it was felt like an electrical shock."[4]

The *Leander* incident and the firestorm of anti-British resentment it ignited followed a quarter century of flare-ups in the struggle for the United States' economic independence from Britain and its survival as a sovereign nation. What neither Jefferson nor any other of America's founding generation could divine was that, even after the British imperial crisis that began with protests over illegal searches and seizures in Boston in 1761 and led to American military victory in 1783, what is commonly called the American Revolution constituted only the first phase of a far more protracted ordeal to achieve true independence. The Treaty of Paris of 1783 only halted the overt conflict of the Revolutionary War and granted political autonomy, but it did not guarantee American economic independence and agency. For fully three more contentious decades that led to another war—the War of 1812—Britain continued to deny the United States' sovereignty.

The second phase of the half-century-long struggle combined a domestic ideological crisis over American identity with unrelenting and ever-intensifying attempts by the British to stifle American trade and to starve her former colonies. From 1783 until combat resumed in 1812, the United States' weak central government and a military enfeebled by Jeffersonian political purges rendered the young nation's chance of survival dubious.

Ignoring their military failure in the Revolutionary War and the consequent treaty of peace, the British Parliament ratcheted up efforts to eliminate competition, first by re-invoking the colonial-era Navigation Act of 1756, requiring that all goods transported between British possessions or to and from England must be carried on British ships—"English goods in English bottoms." Banning long-existing trade between New England and its Canadian neighbor, the Navigation Act also barred long-flourishing commercial ties with British Caribbean colonies. Moreover, Britain insisted that its treaty allies, Spain and Portugal, embargo American trade and forbid trade with any of their three colonies. Britain also prohibited vital exports from England to the United States, including sheep, wool and woolens. All the while, in violation of the peace treaty, Britain refused to remove its troops from fortified trading posts around the Great Lakes and along the Canadian-American frontier. Throughout this perilous half century, the underlying cause of contention was America's right to free trade.

As the Napoleonic Wars spread over Europe in the 1790s, Britain, ignoring America's status as a sovereign nation, denied the United States' neutral maritime rights. Flouting the rights of American merchant-ship owners and sailors, as in the case of the *Leander*, the Royal Navy stopped, searched and seized ships on every ocean.

During the more than two decades of almost constant warfare in Europe that followed the French Revolution, Britain and France formed and realigned alliances. Attempting to blockade each other into submission, the combatants enmeshed the United States in rules aimed at preventing shipments to each other's enemy. Admiral Nelson's decisive victory over the French and Spanish fleets at Trafalgar in 1805 had forced Napoleon to abandon his dream of invading the British Isles, but the French emperor retaliated, setting out to destroy the British economy by cutting off its vital import-export trade with the Continent. In turn, Britain deployed its nine-hundred-ship navy, cordoning off Europe with a blockade that severed France from its overseas empire and high-handedly banning neutral nations from trading with French-controlled ports.

The War of 1812 came on by decrees. After Napoleon achieved a brilliant victory at Jena in 1806, he inaugurated his Continental System with the Berlin Decree, a blockade in reverse that closed all European ports to Britain and subjected all goods of British origin to confiscation. After his victory at Friedland in 1807, he extended the system to include Russia and the Baltic states. In January 1807 Britain responded to Napoleon by issuing Orders in Council that expanded its own blockade. The first of fourteen such orders in 1807 allowed the Royal Navy to control the European coastal trade by banning direct neutral trading with the ports of Britain's enemies. A subsequent order required neutral ships to call at British ports, unload for inspection, pay customs duties of 25 percent and purchase an expensive license before going on to enemy ports. Napoleon retaliated with his Milan Decree, extending to neutrals the embargo on goods destined for the ports of Britain and her allies, Spain and Portugal. He also ordered confiscation of any ship obeying Britain's Orders in Council.

All through the tempestuous 1790s and into the early nineteenth century, the United States had been dragged ever deeper into the worldwide conflict, not only exacerbating tensions between the United States and Britain but, after Robespierre beheaded Louis XVI and Marie Antoinette, dividing Americans' sympathies as well. Many southerners sympathized with the French while New Englanders, longtime enemies of the French in Canada, tended to side with their traditional North Atlantic trading partners.

Beyond cataclysmic battles on land and sea, a new and devastating form of economic warfare emerged. Invoking an evolving international doctrine of neutral maritime rights, America's seagoing merchants defied the new British restrictions, absorbing the bulk of the French Caribbean carrying trade as they developed the world's second largest merchant fleet. The American carrying trade increased fivefold between 1792 and 1807 as the United States became the world's largest neutral maritime power, helped along by the many seamen who deserted the Royal Navy, exchanging brutal, lifelong discipline for more lenient, limited tours of service on U.S. ships.

After the Royal Navy had resorted to blockading—an act of war according to international law—it stopped and searched some 400 American vessels, scouring them for British deserters, to maintain full complements aboard its blockading ships. By 1807, of the 55,000 American sailors involved in overseas trade, fully 40 percent had been born in England and Ireland. Britain refused to acknowledge the revolutionary American doctrine of naturalization. In all, the British impressed 9,991 American sailors between 1796 and 1812, by any measure the majority of them native-born Americans. The British assigned these men to convoy duty in the Indian Ocean, in effect imprisoning them, as they endured indefinite sentences under harsh naval discipline far from any chance of seeing their homes and families again.

In what Winston Churchill aptly called an "unofficial trade war," the

Leander incident was part of an escalating British campaign to snuff out commercial competition from England's upstart former colonies.[5]

Finally, as more Americans demanded that their government confront British policies, the American David declared war on the British Goliath in June 1812. From the foremasts of American frigates, banners proclaiming "Free Trade and Sailors' Rights" fluttered.

Amid the public clamor for war, onetime pacifist president Thomas Jefferson tried to explain America's determination, despite the overwhelming might of its former overlords, to persist in the lopsided hostilities. When she learned in July 1812 of America's declaration of war, Paris *saloniste* and diplomat Madame Germaine de Staël, Jefferson's old friend, wrote to the now former president protesting the United States' attack on Britain, which she deemed the "sole barrier" against the attempts of Napoleon to impose a "universal monarchy."[6] Jefferson secretly wrote back: "My dear Madam; the object of England is the *permanent dominion of the ocean*, and the *monopoly of the trade of the world*." Americans, he declared, refusing to revert to the status of Britain's colonial dependents, would continue to fight until the British stopped presuming that they still had the right to dictate where and with whom and what they could trade.[7]

—— ✦ ——

"Salutary Neglect"

The half-century-long struggle for American independence from Britain commenced almost immediately after a stunning series of British victories in the last French and Indian War, which itself had brought an end to a century and a half of chronic struggle for domination of North America. In London, all through the *annus mirabilis* of 1759, chiming church bells and booming Tower cannon proclaimed the arrival of every dispatch of a global British victory. Peace with the French promised peace with the Indians, removing the threat of attack from the entire 2,000-mile backcountry of the British-American colonies. With the French vanquished, settlers could surge across the Appalachians from overcrowded coastal colonies into the Ohio Valley and beyond to stake out land. Merchant-investors could now subdivide the forested, fur-rich empire, and trade with the Indians would be exceedingly lucrative.

For Britain's ruling class, the prospect was equally alluring. Long-anticipated rewards of a century of oppressive land taxes and humiliating loans would be incalculable. Breathlessly, Horace Walpole dashed off excited letters: "Victories come so tumbling over one another from distant parts of the globe that it looks like the handiwork of a London romance writer," he wrote to an intimate. To another, "The Romans were 300 years conquering the world. . . . We subdued [it] in three campaigns."[1]

To Britain's American colonists, money flowed. Convoys of ships crammed with luxury goods overflowed waterfront wharves, selling as fast as they could be unloaded. In New England alone sixteen shipyards employing a thousand artisans turned hardwood forests into craft to carry wares to the quarter million inhabitants from present-day Portland, Maine, north up to the St. John River to Quebec Province and west over the Berkshires to Lake Champlain.

Amid the jubilation, at 7:30 on the morning of October 25, 1760, seventy-seven-year-old King George II dropped dead, leaving to his grandson, George III, the world's largest modern empire. At Kew House, the unmarried Prince of Wales still lived with his mother, Princess Augusta, and his siblings. At twenty-two, he became the youngest monarch since Elizabeth I.

By nightfall, the tall, thin prince arrived at St. James Palace to confer with his grandfather's chief ministers. There, he received the obeisance of two archrivals: accipitrine William Pitt, the Great Commoner, a spellbinding orator who, as prime minister, had amalgamated British gold with Frederick the Great's Prussian steel; and the stoop-shouldered, obsequious Duke of Newcastle, master of forging Parliamentary majorities with royal bribes and government contracts.

In the customary year of interregnum before the new king's crowning, as courtiers jockeyed for tickets to the coronation, newspapers in America reverently reported the royal funeral:

> The Royal Body, carried by 12 Yeomen, was covered by a large Pall of purple Velvet and lined with purple silk, with a fine Holland Sheet, adorned with ten large Escutcheons of the Imperial Arms, Painted on Satin, under a Canopy of purple Velvet.[2]

Finding itself with a far-flung empire, the British Parliament plunged into a thorough review of its taxes in America. A glimpse at the national debt would have horrified any new minister and made him desperate for new revenues. According to the exchequer, it stood at a staggering £137 million, carrying annual interest of £5 million while the cost of administering the empire—including newly conquered territories—had ballooned to £8 million annually. Facing these immense war debts, the Ministry concluded that American colonists had profited most from war and should now begin to pay their fair share of the bills.

For nearly a century, since Parliament first passed a series of Acts of Navigation and Trade in 1663, British attempts at regulating colonial North America's maritime commerce had collided with the colonists' notion of their right to trade freely. The Acts, ratified at a time when global Dutch trade threatened to engulf British overseas commerce, mandated that any colonist-owned cargo must touch a port of England before being sold, no matter its destination. The first Act stated explicitly that no goods from Asia, Africa or America could be brought into England, Ireland or the colonies except in English ships crewed by a majority of Englishmen.

American colonists had found the thrust of the Act unequivocally threatening: they must buy all manufactured goods from or through Britain and were not free to establish their own manufacturing plants. In addition, in order to protect England's growers, the Mother Country would buy only a fraction of America's harvests. To further defend the profits of British merchants, Americans could export to Britain and to Britain alone certain "enumerated" commodities—and then only in British ships to British ports. But the Acts, fathered by Charles II at a time when England scarcely had a merchant fleet and its colonies none, remained little more than words on paper for nearly a century; British enforcement was haphazard at best and prohibitively costly.

A clever and careful status quo had existed almost since the settling of the first British colonies in North America in the early seventeenth century. Colonies in the West Indies depended on mainland North American colonies for imports such as horses, fish and flour, livestock and lumber, barrel staves and naval store—even the ships that brought them. In exchange, islanders provided mainland colonies with unlimited sugar and molasses to make rum. Yet the West Indies could not produce enough of these two basic commodities to keep pace with mainland colonial growth. British officials turned a blind eye as North America offset the shortfall by trading with the islands of rival Spanish, French and Dutch empires.

In peacetime, goods flowed freely between the West Indies and American mainland ports. The British home government remained content to make ample profits from manufactured goods—furniture, glass, fine clothing, wines, carriages—exported to the colonies by English factors. Despite creating a trade balance favorable to the British, Americans preferred British manufactured goods that were cheaper and better made than similar products of Europe. Cadwalader Colden, lieutenant governor of New York, observed that colonial merchants' profits seldom resided in that province for six months before being remitted to Britain and exchanged for luxury goods.

These *laissez-faire* practices, making up an unofficial British colonial policy of "salutary neglect," lasted until the 1730s. Then the British government, pressured by West Indian plantation owners who sat in Parliament, demanded a monopoly on the rich sugar trade. Asserting Parliament's right to regulate colonial trade, they forced through the Molasses Act of 1733. Provisional for five years, it was renewed over and over again. This new duty was steep—six pence to the gallon—too much for mainland merchants, who simply began to evade the duty, quickly devising systematic practices that circumvented it. What had been, a day before Parliament passed the Act, acceptable commercial practice had overnight become illegal. Previously legitimate merchants, if they did not abandon their businesses or face ruinous duties, now, in the eyes of the British, became smugglers.

Mainland merchants quickly learned that sugar and molasses could either be brought from French or Spanish ports directly to the mainland or brought by cynical British West Indian merchants, and illicit cargoes landed clandestinely along thousands of miles of American seacoast at a profit—or in port at a deep loss at the customhouse.

Thomas Hancock, father of Declaration of Independence signer John Hancock, sent instructions to his ships' captains in the Netherlands with cargoes bound for Boston to unload in Cape Cod. Evading customs duties, they shipped the goods overland to market in Boston. In New York, Governor Charles Hardy reported in 1757 that ships from Holland "stop at Sandy Hook [New Jersey] and smuggle their Cargoes to New York, and carry their Vessels up empty." When he tried to break up this trade, merchants quickly altered their route, "sending their Vessels to Connecticut"—and then smuggled their contraband into New York duty free.[3]

Captains landed partial cargoes surreptitiously at one destination, then, presenting false papers (secured by bribing Caribbean customs officials), they paid duties on the stated cargo in port to customs officers. Even without false papers, thinly stretched mainland customs collectors— there were never more than fifty at any time before 1760 for all of British America—could be bribed to overlook part of the shipment.

Great family fortunes—the Browns' of Rhode Island, the Hancocks' of Boston, the Trumbulls' of Connecticut, the Whartons' of Philadelphia— burgeoned in this perfectly corrupt system. Every Connecticut and Rhode Island shipper who dealt with the Spanish and French in the Caribbean in the molasses trade between 1733 and 1765 was a smuggler, at least according to Colonial Office records in London. *Nothing* was credited for these two colonies in an "account of all the duties collected under the Molasses Act," even while "of all northern provinces their industries were most dependent on the French sugar islands."[4]

As historian Arthur Meier Schlesinger put it,

> If any serious attempt had been made to enforce the statute, the prosperity of the commercial provinces would have been laid prostrate. It was the West Indian trade, more than anything else, which had enabled them to utilize their fisheries, forests and fertile soil, to build up their towns and cities, to supply cargoes for their merchant marine, and to liquidate their indebtedness to British merchants and manufacturers.[5]

Molasses, a staple of New England life, grew steadily in demand for cooking, home-brewing beer and, most important, making rum. By 1770 fully 143 distilleries in Rhode Island and Massachusetts produced 5 million gallons of rum a year. While many New Englanders preferred rum— sailors refused to work without their daily allowance—much of it went to Indians in exchange for furs. Much more fueled the Triangular Trade: barrels of rum from New England bought slaves on Africa's west coast. Shipped to the tobacco plantations of the southern mainland colonies and to the sugar plantations of the West Indies, slaves labored for life on plantations that earned their masters credits to purchase manufactured goods in England.

Tiny Newport, Rhode Island, earned a reputation as one of the greatest violators of British trade restrictions. Boasting twenty-two of the colony's thirty distilleries, Newport's merchants drew special recognition from British admiral John Montagu as "a set of lawless piratical people . . . whose sole business is that of smuggling and defrauding the King of his duties." While only a "trickle of revenue" reached the Crown to repay thirty-one years of effort to wring duties from New England merchants, merchant profits purchased an array of luxurious consumer goods from Britain: coffee and chocolates, tea, wine and brandy, silks and satins.

Defying the fundamental principle of British mercantile law—"English goods in English bottoms"—New England ship owners imported from Dutch Caribbean islands an even broader array of goods. William Bollan, Massachusetts' agent at Court, reported to the British Board of Trade and Plantations in London that the Dutch were furnishing British Americans with "Reels of Yarn or spun Hemp, paper, Gunpowder, Iron, Goods of various sorts used for Men's and Women's Clothing." Bollan worried that widespread scoffing at British trade restrictions "have already begun to destroy the Vital parts of the British commerce." He urged London officials to "do everything in our power towards cutting off this Trade So very pernicious to the British Nation":

> The persons concerned in this Trade are many, Some of them of the greatest Fortunes in this Country, and who have made great Gains by it, and having all felt the Sweets of it, they begin to Espouse and Justify it. Some openly some Covertly, and having perswaded [sic] themselves that their Trade ought not to be bound by the Laws of Great Britain, they labour, and not without success to poison the Minds of all the Inhabitants of the Province. . . ."[6]

By mid-century, New York's share of the West Indies trade surpassed Boston's and Philadelphia's, and rivaled its profits from the fur trade. Merchants shipped provisions to the British West Indies in exchange for sugar and molasses, which they then shipped to Britain and traded for credits in manufactured goods sent to New York, yielding three profits from each transaction. Most of New York's exports went to British Barbados, where trading firms shipped a portion to French and Spanish islands. New York's exports to Britain included tobacco, whale oil and beaver pelts; to the West

Indies, flour, bread, peas, pork and the occasional horse. Much of New Yorkers' profits went on to Britain with long lists of purchases.

Despite Britain's growing list of trade restrictions, the port flourished, the number of ships owned by New Yorkers quadrupling from 99 ships in 1747 to 447 by 1762; the number of merchant seamen multiplied fivefold. Efforts to collect duties lagged: for every ship seized by customs officials, an estimated dozen avoided detection and the inconvenience of customs.[7]

From the colonists' point of view, circumventing increasingly stringent British regulations became an economic necessity on which depended the welfare not only of ship-owners, their crews and the constellation of on-shore maritime enterprises but also of farmers, merchants and virtually anyone else doing business in colonial America. The outbreak of the climactic Seven Years' War between Britain and France in 1756 divided the loyalties of American merchants. Some profited from both sides, a practice that the British considered treason. Becoming enriched from contracts, subsidies and bounties to supply provisions to British and colonial troops, many Americans armed their ships to act as privateers—a deputized form of piracy—and harried French supply lines and sold captured ships and cargoes at auction for handsome profits. Others took advantage of wartime shortages on the mainland to trade with the French and their Spanish allies in the Caribbean.

New York City, headquarters of the British Army and nexus of its supply lines, became the leading privateering port. Its financiers included the mayor, provincial Supreme Court justices and high-ranking American officers. Sir Peter Warren, leader of colonial forces in the siege of Louisburg, owned a three-hundred-acre farm covering much of today's Greenwich Village. He sent his privateer, the *Launceston,* to sea and captured fifteen French ships. Between 1754 and 1763, New York City's fleet of 128 privateers harvested 80 French ships valued at £1 million.

Historian Peter Andreas details one wartime practice condemned by British officialdom: the sale of "flags of truce" by royal governors to ship captains. Sometimes blank and other times carrying fictitious names, these papers facilitated sale of illicit cargoes to the enemy in the French West Indies. Intended to allow prisoner exchanges, the sale of false flags became a lucrative source of income, especially for Rhode Islanders. In

1758 Francis Fauquier, royal governor of Virginia, reported how the scheme worked:

> The Rhode Island Men knowing there were 60 french prisoners at Boston, sent four Ships from Providence to Boston at their own Expence, and put fifteen on board each ship by which they skreen'd four cargoes of provisions . . . to [French] Port au Prince.[8]

Rhode Island's wealthiest merchants, the Browns, repeatedly bank-rolled "flag of truce" missions, usually successfully. But the Royal Navy captured several of their vessels. Admiralty courts condemned them for engaging in "wicked, illegal unwarrantable, clandestine and prohibited trade." When the Browns' *Speedwell* made its seventh and final voyage, it carried only one French prisoner of war as a screen provided by a "flag of truce" issued by Governor Stephen Hopkins.[9]

So widespread did the practice of using false papers of all kinds become that by 1760, as the war wound down, reports of merchants' and government officials' questionable patriotism began to reach the highest levels in Britain. James Hamilton, lieutenant governor of Pennsylvania, wrote in exasperation to Prime Minister Pitt that his predecessor, William Denny, had sold blank flags of truce virtually at wholesale. Few French prisoners came Denny's way—barely enough, Hamilton reported, that they could have been transported in "one or at most two small ships." For each pass, Denny or his agents pocketed "three to four hundred":

> Having once relished the sweets of this traffick, he became more undis-guised . . . open'd a shop at lower prices to all Customers . . . [including those] of the neighboring provinces [New Jersey and Maryland], to which they came and purchased freely. . . ."

Hamilton concluded that the "very great part of the principal merchants of this city [Philadelphia]" had traded illegally with French Caribbean islands. Passing along similar reports from other provincial governors, the Board of Trade and Plantations in London reported to its parent Privy Council that, indeed, all the American mainland colonies had traded with the French enemy.[10]

In a circular letter to provincial governors, a frustrated Pitt denounced the practice "by which the Enemy is, to the greatest Reproach & Detriment of Government, supplied with Provisions . . . they are principally, if not alone, enabled to sustain, and protract, this long and expensive War."

Pitt ordered the captains of Royal Navy ships in North American waters to raid French and Dutch islands in the West Indies acting as way stations between the North American merchants and the French enemy. But the cost of the combined customs service and Royal Navy crackdown, an estimated £8,000 annually, far exceeded the resultant revenues, up from a meager £259 in 1755 to £1,189 in 1761. The employment of the king's ships as customs collectors had added little to the revenues of the past thirty years. In all, the Navigation Acts had produced only £35,000 in thirty years; the Molasses Act, £21,000 in thirty-five years.[11]

IN OCTOBER 1761, three weeks after the coronation of George III, Pitt resigned. Lord Bute, the king's boyhood tutor and the queen mother's choice, replaced him as first minister. Bute was fairly typical of the inept aristocratic amateurs who ruled the sprawling realm. Only 125 nobles comprised the oligarchy: of these, only twenty-five revolved through the doors of committee meetings of the Privy Council. One after another began to tinker with the trade laws as they tried to make sense of administrating the vast new First British Empire, each plunging into a thorough investigation of the country's policies toward America after nearly a century of winking at trade laws.

The British perceived Americans to be far wealthier than the overburdened taxpayers of the Mother Country. Officers returning from America spun yarns of opulence and decadence, of the wives of rich Boston merchants living in three-story mansions of brick and stone, wearing silks and laces as they promenaded on the mall. In the South, they reported, plantation owners, led by liveried outriders, rode in carriages pulled by six matched horses with coats-of-arms on the doors. In the shade on languid summer days, so the stories went, black slaves poured fine imported Madeira and served up delicacies—chilled grapes, soft-shelled crabs—to their masters.

Not all of these stories were far-fetched. In Portsmouth, New Hampshire, Governor Benning Wentworth, made rich by selling timber to the

Royal Navy and selling off large swaths of frontier land, lived in a fifty-four-room waterfront mansion. In Norwich, Connecticut, two London-trained physicians, the Lathrop brothers, parlayed their apothecary shop—the only one between Boston and New York City—into a lucrative government contract for medical supplies for all British forces in New England and Canada. At home, their apothecary deliveries arrived in a long, low yellow carriage pulled by four horses, with their apprentice, young Benedict Arnold, at the reins. In Philadelphia, some eighty-nine citizens were wealthy enough to drive around their small city in carriages.

Operating on the assumption that much of this wealth derived from illicit trade, as soon as a British victory in Canada became assured, customs agents in Boston descended on the city's waterfront. Expecting to find and confiscate contraband goods from trade with the French, they armed themselves with unrestricted writs of assistance—general search warrants—authorizing them to enter and search warehouses and ships. No large-scale seizures had taken place by the time George II died: the writs automatically expired at a monarch's death.

But in the autumn of 1760, customs agents seized a Dutch ship carrying an illicit cargo worth £10,000. Massachusetts merchants cried foul: in England, search warrants could only be issued by the chancellor of the exchequer. How, then, could a mere local surveyor of the customs be allowed to single out Massachusetts merchants when every tide in Rhode Island brought in rich untaxed cargoes? Moreover, Boston merchants knew that it was accepted practice for customs collectors to profit handsomely from the sale of any goods they confiscated: one-third went to the royal treasury, one-third to the colony's treasury and the remainder to the customs collector. So hated were the informants triggering the searches that the customs collectors didn't even have to identify them, even to the Admiralty, only the amount arranged, and from that came the Crown's share.

When sixty-three shipping merchants objecting to the seizure of the Dutch vessel protested to provincial Chief Justice Jonathan Sewall, he called a hearing for February 1761. On legal grounds, the case hinged on whether the Massachusetts Supreme Court possessed the same powers of search and seizure as the Court of the Exchequer in Britain. In a packed courtroom in Boston in February 1761, before Royal Governor Francis Bernard and five judges of the Superior Court, colonial merchants on rows of benches facing the Crown lawyers took the first step toward confrontation between empire and colonist. Lawyer James Otis considered unrestricted general warrants as unconstitutional, basing his contention on seventeenth-century English philosopher John Locke's *Second Treatise on Government*'s principle of an Englishman's right to keep his home secure against search and seizure. Defending English subjects' right not to be taxed without their consent, Otis launched into a fiery five-hour attack. "This writ is against the fundamental principles of English law," he began. Not since the Star Chamber proceedings of the Stuarts had general warrants been exercised. A British officer could only break and enter in case of a felony, and then only with a special warrant:

> All legal precedents are under control of the fundamental principles of English law. If an act of Parliament should be passed a law in the very words of this petition for writs of assistance, it would be void. An act against the constitution is void. An act against natural equity is void.[12]

Three dozen Boston merchants listening intently to Otis knew that, while colonists had always believed they held rights assured by "the laws of God and Nature," no one had ever objected to Parliament's authority to make laws regulating trade. But Boston's merchants objected to any excise tax—an internal tax raising revenue for the government's use without a vote by the colonists' representatives. External taxes based on external legislation passed by Parliament had long been accepted. The Woolen Act of 1699 outlawed transporting any woolens by water: as soon as anyone transported wool over a stream, it became contraband. Thus, no colonial woolen trade could develop. The Hat Act of 1732 barred exportation of American-made hats; the Iron Act of 1750 forbade slitting mills, plating forges and steel furnaces. Americans couldn't even fashion a nail: pigs of raw iron had to be shipped to Britain and manufactured for export to the colonies.

Leaving the courtroom that evening, young lawyer John Adams understood that Otis had just appealed to beliefs he had learned in childhood: his right to liberty as inalienable as his right to life. Otis, asserting the rights of British subjects, had defied Parliament to abridge if not abrogate those rights. At the end of the hearing, Massachusetts' provincial governor bucked the case up to the Board of Trade in London for a decision, certain that it would, as everyone knew, take years. It was, indeed, fully six years before the attorney general and solicitor general of England upheld Otis, declaring that writs of assistance were invalid in America. Such writs could only be issued by the Court of the Exchequer. Meanwhile, searches and seizures and fines went on, ruining more Boston merchants. But on that day of Otis's challenge, many Bostonians became ready for the first time to defy the distant Parliament. More than half a century and a revolution later, Adams wrote, "Here this day, in the old Council Chamber, the child Independence was born."[13]

THREE

"Force Prevails Now Everywhere"

From the salutary neglect of King George II, British policy in America shifted immediately and radically under George III and the Tories. The young king's kaleidoscope of cabinet ministers understood that they had a mandate to drastically overhaul the government's American affairs. Both the members of the Board of Trade and Plantations—still espousing the seventeenth-century doctrine of mercantilism—and many ordinary English subjects believed that the colonies existed to supply the mother country with raw materials to fashion into manufactured commodities and sell at a profit to the colonists, keeping them dependent on the mother country for everything from hats to shoes. Yet, after accepting imperial limitations for decades, many Americans who had fought alongside the English against the French no longer were willing to accept tightening British controls.

While Britain's victory should have brought a massive expansion of trade by English colonists into the void left by the expulsion of the French, for many Americans peace only induced a long depression. During wartime, in exchange for feeding, housing and transporting British troops and supplies and the colonial troops who had made up fully half of the fighting men, the colonies had not only received hard-money subsidies that paid their militias but also bounties for hemp, oak and pine needed for shipbuilding; wheat, corn and cotton; barrel hoops and stave—anything that could assist in the worldwide struggle. The evaporation of these subsidies brought on the collapse of colonial economies. The first serious attempt to regulate American trade and enforce customs duties further shocked the markets. One sharp-eyed British visitor wrote home that Connecticut may have been the most cash-strapped colony. He "would not give £800 for the entire province." He had been "all over it" and came away convinced that "they are all mortgaged to the full."[1]

As the depression deepened, the colonists' viewpoint increasingly diverged from British sensibilities. Britain's war debt amounted to eighteen pounds per subject at home, only eighteen shillings in the American colonies, rendering new taxes or increased levies in the British Isles unthinkable. But the debt in some colonies was nearly as high. Rural New Jersey, with its mountainous northwest border to protect from Indian raids, with ports that harbored British ships and with the main road and bridges between New York and Philadelphia to maintain, produced only agricultural and forest products. Like other colonies, New Jersey's Assembly had been allowed to issue vast amounts of paper money, much of which debt-ridden colonists sent to Britain to retire longstanding accounts incurred in pounds sterling. When the boom swung back at war's end, artificial prosperity deflated. The second smallest populace in America woke up saddled with a £300,000 debt, the highest in America, amounting to fifteen pounds for every male between eighteen and sixty, rivaling the eighteen-pound burden in Britain!

The ordinary Englishman had grown restless paying for a bloated government and military and increasingly irate at reports that so many Americans had profited from trading with the enemy. British public opinion was resentful and strongly supported a government crackdown on the perceived American evasion of a fair share of the tax burden. A belief prevailed that the old Acts of Navigation and Trade should be enforced; Britain was entitled to reap the rewards for the colonial trade she had engendered, financed and defended against the French in Canada.

EVER SINCE THE French had abandoned Fort DuQuesne in what is now Pittsburgh, land-hungry colonists had poured over the new military road from Philadelphia into the Ohio Valley. Their incursion violated Pennsylvania's promise to Indians assembled at the 1758 Treaty of Easton that there would be no further settlements west of the Alleghenies. In October 1761, Colonel Henry Bouquet, in command of British forces at the fort (renamed Fort Pitt), ordered a halt to settlement west of the mountains. That December, the Earl of Egremont, secretary of state for the Southern Department, decreed that all new land grants adjacent to Indian territories must receive Crown approval. At the same time, Lord Shelburne, president of the Board of Trade—the man charged with formulating a policy for lands ceded by the French under the 1763 Treaty of Paris—recommended that the Appalachians, except for a small reserve in the Ohio Valley already set aside for veterans, become the western boundary line between English settlements and a vast Indian reserve. Shelburne envisioned creating three new provinces: Quebec, East Florida and West Florida.[2]

When the French turned over Detroit to the British, the Indians, led by the Ottawa chief Pontiac, demanded the British reduce prices for trade goods and supply them with ammunition. Rebuffed, Pontiac led a revolt. Besides besieging Detroit, he captured and destroyed every British post west of Niagara. Only Detroit and Fort Pitt held out. Lord Amherst, general in chief of the British army, proposed spreading smallpox among rebellious Indians. Colonel Bouquet declined, fearing it would spread among his own troops. Instead, he suggested instead hunting the Indians with "English dogs." Pontiac's five-month-long rebellion ended when Bouquet, suffering heavy British losses, defeated the Indians at Bushy Run in western Pennsylvania.

Before Shelburne's reform proposals could be implemented, the king replaced him at the Board of Trade with a less sympathetic minister, the wily Anglo-Irish Wills Hill, Lord Hillsborough. He promptly eliminated any provision for lands for veterans in the upper Ohio Valley and ordered colonists already settled west of the mountains "forthwith to remove themselves." The Board of Trade's new policy reflected Hillsborough's analysis that His Majesty's possessions in North America were so many times more extensive than in Great Britain and that "[i]f they were equally inhabited, Great Britain could no longer maintain dominion over them. . . . It is therefore evidently her Policy to set bounds to the Increment of People, and to the extent of the Settlement of that Country."[3]

The Board of Trade reported that King George himself had personally "approved and confirmed" the principle that the western expansion of the colonies should be limited "to such a distance from the seacoast, as that those settlements should lie *within the reach of the trade and commerce of this kingdom*" (emphasis mine). By limiting westward expansion to the coastal colonies east of the Alleghenies, British policy shifted radically from "benign neglect" to "the exercise of that authority and jurisdiction" needed to hold the colonies "in due subordination to, and dependence upon, the mother country."[4]

Hillsborough's decree echoed extreme voices in Parliament who, even before the French and Indian War, were demanding that "the colonies should be governed like Ireland, keeping a body of standing forces" with "the abridgements of their legislative powers, so as to put them on the same foot that Ireland stands." (Hillsborough himself was an Irish peer.) All through the war, a Parliamentary faction insisted that future appointments of governors "should be settled by Parliament so as to make them independent of the people."[5]

Hillsborough's sweeping Proclamation of 1763, rushed through the Privy Council and signed by the king, further forbade purchases of Indian lands east of the line, placed the Indians under the British military commander in chief in America and established English law in conquered French-speaking Quebec. The North American continent west of the mountains, so hard won by British and American colonial troops, now became a vast Indian reserve, its lucrative fur trade to be exploited exclusively by the British. Additionally 10,000 British troops—twenty battalions—were sent in to police the settlers as much as the Indians.[6]

George Washington had been leading a small force of Virginia militia and Indians into the Ohio country to stake out lands promised to American veterans of King George's War when he had accidentally triggered the French and Indian War. Washington fought the French and Indians for five years, emerging as a brevet British brigadier and America's first war hero. At first he scoffed at the Proclamation Line. But then, before there was such a notion, he decided to form a corporation with his brother Jack and four Lees to apply to the Crown for a 2.5-million-acre land grant at the confluence of the Ohio and Mississippi Rivers.

If settling on lands now reserved for the Indians posed any ethical or legal impediment to Washington, he dismissed it in his petition to the king. The Indians themselves, he argued, had vacated the 1758 peace treaty by fomenting Pontiac's Rebellion. To Washington, Pontiac's violent crusade illustrated the folly of the new British policy. By "attack[ing] his Majesty's fortifications and most barbarously murder[ing] in cold blood the King's officers and troops[, t]hey have also invaded most of the colonies east of the Alleghenies, murdering multitudes of his Majesty's subjects and destroying the country before them with fire and sword." To Washington, it was only good policy "to [get] that country settled as quickly as possible." His application for a corporate land grant arrived in London just as the king signed the ban on any further migration west of the mountains. Washington, a member of the Virginia House of Burgesses, kept "his initial reaction a profound secret." As a burgess, "I might be censured for the opinion I have given in respect for the King's proclamation."[7]

Years later, he said he considered the British closing of the frontier to legal settlement one of the major precipitants of the Revolution. On the eve of the Revolutionary War, he still pursued a major land grant in the Ohio Valley. He was not alone among Revolutionary leaders: Benjamin Franklin and his son, William, royal governor of New Jersey, had formed a land company that included members of Parliament, seeking a royal charter to a 20-million-acre tract in the Indian reserve. The Illinois Company was to encompass five of the modern Midwest states.

CONVINCED IT NEEDED an army to maintain order in America, the British cabinet reshuffled itself once again. After an anti-Scottish mob overturned his carriage in the streets of London, the unpopular Lord Bute resigned as prime minister. The queen mother once again chose his replacement: George Grenville. William Pitt's pinchpenny brother-in-law, Grenville was known for being so compulsively frugal that he "considered a National savings of two Inches of Candle" equal to Pitt's great military victories. As First Lord of the Admiralty, Grenville sponsored an act of Parliament that, for the first time, allowed the Royal Navy to assist in enforcing trade laws.

The size of the national debt horrified the new prime minister. Despite the spread of the postwar depression worldwide, in March 1764 Grenville chose this singularly inopportune moment to press Parliament to pass the American Revenue Act. Better known as the Sugar Act, it became the first law ever enacted by Parliament specifically to raise money for the Crown by taxing American colonists. Based on a six-month investigation into "the Clandestine trade," the Treasury reported to the king that customs revenues from America were "inconsiderable," not even keeping pace with increasing commerce. Through "Neglect, Connivance and Fraud," the "Salutary Provisions of many wise Laws to secure it to the Mother Country are in great measure Defeated." More revenue would be needed to defend the colonies; the "vast increase in Territory and Population makes the proper Regulation of their Trade of immediate Necessity." Otherwise, "dangerous Evils" would make it "utterly impracticable" to remedy them later.

The Treasury's alarming report induced Parliament once again to extend the Molasses Act of 1733 and to double the duty on refined foreign sugar. But the House of Commons went much farther than merely continuing to tax the lucrative sugar trade. It introduced a protective tariff that imposed new or steeper duties on direct importation of foreign textiles, coffee and indigo, and Madeira and Canary Islands wines—the favorites of Americans—while doubling the duties on foreign goods, already required to be shipped through England. Further stifling American trade, the Act added iron, hides, whale fins, potash, pearl ash and raw silk to the list of "enumerated" products that Americans could sell only to Britain. In addition, the Act outlawed importation to America of French wines and foreign—primarily Dutch—rum. To James Otis in Boston, the new law was a dangerous experiment, a test of colonial opposition on the road to incrementally increased demands. If Britain imposed taxes on Americans "without consent, they cannot be said to be free. This barrier of liberty being once broken down, all is lost."[8]

Perhaps worse for the Americans, Grenville, given to anti-American ranting on the floor of Parliament, pushed through another onerous companion piece of legislation. The Currency Act outlawed the printing or coining of colonial money, a practice already banned in New England. Still, some £250,000 in legal tender currency was circulating in Virginia, introduced to pay clergy after the tobacco crop, their age-old method of payment, failed in a drought. The new law mandated that all fines and taxes henceforth be paid in scarce sterling.

Grenville also won Parliamentary approval for stricter enforcement of existing trade laws. Royal Navy officers became customs officers aboard navy cutters stationed off the American coast. The first navy ship attempting to inspect a suspected smuggler off Rhode Island set off a riot. Islanders turned harbor guns on the navy ship and shelled it. Parliament also authorized a Vice Admiralty court at Halifax with jurisdiction over all British American colonies, eliminating trial by jury, the lynchpin of English law since the Magna Carta. The new law allowed prosecutors and informants to sue in distant Admiralty courts instead of local ones. Also abrogating the right of the accused to sue for illegal seizure, an Admiralty court placed the burden of proof on the accused, required the posting of bond for trial costs and added new and stricter registration and bonding procedures for ships carrying all types of cargo. To sharpen the teeth of Grenville's reforms, Parliament nullified any existing colonial law that conflicted with the new edicts.

For one young Connecticut merchant mariner, peace had meant an end to the threat of seizure by the French during trading voyages around the Caribbean and along the Canadian Maritime coast. With the proceeds of selling his father's house, Benedict Arnold bought a forty-ton sloop, naming it the *Fortune*. Advertising in the *Connecticut Gazette* for "large, fat, genteel horses," barrels of pork, bales of hay and bags of oats, he crowded every inch of his hold, strapped lumber on his deck, and set sail south toward the Caribbean and trading stopovers in St. Kitts, Martinique and the Bay of Honduras before heading back north, running down east to Nova Scotia, Newfoundland, the St. Lawrence River, Quebec and Montreal. Exchanging lumber and livestock for Spanish gold, salt and cotton—in short supply in Connecticut—he traded shrewdly and expanded gradually. But some customers couldn't pay him; he lost 50 percent on two voyages in 1764, the year the Grenville acts took effect. Waiting sometimes three years to be paid, his every bill of exchange protested, by age twenty-six Arnold was nearly ruined.[9]

In Salisbury, Connecticut, on the colony's northwest frontier, young Ethan Allen had purchased a handsome hillside home with the profits from establishing New England's first iron foundry, but now he wanted to sell both and invest in a mine. He took a beating, being offered less than half what he had paid for it. At the settlement, when the buyer showed up

short of the agreed-upon purchase price in cash, a fistfight broke out. The
town constable hauled buyer and seller before Justice Samuel Huntington—a
future signer of the Declaration of Independence—for "disturbance of many
of His Majesty's good subjects." Huntington fined Allen a stiff ten shillings,
to be paid in silver or gold coins, cash Allen could scarcely afford.[10]

In New Jersey, James Parker, printer and secretary of the British American postal service, took the measure of the crisis in a letter to New Jersey's attorney general, Cortlandt Skinner:

> There is such a general scarcity of cash that nothing we have here will
> command it and real estates of every kind are falling at least one-half in
> value. Debtors that were a year or two ago responsible for £1,000 can not
> now raise a fourth part of the sum. . . . There is an entire stop to all sales
> by the sheriffs for want of buyers, and men of the best estates amongst us
> can scarce raise money enough to defray the necessary expenses of their
> families.[11]

Each term, Parliament enacted new measures to harness American
trade. When Parliament decreed that it would for the first time strictly enforce higher imposts, Samuel Adams, a malt brewer and lawyer whose
father's fortune had been wiped out by British currency restrictions, fore-
saw the consequences of taxing American colonists without granting them
representation in the House of Commons. He regarded the new regulations
as the resounding tocsin of an alarming infringement of colonial rights:

> If our trade may be taxed, why not our lands? Why not the product of our
> lands and everything we possess or make use of? This we apprehend an-
> nihilates our charter rights to govern and tax ourselves. It strikes at our
> British privileges which, as we have never forfeited them, we hold in com-
> mon with our fellow subjects who are natives of Britain. If taxes are laid
> on us in any shape without our having a legal representation where they
> are laid, are we not reduced from the character of free subjects to the mis-
> erable status of tributary slaves?[12]

Perversely, Parliament responded to initial American objections by imposing the Stamp Tax on the colonies. Intended to raise £60,000 annu-

ally, taken together with the year's projected customs imposts, it was supposed to yield one-third the cost of the military occupation of the colonies. Items, long taxed in England, included bills of lading, dice and playing cards, mortgages and liquor licenses, printed pamphlets, newsprint and newspaper advertisements, almanacs, calendars, surveying documents—and even college diplomas, which bore an outrageously steep fee. At a time when roughly half the students at Harvard were studying for the ministry on scholarships, the tax stamp cost £50, roughly equivalent to $5,000 in 2016. Graduating from Queen's College (today's Rutgers), future revolutionary William Paterson could not afford to pay the fee until he worked for two more years in his father's store. At a time when cash was sparse and unemployment high, the tax had to be paid in sterling or gold.

The burden fell heaviest on lawyers, printers, tavern owners, merchants and ship owners, broadening the base of opposition to parliamentary power seemingly overnight. Merchants, sailors and lawyers rioted all up and down the Atlantic seaboard. Under pressure from a new secret society called the Sons of Liberty, all the lawyers in New Jersey refused to conduct any business requiring the obnoxious stamps, which put a stop to all legal business in the colony. In Boston, crowds chased the stamp commissioner through the streets, sacked the home of the royal governor and literally pulled it down with blocks and tackles as he escaped out a window. The Boston town meeting denounced taxation without representation in Parliament and proposed intercolonial action. Massachusetts' House of Representatives authorized forming a committee of correspondence to coordinate protests. Delegates from nine colonies assembled in New York City for an unsanctioned Stamp Act Congress.

In August 1764 America's first trade boycott materialized. A total of 250 Boston merchants agreed to forego importing English lace and ruffles, and the town's mechanics followed suit by pledging to wear only leather work clothes made in Massachusetts. The movement spread to New York City, where two hundred merchants boycotted European goods until the Stamp Act was repealed and Britain's trade regulations ameliorated; in Philadelphia, four hundred merchants followed suit. In all, fully a thousand American merchants joined the boycott. On November 1, the day the Stamp Act went into effect, virtually all business in America was suspended, but by then no tax stamp could be found. The royally appointed stamp commissioner for each and every colony had been intimidated into resigning.

As the day the Stamp Act was to go into effect approached, Philadelphia was near civil war. Mobs were assembled at night by muffled drums. Probably because Franklin had arranged the appointment of a friend as collector for Pennsylvania, one faction suspected him to be behind the odious legislation. Deborah Franklin wrote her husband that only the existence of another, pro-Franklin mob of eight hundred tradesmen and mechanics ensured her protection and that of his old friends:

> I was for nine days kept in one continued hurry by people to remove. Several houses [were] threatened to be pulled down. Cousin Davenport come and told me it was his duty to be with me. Toward night, I sed he should fetch a gun or two as we had none. I sent to ask my brother to come and bring his gun also, so we made one room into a magazine. I ordered some sort of defense upstairs such as I could manage myself. I was very sure you had done nothing to hurt anybody nor I had not given any offense to any person."[13]

Alarmed, the British commanding general for North America, Sir Thomas Gage, wrote home to the Ministry that the protests were well organized:

> The lawyers are the source from which these clamors have flowed. . . . [Merchants] in general, assembly men, magistrates . . . have been united in this plan of riots. . . . The sailors who are the only people who may be properly styled Mob are entirely at the command of the Merchants who employ them.[14]

As protests spread throughout the colonies, Virginia governor Francis Fauquier refused to call the fall session of the House of Burgesses. Like other southern planters, George Washington was hit hard by the new tax. For every deed he recorded or lease he executed, for the insurance on crops he had to send to England, for every document he filed in court, he had to come up with four shillings in specie—what he paid a farm manager for a week. After a day surveying the fields or hunched over his ledgers, he liked to play cards or dice with guests around his Mount Vernon gaming table. Now, every pair of dice or deck of cards required a ten-shilling stamp—enough to buy a pair of workhorses or a cask of Madeira. Every page of the *Virginia Gazette*, filled with letters and essays protesting the tax, had to bear a one-penny stamp.

As Washington rode into Williamsburg, he had to coax his horse through knots of rough-hewn farmers who had ridden all the way from the Shenandoah Valley. It was they who would be most affected by any new tax; it was they who bartered for everything they hunted or grew. Where were they supposed to get sterling? Every loan for seed money, every lease and every lien against future harvests already required gold or silver for courthouse fees. Washington could see that these upcountry farmers in buckskin leggings and hunting shirts were in an ugly mood.

That year, Washington had planted no tobacco. He had calculated that three-fourths of the profits of his tobacco crop were being siphoned off by taxes, transportation charges, unloading, weighing, warehousing and reloading in London. A pioneer in diversified farming, he had gradually shifted to wheat and corn that he could market in the American colonies. For the four months since a ship had brought news of the latest new levy, Washington had stayed on the sidelines of politics, but he was growing more and more agitated at a system binding Americans ever more tightly to England. Washington protested the stamp tax to the London commission merchants who sold his tobacco crops and bought all the goods he was not allowed to produce. He felt he was being robbed by middlemen and customs agents and now by stamp men.

Punitive British levies would only drive other Americans to make themselves less dependent on imported English items by developing their own crops and manufacturing goods for their own markets. Calling the tax an "ill-judged measure," Washington for the first time publicly criticized British trade policy:

> What more can they desire? All taxes which contribute to lessen our importation of British goods must be hurtful to the manufacturers of them. . . . Our people will perceive that many luxuries, which we have hitherto lavished our substance to Great Britain for, can well be disposed with while the necessaries of life are to be procured for the most part

within ourselves. . . . Great Britain may then load her exports with as heavy taxes as she pleased but where will the consumption be? Where then lies the utility of these measures? There is not [any] money to pay the stamp. . . . Who is to suffer most in this event, the merchant or the planter?[15]

British merchants could have answered Washington's rhetorical question: exports to America dropped from £2,249,710 in 1764 to £1,944,108 in 1765, a 15 percent decline. Many merchants had not voluntarily joined the boycott movement. The Sons of Liberty emerged as a new and potent political force. One estimate is that upward of 10,000 men joined the radical group. The Reverend Ezra Stiles, professor of moral philosophy at Yale College, wrote that three-fourths of the men in Connecticut were "ready to take up arms for their liberties." They numbered "very boys as well as the hardy rustic" and they were "full of fire and ready to fight."[16] As Dr. Benjamin Gale, himself a founder, put it, their assemblages were a "babel," at once including "several pimps and smugglers."[17]

On March 22, 1765, two months after Benjamin Franklin returned to London as agent for the Pennsylvania Assembly, Parliament passed the Stamp Act. The Boston-born printer, leading distributor of Bibles in America, storeowner and owner or partner of every newspaper in America, set out to eliminate the stamp tax. Thomas Penn, son of the province's founder, had been warned that "the reputation gained by [Franklin's] electrical experiments, which will introduce him into all sorts of company" could "prove [him] a dangerous enemy." Full of scorn, Penn discounted Franklin's influence. "Mr. Franklin's popularity is nothing here. He will be looked very coldly upon by great people." When Franklin managed to arrange an audience with Lord Granville, president of the king's Privy Council, he received a jarring dressing-down:

You Americans have wrong ideas of the nature of your constitution. You contend that the king's instructions to his governors are not laws, and think yourselves at liberty to regard or disregard them at your own discretion. But those instructions are not like the pocket instructions given to a minister going abroad for regulating his conduct in some trifling point of ceremony. They are first drawn up by judges learned in the law; they are then considered, debated and perhaps amended in Council, after which they are signed by the King. They are then, so far as relates to you, *the law of the land,* for the king is the LEGISLATOR OF THE COLONIES.[18]

After reporting the encounter to Philadelphia, Franklin set to work organizing a repeal movement. For nearly a year, he lobbied relentlessly against the Stamp Act. Under an assortment of pseudonyms, he bombarded newspapers with letters, distributed hundreds of copies of a cartoon he had drawn and published in his *Pennsylvania Gazette,* a depiction of a dismembered British Empire against a backdrop of idle ships. Franklin maneuvered himself into the position of primary spokesman among the sixteen American agents in London. All over England merchants were suffering from the American boycott of their goods. Franklin spearheaded a committee that visited thirty towns, circulating petitions to Parliament to repeal the act. By January 1766 the petition of London merchants was attributing bankruptcies to the loss of the American market.

When the House of Commons reconvened, Grenville called for the use of troops to enforce the Act. Countering, Pitt called for repeal and praised Americans for disobeying a tax approved by a government body in which they lacked representation. In February, sitting as a committee of the whole, Parliament summoned colonial agents to testify. Franklin stood at the bar, answering in rapid succession 174 questions he had carefully planted. Five queries went to the heart of the matter:

Q.—*Do you think it right that America should be protected by this country and pay no part of the expense?*
A.—That is not the case. The colonies raised, clothed and paid during the last war near 25,000 men and spent many millions.

Q.—*Do you not think the people of America would submit to pay the stamp duty if it was moderated?*
A.—No, never, unless compelled by force of arms.

Q.—*Can anything else less than a military force carry the Stamp Act into execution?*
A.—I do not see how a military force can be applied to that purpose.

Q.—*Why may it not?*

A.—Suppose a military force [is] sent to America, they will find nobody in arms; what then are they to do? They cannot force a man to take stamps who chooses to do without them. They will not find a rebellion; they may indeed make one.

Q.—*If the act is not repealed, what do you think will be the consequences?*

A.—The total loss of the respect and affection the people of America bear to this country, and of all the commerce that depends on that respect and affection.

On March 4, 1766, Parliament voted to repeal the Stamp Act by a 275-167 vote. But then the House of Commons immediately and unanimously added, at the end of the repeal bill, couched in the same terms as the Irish Declaratory Act of 1719, its assertion that Parliament had full authority to make laws binding the American colonists "in all cases whatsoever."[19]

AMID CELEBRATORY BONFIRES, as the College of New Jersey (today's Princeton) planted plane trees and the New York Assembly commissioned equestrian statues of King George and William Pitt, Jonathan Trumbull, the deputy governor of Connecticut, expressed alarm at learning of Parliament's declaration even as he received instructions that American colonists were now required to provide quarters and rations for the occupying British troops. Trumbull had become one of New England's leading merchants and political figures. He attended Harvard as a divinity student until his older brother disappeared at sea, after which he joined the family business in western Connecticut. His father, beginning as an uneducated farmer, had built an extensive trade in raising beef cattle and hogs, herding them into Boston where meatpackers exported them to England and Ireland and exchanged them for luxury goods that Trumbull distributed to stores all over Connecticut. In Lebanon he became the region's principal shopkeeper, dispensing, among other items, lace, gloves, gunpowder, flints, knives, needles and thimbles, pepper, molasses, rum, drugs, paper, pails, buckles, buttons, combs, earthenware and pewter ware, raisins, butter and pepper.

In the wake of the French and Indian War, Trumbull and his partners had built up a transatlantic trading company that dispatched from its home port of New London some sixty ships: twelve-ton coastal sloops to haul produce to markets in Boston and Rhode Island; eighty-ton brigantines carrying horses, cattle and lumber to the West Indies to exchange for sugar and molasses; and two-hundred-ton brigs carrying salted meat and cod to the Mediterranean, and flaxseed and lumber, potash and whale fins, skins and furs—he employed Mohegan trappers and hunters—to England and Ireland. Provisioning Nantucket Island with farm produce, beef and pork, Trumbull traded them for whale oil, which he then shipped to England and exchanged for finery and furniture to sell in his capacious Lebanon emporium.

Marrying Faith Robinson, a direct descendant of *Mayflower* Pilgrims John and Priscilla Alden, Trumbull entered New England's Puritan elite. He built, furnished and held social sway from a hilltop mansion in Lebanon in the Connecticut Valley, behaving as something of an English country squire. The town's foremost citizen, he rode through his fields in a fine carriage and extended hospitality in fine clothes tailored in Boston from fine English fabrics. Part of his standing as a rural grandee depended on dispensing credit until, by 1764, his books carried more than £10,000 in debts, much of it too old and uncollectable by the time the Parliament outlawed colonial currency. Trumbull then accepted payment in livestock, tobacco, firewood, flaxseed and lime, furs, grain and produce, even bartering for farm labor, carting and carpentry, but his British creditors insisted on payment in sterling or gold.

Trumbull worried about Parliament's "new Fetters." He feared the British would deploy redcoats to break up protests against the new tax measures. He heard talk of the need to separate the colonies from the Mother Country. To Samuel Johnson, Connecticut's agent in London, Trumbull wrote that he still considered the interests of Britain and America "mutual and inseparable." As long as the colonies wanted the protection and manufactured goods of the Mother Country, it couldn't be in Americans' interest to separate; as long as the colonies provided raw materials, commodities and services "beneficial to the native country," it would always be in the Mother Country's interest to keep the colonies "dependent and employed. If violence, or methods tending to violence, be taken to maintain this dependence, it tends to hasten a separation." In February 1767, when General Thomas Gage demanded that Connecticut provide quarters and provisions for his troops stationed there, Trumbull refused, seeking the approval of the Connecticut General Assembly.[20]

AT FIRST, BENJAMIN Franklin did not foresee an intensive struggle over Parliament's disclaimer at the tag end of its act repealing the Stamp Act. To most veteran London observers, the Declaratory Act merely seemed a face-saving measure, having no weight because the colonies had always had the right to make their own laws and then submit them to the king for pro forma ratification. But as years of unrest rolled by like the constant menace of a gathering storm, it became evident that the king was infuriated by mobs on both sides of the Atlantic as he reshuffled his cabinet once again. He replaced the tired, old, moderate Pitt with a high Tory regime intent on abridging colonists' rights as venerable as their seventeenth-century charters. He replaced Pitt with Charles "Champagne Charlie" Townshend, a bibulous rural nobleman who preferred to stay on his country estates, experimenting with crop rotation and fertilizing his fields. To his son William, the royal governor of New Jersey, Benjamin Franklin wrote that "no middle doctrine can be well maintained. Something might be made of either of the extremes, that Parliament has a power to make all laws for us, or that it has a power to make no laws for us."[21]

It took Townshend's colleagues by surprise in May 1767 when he announced new duties on American imports of glass, lead, paint and paper to defray the salaries of civil officers and judges in America. Further, Townshend declared a cutback in frontier garrisons and concentrations of troops in port towns prone to protest. Moreover, Townshend reorganized the customs service under an American Board of Customs Commissioners headquartered in Boston, center of opposition to British tax measures.

To streamline enforcement, Townshend replaced the old Admiralty court in Halifax with superior courts in Boston, Philadelphia, New Orleans and Halifax. His final innovation created an office of secretary of state for the plantations. Its first incumbent, approved by the king, was hardline Anglo-Irish peer Wills Hill, Lord Hillsborough. The Duke of Newcastle, advocate of the discarded policy of "salutary neglect," characterized Hillsborough as addicted to the use of force: the "Doctrine of doing everything by Force prevails now Everywhere." In an interview with

Franklin, Hillsborough summed up his view: the Americans were troublesome children who must be punished into obedience.[22]

Parliament's administration of a purgative proved disastrous. In less than eight months, a new wave of riots and another crippling boycott on English imports forced Parliament to rescind all of Townshend's duties but a token duty on tea. Angry town meetings from Boston to New York City condemned the broad-based assault on colonists' rights. In Philadelphia, Quaker lawyer John Dickinson, in his "Letters from a Farmer in Pennsylvania"—which denied the right of Parliament to tax in order to raise revenue in the American colonies—declared the Townshend duties unconstitutional. A boycott of British luxury goods by Boston merchants took effect on January 1, 1768; Newport, Providence and New York City followed suit.

Early in 1769 Boston merchants tightened the ban to include almost all British goods, allowing only supplies for the fisheries. New York merchants cancelled all orders sent to England after August 15, 1768, boycotting all British imports until Parliament repealed the Townshend Acts. Tradesmen vowed not to deal with merchants who refused to join the boycott. By autumn 1769 merchants in Philadelphia, Maryland, South Carolina, Georgia, North Carolina, Delaware and New Jersey joined them. Virginians further banned importation of slaves. Stimulating wool production and encouraging a homegrown textile industry, Virginia planters pledged not to slaughter lambs weaned before May 1. College students promised to give up sipping foreign wines and, at the 1770 commencement of the newly founded Queen's College, with royal governor William Franklin on the dais, graduates showed up in homespun gowns instead of the traditional imported academic robes. Housewives vowed to stop serving tea imported from England and renounced fashionable silks and satins.

A few merchants balked. In Boston, merchant Theophilus Lillie dared to publish a letter in which he complained that he was being deprived of his livelihood in the name of liberty. On February 22, 1770, a crowd of adolescent boys with a sign marked "IMPORTER"—identifying him as a boycott violator—picketed his store. A sympathetic merchant nearby, Ebenezer Richardson, tried to tear down the placard. The crowd chased him home and hurled rocks through his windows, injuring him, his wife and their daughter. An older rioter pounded on his door, shouting, "Come

out, you damn son of a bitch, I'll have your Heart and your Liver out!"
From an upstairs window, Richardson fired a round of swanshot into the
crowd, killing eleven-year-old Christopher Seider and wounding another
boy. Only the arrival of a leader of the Sons of Liberty saved the badly
beaten merchant. After Richardson's conviction for murder, the king par-
doned him. Christopher Seider's funeral turned into a march of revulsion
at the new British constraints. John Adams witnessed a "vast Number of
Boys" walking ahead of the coffin while thousands of women and boys
followed it.[23]

NORMALLY BRITAIN SOLD fully one-third of its exports in America, and
tens of thousands of jobs depended on the transatlantic trade. Consequently, the anti-Townshend embargo hit British commerce even harder
than the Stamp Act crisis. Imports dropped from £2,157,218 in 1768 to
£1,336,122 in 1769. In New York, exports dropped 86 percent, from £490,673
to £75,930; in Philadelphia nearly by half, down from £441,829 to £204,978.
Overall, British exports to the colonies plummeted 40 percent in one year.
The boycott affected American colonists as well. Washington, who wound
up urging a continent-wide boycott of British goods, also wanted to encourage domestic industry. He wanted to manufacture iron, as his father
had done, but British law now forbade him. In a typical year, he had to buy
many essentials that his artisans could have been trained to produce at
Mount Vernon. One order included nails, saddler's tacks, blacksmith's
files, axes, hoes, keys, locks, adzes, bung-borers, screws, scythes, iron,
wire, sieves, fishing seines and lead sinkers.

AS THE TOWNSHEND protests intensified, in October 1768 Lord Hillsbor-
ough, at the request of nervous customs officials in Boston, ordered two
regiments of grenadiers and artillery to garrison unruly Boston. General
Gage had appealed for troops after customs collectors, chased through the
streets and threatened with having their houses torn down, took refuge on
Castle Island in the harbor under the protection of the fifty-gun frigate
Romney, which had been dispatched from Halifax in May for the purpose.
Only two weeks later, the Customs Commissioners received an urgent appeal to send troops to Long Wharf. A crowd had locked a wharf official in
the cabin of John Hancock's sloop *Liberty* while they unloaded a cargo of

untaxed Madeira wine. The Customs Board ordered *Liberty* seized and towed to an anchorage near *Romney*.

Gage rotated forces from frontier stockades to the seaports, from Canada to Boston, to reinforce its garrison. Into a town of 16,000, he injected 4,000 redcoats to bivouac on the common, where the stench of their latrines wafted over the town. As the historian David Hackett Fischer points out, Gage chose his troops unwisely, selecting "for that difficult assignment the 29th Foot, a regiment notorious for poor discipline, hot-tempered officers and repeated violent clashes with civilians in Canada and New York."[24]

No sooner had the first British occupation forces walked up Long Wharf and pitched their tents than the first serious flare-up occurred. A butcher taunted one of the soldiers, who knocked him down. His commanding officer applauded the "lesson." Fined by a local justice of the peace, the British soldier refused to pay up, instead slashing the constable who attempted to arrest him. When soldiers built a guard box on private property, the owner led a crowd that attacked with sticks, bricks and stones, seriously injuring two soldiers. Insults provoked more injuries.

As the home government "yielded by bits" to unpopular demands, Gage's attitude hardened. He wrote to his superiors in London, "Democracy is too prevalent in America, and claims the greatest attention to prevent its increase." New England's laws were bizarre, the people litigious, wrote Gage, who was married to the daughter of a wealthy New Jersey merchant. "Every man studies law, and interprets the law to suit his purposes." They were, he concluded, "already, almost out of reach of Law and Government."[25]

The persistence of the American boycott alarmed the Board of Trade, which informed royal governors that it was considering ameliorating the odious Acts. The death of Townshend in early January 1770 provided the King an opportunity to appoint a new prime minister, his old school chum, Lord North. While North hesitated to rescind all the Townshend duties for fear of appearing weak, when he called for partial repeal, the cabinet supported him 5-4. The House of Commons approved North's plan—to repeal all but a token duty on tea, lowering its tax to a modest three pence in the pound and promising Parliament would impose no new taxes on the American colonies. Over the next three months, Americans abandoned the trade boycott town by town—and merchants rushed orders to London to restock their shelves.[26]

ON MARCH 2, a soldier was walking past a Boston rope yard when a voice called out, "Soldier, will you work?" "Yes," the soldier replied. "Then go and clean my shit house." The soldier struck the rope-maker, who then beat the soldier until he retreated. The soldier returned with his comrades, and the brawl spilled over to the next day as more and more men on both sides arrived, wielding cutlasses and clubs. The fighting briefly subsided on Sunday, March 4. But that night, as bands of soldiers and civilians roved the ice-crusted snow in full moonlight, they collided at the Customs House. An apprentice insulted a British officer, who cuffed him. A sentry, Private Hugh White, hit him again. As word spread, a score of men and boys arrived: one shouted at White, "You Centinel, damned rascally Scoundrel Lobster Son of a Bitch." When White threatened to bayonet the man, the crowd pelted him with hard-packed snowballs and chunks of ice. Someone yelled "Fire!" and church bells began tolling. The signal to come put out a blaze drew a crowd—some were equipped with buckets to carry water, but others brought swords and clubs.

For an hour, Captain Thomas Preston, officer of the day, watched nervously. When the crowd only grew, he called out the guard, six privates and a corporal. In a column of twos, bayonets fixed to muskets, they pushed through the crowd. Preston deployed his men in a semicircle with their backs to the Customs House wall, facing out, and ordered them to load. More men crowded in. Some shouted, "Kill them, kill them"; more ice and snow struck the sentries, who lowered their half-cocked muskets menacingly. A chunk of ice struck Private Hugh Montgomery. In pain, he fell; when he got up, he fired. After a short pause, the other soldiers fired, reloaded and fired again, hitting eleven men. Three dropped dead, two died later; six were wounded but survived. As at least a thousand Bostonians raged through the streets, Royal Governor Thomas Hutchinson jailed the soldiers for their protection. Courageously, John Adams took Preston's case, brought to trial after long delays, and won his acquittal. Two soldiers, convicted of manslaughter, pleaded benefit of clergy and were branded. All over America, colonists talked of The Massacre.[27]

By aggressively escalating its attempts to extract revenues from its American colonies, Britain's ministers, after a century of failures, had turned modest gains into a fiasco. Seizures of ships for widespread smuggling became virtually impossible. In a showcase trial, the British could produce so little evidence of illegal activity by John Hancock's *Liberty* that they ended up dropping the charges, making Hancock a hero. Instead of prosecutors, it was customs officers who became targets of ritualistic punishment by the Sons of Liberty. When a Salem, Massachusetts, customs officer refused a bribe and tried to seize a ship, he was tarred and feathered and hauled around town in a cart wearing a sign branding him as an informer. In Providence, collector James Saiville was stripped, painted with turpentine and feathers, beaten and jostled around the port in a wheelbarrow.

In November 1770 in Salem, New Jersey, customs collector James Hatton tried to seize a coasting vessel that was emptying goods from ships anchored in Delaware Bay, only to have the smugglers' ship recaptured by a mob. Hatton, himself arrested and jailed for wounding a crewman, sent his son to recover the vessel. He found it in Philadelphia's harbor, but he was attacked by its crew, who beat him, tarred and feathered him and poured hot tar in his wounds. But no witnesses would testify. Philadelphia's deputy customs collector, John Swift, reporting to the American Board, explained why he dropped the case:

> The hands of Government are not strong enough to oppose the numerous body of people who wish well to the cause of smuggling. . . . What can a Governor do, without the assistance of the Governed? What can the Magistrates do, unless they are supported by their fellow Citizens? What can the King's officers do, if they make themselves obnoxious to the people amongst whom they reside?[28]

As the British government, employing the Royal Navy in an effectual blockade as well as troops and customs officers ashore, exerted more pressure on American merchants, those oppressed passed from enterprising colonial businessmen under the century-long policy of benign neglect to determined and systematic smugglers against ever more numerous regulations and taxes to outright resistance, moving closer to rebellion against the Mother Country. There are few better examples than John Brown of Providence, who had attained the status of a merchant prince.

On June 10, 1772, the Royal Navy customs schooner *Gaspee* ran aground on the shoals at Namquit Point in Narragansett Bay, seven miles below Providence, while pursuing a suspected smuggling packet. After dark, Brown organized eight boatloads of men and attacked the schooner. Seriously wounding Lieutenant Dudington, its commanding officer, they put him and his crew ashore, ransacked the vessel and set it afire. Moments later, it exploded and burned to the waterline.

Thoroughly alarmed, Massachusetts' Royal Governor Thomas Hutchinson reported to London that 80 percent of the "prodigious" amount of tea consumed by Bostonians was smuggled from Holland through the Dutch Caribbean colony of St. Eustatius to avoid paying the British three-penny customs duty. He warned that if Britain "shows no resentment against that Colony [Rhode Island] for so high an affront," it could encourage colonists to adopt measures "to obtain and secure their independence." His appeal to London prompted Lord North to offer a £500 reward and appoint an investigating commission made up of royal governors and chief justices to identify the rioters and send them to Britain to stand trial for treason. But no witness came forward and the commissioners had to leave town. No arrests were ever made, and Brown would later boast in writing of his exploit.[29]

As angry men all over America read the Crown order in the *Gaspee* affair in their newspapers, they set up committees of correspondence to coordinate their protests against British innovations endangering civil liberties, including the right to a speedy trial by a jury of one's own peers guaranteed by Magna Carta. Against this backdrop, Parliament passed the Tea Act of 1773 to enable the British East India Company to recoup revenues lost to massive Dutch tea smuggling through St. Eustatius. Many of the stockholders, including the colonial secretary, Lord Dartmouth, had paid £1,000 per share in the monopoly; its share price in 1773 plummeted to £160. With a vast surplus of 17 million pounds of tea on hand in Britain, the nearly bankrupt company appealed to the government for relief. Parliament heard that 1 million pounds of smuggled tea was slipping past customs into Philadelphia alone each year. The Act forgave all duties on tea exported to America but retained Townshend's three-pence-in-the pound import duty, undercutting both legitimate Boston merchants and smug-glers. Instead of time-honored auctions, the tea was to be consigned. The company chose the consignees from the friends of the government: in Massachusetts, they were two sons and a nephew of Royal Governor Hutchinson. Fully half a million pounds of tea sailed directly toward American ports in September, the Boston consignment aboard the *Dartmouth*, the *Eleanor* and the *Beaver*, all ships owned by Nantucket whale oil exporter William Rotch. Their arrival on November 17 triggered a mass meeting and a demand that the tea be sent back. Governor Hutchinson refused.

Shortly after dark on December 16, some 8,000 Bostonians—more than half of the port's population—gathered in a cold, driving rain around Old South Church. When Captain Francis Rotch of the *Dartmouth* reported the governor's refusal to allow the ship to clear the harbor for England with-out paying the duty, Samuel Adams, moderator of the meeting, proclaimed from the pulpit, "I don't see what more Bostonians can do to save their country!" At this prearranged signal, a shrill bosun's whistle split the air and a war whoop erupted. In the doorway, several dozen men threw off their coats. Their faces blackened, they wore old blankets around their shoulders and carried hatchets. "The Mohawks are come," shouted one as they raced toward Griffin's Wharf to man three longboats that carried them to the towering tea ships.

In the moonlight, an estimated 3,000 Bostonians watched silently as the "Mohawks" split into teams. Ordering ashore the customs officers, the "Mohawks" disappeared into the holds of the three tea ships and, with blocks and tackles, hoisted up 342 lacquered Chinese chests of blended Darjeeling and Ceylon tea valued at £9,659 and six shillings—approximately $1.7 million in 2017 currency—to the decks where, in three hours, they were methodically split open with axes and their 90,000 pounds of tea shoveled methodically into Boston Harbor. One eyewitness was John Adams: in his diary he recorded that there was to the protest a "Dignity, a Majesty, a Sublimity."[30]

The Sons of Liberty mimicked the raid in New York City. In Annapo-lis, they used the tea chests as kindling to set fire to the *Peggy Stewart*. In Greenwich, New Jersey, where the tea was offloaded to be hidden before transshipment to Philadelphia, the consignment, soon discovered, went up in flames. In Charleston, the Sons of Liberty forced the tea consignees to pour the tea into the harbor.

General Gage was on home leave in England when news arrived of the Tea Party. Since the lethal 1770 riots he had urged the Ministry to annihilate Massachusetts' charter and abolish the town meeting's "democraticall despotism." The Tea Party convinced the king that Gage's assessment was correct. He ordered Lord North to push through Parliament a set of Coercive Acts. Gage became royal governor as well as commander in chief. Returning to Boston, he promulgated what Bostonians called the Intolerable Acts that effectively annulled Massachusetts' charter. Henceforth, town meetings could only be called with his permission. The Crown would appoint an executive council, effectively stripping the general assembly of its crucial taxing and spending authority. All judges would be appointed and paid by the Crown; juries chosen by the sheriff. Until Bostonians repaid the value of the tea, Parliament cut off all trade by land and sea with the port town and rescinded fishing rights in the Atlantic. On February 10, 1775, the Ministry introduced the New England Trade and Fisheries Act—the so-called Restraining Act—intended to "starve New England" into submission by restricting its trade with Britain, Ireland and the West Indies as well as prohibiting fishing in the North Atlantic. The bill also threatened many British merchants with ruin. In vain, Irish conservative Edmund Burke grandiloquently assailed it in a 25,000-word speech as "prudent management," not heavy-handed force. He praised the "commerce of your Colonies," calling it "out of all proportion beyond the numbers of the people." Yet the bill passed by more than three to one, and on April 13, the bill was extended to all the American colonies.[31]

On June 1, 1774, the day the Restraining Act took effect, church bells pealed solemnly all over New England, shop windows were draped in black and normal business came to a standstill. Other colonies kept Boston provisioned for free, driving donated flocks of sheep and herds of pigs across the narrow neck connecting the town and the mainland—between British cannon. In Virginia, if George Washington harbored any lingering doubts about British intentions, they evaporated when he learned about yet another punitive Parliamentary stricture—the Administration of Justice Act—that ordered Boston's Committee of Correspondence to disband and threatened criminal prosecution against anyone who sought to disrupt trade with Great Britain. The king's decree made Washington and all other Associators, as the signers of the trade boycott called themselves, liable to prison and, under the new law, subject at the discretion of a royal governor to extradition to England to stand trial—"where it is impossible," he wrote to neighbor Bryan Fairfax, "that justice shall be done."[32]

Washington had long sat silently in the House of Burgesses, absorbing impassioned debates. Now the specter of a trial for treason haunted his letters to his old friend and he began to speak out strongly against the British assault on American civil liberties, calling it "the most despotic system of tyranny that ever was practiced in a free government. I think the Parliament of Great Britain hath no more right to put their hands into my pocket without my consent than I have to put my hands into yours for money."[33]

The same day Parliament passed the Coercive Acts, it overwhelmingly approved the Quebec Act, replacing the military laws in force since the end of the French and Indian War with a highly centralized form of civil government. This further outraged Puritan New England. The counter-revolutionary Act was the personal creation of Quebec's military governor, French-speaking Sir Guy Carleton. He sought to win over the conquered French *habitants* by honoring their traditions, their laws and even their Roman Catholicism. This outcome dismayed some 3,000 New England traders and settlers who had flocked in to take over the good lands and the Indian fur trade.

The Quebec Act, considered by Bostonians a reprisal for the Tea Party, created a vast colony entirely unlike any other province. Extending Quebec's borders to the Ohio River, deep into territory claimed by Connecticut, Massachusetts and Virginia, the Act blocked westward expansion. George Washington and other veterans of Britain's wars with France had long expected land grants in the Ohio Valley; Benjamin Franklin, his son (the royal governor of New Jersey) and Philadelphia mercantile houses had invested heavily in multimillion-acre colonization schemes in the Illinois country, which were now cut off by a vast fur-producing Indian reserve.

This Act created a single-house legislature appointed by the king to advise the governor, with no lower house elected by the people; it preserved French land-tenure law and abolished habeas corpus and trial by jury. The Quebec Act was widely regarded as a model of the form of government the British planned to impose on their colonies to the south. At a time when

Catholicism was still suppressed in Britain, establishment of the religion in Quebec meant that, for the first time since the Reformation, there were in the British realm bishops supported by tithing of the crops and incomes of all citizens. Injection of the religious issue brought an immediate and harsh reaction.

At Yale College, Reverend Ezra Stiles called the Quebec Act the outstanding American grievance against the British government. Thousands of New England troops who had marched at the side of Britain to evict the French from Canada now felt betrayed.

Protest against the Quebec Act would be incorporated in the most radical Massachusetts document, the Suffolk Resolves, precursor of the Declaration of Independence. Dr. Joseph Warren, the Resolves' author, called the new Canadian charter "dangerous in an extreme degree to the Protestant religion and to the rights and civil liberties of all America. . . . We are indispensably obliged to take all the measures for our security . . . to acquaint ourselves with the art of war as soon as possible."[34]

Adopted at a province-wide convention, the Resolves declared the Coercive Acts unconstitutional and recommended ignoring them. The convention urged Massachusetts' citizens to form a provisional government to collect taxes and withhold them from the royal government until the Coercive Acts were repealed. Meanwhile, citizens were to arm and form their own militia. Finally, the Resolves recommended stringent economic sanctions against Britain.

Carried immediately to Philadelphia by Paul Revere, the Resolves received the endorsement of the First Continental Congress, which ordered them printed and distributed throughout North America and Britain. The conservatives in Congress responded by urging members to endorse a "plan of a Proposed Union between Great Britain and the Colonies," drawn up by Joseph Galloway, Speaker of the Pennsylvania Assembly, Benjamin Franklin's erstwhile political lieutenant, and supported by his son, Governor Franklin. Resembling Benjamin Franklin's 1754 Plan of Union, the Galloway plan offered a conservative alternative to the Suffolk Resolves to govern "the general affairs of America."

Calling for a grand legislative council elected triennially by the legislatures of all the colonies and meeting annually, the plan proposed a president appointed by the king and serving at his pleasure. Whereas Benjamin's plan had merely called for a union of all colonies to facilitate defense against Indian attacks and to arbitrate land claims, Galloway's plan went much further: the American legislature was to be connected to Parliament and would send delegates from America to sit in the House of Commons. This particular provision, proposed by Governor Franklin, would provide virtual representation of Americans in Parliament and addressed a major cause of the unrest of the 1760s. Either Parliament or the American council could propose laws for the colonies but both must approve them. The underlying principle of Galloway's Plan of Union was that no law could bind America without her consent.

Galloway—Pennsylvania's chief delegate to Congress—had the support of moderates in South Carolina, New York and the Middle Colonies. When Galloway presented it to Congress, Sam Adams introduced a motion to table it, which carried by a 6-5 vote. Soon after Galloway shelved his plan, he received a strong hint to withdraw it from consideration. A box delivered to his Market Street mansion contained a hangman's noose and orders to use it himself or else a mob would; also in the box was a torn life insurance policy. Galloway abruptly withdrew his motion and retired to his farm. Following its policy of making unanimous each delegation's votes, the First Continental Congress withdrew Galloway's plan, then voted to expunge the motion from its minutes. In 1922, 148 years later, a remarkably similar plan became the framework of the British Commonwealth of Nations.

In place of the Galloway plan, the Continental Congress drafted a Declaration and Resolves, a conciliatory olive-branch petition listing its grievances, and sent it to London. Virtually identical to the Suffolk Resolves, the petition criticized revenue laws imposed by the Parliament since 1763 and protested the extension of Vice Admiralty jurisdiction, dissolution of colonial assemblies and the stationing of a standing army in seaport towns in peacetime. Among ten resolutions, the petition spelled out the rights of colonists, including "life, liberty and property," and the exclusive power of provincial legislatures "in all cases of taxation and internal polity," subject only to royal veto. Congress sent off its olive branch to London, pledging economic sanctions until the repeal of the thirteen Parliamentary acts passed since 1763 that violated American charter rights. The colonial secretary, Lord Dartmouth, placed it at the bottom of a pile of eighty-three petitions.

All that winter, the drift toward war continued. When George Washington returned home in late October to Mount Vernon from the First Continental Congress, he found militia drilling in every town. In November, as Lord North laid the petition before a reconvening Parliament, King George gave a belligerent opening speech from the throne in which he denounced Congress's "most daring spirit of resistance and disobedience to law." Even an impassioned pro-American speech by the aged Lord Chatham—the brilliant William Pitt, engineer of the great British victory over France a decade earlier—could not stem the anti-American tide. Chatham's bill to recall the troops from Boston went down noisily to defeat, 68-18. Chatham's call for repeal of all acts that had enflamed Americans in exchange for American acknowledgment of Parliamentary supremacy was again shouted down, 61-31.

For more than a year, English merchants in Montreal had been corresponding by courier with Samuel Adams and the Boston Committee of Correspondence. A secret Montreal committee met with Adams's emissary to assure Massachusetts Patriot leaders that many Montreal merchants, transplanted from New England after the French and Indian War, were willing to support Boston's cause. In February 1775 Adams sent a letter to the Canadians, inviting them to set up their own committees of correspondence. In early April Adams again sent the courier back to Montreal, this time to invite the English Canadians to send two merchants as a delegation to the Continental Congress in Philadelphia to represent the 3,000 transplanted New Englanders now living in Quebec Province. Many merchants, fearing reprisals, could agree only to set up a secret committee of correspondence, with John Walker, the province's wealthiest merchant, as chairman.

On May 1, 1775, the day the Quebec Act officially took effect, a crowd gathered at the Place d'Armes at Montreal's center. There, King George III's bust had been smeared with a coat of black paint, and a rosary of potatoes and a wooden cross, inscribed "Behold the Pope of Canada, or the English fool," had been draped around its neck. Indignant British officers offered a fifty-pound reward for the culprit. David Franks, a young Jewish merchant, later admitted his handiwork. The next day, a French merchant told bystanders that the proper punishment for such an insult was hanging. At that, young Franks punched the Frenchman as another merchant named Salomon shouted that it must have been done by a French Canadian. When a Frenchman retorted it was more likely a Jew, Salomon punched him in the face. Both Franks and Salomon were dragged off to jail, even though the news of open warfare in Massachusetts had not yet reached Canada.

SETTING OUT SYSTEMATICALLY to disarm Massachusetts, General Gage had dispatched from Boston crack troops to seize town powder magazines. For nearly a year, a network of thirty "observers" coordinated by the Boston Committee of Safety provided intelligence of British movements. Alerted by post riders on fast Narragansett horses led by Paul Revere, townspeople all over the Bay Colony stood silently, sullenly by, watching while columns of the detested redcoats, locally called "bloody lobsterbacks," sortied from Boston to seize the colony's supply of gunpowder and weapons.

On September 1, 1774, as many as 20,000 armed militiamen, many of them combat-seasoned veterans of the French and Indian War, swarmed around Boston when British troops marched to Charlestown to seize the town's 125-barrel supply of gunpowder. Some militiamen, primed to fight raw British recruits, rode one hundred miles or more from every direction, only to turn back in disappointment when they learned that, since the British had drawn no blood, there was no legitimate provocation to shoot them. Alarmed, Gage ordered Boston Neck fortified with twenty-four heavy guns.

On December 14, 1774, Paul Revere warned that 2,000 British regulars were about to march to the coastal town of Portsmouth to seize New Hampshire's munitions. The local Sons of Liberty, led by John Sullivan, broke into the lightly garrisoned Fort William and Mary, overpowered the guards and carted off guns and gunpowder.

After a second Provincial Congress convened at Cambridge on February 1, 1775, to decide on plans for war, Gage's Loyalist informants alerted him that carriages for twenty cannon were being built at Salem. A 150-man detachment of the 64th Regiment boarded a transport and sailed to

Marblehead to land and attack the Salem forge at night. They found their route blocked: Salem men and women had hoisted the drawbridge across the North River. When the Regulars lowered their guns to fire, towns-people warned them that, if a single man pulled a trigger, they would all be killed. In March, when Brigadier Hugh, Lord Percy rode at the head of a full brigade of 1,200 regulars out into the countryside, post riders sounded the tocsins and, again, as thousands of militia turned out, Percy turned back. In effect, the Patriots of Massachusetts were blockading the British inside Boston.

As Gage awaited further instructions from London, Massachusetts towns organized crack units of seventy rapid-response minutemen to turn out on a moment's notice. The resistance movement not only was spread-ing throughout New England but also was winning growing sympathy in other colonies, especially among the merchant class. In Connecticut, the general assembly commissioned two new independent military compa-nies, each recruited, outfitted and paid by wealthy ship owners. In New Haven, Benedict Arnold, son-in-law of the sheriff and owner now of thir-teen merchant ships and a thriving apothecary and luxury goods store, received the assembly's commission as captain of the 2nd Connecticut Foot Guards, recruited Yale College students and outfitted them in scarlet.

In Connecticut, Governor Trumbull anonymously drafted resolutions for the general assembly, ordering all towns to double their arsenals of powder, balls and flint. Connecticut also coined six new regiments of mi-litia, upward of 6,000 men in a colony of 100,000 citizens. The Connect-icut Assembly dispatched fast ships to the Caribbean to purchase weapons and gunpowder and ordered all militia to train for twelve days, double the normal term of service, paying them six shillings a day, double the wages of a skilled artisan.

In March 1775 a purge of leaders of old militia units swept a dozen top officers from their posts, including any suspected of being Loyalists. In-variably, their offices went to the most radical Patriots, the Sons of Liberty. Intimidated by Patriot crowds, more than 1,100 Loyalists from all over New England fled that winter from their homes into Boston, seeking Brit-ish protection. Throughout the colonies, objections to the trade boycott and militia mobilization had become dangerous, subject to a visit by mem-bers of the estimated 10,000-member Sons of Liberty.

An article in the *New York Journal* illustrated that suppression of dissent, formerly kept deliberately at the level of ostracism and intimidation, now became cruel, systematic and ritualized. Thomas Randolph, a cooper in Piscataway, New Jersey, "had publicly proved himself an enemy to his country by reviling and using his utmost endeavors to oppose the proceedings of the Continental and Provincial Conventions and Committees in defense of their rights and liberties." His sentence: tarring and feathering.

In freezing December weather, the local Sons of Liberty stripped off his clothing. They broke open a fresh barrel of pine tar and heated it in an iron cauldron until it was bubbling hot and thin enough to spread, then applied it to Randolph's head and face and body and arms and legs and groin and feet with ladles and brushes until all of his writhing, squirming skin was covered and beginning to shrivel and blister and give off a rancid steam into the crisp winter air. He must have screamed and prayed and pleaded for mercy. Then the Patriots slit open his mattress with their knives and, dancing and cheering around his strange-looking form, sprinkled sharp-tipped goose feathers all over his roasting, stinking flesh. If, as sometimes happened, the sizzling tar ignited a few of the feathers, they could be beaten out readily enough, even though, by this time, the slightest touch would make Randolph scream again. As the *Journal* recounted, Randolph was "carried in a wagon publicly round the town. He soon became duly sensible of his offense, for which he earnestly begged pardon and promised to atone, as far as he was able." After a half hour, Randolph was released and allowed to return to his home. "The whole was conducted with that regularity and decorum that ought to be observed in all public punishments."[35]

ON APRIL 14, 1775, as drilling militia practiced the manual of arms on town greens, General Gage opened fresh orders from Lord Dartmouth. Gage now had authorization to march into the countryside "with large detachments to secure obedience through every part of it." Both Massachusetts and Connecticut were to be stripped of their seventeenth-century royal charters, and Boston's radical leaders, especially brewer and town-meeting moderator Samuel Adams and militia commander John Hancock, were to be arrested and shipped in irons to London to be tried for high treason.

FOUR

"For Cutting Off Our Trade"

On April 19, 1775, a decade of ideological ferment and partisan protests over Britain's fumbling attempts to formulate imperial trade policies finally turned into open rebellion in a deadly clash of arms between Massachusetts militiamen and British regulars on the outskirts of Boston. Acrid blue clouds of musket smoke still hung over the bayonetted corpses of the Revolution's first casualties when the Massachusetts Provincial Congress, in hiding in Watertown, summoned its most trusted courier, Israel Bissell, and handed him a single document. Bissell was to ride west, then south as far as New York City, spreading the news of the British invasion. At every town he was to obtain the countersignatures of the chairman of the Committee of Safety to this missive:

> *Wed. morning near 10 of the clock*
> *Watertown,*
>
> *To all friends of American liberty: let it be known that this morning before break of Day a British brigade consisting of about 1000 or 1200 men landed at Phips farm at Cambridge and marched to Lexington where they found a company of our colony militia in arms, upon whom they fired*

without any provocation and killed six men and wounded four others. By
an express from Boston we find another brigade are now upon their
march from Boston supposed to be about 1,000. The bearer, Israel Bissell, is
charged to alarm the country, and all persons are desired to furnish him
with fresh horses, as they may be needed. I have spoken with several who
have seen the dead and wounded.[1]

What actually happened that spring day became shrouded in folklore
and would be transformed into a story repeated from poet, parent and
teacher to child and new citizen ever since. At three o'clock on a cool,
windy morning, seven hundred elite British light infantry and grenadier
guards marched to the south end of Boston Commons and boarded launches
from the men-of-war that took them up the Charles River to Cambridge.
There they stepped off, without rations or bedrolls, for an expected twelve-
mile sortie to Lexington, where, according to Loyalist informants, Patriots
were stockpiling munitions. Informed by a spy, probably Gage's American-
born wife, Margaret Kemble Gage—he later sent her home to avoid worse
embarrassment—Gage's primary targets, Samuel Adams and John Hancock,
had fled farther west and were concealed in the basement of a Puritan
church in Woburn.

When Major John Pitcairn encountered Lexington's militia formed up
on the town's green, he rode up and ordered them to disperse. By not immediately heeding his command, they crossed an invisible line that made
them rebels in arms against the king. Wheeling his horse and giving a
command to his men to surround and disarm the militia, Pitcairn saw a
gun in the hands of "a peasant" behind a stone wall "flash in the pan without going off." But two or three more guns, also fired from cover, did go
off. Instantly, without orders, "a promiscuous, uncommanded but general
Fire took place," Pitcairn later recounted, insisting he could not stop it
even when he swung his sword downward, the signal to cease firing. When
the British did stop firing, eight Americans lay dead; ten more, badly
wounded, were carried to nearby houses as the Regulars regrouped and
dog-trotted toward Concord to seize the fourteen cannon and upward of
one hundred barrels of gunpowder reportedly concealed there.[2]

When hundreds of Patriots refused to retreat and continued to fire
on the Regulars, any veneer of civility between occupier and colonist

vanished. Guided by Loyalists, grenadiers battered down doors with the brass-jacketed butts of their heavy Tower muskets in a targeted quest for concealed weapons. Dragging terrified families into Concord's streets, the Regulars ransacked and looted houses, shooting and bayoneting anyone who resisted.

As the British column reformed to countermarch to Boston, a swelling mass of well-officered militia galled them from rooftops, firing accurately out of windows, from trees, from behind stone walls. Four thousand men in moving rings of skirmishers swirled around the retreating redcoats, firing into their thinning ranks, sometimes with long guns meant for duck gunning. Riders with saddlebags bulging with a seemingly limitless supply of poorly shaped bullets resupplied clumsy muskets rarely able to hit anything beyond one hundred yards. Some historians estimate only one in three hundred lead balls hit anyone.

By the time the Regulars reached Metonomy, all of 5,500 militiamen had joined the melee in what was fast developing into the first major battle of the Revolution. Outnumbered six to one, the Regulars responded savagely, giving no quarter even at some undefended buildings, putting to death everyone they found inside. More than one hundred bullet holes riddled one tavern where grenadiers shot and bayonetted the proprietor, his wife and two topers and bashed in their skulls. In a bloodlust saturnalia, marauding British soldiers carried away anything they could cram into knapsacks, even communion silver, set fire to buildings and slaughtered livestock. One young boy responded to the carnage by scalping a wounded redcoat with a hatchet and hacking off his ears. In all, seventy-three British soldiers died and two hundred more suffered critical wounds before, reinforced, they fought their way back to their boats and the men-of-war.

Overnight, an estimated 16,000 militiamen swarmed from all over New England. Trained by the British in the French and Indian War, militia officers laid out siege lines and organized work parties that built a thin sixteen-mile line of earthworks. The dozen-year-long clash between neophyte British imperial officials, who were seemingly capable of designing legislation that only provoked American colonists and produced protests that, in turn, precipitated ever more repressive—and equally unenforceable—British edicts, now culminated in a mass of infuriated

New England militiamen. Abandoning their spring planting, their shops and their shipyards, they rushed to avenge the years of British arrogance, escalating taxes and overbearing government regulation.[3]

When weary post rider Israel Bissell swung down at New Haven at noon two and a half days later, Benedict Arnold, owner of thirteen merchant ships and an organizer of the Sons of Liberty, rounded up the sixty-three members of his 2nd Connecticut Company of Foot—some of them Yale College undergraduates—and ordered them to pack their kits and be ready to march the next morning. At dawn on April 22 they surrounded the tavern where New Haven's selectmen had been debating the grim news. At gunpoint, Arnold, son-in-law of New Haven's sheriff, demanded the keys to the town's powder magazine. Seizing ammunition, Arnold and his red-uniformed volunteers stepped off briskly toward Boston, a streak of scarlet against the bare spring landscape.

They soon encountered Samuel Holden Parsons, colonel of the New London County militia and a member of the General Assembly's extralegal committee of correspondence. Returning from leading the militia of the colony's largest port to reinforce the American lines around Boston, Parsons was rushing toward Hartford for an emergency meeting of Connecticut's principal Patriots with Royal Governor Jonathan Trumbull. He paused long enough to complain to Arnold of the Americans' inherent weakness in the face of certain British counterattack. Without artillery, militia would be helpless. Arnold boasted to Parsons he knew where to find hundreds of serviceable cannon, buried intact by the French around Lake Champlain as they retreated to Canada.

When Trumbull learned from Bissell of fighting in Massachusetts, he threw open the doors of his warehouses in Lebanon and, with his sons Jonathan and John—future history painter of the Revolution—joined neighbors in openly defying Britain's Intolerable Acts. His nineteenth-century biographer described the scene:

There he was, himself, his sons, and his son-in-law . . . in the midst of a crowd of neighbors and friends, aiding with his own hands to collect the needed stores, of all kinds . . . in the midst of barrels and boxes, horses, oxen, and carts, himself weighing, measuring, packing, and starting off teams, dealing out powder and ball.

Trumbull sent off three regiments of militia, including five hundred men from the Lebanon area, with sixty barrels of gunpowder and forty tents, the first of many long wagon trains of supplies and herds of cattle.[4]

While Arnold briskly marched toward Boston, Parsons galloped west to Hartford, arriving just as Trumbull, abdicating his office as royal governor, convened an emergency joint meeting of the Connecticut Committee of Correspondence and the Hartford Committee of Safety. Massachusetts' delegates to the Second Continental Congress had just arrived by fast sloop down the Connecticut River. Samuel Adams, whose father's fortune had been ruined by British currency regulations, and Colonel Hancock, scion of Boston's commercial dynasty, came ashore exhausted after a sleepless week on the run. They had been escorted from their Woburn hiding place by armed militia after they had waited a nerve-wracking five days for the other Massachusetts delegates, John Adams, Thomas Cushing and Robert Treat Paine.

Connecticut's contingent at Hartford included some of the colony's wealthiest merchants, blocked by royal decree from enjoying a greater share of the lucrative fur trade now being taken over by British merchants. Parsons was a major land speculator, as was Silas Deane, a blacksmith's son who had married wealthy women twice, his second wife the granddaughter of a former governor. Deane served as secretary of the assembly's Committee of Correspondence. A prime mover in the Susquehannah Land Company of Pennsylvania, a frontier land-developing scheme, Deane was the colony's leading expansionist and was closely allied with Governor Trumbull, also a stakeholder in the Pennsylvania land company. Christopher Leffingwell's family had founded Norwich and had managed a flourishing network of agricultural and mercantile businesses, including the manufacture of paper, a scarce commodity, and chocolates. It was Leffingwell who had bankrolled Arnold's march and paid his men; he was captain of the Norwich Light Infantry, a cavalry unit composed of businessmen and their clerks.

After John Adams described the chaotic conditions along Patriot siege lines, Trumbull, the only royal governor to become a revolutionary governor, without waiting for authorization from Congress or the Connecticut assembly, agreed with the others that they must act swiftly to buttress the Patriot army. They "borrowed" £3,000 (about $500,000 today) on their personal security from the colony's treasury to bankroll an expedition to seize the cannon in the Lake Champlain forts.

THEIR TOWN AND colonial powder magazines systematically stripped of munitions and devoid of artillery, the Hartford conferees knew that only to the west in the Green Mountains could they hope to muster a large, trained force to attack the British forts at Ticonderoga and Crown Point on such short notice. As soon as he heard of the fighting outside Boston, Ethan Allen, colonel-commandant of reputedly 2,000 armed settlers, offered to lead the Green Mountain Boys militia in seizing the lake forts and an estimated two hundred French cannon. During a four-year armed standoff against New York's royal government over ownership of the land claims in the region, Allen had recruited and trained the largest paramilitary force in British America.

At its extralegal meeting, the Connecticut Committee of Correspondence sent Allen a commission as colonel in charge of the expedition. From his headquarters in Bennington, Allen dispatched couriers throughout the mountain settlements to raise the Boys. At the same time, Benedict Arnold, having alerted Massachusetts' Provincial Congress of the forts' armaments and vulnerability, rode west with a Massachusetts colonel's commission to lead the attack. After a brief face-off over leadership, Allen and Arnold agreed on a joint command.

Ticonderoga's garrison did not know that war had broken out. Military dispatches did not travel overland from Boston: Royal Navy dispatch ships carried them from Boston to Halifax to Quebec to Montreal to southern Quebec. On May 10 the communiqué describing the first fighting three weeks earlier sat unopened aboard the sloop-of-war *George*, tied up at St. Jean-sur-Richelieu, 125 miles north of Fort Ticonderoga. Occupying the fort was a peacetime detachment of the 26th Regiment of Foot, mostly veterans, their wives and children, forty-six Regulars expected to put up a fight until reinforcements came from Montreal.

Late the afternoon of May 9, Ethan Allen lined up three hundred Boys who had set aside their spring plowing and rushed to Hand's Cove, where they waited anxiously in the rain for boats to ferry them the mile across Lake Champlain's southern tip to assail the fort. Six hours later, as wind whipped the lake into whitecaps, no boats had appeared. A fierce storm lashed the lake half the night, nearly wrecking the expedition. At three in the morning a single lumbering thirty-foot scow sailed by a terrified young black slave finally tacked into the cove. It had taken an hour and a half to ferry a score of men to Willow Point, a quarter mile north of the fort. By first light, Allen and Arnold were able to lead only eighty-three men up a steep slope toward the looming granite walls of the main, star-shaped fortress. It would take many more hours to shuttle the remaining militia across the lake.

A narrow, low wicket gate barred a sentry box inside. The lone guard had dozed. Arnold squeezed through first. The startled guard aimed his musket and pulled the trigger but the gun misfired. The terrified soldier threw down his gun and ran, yelling, toward the barracks. A second sentry appeared; his shot went high. As he lunged at Allen with his bayonet, Allen, sidestepping, swung his heavy cutlass at the man's head, striking a wooden comb in the British soldier's carefully coiffed and powdered hair and sending him sprawling with only a slight cut—the only blood spilled during the attack.

While Arnold led men up into the barracks to wake each sleeping soldier at gunpoint, Allen, yelling "No quarter! No quarter!" ordered the stunned sentry to lead him to the commandant's quarters. As Allen roared, "Come out of there, you damned old rat," Captain Walter Delaplace took time to don his full dress uniform and his sword before he emerged to ask Allen what terms he would give. Allen demanded immediate capitulation. With that, Delaplace surrendered his sword, his pistols and the mightiest fortress in colonial America.[5]

Two days later on Allen's orders, his cousin, Captain Seth Warner, and forty Boys captured a sergeant, nine regulars, women and children at Crown Point, where 111 cannon had been abandoned by the French. Allen sent off to the Second Continental Congress, convening that very day three hundred miles to the south in Philadelphia, an inventory of seventy-eight serviceable cannon, from three-pounders to forty-two-pounders and siege mortars; three howitzers and a number of swivel guns; as well as 18,000 pounds of musket balls and 30,000 flints. This unbelievable treasure of state-of-the-art weaponry would enable the Americans to fight the British on more even terms.

The news that Allen and Arnold, commissioned respectively by Connecticut and Massachusetts, had captured British forts in New York jolted a Continental Congress far from ready for such an overt act of war. Without even a military committee to study what to do about the British attack near Boston, the ferocious response by Massachusetts militia left a divided Congress reeling.

The idea of seizing the King's forts horrified conservatives. On May 26, the same day it sent another conciliatory message to the king, Congress passed a resolution to put the colonies "into a state of defence"; but a week later, it voted against supporting "any expedition of incursion" into Canada. With thousands of combat veterans entrenched in siege lines around Boston, Congress could only pass a resolution to take a tentative first step toward creating a continental military.

PREPARING TO RETURN to Philadelphia and a Second Continental Congress, George Washington was reviewing the Alexandria militia when an express rider arrived at Mount Vernon with an urgent message. Early the morning of April 21, the captain of the armed British schooner *Magdalen* had landed with fifteen marines and, on orders of the royal governor, Lord Dunmore, seized all twenty barrels of the colony's meager store of gunpowder from the brick magazine in Williamsburg. An angry crowd had agreed to wait before marching to the governor's palace. The town council asked Dunmore to return the powder, insisting that it was for their own protection in case of an Indian attack or a slave uprising. Dunmore refused and issued weapons to his household.

The next day, another rider charged up the lane to Mount Vernon to report sketchy details of fighting in Massachusetts. The news that Americans had stood and fought the British thrilled Washington. Caught between two fires, Washington wondered whether he should stay in Virginia in case fighting Lord Dunmore became unavoidable or if he should go to Philadelphia where Congress would obviously have to decide what to do about a far broader threat. At this tremendously inopportune moment he received a haughty letter from Lord Dunmore declaring that he was nullifying the 1754 Ohio grant for veterans because the veterans' surveyor had not sworn the correct oath. Infuriated, Washington decided his place was with the continental resistance movement; his own private interests would have to wait. Packing his blue and red British brigadier's uniform in his portmanteau, he turned over his business affairs to his brother-in-law, Fielding Lewis, his farms and Mount Vernon to his cousin, Lund, sent off some cash to his mother and sadly said goodbye to his wife, Martha. He would be home in July, he assured her.

As WASHINGTON'S CARRIAGE jounced toward Philadelphia, five hundred horsemen rode out to escort him. New England's delegates received an equally enthusiastic cavalcade the next day. At the Pennsylvania State House (today's Independence Hall) delegates sat colony by colony around green baize-covered tables as Massachusetts' delegation reported mobilization of 13,600 men but a terrible shortage of gunpowder. Washington attended in uniform to make the statement that at least one delegate favored firmer measures. As if in response, a majority elected him to chair a committee to study New York's defenses.

Exactly one month after Lexington, his committee reported back, urging general defense preparations, recruitment bounties, garrisons, as well as a final attempt at reconciliation. Six days of debate later, six resolutions emerged to prepare New York City for the inevitable counterattack. Each week brought Washington fresh duties. The new president, John Hancock, appointed Washington to the board for financial management. All the other members were merchants. Washington's obvious experience as a military logician next led to his appointment as chair of the committee on supply. It didn't take much time to discover that there was little ammunition to collect and the colonies were nearly destitute of other munitions. Few solutions emerged. All that Washington could do was to urge interior towns to send gunpowder to the ill-equipped volunteers barricading Boston.[6]

He also recommended, and Congress agreed, to form ten companies of "expert riflemen" from the backwoods of Virginia, Maryland and Pennsylvania to be sent to Boston and placed under the command "of the chief officer in that army." But just who would that be? Most of the veteran field-grade officers were too old, left over from the French war. Washington, with five years of command experience, was forty-three, the perfect age. On May 14 John Adams argued that unless the commanding general came from outside Massachusetts, other colonies would fear New England domination. The obvious choice was a Virginian. Virginia outnumbered New York and Massachusetts five to one; its troops, crops and money were vital to intercolonial success. When Adams said the one man he had in mind was from Virginia, Washington stood up and practically ran from the room. Ushered back in, he heard that "all America" wanted him. But, as Washington confided to Patrick Henry with tears in his eyes, he did not relish the command: "From the day I enter upon the command of the American armies I date my fall and the ruin of my reputation." With no other name placed in nomination, Washington accepted. On June 22, after refusing a proffered five-hundred-pound annual salary, Washington packed his papers and his portmanteau—just as a messenger arrived with news of a terrible battle.[7]

At a secret meeting on June 15, the very day Congress appointed Washington commander in chief, the Massachusetts Provincial Congress, upon learning that Gage intended to occupy the Charlestown peninsula, voted unanimously to fortify Bunker Hill, the highest of three hills overlooking Boston. That night, nine hundred young farmers double-timed past Bunker Hill to Breed's Hill and marked out a small redoubt roughly forty-five yards square. Joined by militia from New Hampshire and Connecticut, they began digging at midnight and ran a breastwork one hundred yards down the hill to an impassable swamp. Expecting a classic British flanking attack, two hundred Connecticut marksmen, including Colonel John Trumbull, the governor's son, took positions behind a rail fence with a stone base one hundred yards to the rear and downhill from the mud fort. Between the Mystic River beach and the fence lay fresh-mown hay. Soon, four companies of New Hampshire frontiersmen reinforced them, throwing up a stone breastwork across the beach to the water's edge. All night the rugged farmers, including seven freed African Americans and Stockbridge Indians, dug a square hole five feet deep, piling the excavated dirt into a six-foot-high wall behind it that would bake hard in the searing sun. They lined the inside of the redoubt with wooden firing platforms but forgot to pierce the front parapet with their two small cannon. Two shots at point blank range did the job.

Like so many battles that followed it, what became known as the Battle of Bunker Hill did not have to happen. The Americans were ill prepared, had few cannon, no skilled artillerymen or military engineers, little ammunition, poor communications, no chain of command, no reinforcements, no escape plan. An army of zealots, many were veterans prepared to take on a British foe who had treated them as if they were an occupied country for many years and were now trying to silence their protests in an all-out invasion of Massachusetts. For all of their handicaps, the Americans had officers seasoned by many of the same battles at which the British leaders had learned their tactics in two wars against the French. And they had surprise on their side.

At dawn, the discovery that the rebels had fortified the entire hill over-night led to a hasty British council of war. There they decided that they would initiate a classic flanking attack at once before other hills could be fortified to cut them off from the mainland. Bostonians crowded into windows and climbed onto rooftops for a better view as British men-of-war maneuvered up the Mystic River, dropped anchor close to shore and disgorged their barges as naval guns rained broadsides of shells into the hill below the fort. By noon, British grenadiers marched through the streets and down to the Charles River to landing craft. American snipers posted in deserted houses in Charlestown began peppering them, their shots falling short. British ships lowered their guns and shelled the town, setting it ablaze and destroying four hundred houses.

At noon the landing boats rode the rising tide up onto the beach. In blazing heat, Regulars wore wool uniforms and carried 125 pounds of weapons and gear, three days' rations of boiled beef and bread and cooking implements on their backs. From the start, the attack went badly. The field artillery became mired in muddy fields. The advance light infantry, trotting up the beach on the right, stumbled into the reinforced rail fence and withering fire. A bayonet charge proved impossible: the rebels fired in rotation. Row upon row of the British—many of them shot in the groin—pitched into the fresh-mown hay. Ninety-six lay dead on the beach.

Meanwhile, the new British commander, Sir William Howe, unleashed six hundred men up the steep hillside over fallen trees, tangles of blackberry and through tall grass toward the silent breastworks where fifty-seven-year-old Colonel Israel Putnam of Connecticut, cutlass in hand, lectured his sharpshooters: "Men, you are all good marksmen. Don't one of you fire until you see the whites of their eyes." At one hundred yards, the red-coats fired a volley, too high, too far away. At fifty yards, they fired again. Again, too high. Up they trudged, bayonets glimmering; the Americans could make out the brass matchboxes on their coats. The best marksmen sighted in on the crossed white sashes intersecting at the belly. As troops crumbled, pitching into the grass, thrashing and screaming, behind the earthworks young boys rammed rusty nails and double-charged buck-shot and bits of glass and lead balls and cloth wadding into the guns and handed them up to the sharpshooters on the parapet.

By noon, British artillery was pounding holes in the crude fort, shells crashing through the useless little sally port, killing defenders with solid-iron shot that skittered along the ground, shearing off arms, legs and heads. Suddenly the little fort became an open grave. As carefully as the sharpshooters had conserved their precious gunpowder, untrained artil-lerymen had squandered it. Sensing victory, Howe ordered his troops to drop their knapsacks and fix bayonets. They charged through scattered fire and stormed over the ramparts. Trapped, 150 men had no way out. The Regulars fired down into the mass of running, stumbling, yelling Americans. A shot in the forehead killed Dr. Joseph Warren, author of the Suffolk Resolves and father of four young children. Of 1,600 Americans, 140 died—two-thirds of them killed after the redoubt fell—and 301 were wounded, with thirty taken prisoner. Proportionately, it was the costliest victory in all British military history: of 2,400 combatants, 1,054 were killed and wounded, a high percentage of them officers.

Inside Boston, even as carts of screaming, moaning, wounded British rumbled through rutted streets, British commander Howe declared that he had only fallen short of totally crushing the American rebellion because he lacked adequate manpower. He immediately demanded 30,000 fresh troops from London.

THE ULTIMATE TOLL of battle included Faith Trumbull, eldest daughter of the governor. She got to talk to her brother, John, just before the British attack. Years later, he wrote that he had time only for "a momentary inter-view with my favorite sister." Faith told John that her husband, Colonel Jabez Huntingdon, was leading his Norwich militia toward the fort. "The novelty of military scenes excited great curiosity," the future history painter wrote. "My sister was part of a party of young friends who were attracted to visit the army." The timing of her visit was most unfortunate. . . . She found herself surrounded not by "the pomp and circumstance of glorious war" but in the midst of all its horrible realities. She saw too clearly the life of danger and hardship upon which her husband and her favorite brother had entered, and it overcame her strong but too sensitive mind.

Faith Trumbull lapsed into a deep depression and, five months later, committed suicide.[8]

GENERAL WASHINGTON RECEIVED details of the battle from couriers as he began a ten-day journey with his staff and an escort of five hundred militia on June 23. Crossing heavily Loyalist New Jersey, he pulled a purple smock over his navy blue uniform and donned a hat with a plume. At New York City, a crowd turned out to cheer him; one hour later, another crowd, including many of the same people from the first, hailed the British royal governor, General Sir William Tryon, returning from England with orders to suppress the rebellion. Washington's second-in-command, Hudson River land baron Philip Schuyler, told him that New York would not be safe so long as the British could counterattack down the Hudson. Schuyler, general in chief of the Northern Department, agreed to lead a full-scale invasion of Canada to seize Montreal and Quebec before the British could reinforce from England. Congress had unanimously authorized a preemptive invasion if the intrusion was "not disagreeable to the Canadians."[9]

Washington arrived without ceremony at Cambridge, Massachusetts, on Sunday, July 2, and set up temporary headquarters in a single spare room in the house of the president of Harvard College. Riding the lines, he quickly grasped the army's weakness. Despite a four-to-one numerical advantage, he had no cannon, no military engineers, very little gunpowder. Washington deplored the conditions he found: 16,000 men living in a shantytown of huts made of sod, planks and fence rails or tents made of linen or sailcloth. Most only had the clothes they had worn when they left home weeks before—homespun breeches, rough linen shirts, leather vests—and carried the family firelock. He found a paucity of nearly everything: uniforms, muskets, gunpowder, cannon, picks, shovels, tents. At his first council of war he was informed by his officers that it was becoming hard to find any new recruits other than "boys, deserters and negroes." Each New England colony officially forbade black men, indentured white servants or apprentice boys; Washington barred the continued service of Indians. In Virginia, Washington had preached an end to the importation of slaves; in Massachusetts, he now was gratified to see how many freed blacks had enlisted.[10]

Where scores of men had been digging trenches, he put thousands to work. He discovered that there were no trained sergeants and few officers to teach the myriad routines of military life and discipline. Fuming about using the "exceedingly dirty and nasty" New Englanders to oppose the spit-and-polish British professionals a mile away, he blamed an "unaccountable kind of stupidity" on "the levelling spirit" and the "principles of democracy [that] so universally prevail." Washington saw himself—and the British saw him—as the Oliver Cromwell of the revolution. Like Cromwell, he was an aggrieved member of the country gentry engaging in a civil war, with the virtuous American colonies oppressed by a corrupt court. But in this case, Parliament was choosing to serve an errant king and finding it necessary to put a powerful army in the field to compel his reforms.[11]

When no more attacks came from the British, Washington reasoned that Howe was waiting for reinforcements. In the meantime, he could use his superiority in manpower to take the offensive. He urged Schuyler, with 4,000 Connecticut militia, to accelerate the Canadian invasion. Not the scantest quantity of gunpowder could be found in New York, Schuyler argued. Governor Trumbull scavenged five hundred pounds of gunpowder from Connecticut's town stocks and managed to send Schuyler £15,000 as well as four hundred barrels of pork. It was August 30 before Schuyler's forces disembarked on Canadian soil, and there they waited for him—he wrote Washington that he was suffering from an attack of rheumatic gout. Schuyler lost another full month when Connecticut troops at Fort Ticonderoga refused to serve under New York officers and a promised Vermont regiment failed to materialize.

The delays also set back Washington's plan for a simultaneous surprise attack—led by Benedict Arnold—on Quebec from the rear, which they would approach through the trail-less Maine wilderness. To win Washington and the command over, Arnold had produced the journal of a captured British engineer who had mapped the Kennebec region of Maine.

On the hot gray Sunday morning of September 3, 1775, the Continental Army formed up for Washington's inspection of the ten-mile cordon of fortifications investing Boston. Washington, his aides and brigade commanders and Arnold, in his red Connecticut Foot Guards uniform, appeared to study every man, every musket. A chaplain later wrote:

> The drum beat in every regiment. . . . All was bustle. . . . The whole army was paraded in continued line of companies. With one continued roll of drums, the general-in-chief with his staff passed along the whole line, regiment after regiment presenting arms.[12]

Many of the men had tired of the heat, the boredom, the grind of camp life. The prospect of action, especially in a cooler place, excited those who had fought only once in five months. Washington had appointed Arnold a colonel of the Continental Army and allowed him to pick the troops who would march to Quebec before the British could reinforce it—only 775 redcoats held the vast province. After the review, Arnold visited each regiment; forming the men in squares, he explained his need for volunteers. By noon he had 6,000, five times what he needed. He chose men under thirty and above average height. Today, every man was an expert woodsman *and* boatman. By nightfall, he had a full regiment of 1,050 men.

Washington was happy to see the riflemen go: while their guns could hit a man in the head at a mile and a half, these "shirt-tail men" in hunting shirts and moccasins had been robbing farms and fellow soldiers and violating military etiquette by sniping British officers at long range against Washington's explicit orders. Washington arranged for a fleet of eleven fishing vessels to take Arnold's newly minted regiment of rangers from Newburyport, Massachusetts, to the mouth of the Kennebec River. The little army would march overland and then sail up the Kennebec as far as Gardinerstown, where 220 shallow-draft boats were being built to carry men and supplies all the way to within 100 miles of Quebec City. He expected the march to take only twenty days. So confident was Washington that the expedition would succeed, when he finally informed Congress, he grossly underestimated the distance and the difficulty of the march. In his orders, he emphasized that the American invaders were to "consider yourselves as marching, not through an Enemy's Country; but that of our friends and brethren." He ordered punishment for "every attempt to plunder or insult any of the Inhabitants." He gave Arnold a strongbox of gold and silver coins. They were to buy everything with cash, stealing nothing.

From the beginning, everything went wrong. Washington had refused the aid of Penobscot Abenaki guides and the expedition got lost. The captured British map turned out to be a fraud. The bateaux had been made of poorly caulked green wood and had all sunk before the expedition reached Canada—which it did in sixty days, the men nearly starved, not in twenty. Fully a third died or deserted. The entire rear guard mutinied and returned to Cambridge. Washington court-martialed Major Robert Enos but all the witnesses were in Canada. Arnold arrived at the St. Lawrence three days too late. Loyalists, Scots Highlanders from Newfoundland and New York, had reinforced the city and thoroughly defeated Arnold's assault. Richard Montgomery, who had finally taken over Schuyler's command and captured Montreal, had been killed in the attack on Quebec on the last day of 1775. Arnold had been critically wounded and all but 150 of his men killed or taken prisoner. Arnold was besieging the walled city with only a few guns and a few French Canadian volunteers. The Canadian expedition could only be rescued with massive reinforcements, but that was impossible until spring. In the meantime, Washington had lost 900 men and his first offensive.

WHEN STILL NO British attack came from Boston, Washington pursued other ways to pressure them and ease his own terrible shortages. He issued letters of marque to six privateering ships crewed by soldiers from Massachusetts port towns. At the same time, Congress directed him to commission two ships to interdict British arms shipments from Halifax. The two ships, the *Cabot* and the *Andrew Doria*, became the first official U.S. Navy vessels. By year's end, as Congress authorized more vessels, Washington's Navy, as it was dubbed, included seven ships with thirteen more scheduled to be built. Congress approved a schedule of prize money to be allotted to officers and crewmen. One-tenth of the money derived from auctioning off captured ships and cargoes was to go to Washington himself for his private use, a typical arrangement for eighteenth-century commanders. The infant navy quickly eased one of Washington's worst problems, capturing a British ordnance brig carrying 2,000 muskets, 100,000 flints, 20,000 rounds of shot and 30 tons of musket balls.

The nearly universal shortage of munitions, especially gunpowder, proved one of Washington's more enduring obstacles. Historian Orlando Stephenson notes, "The greater part of the gunpowder stored in the colonial magazines had lain there since the Seven Years' War, the few powder-mills were in ruins, the manufacture of the explosive almost a lost art." As Americans' determination to fight had grown, radical leaders had rushed to procure whatever they could however they could, often by seizing private property or Crown supplies. In December 1774 New Hampshire militia had attacked Fort William and Mary in Portsmouth, seizing 10,100 pounds of gunpowder. In May 1775 the Sons of Liberty appropriated six hundred pounds from Savannah's powder magazine; in July, they boarded a royal navy ship and carried off 12,700 pounds. In a matter of months, the rebellious colonists secured another 3,000 pounds in New Hampshire, 12,000 in Massachusetts, 4,000 each in Connecticut, Maryland and Pennsylvania and 17,000 in Rhode Island, but heavily Loyalist New York and New Jersey yielded almost none. Under the guise of post office business, Benjamin Franklin, a member of Pennsylvania's Committee of Safety and a delegate to the Continental Congress, smuggled wagons to Washington's camp loaded with 4,000 pounds of powder gathered in Philadelphia, stopping along the way to berate his son, William, the last holdout as a royal governor, for refusing to come over to the revolutionary cause.[13]

Washington pleaded for even the smallest quantities. Half of the 80,000 pounds procured in the opening weeks of the war had found its way to the fighting around Boston. By the time Washington arrived, half the powder collected in all the colonies had been expended recklessly. He found only thirty-six barrels at Cambridge. When he took an inventory on August 3, he found only enough powder in the whole army to furnish "half a pound to each man exclusive of what was held in their horns and cartridge-boxes." By the end of August he could no longer employ his artillery, all his cannon silenced except a nine-pounder he fired peripatetically from Prospect Hill. Looking down on Boston from this vantage point, Nathanael Greene wrote back to Governor Henry Ward in Rhode Island: "Oh, that we had plenty of powder; I should then hope to see something done here for the honour of America."[14]

Not a single powder mill operated in the British colonies at the outbreak of war. On Christmas Day, 1775, Washington wrote, "Our want of
powder is inconceivable. A daily waste and no supply administers a gloomy
prospect." By January, after nine months of war, nearly all the powder
found in colonial America had been used up. The scarcity of powder im-
pelled the Second Continental Congress to act with unaccustomed celerity
to produce or import an adequate supply. While some delegates maintained that the manufacture of gunpowder was the prerogative of colonial
governments, Congress pushed through an elaborate plan for producing
saltpeter and powder. John Adams wrote James Warren on June 27, 1775,
that "Germans and others here have an opinion that every stable, Dove
house, Cellar, Vault, etc., is a Mine of Salt Petre. . . . The Mould under stables, etc., may be boiled Soon into salt Petre it is said. Numbers are about
it here," he added, sending along the proclamation with instructions for
processing that Congress was sending to each colony's government. After
Lexington, Concord and Bunker Hill, Massachusetts needed no urging.
Every colony passed legislation, promising financial support and handsome
bounties for the first to manufacture specified quantities of gunpowder,
saltpeter or both, but all sulphur had to be imported.[15]

In January 1776, at Weymouth, Massachusetts, not far from Washington's headquarters, a group of fledgling chemists celebrated their production of saltpeter before a committee of the Provincial Congress, who
deemed it "very good." In Pennsylvania, merchant Oswald Eve "established the making of powder in this Province which had not been carried
on to any extent before." By the autumn of 1777, saltpeter extracted in each
colony enabled production of 115,000 pounds of gunpowder, nearly all of
it in 1776 at the peak of revolutionary enthusiasm. Gradually, vast quantities of saltpeter would be imported, mainly from the Netherlands, until,
by late 1777, nearly 700,000 pounds of gunpowder was produced from
imported saltpeter. Added to 1.5 million pounds of imported gunpowder,
American forces had 2.4 million pounds of gunpowder to draw on during
the first half of the war, nearly 90 percent of it imported from Europe
through Dutch and French colonies in the Caribbean. America was learning how to arm itself.[16]

At the beginning of 1776—that pivotal year of revolution—George
Washington was still gloomy about the prospect of equipping an army

"without any money in our treasury, powder in our magazines, arms in our stores . . . and by and by, when we shall be called upon to take the field, shall not have a tent to lie in." Had Howe known the Americans' desperate shortages, he might have rolled over the Continental Army and ended the Revolutionary War. As the colonies went to war, they could only find weapons in gun shops, trading houses and private homes, which held an array of muskets, rifles, fowling pieces, pistols and blunderbusses. Some volunteers had no weapons at all, possessing only pikes or swords. What few iron forges existed lay hidden in remote reaches of colonies. In the Pine Barrens of New Jersey, bog iron turned into cannonballs. In Salisbury, Connecticut, a forge founded by Ethan Allen to produce iron caldrons for boiling potash underwent conversion to produce cannon, some at first dangerous only to the gunners themselves. Connecticut also set up a small musket factory at Waterbury; Pennsylvania expanded its weapons industry, centered in Lancaster County and drawing on iron mines and foundries in Warwick, Reading and Carlisle. More commonly, gunsmiths, in towns or on the frontier, worked alone or with one or two apprentices to make highly individualistic weapons—they could only produce, on average, one gun a day. Very few guns except those seized from royal stores matched.

At one point Washington even considered sending hundreds of unarmed militia home before Congress decided to confiscate weapons from Loyalists. In his memoirs, General William Moultrie of South Carolina remembered with awe that the colonists dared resist British might "without money, without arms, without ammunition, no generals, no armies, no admirals and no fleets." The people of Charleston lacked weapons and ammunition until they broke into royal magazines and took some 1,000 muskets, then seized an English brig carrying 23,000 pounds of gunpowder. The "want of powder was a very serious consideration," wrote Moultrie, "for we knew there was none to be had upon the continent of America." In Pennsylvania the Committee of Safety, chaired by Franklin, advertised for weapons in the newspapers. The few cannon available in New York City lined the parapets of Fort George—until King's College (today's Columbia University) students led by twenty-year-old Alexander Hamilton dragged them away under fire from the British man-of-war *Asia* to arm the first artillery company in the Continental Army.[17]

The revolutionaries' fortunes improved dramatically in early March 1776, when Washington's putative colonel of artillery, erstwhile Boston bookseller Henry Knox, appeared in camp with sixty pieces of French field artillery captured at Ticonderoga and Crown Point. Waiting until ice and snow paved his route, Knox and three hundred teamsters with their oxen had dragged the cannon first across the frozen Hudson River and then east along the route of the present-day Massachusetts Turnpike. On the morning of March 2, 1776, Washington's newly acquired artillery opened a booming barrage from the north shore of the Mystic River, diverting British attention away from where 2,000 men were hastily constructing an ice fort out of huge wicker baskets filled with snow and doused with water. By the morning of March 5, the sixth anniversary of the Boston Massacre, American gunners looked down on all of Boston and the entire British fleet. After two days of fierce winds and driving rain, Howe aborted a planned counterattack. By March 7, Howe began evacuating the city, sending off a regiment each day embarked on transports—after the soldiers plundered every shop and house in the town. Crowding onto any vessel they could hire, some 1,100 New England Loyalists and all they could carry joined the retreating British flotilla and sailed into exile at Halifax.

If it hadn't been for guns and ammunition purchased in Europe and the West Indies, the American Revolution would have collapsed. As early as October 1774, when the British Privy Council banned the importation of weapons to the American colonies, a brisk contraband trade sprang up, centered in St. Eustatius. Gage warned London that colonists were "sending to Europe for all kinds of Military Stores," some of them from "unscrupulous" British merchants. In the summer of 1775 Maryland's Convention sent commercial agents to St. Francois in the Caribbean to transship arms purchased in Europe by small vessels. Agents also slipped into France to procure munitions directly from Europe. Pennsylvania's Committee of Safety followed suit in August, ordering munitions from the French and Spanish West Indies. The few guns produced in Pennsylvania cost twelve dollars apiece, French muskets half that.[18]

In July, a full year before the vote on independence, Congress resolved that any ship transporting munitions for "the continent" could load and export produce in exchange, clearly in defiance of the British Orders in

Council. Two weeks later Congress appropriated $50,000 for selected merchants to buy gunpowder for the Continental Army—at a 5 percent commission. By September Congress created the Committee of Secret Correspondence, its members—merchants John Alsop and Philip Livingston of New York and Thomas Willing and Robert Morris of Philadelphia— empowered to draw on the Continental treasury to buy 1 million pounds of powder, 10,000 muskets and 40 field pieces.

In September 1775 Congress created the Secret Committee of Trade, putting Morris in charge of the business side of the war and capitalizing on the commercial contacts of Willing and Morris in Europe. Becoming known as the "financier of the Revolution," Morris wrote to Connecticut merchant Silas Deane, "It seems to me the oppert'y of improving our Fortunes ought not to be lost, especially as the very means of doing it will contribute to the Service of our Country at the same time."[19]

As the Treasury dried up, Congress voted to allow exchange with Caribbean islands of cod, lumber, tobacco and indigo for arms and ammunition, and they also commissioned agents to order and funnel supplies from Europe and the West Indies to the Continental Army. In May 1776, as Congressmen rode home to ask their conventions for authority to vote for independence, Deane landed in France to negotiate arms shipments. By December he wrote Congress that he had shipped 200,000 pounds of gunpowder and 80,000 pounds of saltpeter from France to Martinique and 100,000 pounds of gunpowder from Amsterdam. By the end of 1776 congressional agents operated openly in all the Dutch, Spanish and French colonies in the West Indies and in European ports.

Historian Peter Andreas writes,

Merchants in France, the Dutch Republic, Spain, Sweden and the West Indies viewed the revolution as an opportunity for expanding their trade and profits. Though the governments of these countries and their dependencies avoided, they seldom interfered with entrepreneurs involved in contraband trade. Some merchants were permitted to remove "outmoded" arms from royal arsenals for a nominal sum even though their destination was obvious. Dutch arms manufacturers were operating their mills at full capacity by mid-1776.[20]

Maryland's agent in the free port of St. Eustastius, Abraham Van Bibber, reported that, while officially the Dutch had imposed an embargo on selling arms and munitions to Americans to mollify the British, "[t]he Dutch understand quite well that the enforcement of the laws, that is, the embargo, would mean the ruin of their trade."[21] "Statia," as it became known, was the first foreign port to salute the American flag; no wonder, Dutch merchants on the island were selling gunpowder to the Americans at six times the going rate in Europe. Their rivals, the French, sent a deputation from a leading Nantes shipping firm to visit Washington at Cambridge; by November 1776 they were covertly supplying his army with thousands of dollars in war supplies.

By mid-1776 a river of arms, ammunition, cloth and quinine flowed through Louisiana into the Carolinas. Gunpowder smuggled in sugar hogsheads arrived in Charleston from Jamaica; from Bordeaux, three hundred casks of powder and 5,000 muskets sailed for Philadelphia—on ships flying French colors—to be hauled overland to Boston. Americans shipped tobacco to England through St. Eustatius; British manufactured goods found their way to New England via Nova Scotia. One Loyalist merchant complained to British vice admiral Molyneux Schuldham in January 1776 that "at most of the Ports east of Boston, [there were] daily arrivals from the West Indies, but most from St. Eustatius; every one brings more or less gunpowder." By the summer of 1776 many of the several thousand American privateering ships—including six hundred carrying letters of marque from Congress—avidly transported contraband arms and goods and hunted for lucrative prize British merchantmen. Following the British evacuation of Boston, fully 365 privateers operated from this one port.[22]

Privateering offered a high-risk path to overnight wealth. From nine highly profitable voyages, Joseph Peabody of Salem, Massachusetts, climbed from deckhand to investor to the port's leading shipping magnate in six years, owning eighty ships and employing 8,000 men. Israel Thorndike, once a cooper's assistant, became a privateer's captain and one of New England's wealthiest bankers. The Cabots of Beverley operated one of Massachusetts' most profitable privateering firms. Washington's quartermaster general, Nathanael Greene of Rhode Island, invested in privateering voyages. He asked one associate to keep his involvement secret and proposed using a fictitious name. When Congress tried to investigate Greene for allegedly diverting public money for his own business ventures, Washington blocked the inquiry to preserve military morale. James Forten, the free black grandson of a Maryland slave, served as powder boy—the most dangerous job—on a privateer; captured on his first voyage, he taught marbles to the son of a British admiral and survived to become America's first black millionaire, owner of a sail-making loft, inventor of the sailing winch and the man who bankrolled the anti-slavery weekly newspaper, William Lloyd Garrison's *The Liberator.*[23]

So profitable was privateering that the Continental Navy and the eleven state navies had difficulty recruiting crewmen. Many sailors deserted Continental Navy ships, lured away by the prospect of a share of a privateer's loot. One wealthy privateer investor, John Livingston, worried that peace would ruin him "if it takes place without proper warning." As historian Peter Andreas opines, "The war at sea was at least as important as the war on land, yet for the colonies it was fought almost entirely by what was essentially a profit-driven mercenary force."[24]

The leading American commercial agent, Silas Deane, sent to Paris in July 1776 to surreptitiously procure arms, posed as a Bermuda merchant. He worked with merchant-playwright Pierre-Augustin Caron de Beaumarchais through a dummy mercantile house, Rodrigue Hortalez et Cie, created to mask official French cooperation. Openly supplying contraband weapons to the rebellious American colonies would violate French neutrality under international law. By late 1777, eight arms-laden ships transported 2,000 tons of munitions to the Continental Army through Martinique for transshipment by American vessels. The French ships brought 8,750 pairs of shoes, 3,600 blankets, more than 4,000 dozen pairs of stockings, 164 brass cannon, 153 (gun) carriages, more than 41,000 balls, 37,000 fusils, 373,000 flints, 15,000 gun worms, 514,000 musket balls, nearly 20,000 pounds of lead, 161,000 pounds of powder, 21 mortars, more than 3,000 bombs, more than 11,000 grenades, 345 grapeshot, 18,000 spades, shovels and axes, over 4,000 tents and 51,000 pounds of sulphur.[25]

WITH ONLY TWO dozen warships to patrol the entire 1,000-mile Atlantic coastline, the British Navy could not enforce the blockade mandated from London in the first year of the Revolution. Instead, Royal Navy ships based in Boston—where seven rode at anchor—raided and intimidated New England towns, prodding a reluctant Congress to create the Continental Navy. On October 7, 1775, Captain James Wallace of the Royal Navy frigate *Rose* led a squadron of sixteen ships—four warships, four tenders, two transports, three schooners and three sloops—toward Bristol, Rhode Island. Earlier that day, Wallace had sent ahead a lieutenant with a list of demands from the townspeople, including three hundred sheep; the citizens refused. Wallace instantly responded by ordering a cannonade. The bombardment lasted more than an hour, with cannonballs crashing into homes, shops, the town church. On Friday the thirteenth, Wallace sailed into Newport. In exchange for "Beef Beer & necessarys for his Ships," he pledged that "he would not fire upon the Town without giving the Inhabitants sufficient warning."[26]

That same day, a committee of revolutionaries stood anxiously in a driving rain on the dock of Falmouth (now Portland, Maine) as a British squadron sailed past. Three days later, Captain Henry Mowat of the *Canceaux* sent a longboat into Casco Bay with an ultimatum: "After so many premeditated Attacks on the legal Prerogatives of the best of Sovereigns" and "the most unpardonable Rebellion" of the town's citizens, he intended to "execute a just Punishment." After frantic negotiations with terrified town leaders, Mowat agreed to hold his fire if the town surrendered its cannon and muskets and gave hostages. Falmouth sent only a handful of muskets and pistols. At 9:40 the next morning, as villagers fled with wagons and carts piled high with their belongings, three ships opened fire. While panicking oxen broke their yokes and stampeded through the throng, Mowat ordered hot shot fired on the town. Soon, the flames spread, fanned by the wind, engulfing the village. Mowat's squadron kept firing until he could later report, "The whole town was involved in smoak and combustion."[27]

Washington rushed news of the raids to Congress, describing the attack on Falmouth as a "horrid procedure" and warning that "the same Desolation is meditated upon all the Towns on the Coast." He also reported that Parliament was sending five regiments of Scottish Highlanders and Irish Catholic regulars on a new fleet that included six ships-of-the-line and 1,000 marines. That day, by an overwhelming vote, Congress gave birth to the Continental Navy. Naming Esek Hopkins—younger brother of Rhode Island delegate Stephen Hopkins—as commodore of a small fleet, Congress gave shipwright John Wharton £100,000 "to fit for sea the first fleet," beginning with the purchase and refitting of merchant-financier Robert Morris's *Black Prince* by its captain, John Barry. The *Sally*, owned by merchants Conyngham and Nesbitt, received a saltier name, *Columbus*. Both merchants drew heavily on the Continental Treasury to refit their ships. Soon, four more ships crowded Wharton's shipyard, undergoing conversions. John Adams, busily rewriting the Royal Navy's Articles of War into *Rules for the Regulation of the Navy of the United Colonies*, listed them: the *Alfred*, the *Columbus*, the *Cabot* and the *Andrew Doria*. From Rhode Island came the sloop *Katy*, renamed the *Providence*. By December 1775 two more schooners, the *Wasp* and the *Fly*, and a sloop, the *Hornet*, comprised the first American fleet.[28]

The first American amphibious operation was a raid on the British base on Providence Island in the Caribbean, where the first landing by American Marines seized a vital two hundred tons of munitions. Never very large, the complement of Continental Navy personnel fluctuated from 600 to 4,000 men and back to 600 by war's end. None of this first squadron of small American navy warships survived the conflict. By war's end, 47 larger vessels had been added to the fleet. By contrast, as many as 70,000 men served aboard the 1,697 privateering vessels—including 301 ships, 541 brigs and brigantines, 751 schooners and sloops and 104 boats and row galleys—listed by Congress. In addition, American agents abroad commissioned some 300 private warships, bringing the total of the United States' commerce-raiding, for-profit private navy vessels to 2,000, bearing 18,000 guns.

The Royal Navy not only failed to stop privateering attacks in North American waters; Continental Navy ships also raided Britain's home waters. John Paul Jones, sailing the French-built *Bon Homme Richard*, so terrorized the West Coast of England that the king, fearing imminent invasion, ordered construction of new coastal fortifications. Sweeping the Royal Navy from its waters by 1779, American privateers captured one hundred ships in 1778 and more than two hundred in 1779, forcing the British to build a fleet of frigates to escort merchant vessels carrying linen between Ireland and England. In the first two years of the war alone, seven hundred British merchant vessels captured by privateers went under the gavel, auctioned off in French and American ports. While the Continental Navy captured some two hundred British vessels worth $6 million in the course of the Revolution, privateers captured prizes valued by customs-paying Americans at $18,000 but, according to historians, with more like $66 million. Lloyd's of London listed 2,208 British vessels captured between 1775 and 1783; their evaluation at auction averaged $30,000, with one ship worth $1 million.[29]

Eleven states emptied their treasuries into their own navies. Several, like Pennsylvania, relied on row galleys to defend their waters against British marine boarding parties or Loyalist vessels. Governor Trumbull of Connecticut signed letters of marque for two hundred Connecticut-based privateering ships and stripped the state's coffers bare to build a frigate. The Puritan patriot proudly christened it the *Cromwell*. Meant to break up raids by Loyalist whaleboats, the largest vessel built by any state navy proved no match for three Loyalist row galleys. Captured on its maiden voyage, the Yankee ship received a biting new name: the *Restoration*.

As NEWS OF deteriorating British conditions in Boston reached Britain, government officials developed a plan for massive retaliation. By late December, a fleet commanded by Commodore Sir Peter Parker and with troops under Lord Cornwallis prepared to sail from Cork, Ireland. Orders reached New York in early January: Sir Henry Clinton and an estimated 1,500 regulars were to rendezvous with Parker's fleet and subdue the South. At the same time, fifteen copper-sheathed warships capable of breaking the pack ice in the Gulf of the St. Lawrence prepared to relieve the British garrison at Quebec under siege by the remnants of Benedict Arnold's expedition. At six o'clock on the morning of May 6, the aptly named *Surprize* hove into view. Two hundred redcoats clambered ashore and joined 800 Highland Emigrants. The redcoats, French Canadians and British militia surged out onto the Plains of Abraham, their bayonets glistening as they chased the Americans halfway to Montreal before sunset. In command in Montreal, Arnold organized a gradual retreat and fought a rearguard that brought the remnants of the invading American army back to Crown Point where they had begun. The first American to attack Canada a year earlier was the last to leave, shooting his horse in the head before he rowed up Lake Champlain toward Fort Ticonderoga.

By June 28 Commodore Parker's British flotilla was in position oppo-site the unfinished American forts in the harbor of Charleston, South Carolina. Their opening hundred-gun salvo at Fort Sullivan sank harm-lessly into spongy palmetto logs and *coquina*—a mix of sand and crushed oyster shells. The American return fire raked the deck of the fifty-gun flagship *Bristol*, tearing off Sir Peter's trousers. Clinton's landing failed: faulty Loyalist intelligence left his men floundering in seven feet of water at a supposed fording place. The British reported "exceedingly well-directed fire," which struck *Bristol* seventy times, killing sixty-four men and wounding 161.

The bomb ketch *Thunder* rained down shells that mostly landed in a morass and never exploded. At eleven that night, abandoning the expedi-tion, Parker ordered the ships to cut their anchor cables and drift away with the tide.

The third British punitive expedition sailed through the narrows into New York harbor, its vanguard landing on Staten Island on July 2, 1776, just as the Continental Congress in Philadelphia debated Thomas Jeffer-son's draft of the Declaration of Independence. After more than a year of undeclared war, as British fleets sailed for America and news of the deba-cle in Canada sank in, on May 15, 1776, Richard Henry Lee had proposed a resolution that would bring the issue of independence to a vote. While delegates rode home for instructions, thirty-three-year-old Thomas Jef-ferson, who later wrote that he "turned to neither book nor pamphlet," had composed the Declaration of Independence that he "intended to be an expression of the American mind."

Knowing his audience in Congress and beyond the walls of the Penn-sylvania State House, he chose the form and rhetoric of Enlightenment science, of syllogistic logic, self-evident assertions and deductively estab-lished conclusions to achieve persuasion. His major premise: that America must reluctantly take a necessary step. After many failed attempts at rec-onciliation, the United States must declare itself equal among the nations of the earth in a document made necessary out of "a decent respect to the opinions of mankind." As his minor premise, Jefferson averred that the king and his ministers had carried out a plot, "a design to reduce" the American colonies "under absolute despotism." It was their duty "to throw off such despotism," to revolt against a bad king. As John Knox had put it in justification of the English Revolution of the seventeenth century, "Resistance to tyrants is obedience to God."[30]

In a withering bill of particulars intended to prove King George III guilty of tyranny, Jefferson marshaled language and tone usually reserved for a common criminal, listing the reasons for indictment:

> For Quartering large bodies of armed troops among us. . . . For protecting them, by a mock Trial, from punishment for any Murders which they should commit on the Inhabitants of these States. . . . For cutting off our Trade with all parts of the world. . . . For imposing Taxes on us without our Consent. . . . For depriving us in many cases, of the benefits of Trial by Jury. . . . For transporting us beyond Seas to be tried for pretended offences. . . . For abolishing the free System of English Laws in a neighbouring Province, establishing therein an Arbitrary government, and enlarging its Boundaries so as to render it at once an example and fit instrument for introducing the same absolute rule into these Colonies. . . . For taking away our Charters, abolishing our most valuable Laws, and altering fundamentally the Forms of our Governments. . . .

Before a world ruled by monarchs, Jefferson summed up, as if before the jury of world opinion, America's desperate need to defend itself:

> He has plundered our seas, ravaged our Coasts, burnt our towns, and destroyed the lives of our people. . . . He is at this time transporting large Armies of foreign Mercenaries to compleat the works of death, desolation and tyranny, already begun with circumstances of Cruelty & perfidy scarcely paralleled in the most barbarous ages, and totally unworthy the Head of a civilized nation.[31]

After three days and nights of debate and eighty-nine amendments and elisions—including any allusion to slavery—the Continental Congress, voting by states, passed the Declaration of Independence by a 7-6 vote. Raced by couriers north and south, public readings of the document stirred—and terrified—large crowds. In New York City, as more of the king's 283-ship armada—including 73 warships (half of the Royal Navy then afloat)—disgorged 31,625 troops, the largest expeditionary force ever to cross the Atlantic, crowds rampaged through the city. Arriving at Bowling Green, they fastened ropes to the fifteen-foot-high equestrian statue of King George III, erected in thanks for the British American victory over France, and pulled it down. After sawing off the king's head, they sent the statue's massive fragments by wagon to Connecticut's northwest frontier where the women of Litchfield set to work, turning it into more than 42,000 bullets.

ON AUGUST 27, 1776, with more than 15,000 professional soldiers and forty cannon ferried across from Staten Island to Long Island, the British attacked Washington's main force on heavily wooded Brooklyn Heights. In a perfectly executed plan, after drawing off the Americans with an artillery barrage, British commander Howe personally led 10,000 men on a nine-mile, five-hour march around the American left flank at Bedford Pass and struck the American rear. At Flatbush Pass, as General John Sullivan tried to fight his way back to the American defenses, his men were trapped by a Hessian bayonet charge. "Through the woods, down the slopes, across the fields" they ran for the fortified camp. Some reached it; many more were killed. Sullivan was among those captured. As the Maryland and Delaware troops started across the eighty-yard-wide, fast-ebbing Gowanus Creek, British artillery and musket fire cut them down. Of 250 Marylanders, only ten survived.

In the first pitched battle of the war, more than 1,000 Americans were killed or wounded and 1,500 captured. Washington's rout would have become total if he had paused when a hurricane hit. Howe paused instead, thereby allowing Washington to muster Marblehead, Massachusetts, fishermen and escape to Manhattan Island. On September 15 Howe struck again at Kip's Bay; Connecticut troops refused to fight. Once again Howe failed to follow up. In a series of retreats and stands, Washington's army dwindled from 20,000 men to 2,000; he lost 2,800 men when Fort Washington fell to a German attack. Retreating across New Jersey, Washington withdrew to Pennsylvania as the Continental Congress fled to Baltimore.[32]

ON OCTOBER 11, the most important naval battle of the Revolutionary War took place between the Adirondack and Green Mountains, on Lake Champlain. There Benedict Arnold, with a fifteen-vessel fleet that was

built in two months, faced a British flotilla assembled from timbers numbered in England and carried on troop transports to Quebec and then
dragged over a muddy log road and reassembled just north of the Canadian
line. The British, intent on severing rebellious New England, had sent a
combined army and navy force to fight its way south from Canada, down
Lake Champlain and Lake George, then down the Hudson to join Howe's
forces in New York and thus end the rebellion. By building a fleet to block
the British, Arnold forced them to spend the summer season of war building a superior force. Snow covered the peaks and the sleeping sailors by
the time Sir Guy Carleton's fleet sailed south—into Arnold's trap behind
Valcour Island. In a savage battle at close range in a narrow channel, Arnold crippled the best British vessels before escaping at night, losing only
one of his own ships. In a four-day-running encounter, Arnold lost two
ships and scuttled eight, carrying his wounded in sails south through the
Vermont forest to safety at Fort Ticonderoga. By the time a stunned Carleton arrived to attack the heavily defended fortress, thick snow was falling. Rustling a herd of cattle, he retreated all the way to Quebec, losing a
season of war. Troops Carleton drove south joined Washington's Christmas crossing of the Delaware River and his surprise attack on Trenton,
where 1,000 Hessians were captured along with their cannon and munitions
at the end of 1776. The Revolution clung to life.[33]

On March 26, 1777, Major General John Burgoyne attended the king's
weekly levee at St. James Palace. In a private audience with George III,
Burgoyne received orders to launch an attack "from the side of Canada"
in a renewed attempt to split off rebellious New England. The king, who
personally approved all army and naval campaigns, had studied Burgoyne's proposal to march south from Montreal, capture Fort Ticonderoga, then hurry south to Albany to link up with Howe's army marching
north from New York City. As Carleton's second in command, Burgoyne
had watched from the rear as his superior, lacking artillery support, failed
to use his army. Burgoyne told the king that he planned to combine heavy
artillery with "savages and light forces." To avoid weakening Canada, Burgoyne was to augment his invasion force with Hanoverian jagers. The
king also insisted that "Indians must be employed."

He evidently was unaware that Howe had submitted his own plan to march not north but south to the Chesapeake, and then north to defeat Washington and capture the rebel capitol. Following this, Howe planned to quick-march north to join Burgoyne at Albany and end the Revolution.

Burgoyne sailed to Quebec to receive his written orders from Carleton and take command of his 8,118 men—3,724 redcoats, 3,016 Germans, 478 artillerymen, 250 Brunswick dragoons without horses, 250 French Canadians and Loyalists and 400 Indians—before marching south with them. The shortage of wagons, carts and horses would prove crippling. When Burgoyne told Carleton he required 1,000 horses, Carleton, scoffing, and without intending to do so, said he would order them. Burgoyne could only buy 400 horses to haul 144 cannon, 30 days' rations for 10,000 men and 1,000 gallons of rum. The cavalry, the eyes and ears of his army, would have to walk. Encountering a rough, unpaved military road as he marched along the heavily forested west shore of Lake Champlain, Burgoyne had to leave behind two-thirds of his heavy guns and forty of forty-nine medium guns by the time he reached Willsboro on June 21, where he convened a five-day "Congress of Indians."

Reading a proclamation intended to impress Loyalists and Indians and terrify rebellious colonists, he threatened, "I have only to give stretch to the Indian Forces under my command, and they amount to thousands, to overthrow the harden'd Enemies of Great Britain and America." His "messengers of Justice and wrath await them in the field," he thundered, promising "[d]evastation, famine and every concomitant horror." Not only a gross exaggeration, his threat to employ thousands of Indians also proved extremely ill advised. Settlers in the region hid the supplies and horses Burgoyne desperately needed. Militias began to form to contest Burgoyne's specter of thousands of scalping knives.

Burgoyne's vanguard found Crown Point abandoned. By July 1 Burgoyne stood before Ticonderoga's looming walls. French-trained Polish engineer Tadeusz Kosciuszko had urged Americans to fortify the highest hill overlooking the fortress. On July 5 British soldiers cleared a path to the summit of Mount Defiance. At the firing of the first cannon, American officers voted unanimously to evacuate the fort and retreat to minimize casualties. In London, when the king heard that Ticonderoga had fallen, he exulted to Queen Charlotte, "I have beat them, beat all the Americans."[34]

As the Americans retreated, Burgoyne made a controversial decision. Without enough boats to transport troops, guns and supplies all at once, he divided his forces, sending his foot soldiers by land and his artillery by boat over Lake George. Time became his enemy. All night he could hear the dull thwack of axes and crash of trees ahead as a growing army blocked the roads, slowing his march to a mile a day. By early August Burgoyne's rations were gone. More than anything, he needed horses to haul food, tents and winter uniforms. Informed by Loyalist spies of an American supply base at Bennington, Vermont, he detached 486 men on foot under German colonel Friedrich Baum. In heavy rain, entrenched on high ground and outnumbered three-to-one by New England militiamen under John Stark, the Germans held out for two hours. Burgoyne sent reinforcements but so did the Vermonters. In continuous flank sweeps and frontal attacks, the Americans killed 200 British, including their commander. Burgoyne lost 1,400 men and his chance for resupply.

Crossing the Hudson on September 13, Burgoyne faced 6,000 Americans entrenched on Bemis Heights—and French heavy artillery. In July General Philip Schuyler had complained to Washington that he had no cannon. Two French vessels, *Amphitrie* and *Mercure*, had come to the Americans' rescue with "more than eighteen thousand stands of arms complete, and fifty-two pieces of brass cannons, with powder and tents and clothing." According to historian Claude H. Van Tyne, 90 percent of the American arms at Saratoga were state-of-the-art, French-made weapons.[35]

In the fierce Battle of Freeman's Farm, Burgoyne's desperate attempt to gain the high ground ran into the murderously accurate fire of Daniel Morgan's riflemen. Burgoyne waited three more weeks for Howe, but he would never arrive. Howe had battled and again outflanked Washington on Brandywine Creek, finally outmaneuvering him and capturing Philadelphia, where he would spend the winter, abandoning any plan to link up with Burgoyne's northern army. After three weeks of waiting, on October 7 Burgoyne finally ventured out of his heavily fortified lines on Bemis Heights, only to be thrown back behind a fierce assault led by Benedict

Arnold. Arnold received a crippling wound, but the British lost another six hundred men. That night, Burgoyne retreated to Saratoga. His hope for reinforcement by Howe in Philadelphia had been dashed by the stubborn American defense of forts on the Delaware River, which blocked reinforcement and resupply. Surrounded by Americans now outnumbering him three to one, his retreat to Canada cut off, he surrendered his remaining 5,700 men. In the greatest American victory of the eight-year-long war, the reckless Burgoyne's loss of an entire British army convinced the French that the Americans could defeat Britain. In February 1778 they signed the United States' first treaty of alliance.

And now it became an entirely different kind of war. In French uniforms with French weapons and trained to maneuver briskly by Baron von Steuben, the Prussian drillmaster, Washington's reinvigorated army left behind a starving winter at Valley Forge and pursued the British as they retreated to New York City, fighting them to a draw in hundred-degree heat at the Battle of Monmouth in June 1778.

For the next five years, the American Revolution expanded to a theater of worldwide struggle between the British and allied American, French, Spanish and Dutch forces.

The British, attempting to cut off further French aid to Washington's forces, curtailed offensives on land, retreating to their main base at New York and launching sporadic attacks on Connecticut, Georgia and, in their only major victory in the South, Charleston, South Carolina. Washington concentrated his forces, defending a strategic quadrant bordered by the northwestern New Jersey foothills, the Hudson Valley, Massachusetts and Rhode Island. Only once did he mount an offensive, driving into Canada the Iroquois who had been ravaging their western New York tribal lands. In the South, savage fratricidal guerilla warfare raged between Loyalist and Patriot neighbors.

Since their victory in the Seven Years' War, the British had neglected the Royal Navy while France had rebuilt its fleets. The weakened British could no longer hope to enforce a blockade; instead, they pounced on the sugar-rich Caribbean islands, contesting for plunder with the French Navy. Many British vessels now were decrepit. When the Revolution began, only half a dozen sloops-of-war and several lightly armed cutters patrolled the 1,000-mile East Coast from Boston to Florida. By the time the

French joined the war, Admiral Lord Howe could on paper deploy eighty-three vessels, including eleven ships-of-the-line, sixteen sloops-of-war and thirteen frigates. But as naval historian James M. Volo notes, many of these ships rode uneasily at their stations "with fouled bottoms, ancient spars and second-hand-rigging." Between 1776 and 1782, seventy-six Royal Navy vessels, including fourteen ships-of-the-line, capsized, sank or were wrecked. The loss of 1,000 miles of American hardwood forests, of the oak and pine that for so long had undergirded British naval superiority, severely limited Britain's ability to modernize its fleets.[36]

Living conditions aboard British ships became so intolerable that many, risking execution, jumped ship to join the crews of American privateers. From 1776 to 1782 nearly 42,000 British sailors deserted and 18,000 died of disease. British seamen at the main base in New York Harbor ate tainted, short-weight rations served up by corrupt pursers, who pocketed sailors' specie pay and substituted worthless counterfeit Continental currency. The Royal Navy attempted to restore its decimated complements by offering captured American sailors the choice of joining British crews or facing a virtual death sentence aboard prison ships. Many skilled American whalers, taken in sea fights with privateers, chose to join the British Navy. Forced to teach the British their arcane craft, they shipped out for the Indian Ocean, many never to return home.

By contrast, the French set out to rebuild their defeated navy in the years between wars, taking the lead in marine design with larger, faster ships-of-the-line. For new-generation warships, the French recruited and trained 10,000 naval gunners. With their new eighty-gun ships, the French enjoyed freedom of access and supply in American ports, making it easier to shield and resupply Washington's army until the French marine joined him in a final joint victory over a second British army, trapped by the French navy at Yorktown, Virginia, in October 1781.

CONTRARY TO MYTHOLOGY, an accurate oral history of the American Revolution would not have an English accent. Revolutionary politics and the ranks of soldiers included Czechs, Poles, Hungarians, Greeks, Danes, Swedes, French, African Americans, Indians, Protestants, Catholics, Jews and Quakers. More Germans fought on the English side than Englishmen. British major general James Robertson, who had served in the colonies for a quarter century, reported that half the rebels were Irish; a modern Irish historian concludes that 38 percent of the British soldiers were Irish.

Charles Thomson, a successful Philadelphia merchant and secretary of all the Continental Congresses, had been born in Ireland; his family migrated to America after enduring frequent crop failures and increasingly repressive British laws and taxes. Thousands of Scots-Irish came to America in the early 1770s when the linen-weaving industry in Ulster collapsed; by 1776, an estimated 300,000 had immigrated there. Many, including Thomson and Patrick Henry of Virginia, John Rutledge of South Carolina and Henry Knox, Washington's chief of artillery, fought through all eight years of the war.

By 1776, at least 225,000 Germans of at least 250 different Protestant sects had migrated to America in the wake of European religious wars. Some came not to settle but to fight on the side of the Americans. Baron von Steuben, a professional Prussian soldier, drilled the Americans at Valley Forge into a tightly disciplined, highly maneuverable army. At the same time, 12,562 of the 29,875 German mercenaries rented to the British by their feudal overlords stayed in America after the revolution.

Ethnic Americans took part in virtually every military engagement. Polish sailors crewed the *Bon Homme Richard* under the Scottish American captain John Paul Jones. Thirteen-year-old Pascal de Angelis fought under Benedict Arnold at the Battle of Valcour Island on Lake Champlain in 1776, the outcome saving the new United States from being cut in two by British armies and navy. Hungarian hussars came to fight under their Polish friend Casimir Pulaski, who commanded four cavalry regiments in the south until he was killed. Tadeusz Kosciuszko, impoverished son of Polish gentry, fled his homeland to study military engineering at Ecole Militaire in Paris before coming to Philadelphia in 1776 to volunteer. Working with Benjamin Franklin, he put 5,000 men to work building a gigantic defense network, including forts on both banks of the Delaware. Sent north, he laid out the defense of the hilly ground around Saratoga for the newly arrived French cannon. Despite a series of British and Hessian attacks and artillery barrages, Kosciuszko's mile-long chain of earthworks and redoubts blocked British flanking attacks until the deadly American counterattack led by Benedict Arnold convinced General John Burgoyne's war-weary veterans to surrender.

Two regiments of Italians fought under the French flag at Yorktown. Greek knights journeyed to America to fight as volunteers under the French Marquis de Lafayette; Greek American patriots suffered the horrors of imprisonment on the disease-ridden prison ship *Jersey*. North and south, African Americans fought on both sides, with both sides offering freedom if they survived. An estimated 7,500 blacks fought under Washington, with more than double that number on the British side. Throughout the war, Jewish Americans fought, suffered and often gave all they had to keep the Revolution and its armies and navies alive.

BY LATE 1778, midway through the Revolutionary War, Washington's task had shifted from countering massive annual British attempts to divide, conquer and crush the infant American nation to figuring out how to afford to continue the fight at all. By that time, the Continental dollar had been devalued to the point where it had about one-fortieth its original purchasing power; by May 1779 prices had soared to four times their prewar level. As the sixth year of the Revolution began, Continental currency had depreciated so badly that Colonel Alexander Hamilton, Washington's principal aide-de-camp, could not afford to buy a horse. His old gray mount had been wounded at Monmouth, and army regulations he had written himself barred him from borrowing one except for military use. As Washington put it, "Even a rat in the shape of a horse is not to be bought at this time for less than £200." That was about $40,000 in depreciated Continental currency. Hamilton's pay: $60 Continental a month. Hamilton made ends meet by investing a small inheritance in privateering ships and taking all his meals at Washington's mess table. That winter the price of a season dancing assembly ticket was $400 Continental. Foregoing his own horse, Hamilton bought the dancing ticket.

With no power to tax, Congress continued to print Continental dollars. The American economy was grinding to a halt. By spring 1780, after the worst winter the army had weathered, Washington faced a mutiny. Because of the latest drop in value of the Continental dollar, supplies stopped reaching the camp at Jockey Hollow in Morristown, in the northwest New Jersey mountains, in March. Washington cut rations to one-eighth the norm for the next six weeks. On May 25 the Connecticut regiments paraded under arms in protest, demanding a full ration and their five months' arrears in pay. At least twice before, finding enough money to pay his troops had nearly scuttled Washington's ambitious plans: Connecticut troops had refused to march with Arnold into Canada until they could send money home for their families' subsistence; gold coins raised by fining Philadelphia Quakers for refusing to drill and fight reached Washington just in time to pay his men before they consented to cross the Delaware to attack Trenton at Christmas in 1776.

This time Washington had to call out the Pennsylvania Line to break up the protest at gunpoint. That day, in a letter encapsulating his army's desperate condition, Washington pleaded for help from a former aide, Joseph Reed, now president of Pennsylvania's Supreme Executive Council:

> I assure you, by every idea you can form of our distresses will fall short of the reality. All our departments, all our operations, are at a standstill; and unless a system, very different from that which has for a long time prevailed, be immediately adopted throughout the states, our affairs must soon become desperate beyond the possibility of recovery. If you were on the spot, my dear Sir, if you could see what difficulties surround us on every side, how unable we are to administer to the most ordinary calls of the service, you would be convinced that these expressions are not strong enough, and that we have everything to dread. Indeed, I have almost ceased to hope.[37]

AT LEAST 10,000 Americans "fell a sacrifice to the relentless and scientific barbarity of Britain," as Ethan Allen, incarcerated by the British for 952 days, put it in his best-selling prisoner-of-war narrative. According to modern research, his estimate is remarkably conservative. The British, according to one UK study, imprisoned between 24,850 and 32,000 Americans in and around New York City during the war, with between 9,150 and 10,000 in the city's prisons, churches and warehouses. Some 11,000 died in the abominable prison hulks anchored off Wallabout Bay. Estimates of the total number who died while imprisoned in New York City range from 15,575 to 18,000—at least four times the toll of American revolutionaries killed in combat. Allen and other American leaders, including Jefferson and Madison, believed that the abuse of prisoners of war by their British captors became a question not of international rules of law nor a reflection on the character of individual British officers and commanders but an existential reflection of official British government policy itself that left a bitter legacy long after the Revolutionary War.[38]

By the signing of the Franco-American alliance in 1778, the problem of the Loyalists had transformed the Revolution into a civil war. In addition to Loyalist enlistments in the British army and navy, the British formed fifty-five regiments of Loyalist Provincial Corps, some 19,000 serving in their ranks. In all, nearly 50,000 Americans served under the royal standard, including 12,000 blacks. An estimated 500,000 of 3 million Americans, including about 25 percent of the white male population, became active Loyalists. In New York and New Jersey, this number included many Dutch tenant farmers who preferred monarchy. In Pennsylvania, many Germans and Quakers attempted to stay neutral. When the British army evacuated Philadelphia in 1778 and Pennsylvania revolutionaries hanged two Loyalists for aiding the Crown, 5,000 Loyalist sympathizers trailed their coffins in protest. Virtually all Anglican clergy fled America or joined Loyalist regiments as chaplains. Large numbers of Iroquois fought in support of British armies before they were driven into Canada in a sustained campaign by Washington.

When the British responded to the Franco-American alliance by concentrating their forces in coastal towns where they could be reinforced by their navy, they increasingly relied on a supposed outpouring of Loyalist support whenever they ventured into the countryside or attacked other port towns. They also placed greater emphasis on recruiting spies, seeking to ascertain which Americans had become disenchanted by the lagging course of the Revolution. Washington's best field commander, Benedict Arnold—hero of the epic wilderness march to Quebec, victor in the most important naval battle of the war at Valcour Island, leader of the decisive charge at Saratoga—after twice being wounded and sidelined, became disgruntled. Passed over for promotion three times, unpaid by Congress for seven years, heavily in debt to British factors and his shipping business in ruins, Arnold became convinced that the Americans he knew could not win the war. For the promise of £20,000 pounds, roughly equivalent to his debts, he personally attempted to betray Washington, West Point and its garrison—including many of his former troops. He ultimately fled America with the departing British and Loyalists, becoming in America's lexicon the very eponym for treason.

As the preliminary peace treaty sped across the Atlantic, Loyalist refugees cleared New York and Charleston harbors for England, Canada or the Caribbean, or walked across the frontier into present-day Ontario. This vast migration of more than 100,000 Americans into exile consisted of more than 5 percent of the population, probably the highest refugee rate of any revolution. Vilified as "Tories," stripped of their legal and civil rights, their lands and businesses confiscated, Loyalists were merely the political conservatives of an era when dissent from popular radicalism was not tolerated. In truth, the United States began as a one-party system. The loss of the Loyalists ultimately caused many of the severe problems that would plague the early life of the new American republic.

FIVE

"To the Shores of Tripoli"

For much of its adolescence as an independent nation, the United States teetered on the brink of dissolution, at first caught between commercial rivals Britain and France and then entangled in their worldwide war. More than once, Congress came perilously close to declaring war on one European empire or the other. An uneasy peace with England emanated, despite its impingement on American trade and persistent tension over breaches of the 1783 peace treaty. Many Americans felt boxed in by the British to the north in Canada, by the Spanish to the south in Florida and to the west across the Mississippi, and by the French in the Caribbean. Many Americans felt entitled to lay claim, by conquest or annexation, to their sparsely populated Canadian neighbor because they believed Britain constantly instigated and armed Indians to harass frontier settlements. Perhaps an equally large number of British, refusing to accept that England, by losing the Revolutionary War, had irrevocably granted American independence, favored subduing and reclaiming their former colonies.

A rift within the cabinets of presidents over the proper direction for the new nation's foreign policy only increased the risk of renewed conflict. Under President Washington, the clash between Thomas Jefferson,

Francophile secretary of state, and Alexander Hamilton, Anglophile secretary of the treasury, metamorphosed into the formation of opposing political parties. For many citizens of the Revolutionary generation, there could only be one American ideology: to oppose the nation's political leadership was to oppose the government—in other words, treason. Many of the founders' ancestors, including Washington's, had fled the bloody partisan warfare of the English Civil Wars of the 1640s that had culminated in the beheading of King Charles I. That event still haunted the American historical consciousness as factional infighting turned increasingly contumacious: witness the death of Hamilton in a duel with archrival Aaron Burr.

In more recent memory, the American Revolution had devolved into a civil war as much as a war for independence from England, pitting pro- and anti-English parties and armies against each other. The two warring factions adopted seventeenth-century English labels. Adherents to the American independence movement called each other Patriots or Whigs, once a derisive Scottish term for curdled milk; Patriots labeled royalist, anti-independence Loyalists as Tories, an Irish word for highway robbers. So deep went the fear that post–Revolutionary War politics would again erupt into civil warfare that the Founding Fathers shunned the word "party." Scottish philosopher David Hume, upon learning that his old friend Benjamin Franklin indulged in political intrigue, recoiled in horror. To Adam Smith he wrote, "I always knew him to be a very factious man and faction next to fanaticism is of all passions the most destructive of morality."[1] Even when, in 1787, leaders of the new nation thrashed out thorny political questions in secret in the State House in Philadelphia during a marathon Constitutional Convention, the Constitution itself made no provision for party politics. Opposition to the new federal Constitution, while strong in many states, appeared to be disorganized and was expected to be short lived.

In France as minister plenipotentiary during this reform convention, Thomas Jefferson had objected to the lack of any formal provision for a two-party system:

> Men by their constitutions are naturally divided into two parties: those who fear and distrust the people and wish to draw all power from them into the hands of the higher classes [and] those who identify themselves

with the people, have confidence in them, cherish and consider them as the most honest and safe, although not the most wise, depository of the public interests.[2]

It seemed obvious to the unanimously elected first president, George Washington, that unless he drew him into his government, Jefferson would organize anti-federal opposition into a political party. The uneasy honeymoon of the first American political system lasted less than two years. Inside Washington's cabinet, the seeds of two quite opposite political parties germinated along lines of interest as well as ideology. Hamilton spoke for the prosperous seaport towns of the North, the banking and commercial sectors, the creditors: trade with England still accounted for most of America's exports and imports. Jefferson, the perennially cash-strapped Enlightenment political philosopher from Monticello, spoke for the South and the West, the farmers, the workers, the impecunious, the debtors. To Jefferson, Hamilton and his Federalists were intolerably aristocratic "monocrats." To Hamilton, Jefferson's Democratic-Republicans were French-style incendiaries who had to be kept in check.[3]

After Benjamin Franklin, John Adams and John Jay negotiated the Treaty of Paris with England, France and Spain, Jefferson traveled widely, visiting Germany, the Netherlands, England and Italy and establishing a system of consulates to facilitate American trade. Jefferson found it impossible to rebuff Washington's invitation—more a command—to serve as the nation's first secretary of state. For a while, Jefferson's closest friend, James Madison, putative father of the Constitution and coauthor of *The Federalist Papers*, had aligned himself with fellow coauthor Hamilton. But Hamilton's pro-business, pro-banking proclivities, his unapologetic coziness with land speculators who were swindling veterans out of their soldiers' bounty lands, repelled Madison. On Jefferson's return from Europe, Madison allied himself politically with his friend. By the end of the First Congress, in the spring of 1791, when Jefferson and Madison took a five-week tour of the Adirondacks and Vermont, they had decided they must launch a political party to oppose Hamilton's, ergo President Washington's, fiscal policies.

In cabinet meetings, in his reports to Washington and in public, the secretive Jefferson attempted to mask his radically pro-French, Anglophobic views. In Paris he had hosted illegal meetings of revolutionaries in the American mission at the Hôtel de Langeac on the Champs-Elysées as he edited drafts of the revolutionary Declaration of the Rights of Man and of the Citizen. But in the temporary American capital of Philadelphia, where the secretary of state's office on Chestnut Street, one block from Independence Hall, abutted Hamilton's treasury office, Jefferson found it difficult to conceal his loathing for the pro-British conservatism of Hamilton.

As the French Revolution metastasized into a pan-European cataclysm, the blood-drenched mass executions of the Reign of Terror—accelerated and orchestrated by the pro-American Robespierre—far from repulsed Jefferson, widening instead the political gulf between him and Hamilton. Writing to William Stephens Smith, Jefferson opined that "from time to time the tree of liberty must be refreshed with the blood of patriots & tyrants."[4]

Jefferson and Madison had managed to keep their pro-French, anti-British political views out of the public eye until, in the spring of 1791, Jefferson sent an unsigned note to a Philadelphia printer, urging him to publish Tom Paine's *Rights of Man*. Paine had become the only American deputy in the Jacobin-controlled French National Assembly. The printer inadvertently included Jefferson's letter as the introduction to Paine's tract, exposing the extent of Jefferson's radicalism. As Jefferson and Madison rode north on a vacation, Vice President John Adams savaged Jefferson in print for endorsing Paine's avowedly radical views.

Meeting in New York City, Jefferson and Madison asked the latter's Princeton roommate, the poet and journalist Philip Freneau, to launch a thrice-weekly newspaper in the nation's capital. In this first step toward the clandestine formation of a political party, Jefferson planned to dip into the State Department's budget and its diplomatic pouch to pay Freneau and produce a partisan critique of Hamilton's policies. Jefferson's *National Gazette* would attack Hamilton's already extant *Gazette of the United States*, each cabinet secretary battering the other's positions under *noms de plume*—and each fully aware that Washington abhorred discord. Washington repeatedly intervened personally, attempting to reconcile his warring lieutenants, but ultimately he failed. His cabinet fracturing, Washington increasingly sided with Hamilton's federalism.

Above all else, Washington dreaded the prospect of disunion. Despite repeated personal efforts, his cabinet divided sharply between Jefferson's Democratic-Republicans and Hamilton's Federalists. The clash became public when news of the execution of Louis XVI reached America. More shockwaves followed as France declared war on Great Britain and the Netherlands. Provoking a heated cabinet debate, Hamilton insisted that the bloody regime change in Paris from monarchy to republic called into question the continued validity of the 1778 Franco-American treaty of alliance. Hamilton contended that the treaty, signed by a monarchy, no longer existed and must be suspended. Jefferson countered that treaties were made between nations, noting that the form of government of the United States had also changed—from a confederation to a constitutional republic—without abrogating its treaty obligations.

The cabinet deadlocked over whether the treaty obliged the United States to help France defend its West Indian possessions against the British. Jefferson argued against going to war for any reason. Hamilton and Jefferson also clashed over the propriety of formally receiving the new French ambassador Edmond-Charles Genêt, who had been appointed by Robespierre, the principal architect of the Reign of Terror, which had taken the lives of so many French aristocrats who had fought by the side of Americans. Washington, determined to steer the Republic clear of the twin shoals of European war and diplomacy, insisted on strict neutrality, even if it meant renouncing the treaty's military obligations. Ultimately bowing to the advice of his secretary of state, Washington upheld Jefferson's opinions on the treaty and instructed that Genêt be received, but "not with too much warmth or cordiality."[5]

Despite Washington's official cool civility, Genêt received a conquering hero's welcome, including an ovation in Congress Hall. Misgauging America's enthusiasm, Genêt ignored its neutrality. Outfitting privateers and recruiting Americans for a sea-and-land expedition against Spanish-held Florida, he ordered the French consul at Charleston to sell as prizes merchant ships taken from the British. When Jefferson upheld Genêt's contention that French prizes were French property that could be sold by a French consul, Washington angrily overruled Jefferson and ordered all French privateers out of American ports, ignoring Jefferson's assertion that neutrality was effectively a pro-British stance because it disregarded treaty obligations to France. When Hamilton twice attacked Jefferson's interpretation in print, Jefferson wrote to Madison, "For god's sake my dear Sir, take up your pen, select the most striking heresies and cut him to pieces."[6]

The Genêt affair came to a head when a French frigate towed a captured British merchantman, the *Little Sarah*, into Philadelphia. Jefferson ordered Genêt to detain the vessel, renamed the *Democrate*, until Washington returned from his Mount Vernon vacation. Genêt refused. In an impromptu cabinet meeting, Hamilton and Secretary of War Henry Knox clamored to set up artillery along the Delaware River to impede the vessel's departure. Jefferson, aware that a French fleet was approaching Philadelphia, feared this would trigger open warfare with France. Defiant, Genêt ordered the partially refitted *Democrate* to drop downriver beyond the reach of Knox's guns.

When Washington arrived, he accused Jefferson of "submitting" to Genêt. It was Jefferson's last fight as secretary of state: he submitted his resignation. When Washington pleaded with him to stay on, Jefferson assured him that his Democratic-Republican Clubs would support the president through the rest of his first term, but that he, Jefferson, was tired of a post that forced him "to move exactly in the circle which I know to bear me peculiar hatred; that is to say, the wealthy aristocrats, the merchants connected closely with England, the new created paper fortunes." Jefferson knew that his archenemy, Hamilton, was resigning and returning to New York City to galvanize support for his Federalist party. At that moment, American party politics burst from its chrysalis.[7]

IN THE SPRING and summer of 1793, as tumbrels carrying thousands of French *aristocrates* rattled over the *pavés* of Paris toward the city's five guillotines, a tidal wave of French refugees swamped the American capital of Philadelphia. The French Revolution's spread to France's Caribbean colonies compelled thousands of plantation owners, their families and household slaves to flee from slave insurrections in Santo Domingo and Martinique to the United States. As many as 25,000 French refugees crowded into coastal cities. Up to 2,000 debarked in Philadelphia, a town of 35,000, according to French journalist and historian Médéric Louis Elie Moreau de Saint-Méry, a Martinique-born delegate to the revolutionary Constituent Assembly and former president of the *electeurs* of Paris. In

Baltimore, the nation's third-largest town—population of 26,514—some 1,000 French families and 500 slaves sought refuge.

Among French aristocrats landing in Newport came Prince Charles Maurice de Talleyrand-Périgord, notorious libertine and former bishop of Beaune. Making his way to New York City, he watched the Fourth of July parade from a Broadway window along with other leading French émigrés. St. Méry, at his elbow, had been savagely beaten and left for dead in a Paris café for speaking out against the excesses of Robespierre and his Jacobins. With his wife and two children, he escaped from France only hours ahead of the issuance of a warrant for his arrest and execution. In his diary, St. Méry described "the annual fete of American independence":

> The Governor [George Clinton] and the people who accompanied him in the fete were preceded by a long procession of French Jacobins, marching two by two, singing the *Marseillaise*. . . . [T]hey interrupted themselves to address invectives to us in the windows where they saw us. . . . The Minister of France to the United States, Genêt . . . was in the procession; and sang and insulted us like all the others. We wept for our country and for him![8]

Saint-Méry moved to Philadelphia and opened a bookstore on the edge of the square mile of elegant Georgian houses known as Society Hill. Setting up a printing press, he also edited a French-language newspaper. For four years, his bookstore, located five blocks from Congress Hall and the offices of Jefferson and Hamilton, served as the unofficial capitol-within-a-capital for the French émigrés. Only one city block away, the courthouse bell announced the start of another day in exile. Having escaped the death rattle of tumbrels, he now heard the rumble of red-paneled Conestoga wagons, their bowed canvas covers luffing as great black workhorses pulled them down the recently cobbled Second Street Pike. By five in the morning on thrice-weekly market days, Pennsylvania German farmers delivered their cargoes of cheeses, sausages and produce, their herds of cattle, sheep and pigs to the covered sheds on Market Street. A block to his east, Saint-Méry could see as many as one hundred ships lined up along the Delaware River waterfront. And around the corner from his bookstore, after a long day, Saint-Méry metamorphosed back into a *saloniste*. In a stately redbrick townhouse that was rented nearby, past and future rulers of France argued American and European politics all night. Among them were the Prince de Talleyrand; Francois-Alexandre-Frédéric, duc de la Rochefoucauld-Liancourt—the king's chamberlain who first informed him that the French Revolution had broken out; the duc de Noailles; and the duc d'Orléans, the future King Louis-Philippe.

ESCAPING THE RIGORS of the office work he so detested as he inspected his Tidewater acres, President Washington convinced himself that Citizen Genêt was fomenting organized resistance to his administration. All over the country, noisily pro-French and anti-Hamilton Democratic-Republican societies were springing up. Washington refused to believe the movement was spontaneous. Its aim, he wrote to his protégé, General Henry "Light Horse Harry" Lee, was "nothing short of the subversion of the government of these states, even at the expense of plunging this country into the horrors of a disastrous war." In a series of messages to Congress, Washington defended his neutrality policy and his decision to expel Genêt.[9]

But there was to be no peace. It was the Jay Treaty, as it became known, that emerged as the central issue of contention between Jeffersonian Republicans and Hamiltonian Federalists, hastening the consolidation of the first political parties. As early as June 1791, during Jefferson and Madison's visit to the new state of Vermont, they learned that the British had built a blockhouse on North Hero Island, fifteen miles south of the Canadian border. A Royal Navy schooner, the *Lady Maria*, was stopping and searching American vessels carrying cargo into Canada. Jefferson wrote to Washington that the warship, normally based at the British customs house on the border,

> was sent to the Blockhouse, & there exercised her usual visits on boats passing to & from Canada. [T]his being an exercise of power further within our jurisdiction became the subject of notice & clamour with our citizens in that quarter. . . . [A] new one is to be built to perform her functions. [T]his she has usually done at the Point au fer with a good deal of rigour, bringing all vessels to at that place, & sometimes under such circumstances of wind & weather as to have occasioned the loss of two vessels & cargoes.[10]

Although the British had agreed in Paris to abandon their frontier forts, nearly a decade after the war's end more than 1,000 redcoats still garrisoned forts and trading posts on U.S. soil. The British refused to remove them until Americans honored another treaty provision: to discharge their pre–Revolutionary War debts with British and Loyalist creditors and allow British subjects access to American courts to sue for recovery. American signatories to the 1783 treaty knew full well that the Continental Congress could only recommend terms to individual states since the Continental Congress had no treaty-making authority. Every state had refused. Many Americans proffered payment with virtually worthless Continental currency. British creditors insisted on abiding by the precise terms of the 1783 peace treaty—that the debts be paid in coin-of-the-realm silver or gold specie, as they had been incurred, together with accumulating interest.

In May 1794, as tensions worsened, Washington dispatched pro-French congressman James Monroe to Paris and sent Federalist John Jay to London. The resultant treaty, devised by Hamilton and generally advantageous to the United States, stipulated withdrawal of all British troops in pre–Revolutionary War forts west of Pennsylvania and north of Ohio. Wartime debts and the Canadian-American boundary would be submitted to arbitration—one of the first major uses of arbitration in diplomacy. Americans won limited rights to trade with British colonies in India and the Caribbean in exchange for limits on the export of American cotton.

When a copy of the treaty reached Philadelphia ten months later, Benjamin Franklin Bache, grandson of Benjamin Franklin and radically pro-French publisher of the *Aurora,* obtained a leaked copy, most likely from Democratic-Republican senators, and rushed it into print before allowing Washington time to discuss its terms with his cabinet and congressional leaders. Riots, organized by Jefferson's Democratic-Republican societies, broke out; as Jay arrived in Philadelphia, he found himself burning in effigy. While Washington mulled his response to the draft treaty, he received yet more jarring intelligence: the British navy was boarding and confiscating American cargo ships bound for France.

On close examination, Washington found little comfort in the draft treaty. After arbitration, the British promised to give up their forts by year's end and spelled out the rights of neutral shippers in wartime. But they rejected all other American terms. The only ports they would open to American shipping were those in the West Indies, and even then they would only allow relatively small vessels of less than seventy tons, capable of exporting only small quantities of American cotton to England's textile mills. The British Isles and Canada remained off limits; the Navigation Act of 1756 remained in force. In their Caribbean possessions, the British would have the right to buy all American cargoes, thus blocking all exports to the French. Worst of all, the treaty made no mention whatsoever of the impressment of sailors from American ships.

In almost every respect Jay's negotiation failed, as Madison, orchestrating the protests in the House, pointed out in angry debates. The Democratic-Republican-controlled House demanded all of Washington's correspondence bearing on the treaty, contending that the House would have to appropriate funds to pay for the expenses of the arbitration commissioners. Washington insisted that the House had no constitutional role in treaty making. After debate raged for three weeks, the House voted 62-37 to demand the papers. Washington refused to comply: "It is perfectly clear to my understanding, that the assent of the House is not necessary to the validity of a treaty." Washington instead forwarded the treaty to the Federalist-dominated Senate, which ratified it by a two-thirds margin. Counseling "prudence and moderation on every side" in his last annual message (forerunner of today's State of the Union speech), Washington outlasted a six-week face-off with the House. In the end, it was the House that yielded, voting to accept Washington's refusal. Washington's prudent silence had won out, buying ten years of fitful peace with Great Britain.[11]

WHEN THEY FIRST came to Philadelphia to serve their terms, congressional delegates clustered in Philadelphia boardinghouses according to their home states. By the end of Washington's second term in 1796, they roomed only with ideological mates. Deepening partisanship had prompted Washington's surprising decision to stay on for a second term. He had feared that, unless he did, the nation, like his cabinet, would split into warring factions, commercial North against agrarian South and West. When he had announced his decision to his long-suffering wife, Martha, to stay on in Philadelphia for four more years after spending most of the last two decades far from their beloved Mount Vernon, she wept. "Poor Patsy," he tried to console her. "Poor Patsy!"[12]

Despite his unopposed reelection, Washington had no reason to expect a more tranquil second term. Any optimism he retained that his continued presence would smooth the ruffles around him proved short-lived. His vice president, John Adams—who never doubted that he was Washington's heir presumptive—barely survived a surprisingly stiff challenge from Governor George Clinton of New York, the leading anti-Federalist now aligned with Jefferson and Madison. Adams's reelection as vice president by a 77-50 vote provided fresh evidence of consolidation of political parties. Washington believed that the split in electoral votes was the result of deep dissatisfaction in the South, especially in Virginia, because of planters' losses at the hands of what they considered unscrupulous, sharp-trading northern businessmen.

The evidence of a permanent split between factions became even more apparent by the time Adams approached Washington late in 1796 to see whether he would consider staying on for a third term. Washington declined: as he had made it clear to trusted confidants, he had too long smarted under the thrice-weekly lashings he received in the Democratic-Republican press. "If you read the *Aurora* of this City," he complained to Benjamin Walker in Virginia, "you cannot but have perceived with what malignant industry and persevering falsehoods I am assailed." He believed that such attacks were intended "to weaken if not destroy the confidence of the public" in his presidency. Opposition journalists were "bad (and if I may be allowed to use so harsh an expression) diabolical." To his protégé Henry "Light Horse Harry" Lee, governor of Virginia, he wrote, "no man was ever more tired of public life." To Abigail Adams, explaining that his decision was final, he told of his "disinclination to be longer buffeted in the public prints by a set of infamous scribblers."[13]

Washington's Farewell Address—the final draft all Washington's thought, all Hamilton's writing—revealed just how far Washington had drifted into partisan Federalist ranks. His advice to Americans: avoid permanent alliances. His isolationist message came from the experience of a single alliance: with France. In a clear reference to the Genêt affair, Washington warned that partisanship "opens the door to foreign influence and corruption, which finds a facilitated access to the govern-ment itself through the channels of party passions. Thus the policy and the will of one country are subjected to the policy and will of another." But far from discouraging bipartisan politics, Washington's "spirit of party" valedictory only fanned them, serving as the opening gun of the 1796 presidential election in which he supported his Federalist vice president, John Adams. Yet even with Washington's blessing, Adams only defeated Jefferson by three electoral votes, 71-68.[14]

Adams had little time to pursue Washington's policy of neutrality. Once the United States declared its independence, the British stopped protecting the shipping conducted by its former American colonies in the Mediterra-nean from attacks by corsairs of the kingdom of Morocco and the three Ottoman regencies along the Barbary Coast of North Africa: Algeria, Tuni-sia and Tripoli. During most of the Revolutionary War, France had ex-tended its mantle of protection. Even though the 1778 treaty with the United States did not explicitly mention the Barbary states, referring only to com-mon enemies, they were included under that broad description.

At the end of the Revolution, the Confederation Congress was slow to accept the overtures of Morocco for a peace treaty with the United States. In March 1783, American vessels sailing out of Marseilles narrowly escaped capture by nine armed Algerian ships. Without further French protection, American merchant ships could expect attacks by North Afri-can corsairs seeking to capture sailors for ransom unless the United States agreed to pay the customary tribute money to avoid further attacks. Euro-pean countries had paid the Barbary states for centuries: between 1 mil-lion and 1.25 million Europeans were captured and ransomed or sold as slaves between 1500 and 1800.[15]

In July 1785 Algerian corsairs captured two American ships, taking twenty-one sailors and forcing them into slave labor. As American ministers plenipotentiary in Paris, Jefferson and Adams had explicit authority from the Continental Congress to negotiate treaties of amity and commerce. While emissaries were reluctantly sent to Morocco and Algeria to make ar-rangements for the release of hostages, Jefferson wrote to James Monroe:

We ought to begin a naval power, if we mean to carry on our own com-merce. Can we begin it on a more honorable occasion, or with a weaker foe? I am of opinion [John] Paul Jones with a half dozen frigates would totally destroy their commerce . . . by constantly cruising and cutting them to pieces by piecemeal . . .

In March 1786 Jefferson joined Adams in London for a meeting with Moroccan envoy Abdrahaman. As they smoked tall pipes and sipped coffee, Jefferson asked the envoy "the Grounds of the pretensions to make war upon Nations who had done them no Injury."

The Ambassador answered that it was founded on the Laws of their Prophet, that it was written in their Koran, that all nations who should not have acknowledged their authority were sinners, that it was their right and duty to make war upon them wherever they could be found, and to make slaves of all they could take as Prisoners, and that every Musselman who should be slain in battle was sure to go to Paradise.[16]

While France paid $209,000 a year to Algeria and Britain paid as much as $280,000, Congress would only authorize paying up to $80,000 for the ransoming of captives from all four Barbary states. On June 23, 1786, Morocco became the first of the four to sign a peace treaty with the United States. Any American captured by a Moroccan or other Barbary Coast ship trading with Morocco was to be set free. But by this time, a more belligerent Algeria had also begun seizing American ships. The captures of the schooners *Maria* and the *Dauphin* announced a hardening of demands by the other three Barbary states. Jefferson and Adams were authorized by Congress to offer only $200 per captive; the Dey of Algiers expected $6,000 for a ship's master, $4,000 for a mate and $1,500 for each sailor. He put his captives to work, clapping them in chains and forcing them to carry timber and rocks to help strengthen his defenses. When Congress dispatched Commodore William Bainbridge to Tripoli to negotiate directly with the Dey of Algiers and inform him that the United States would not meet his demands, diplomatic efforts broke down.

President Washington, himself an exporter of grains to the Mediterranean, was well aware of the extent of the United States' carrying trade in the region: American ships brought sugar, flour, rice, salted fish and lumber to France, Spain and Italy and returned with wine, citrus fruits,

figs, olive oil and opium. To assure immunity from Barbary state depredations, Washington felt he had no choice but to pay tribute. He could
muster little support for building and maintaining an expensive navy. Indeed, in Congress, Madison led Democratic-Republican resistance to a
navy in the House of Representatives. But by January 1794, as Algerian attacks accelerated, a divided House authorized "a naval force adequate to
the protection of the commerce of the United States, against the Algerine
corsairs."[17]

A select committee dominated by representatives from northern ports
gathered intelligence on the size and armor of the Algerian vessels and
concluded that a small cruising squadron of well-armed warships would
be more than adequate to protect American shipping. On March 10, 1794,
the House, by a 50-39 vote, passed the Act to Provide a Naval Armament; a
voice vote in the Senate sped the measure to Washington's desk, where, by
a stroke of his quill, the United States Navy was born on March 27. The act
provided for $688,888—roughly two-thirds of one year's tribute to the
Barbary states—to buy or build six frigates armed with thirty-eight to
forty-four guns.

On May 10, 1797, the 1,500-ton, forty-four-gun oaken frigate *United
States,* America's largest and costliest weapon to date, slid off the ways into
the Delaware River to the cheers of some 30,000 onlookers, roughly equal
to the capital's population. The frigate carried state-of-the-art weaponry:
short-range carronades, developed since the Revolution, called "smash-
ers" because they could hurl thirty-two-pound balls four hundred yards,
splinter an enemy ship and kill its gun crews, and long guns that could hit
a target two-thirds of a mile distant.

Within weeks, Adams reversed Washington's policy of paying tribute
and negotiated a new accord, the Treaty of Tripoli, aimed at establishing
"firm and perpetual Peace and friendship" and providing a one-time cash
payment of $56,486 for the Dey of Algiers. Signed by Adams on June 10,
1797, the treaty attempted to silence critics of an alliance with a Muslim
state. Article 11 read,

> As the Government of the United States of America is not, in any sense,
> founded on the Christian religion; as it has in itself no character of en-
> mity against the laws, religion, or tranquility, of Mussulmen; and, as the

said States never entered into any war, or act of hostility against any Mahometan nation, it is declared by the parties, that no pretext arising from religious opinions, shall ever produce an interruption of the harmony existing between the two countries.[18]

Even as the incubus of the United States Navy sailed toward the Mediterranean, President Adams learned that he was to enjoy little respite. Immediately he had to face the prospect of a war with France, which regarded the Jay Treaty with its enemy Britain as a betrayal, an Anglo-American alliance in disguise that abrogated the 1778 Franco-American treaty. France unleashed its navy and privateers on American commerce. Between 1795 and 1801, the French seized an estimated $25 million in American ships and cargo. Adams's Federalist partisans urged mobilization for war, branding their Francophile Democratic-Republican opponents as traitors. Exploiting a public backlash against its former treaty ally, Adams's Federalist government purchased massive amounts of munitions from the British at the very moment that the British were suppressing an independence movement in Ireland.

The Irish rebellion of 1798 had its roots in the American Revolution. The British, the island's overlords, had needed to draw down garrisons of Regulars to quell the American uprising. The Irish Volunteers ostensibly were intended to defend Ireland against invasion by America and her ally, France. Upward of 40,000 attorneys, doctors, clergymen, academics and artisans signed up. Thousands of red-jacketed Volunteers drilled and paraded in Belfast and Dublin in their "smart new uniforms of scarlet turned up with black velvet, black hats, white waistcoats and breeches."[19]

British authorities began to worry about the newfound enthusiastic patriotism of Ulster Volunteers. Although an independent kingdom, Ireland was beholden to the British monarch and governed by a parliament subordinate to its counterpart in London and to privy councils in Dublin and at Westminster. The Volunteer movement spawned debate on its relationship with Britain, initially over restrictions on trade with the mother country: British policy embargoed Irish exports to market, channeling Irish provisions to the military.

Following the example of American revolutionaries, Dublin importers in 1779 boycotted consumer products imported from England. Mass demonstrations outside Dublin Castle peaked when the Dublin Volunteer Company of Artillery dragged two field pieces to Trinity College Green, brandishing placards reading "Free Trade, or This." Relenting, the lord lieutenant requested and received concessions from London, allowing Irish goods onto the British market. As the British Ministry eased its grip, radical leaders in the Irish Parliament and in Dublin pubs pressed for further reforms. With the motto "[N]o illuminations, no rejoicings . . . until our constitution [is] made free," the Volunteers staged orderly demonstrations with parades, protests and mock battles. In 1782 the newly installed Rockingham administration in London, negotiating an end to the American war, declared an end to British control of the Irish Parliament.[20]

But it wasn't enough to appease the Irish patriots. As demands for reform spread, radicals organized the Society of United Irishmen. Its membership, burgeoning to 300,000 by the 1790s, was comprised of Presbyterians in the North and Catholics in the south. Both resented the Anglican squirearchy, which owned 90 percent of the land and controlled virtually all seats in Parliament, government posts and military commissions. Embracing old religious enemies, the United Irishmen spelled out in the *Belfast Northern Star* their demands for universal male suffrage, emancipation of the Catholic peasantry and an end to British rule. Jubilant when the French Revolution broke out, they toasted each other, "A fourth and fourteenth of July to Ireland: we will die to achieve them." The radicals' leader, Theobald Wolfe Tone, later wrote that "the French Revolution changed the politics of Ireland in an instant, dividing society into Aristocrats and Democrats."[21]

Alarmed British officials' highly paid spies, infiltrating the movement, reported that the movement's leaders had appealed secretly for military aid from revolutionary France. In Dublin the newly formed Independent Corps of Volunteers, calling themselves the National Guard, dressed as *sans culotte* revolutionaries, the crown on their coat buttons replaced by the Frisian cap of liberty; in Belfast, the *Northern Star* carried articles on "the Advantages and Defects of Missile and Hand Weapons" and of "squadrons of pikes." Reacting, Irish Loyalists formed Orange Lodges and prepared for civil war. In December 1792, when France declared war on England, the Dublin Society of United Irishmen issued an "Address," calling on Volunteers to arm immediately. When the Irish Privy Council promptly banned the Volunteers from assembling in arms and ordered the arrests of five radical leaders for seditious libel, the remaining United Irish leadership went underground and began stockpiling weapons.[22]

It would be fully four years before a French expedition prepared to aid Irish revolutionaries. After conquering Italy, Napoleon allocated 14,000 veterans under his best general, Lazare Hoche. An armada of thirty-five ships sailed from Brest and eluded the British blockade, only to arrive in Bantry Bay during a hurricane-force winter storm that made it impossible to land the troops and scattered the fleet. As one battered vessel after another cut its anchor cable and sailed back to France, Hoche abandoned the expedition.

The British government, invoking martial law, set out to suppress the Volunteers. Silencing the *Northern Star,* government forces confiscated all private arms, carried out house burnings and tortured and murdered suspected revolt leaders.

Their ranks still exceeding 200,000 men, the United Irishmen delayed open rebellion as they waited for another promised French expedition. Their plan was to take Dublin and the surrounding Pale counties in a revolt timed to tie down reinforcements from scattered British garrisons, allowing uprisings to erupt simultaneously all over Ireland. The signal to rise was to be the interception of mail coaches from Dublin. But informers who had infiltrated the United Irishmen revealed the rebels' assembly points to Dublin Castle. One hour before the appointed rising, British troops massed at the rendezvous locations and rounded up rebel leaders as the rank and file fled, dropping their weapons.[23]

When a general uprising erupted spontaneously in Dublin on May 24, it quickly spread among Catholic peasants in the South, with the heaviest fighting breaking out in County Kildare. Poorly led and armed only with crude pikes, they first defeated the outnumbered British regulars and Loyalist militiamen. As the rebellion became violently sectarian, Catholics killed large numbers of Protestants and forced many others to flee. When Catholics slaughtered Protestant prisoners, the government publicized the massacre in the Presbyterian North, successfully fanning ancient religious animosity. Some 20,000 British reinforcements from England crushed the rebels in a series of battles, and, in the gorse-covered hills of County Wicklow, Loyalists massacred rebel prisoners. Without artillery or cavalry, the Catholic rebels were ultimately vanquished by government forces at Vinegar Hill on June 21, 1798.

Two months later, 1,100 French soldiers led by General Joseph Humbert slipped through the British blockade and disembarked in County Mayo. As he marched toward Dublin, 5,000 untrained rebels joined him. At heavily defended Castlebar, he surprised the garrison by taking a path through bogs and over hills that the British considered impassable. The ambushed soldiers fled so quickly that their rout became known as the Castlebar Races.

But now Humbert faced Lord Lieutenant and General Charles Cornwallis, viceroy of Ireland, whose surrender at Yorktown brought to an end the American Revolution. After serving as governor-general of India and being in charge of all British ordnance in Europe, he now possessed extraordinary wartime powers. Embarking 3,000 troops on canal boats, he linked up with fresh troops from England and pursued the French north to Sligo, then south toward Dublin. This time, the countryside didn't rise. Cornwallis kept his force between the French and the capital and, at Ballintra on September 8, after a brief battle, the French surrendered.

Hardly a month later, in October 1798, the French once more attempted to support the Irish rebellion. A powerful British naval squadron intercepted French ships carrying 3,000 troops and, after a three-hour naval battle off County Donegal, the French fleet surrendered. Theobald Wolfe Tone, brought to Dublin Castle in chains to face a court-martial, insisted that, as a French general, he was entitled to be treated as a prisoner of war. Unfazed, the British convicted him of treason and ordered him hanged. His brother smuggled a razor to Tone who attempted to slit his own throat, but he only succeeded in cutting his windpipe. He died a week later of septicemia, the Irish rebellion of 1798 dying with him.[24]

After each battle, large numbers of rebel prisoners were executed, many hanged on improvised portable gallows carried by British soldiers. Loyalists massacred the wounded and prisoners. Historian Alan Taylor found that "victors flogged and murdered hundreds, burning their houses and Catholic chapels, making a grim landscape of scorched villages. Executed and rotting bodies hung in chains from the roofs of county courthouses, while city walls bristled with heads stuck on spikes. The rebellion claimed at least 20,000 lives, most of them defeated rebels."[25]

As embittered Loyalists meted out revenge, the scale of the violence stunned Cornwallis, who had once hoped for lasting reforms, including Catholic emancipation. He later wrote in disgust of the "wretched business of Courts-martial, hanging, transporting, etc., attended with all the dismal scenes of wives, sisters, fathers, kneeling and crying." Cornwallis executed eighty-one radicals and imprisoned 410 more in the Scottish Highlands, and he transported far more to the British penal colony in Australia or conscripted them to service for life in the Royal Navy.

In the next two decades, nearly two-thirds of the immigrants to the United States came from Ireland, three-fourths of them from Ulster, one-fourth Catholics, mostly seeking refuge in the port cities of New York, Philadelphia and Baltimore. One Ulsterman wrote home that "the lowest here [unlike those of poor Ireland] are well-fed, well-dressed, and happy. . . . They stand erect and crouch not before any man."

In 1799 alone, according to the eyewitness French journalist Moreau de Saint-Méry, 13,000 Irish refugees arrived in Philadelphia as indentured servants, and each year the city received 4,000 to 5,000 more. By 1812 Irish immigrants made up 12 percent of Philadelphia's population. Many would later move on to take up inexpensive federal lands on the frontiers where they would fight fiercely against the hated British and their Indian allies. Survivors of the United Irish, the militants making up this revolutionary diaspora would form the nucleus of anti-British—and anti-Federalist—riots during the War of 1812 and would provide a significant proportion of volunteers who served in the American army and aboard navy and privateering ships.

THE TIDAL WAVE of refugees fleeing turmoil in Europe and the Caribbean severely strained the fabric of American politics. After bloody sectarian strife in Ireland, when the survivors of the United Ireland movement arrived in the United States, they downplayed former religious differences and simply saw themselves as enemies of Britain. Any British sympathizers, as they considered the Federalists, became their new enemies. Casting their ballots for Jefferson's Democratic-Republicans, they strengthened his urban base. From Albany to Charleston, they organized the American Society of United Irishmen, their members swearing to pursue "the attainment of liberty and equality to mankind in whatever nation [I] may reside."

Alarmed, certain that the Irish republicans intended to assist a French invasion of America, Connecticut Federalist congressman Uriah Tracy wrote to Federalist Oliver Wolcott that, "with a very few exceptions," the Irish immigrants were "United Irishmen, Free Masons, and the most God-provoking Democrats on this side of Hell."

Further driving up the temperature in a climate already boiling with xenophobia and nativism, radical journalists arrived in Philadelphia, introducing a scurrilous form of press warfare not seen before in America. The Federalists' champion, William Cobbett, a former British army sergeant, squared off against William Duane, an Irish bigamist and former mercenary of the British East India Company. Cobbett's shrill *Porcupine's Gazette* declared that "every United Irishman ought to be hunted from the country, as much as a wolf or a tyger."[26]

New York–born, Ireland-raised Duane had offended British authorities in India, where he published a Calcutta paper and fathered three illegitimate children. Adulating the French Revolution for exposing official corruption, Duane had been deported from the subcontinent for "attempting to disseminate the democratic principles of Tom Paine." Brought to London in chains, Duane rejoined his Irish wife and three legitimate children and edited a radical newspaper there until immigrating with his family to Philadelphia in 1798. Buying the *Aurora*, America's most radical and influential newspaper, in 1798, Duane's work became the favorite of invective-loving anti-Federalist breakfast table readers all over the nation. While Adams's administration appeared to turn two blind eyes, federal troops broke into Duane's office and beat, kicked and flogged him. The Federalist *Gazette of the United States* told its readers that Duane "was not an American but a foreigner, and not merely a foreigner, but a United Irishman, and not merely a United Irishman, but a public convict and fugitive from justice."[27]

ACROSS THE ATLANTIC, the rumble of tumbrels gave way to the thud of the boots of France's republican armies. The five-man governing Directory shared power until Napoleon Bonaparte wrested away full control of the Revolution in December 1799. In the previous two years, French privateers had captured some four hundred American trading vessels. Boarding *Cincinnatus*, out of Baltimore, French privateers tortured the American captain with thumbscrews in a vain attempt to wring from him an admission that he was carrying British cargo. Meanwhile, Napoleon took command of all French forces on land and sea before invading Italy and Austria and preparing to cross the English Channel.

Seeking a new treaty of amity and commerce with France, Adams appointed James Monroe the new minister there. At the opening congressional session in May 1797, Adams had accused the French of treating their old American allies "neither as allies or friends nor as a sovereign state." He urged Congress to show the French that the Americans were not "the miserable instruments of foreign influence" who had no regard for "national honor, character, and interest." Adams's provocative speech shocked Jefferson, who had been sworn in as vice president two months earlier and presided over the Senate. As former envoy to France, Jefferson worried that Adams's slur would bring on war. When Monroe arrived in Paris to present his credentials, the French, still seething, not only refused to receive him but ejected him.[28]

As the crisis deepened, Adams dispatched special envoys Charles Cotesworth Pinckney, John Marshall and Elbridge Gerry to Paris. For six months Adams heard nothing. Then a batch of coded reports arrived in Philadelphia by courier ship, informing him that the diplomatic mission had failed. From one dispatch Adams learned that Napoleon had decreed that French ports would now be closed to any neutral American ship carrying anything produced in England or any British colony. The United States, as the nation with more merchant ships than France, was now barred from trading directly with either of the warring European giants, a devastating blow to America's carrying trade. (By 1794, exports alone stood at $33 million.)

From another dispatch, Adams learned that his emissaries had been kept waiting for weeks before being promised a fifteen-minute interview with the new foreign minister, Talleyrand, who, during two years in exile in Philadelphia, had dined frequently with Hamilton and had a nodding acquaintance with then–vice president Adams. After more obfuscation, the American envoys received a summons to the Garde Meuble Palace—today the Talleyrand wing of the American embassy, overlooking the Place de la Concorde, the site of thousands of beheadings by guillotine. There the Americans met with three secret agents, identified in the dispatch only as X, Y and Z. Talleyrand might be favorably disposed to meeting with the Americans, but before negotiations could proceed, they would have to pay a *douceur*—a bribe—of $50,000, an enormous amount of money, personally to Talleyrand and then agree to a $10 million loan to France in compensation for Adams's insult. There was no mention of the American demand for compensation for the hundreds of ships seized by the French. Directly asked whether they would agree to the bribe, all three Americans refused; Pinckney responded, "No! No! Not a sixpence!"[29]

Incensed, Adams informed Congress that peace negotiations had failed and that the former allies would not exchange envoys. Outraged, Congress insisted by a 65-27 vote that the entire secret diplomatic correspondence be turned over to the House. The Senate voted that the documents be printed, but then be read only in executive session. Within days, however, their contents leaked to the public, fomenting fresh anti-French fury. Brushing aside any possibility of a diplomatic settlement and acting without an official declaration of war, Congress granted Adams emergency war powers. Rushing war preparations, the House voted a substantial $1 million to buttress harbor fortifications, build cannon foundries and purchase massive quantities of arms and munitions. The navy would be expanded: by 1801, there were to be thirteen frigates in service as well as six ships-of-the-line under construction. To finance mobilization, Congress for the first time imposed a direct federal tax on land, houses and slaves. In May 1798 Congress passed a bill that empowered American warships to capture any French privateer or naval ship found in American waters, and it rescinded the Washington administration's ban on arming merchant vessels.

Congress then created the Navy Department, henceforth to be separate from the War Department, with its own cabinet-level secretary. Another bill expanded the army from its peacetime strength of a scant 840 men to 10,000. Federalists' demand for 25,000 met with defeat. On each vote, the margin was narrow. Many Americans, especially in maritime New England, wanted peace, not war. Jefferson spoke to them when he called Adams's bellicose policy "insane" and his message to Congress little short of "a declaration of war." Jefferson wrote to a fellow Virginian that he still hoped the "reign of witches" would soon end, that "the people" would recover "their true sight, restore their government to its true principles."[30]

For two months at the beginning of his one-term presidency, Adams and his old rival Jefferson had seemed friends again. They had served together in the Continental Congress on the committee that drafted the Declaration of Independence, their families living together in Paris during the protracted Revolutionary War peace talks. But now their friendship ended. Two days before Jefferson departed for his summer vacation at Monticello, Congress passed the first of four laws meant to stifle all criticism of the administration, all opposition to the Federalists by Jefferson's Democratic-Republicans. Leading Federalists suspected that Jefferson and his followers were plotting an upheaval similar to the French Revolution to overthrow the government.

As the unrest sweeping Europe lapped America's shores, calls for secession came from several states. The fledgling nation seemed ready to rip itself apart. Federalists blamed French refugees and French-sympathizing Irish immigrants. Adams persuaded an increasingly xenophobic Congress to attenuate the naturalization process for new citizens from five to fourteen years. To guard against what it perceived to be the threat of anarchy, the Federalist-dominated Congress passed a temporary alien act under which the president could deport any alien he considered "dangerous to the peace and safety" of the nation. Only after receiving a deportation order could an alien offer evidence in his defense. Congress then passed a second and permanent alien act allowing the president to imprison or deport all aliens of an enemy power in wartime. On July 14, the anniversary of the fall of the Bastille prison in Paris on the first day of the French Revolution, Congress passed the Alien and Sedition Act by a narrow 44-41 vote. To be enforced in peacetime or war, the Act made it unlawful for American citizens to combine or conspire to oppose any government measure, to prevent government officers from doing their duties or to aid "any insurrection, riot, unlawful assembly or combination."

But the Act also targeted any person writing, speaking or publishing "any false, scandalous and malicious writing or writings against the government of the United States, or either house of the Congress of the United States, or the President of the United States." The Act was to expire the last day of Adams's presidency. The Sedition Act undoubtedly had as its principal targets Vice President Jefferson, the Democratic-Republican societies and anti-administration newspapers that were criticizing Adams's government. The punishment: a stiff fine of up to $2,000 and two years in prison. The demonic intensity of the debates in Congress and the swiftness of the bill's adoption horrified Hamilton. "Let us not establish a tyranny," he cautioned. "Energy is a very different thing from violence."[31]

But even before Adams signed the Sedition Act, alarmed French refugees prepared to leave the country. In late June, Saint-Méry wrote in his journal, "People acted as though a French invasion force might land in America at any moment. Everybody was suspicious of everybody else. Everywhere one saw murderous glances." While no émigré was ever deported, as soon as the Alien and Sedition Act passed, a dozen crowded ships sailed for France or Santo Domingo. Those who did not flee were kept under close surveillance by agents of ultra-suspicious Secretary of State Timothy Pickering. On the day the act passed, Saint-Méry obtained a passport for himself, his wife and his children. After four years at the heart of the French community in Philadelphia, he learned that President Adams "had made a list of French people to be deported": "Now M. Adams had often come to my house, to my study and to my shop during his term as Vice-President and we had exchanged books as gifts. But after he became President, I never saw him."

As a favor, Senator Langdon of New Hampshire went to see Adams "to find out what [Saint-Méry] was charged with." He replied, "Nothing in particular, but he's too French."[32]

During the eighteen months that the Sedition Act was in force, circuit-riding Supreme Court justices traveled from town to town, reviewing suspect newspaper articles, pamphlets and books. By the time they had finished their inquisition, they had prosecuted twenty-five writers, editors and printers in fourteen separate cases, convicting and imprisoning ten.

THAT SUMMER OF 1798, as each ship from Europe brought fresh news of battles and insurrections, pro-war and pro-peace gangs waged battles in the streets of Philadelphia until the city's elite cavalry, the First City Troop, broke them up. When the Democratic-Republican *Aurora* persisted in lampooning the war preparations, a mob attacked its editor Duane's home and smashed its windows. Reluctantly, Adams consented to have sentries posted at the doors of the President's House at Sixth and Market Streets. Jefferson, who let it be known that he considered the new navy a waste of taxpayers' money, wrote to his daughter, Martha, at Monticello that he was afraid to go outside at night: "Politics and party hatreds destroy the happiness of every being here. They seem, like salamanders to consider fire as their element."[33]

While Adams resisted pressure from Hamilton and the pro-war wing of the Federalist Party for an outright declaration of war against France in the Senate, he yielded to their demand for a massive military buildup. Between March and July 1798, Congress passed twenty acts: to modernize and consolidate the young nation's defenses in case of a French invasion and to revoke the 1778 Franco-American treaty. Adams summoned sixty-six-year-old Washington out of retirement, appointing him commander of the enlarged army. Washington agreed to accept the command on the condition that he would remain at Mount Vernon and turn over most of his duties to Hamilton, who, as inspector general, assumed the rank of major general. Opportunistically, Hamilton set about purging the officer corps of Democratic-Republicans.

In the so-called Quasi-War, the Navy patrolled the Caribbean, where most American shipping losses had taken place. The undeclared war began with the French capture of the American schooner *Retaliation* off Guadeloupe in November 1798. Two months later, in the first naval victory of the new cruising navy, the French frigate *l'Insurgente* surrendered to the American frigate *Constellation*. The Americans defeated two more French frigates, captured eighty-two French privateering vessels and recovered more than seventy American merchant vessels. As reports of each victory reached shore, American pride and bellicosity reached new heights.

By September 1800, as Adams's presidential term ended, no French invasion had come. Amid mounting criticism of burdensome taxes for war materials, ships and fortifications, Adams worried about his chances for reelection. When Foreign Minister Talleyrand published in Paris his assurance that the next American minister would be received with respect, Adams appointed a trusted old friend from his years in the London embassy, William Vans Murray, to the premier diplomatic post in Europe to seek a new treaty. He did so without consulting anyone, completely surprising Hamilton's pro-war Federalists. Hamilton pressured Adams but failed to persuade him to change his course. Adams stubbornly enlarged the delegation leaving for Paris to negotiate with Talleyrand. A divided Senate ratified the resulting Treaty of Morfontaine, releasing the United States from the joint defensive alliance. Taken together with the Jay Treaty of 1796 with England, this left the United States, as Washington had wished in his Farewell Address, free of any permanent, entangling alliances, a neutral nation with defined neutrality rights. As French and English navies attacked each other on all of the world's oceans, the U.S. merchant marine, despite its early losses in the Caribbean, was free to carry cargo for both combatants. Emerging from the crises of the 1790s, the maritime nation nearly tripled its carrying trade—and America basked in unprecedented prosperity.

FOR MOST OF their terms, President Adams and Vice President Jefferson avoided each other. From his Virginia aerie at Monticello, Jefferson, with Madison, clandestinely attacked the Alien and Sedition Acts, labeling them a blatant attempt to silence Democratic-Republicans and their news-papers. An intended target of the Sedition Act, Jefferson worked in secret, but by late 1798 he began casually mentioning to visiting members of state legislatures of Virginia, Kentucky and North Carolina that he was sure that their states would react strongly to the decrees. He had drafted an anonymous resolution attacking the acts as unconstitutional and handed copies to his visitors—he could not risk mailing them—to introduce into the Kentucky and North Carolina legislatures. His neighbor Madison rode over from Montpelier to show Jefferson similar documents he had secretly drawn up. In the opening sentence of his Kentucky Resolutions, Jefferson affirmed that the "several states" were not united on "the principle of un-limited submission to their general government." The states had only del-egated "certain definite powers." When the national government "assumes undelegated powers, its acts are unauthoritative, void, and of no force."[34]

In November 1798 the Kentucky legislature adopted Jefferson's resolu-tions, declaring the Alien and Sedition Acts null and void and calling on other states to express their outrage. Later that month, Virginia followed suit. The two states were planting the seed, borrowed from Jefferson, of the doctrine of a state's right to nullify federal law, firing the first shots of the presidential election campaign of 1800 in doing so. Jefferson must have known that the second-highest officer of the government could be charged with sedition under the Act if he openly associated himself with a protest movement to declare two laws of the current Congress unconstitutional. All in secret, Jefferson and Madison, without making a single speech or consigning a word between them to writing, conducted a vast underground campaign that spawned pamphlets and hundreds of letters that circulated among Democratic-Republican newspapers and supporters. *Sub rosa*, a second national political party grew out of resistance to the Alien and Sedition Acts. More than ever, the Jefferson-Madison campaign intensified hatred against Federalists. After visiting Virginia, the Federalist governor of North Carolina wrote to Supreme Court Justice James Iredell that he feared Virginia's leaders were "determined upon the overthrow of the General Government. . . . [T]hey would risk it upon the chance of war. . . . [S]ome of them talked of 'seceding from the Union,' while others boldly asserted . . . the practicability of 'severing the Union.' "[35]

George Washington's recurring nightmare had long been that divisive partisan politics would break up the Union. Within months of his death in December 1799, the party that he had reluctantly espoused, the Federalists, imploded. His protégé, Alexander Hamilton, potentially Adams's opponent, had effectively disqualified himself from the presidency by admitting in print that he had carried on a year-long, illicit affair with the wife of a subordinate in the Treasury. Hamilton also had turned against Adams. But any natural advantage that incumbent Adams might have enjoyed was more than offset by the unpopularity of the Alien and Sedition Acts and federal taxes financing the military buildup. In the first knockdown, drag-out campaign, Americans proved that they preferred newspapers to pamphlets or books and, further, preferred newspapers crammed with scandal. The Federalists blundered again when they attacked Jefferson's deistic views on religion: it backfired, but the attack underlined his championing of the Virginia Statute of Religious Freedom. The assault on his Enlightenment philosophy led to the revelation that it was Jefferson who had authored the Declaration of Independence. While Jefferson and Madison organized a political party, with Jefferson as its candidate, the Federalists turned on each other. At Hamilton's insistence, Federalists in Congress voted to support two candidates equally, Adams and Pinckney, allowing the Electoral College to decide the outcome. Secretly, however, Hamilton pushed Jefferson's candidacy, not Adams's. "If we must have an enemy at the head of the government," he wrote, "let it be one whom we can oppose & for whom we are not responsible, who will not involve our party in the disgrace of his foolish and bad measures."[36]

In Electoral College voting, Jefferson and Aaron Burr of New York tied. The deadlock threw the election into the old Federalist-controlled House of Representatives, which vowed to vote continuously, eating and sleeping in the unfinished Capitol, until a president was chosen. After five inconclusive days and thirty-five ballots, James A. Bayard, the sole congressman from Delaware and a staunch Burrite who had refused to vote for Jefferson, forced the Federalists' hand by announcing he would switch to Jefferson. On the thirty-sixth ballot, Bayard and several Federalists from Vermont and Maryland put blank pieces of paper in the ballot box. In bloc voting by state, this allowed Jefferson to win, ten states to four.

Jefferson ordered a halt to all prosecutions under the Alien and Sedition Acts and ordered all fines refunded. In his inaugural address, he called for reconciliation with the defeated Federalists, but then he set to work dismantling their party's political base by purging its members from federal patronage jobs. Furious at Adams's midnight appointment of federal magistrates, he found he could not remove them: the Judiciary Act of 1801, passed by lame duck Federalists *after* Jefferson's election, protected them. But Jefferson *could* replace all Federalist marshals and district attorneys. According to his own careful record, of 316 federal offices subject to presidential appointment and removal, he saw that 158, exactly half, would be filled by Democratic-Republicans, 132 by Federalists and 26 by independents. Jefferson was keeping faith by the numbers. He filled most key federal and state offices with Jeffersonians.

The third president ushered in the spoils system; it would plague American politics and government throughout the nineteenth century. Pressing his bloodless revolution, he systematically eliminated entrenched Federalist aristocrats from every level of administrative office, banishing from power many of the scions of the oldest and best-established families in America and inflicting permanent damage on the party of Washington, Adams and the hated Hamilton. Not only did he oust top elected officials but he removed the second tier as well by personal intervention, wielding his power in Congress to eliminate whole departments. He replaced eighteen of thirty federal judges, thirteen of twenty-one U.S. attorneys, eighteen of twenty U.S. marshals. He purged Hamilton's old power base at the Treasury, sacking fifteen of sixteen revenue supervisors, twelve of twenty-one inspectors, all but one collector of customs. No purge in nineteenth-century American politics surpassed the thoroughness of Jefferson's housecleaning. What he denominated the Revolution of 1800 shattered the Federalist Party, permanently damaging its underpinnings in every state while at the same time breaking the power of the New England Federalist aristocracy and shifting its influence to the South.

With a Democratic-Republican majority in both houses of Congress, Jefferson and his secretary of state, Madison, wrote Congress's agenda, affecting sweeping reforms. Reducing the residency requirement for naturalization from Adams's fourteen years back to the original five, he assured the aggrandizement of his political base among new Americans. Virtually dismantling the Federalists' fiscal and military programs, he slashed federal spending by attacking military expenditure, which Federalists had linked to growth in American trade. The Federalists had increased the peacetime military from 840 soldiers in frontier outposts in 1789 to 5,400 by 1801; Jefferson cut it back to 3,300 men. He also cut back the navy: with six frigates on active duty and seven more frigates and six state-of-the-art ships-of-the-line under construction, he spared only the frigates. He ordered most of the ships decommissioned and mothballed in an eight-hundred-foot-long dry dock, which was constructed at the Washington Navy Yard at his command. The keels of seventy-four-gun ships-of-the-line never were laid; the costly lumber warped in navy yards up and down the Atlantic coast.

Jefferson opposed a costly arms race that, he believed, could only bring about constant friction and the threat of war with much wealthier naval powers. Just before his inauguration, Congress passed legislation that gave the president discretion in officering and manning the six commissioned frigates. If war broke out with the Barbary states, these ships were to "protect our commerce & chastise their insolence—by sinking, burning or destroying their ships & Vessels wherever you shall find them." Advised of Jefferson's swearing-in early in 1801, the Dey of Tripoli demanded a gift of $225,000 from the new administration, more than 2 percent of all federal revenues in 1800. Long opposed to paying tribute, Jefferson refused. On May 1, 1801, Tripoli signaled that it was declaring war on the United States by cutting down the flagstaff in front of the American consulate.[37]

While Congress never voted a formal declaration of war, it authorized Jefferson to instruct captains of all American ships to seize all vessels of the Dey. The American squadron joined forces with the Swedish navy, which had gone to war the year before. From bases provided at Palermo, Messina and Syracuse by the Kingdom of the Two Sicilies, the allies launched operations against the walled port of Tripoli. Under the command of Commodore Edward Preble, the American flotilla of eight warships, including four of the six frigates, was sent to the Mediterranean as soon as they came off the ways. Preble set up a blockade of the Barbary ports and attacked Tripoli's ships. The North African city mounted 115 pieces of heavy artillery to guard its outer harbor, 25,000 troops, a fleet of ten 10-gun brigs, two 8-gun schooners, two large row galleys and nineteen gunboats.

In the first engagement, on August 1, 1802, the schooner *Enterprise* defeated the more powerful fourteen-gun corsair *Tripoli*, but in October 1802, while patrolling Tripoli's harbor, the frigate *Philadelphia* ran hard aground. Taking its captain and crew hostage, the Dey stripped the *Philadelphia*'s guns to turn on the American fleet. In a daring raid on the night of February 16, 1803, twenty-five-year-old Lieutenant Stephen Decatur and an all-volunteer crew sailed the captured *Tripoli* ketch, rechristened *Intrepid*, into the harbor and close enough to the *Philadelphia* to board it. Their deception was successful, and Decatur and his disguised men boarded the American frigate, overpowered its crew and, with covering fire from the American squadron, set the *Philadelphia* ablaze, destroying it to deprive Tripoli of its use. British admiral Horatio Nelson hailed Decatur's raid as "the most bold and daring act of the age." By June 1805, the Dey of Tripoli was ready to sign a peace treaty and, after a final ransom payment of $60,000, carry out a prisoner-of-war exchange. The tribute, twenty barrels of silver coins, arrived on a U.S. Navy ship.

SHIFTING TO A strict defensive posture at home, Jefferson built up coastal fortifications, launching an extensive building program that cost a staggering $2.8 million between 1801 and 1812, three times what the Federalists had spent in the 1790s. He also created what his critics dubbed a "mosquito navy": 278 small but expensive gunboats that required 40-man crews, carried only two small cannon, could be sunk with a single cannonball, and capsized easily in open water. The boats cost $1.5 million, which could have been spent to add a fleet of eight new forty-four-gun frigates or four new seventy-four-gun ships-of-the-line. Jefferson and the Democratic-Republicans were willing to cut the nation's regular forces because they believed, as an article of faith, that they could rely on the state militias and their naval equivalent, privateers, that were more democratic in character and posed no threat to democratic institutions. When, after his reelection in 1805, Jefferson cut the Navy's budget in half again even as he ordered more gunboats, many of his experienced naval officers resigned.

An off-again, on-again pacifist, Jefferson meanwhile created the United States Military Academy at West Point, building on the base of the small Corps of Discovery that he commissioned to explore the vast Louisiana Territory he purchased from Napoleon. Even as the Napoleonic Wars ravaged Europe and ended the Age of Reason, Jefferson clung to reason as a deterrent against war. To the Earl of Buchan he wrote in 1803, "My hope of preserving peace for our country is not founded on the greater principles of non-resistance under every wrong, but in the belief that a just and friendly conduct on our part will procure justice and friendship from others." In his years as American minister to France, Jefferson had frequented the influential *salon* of Madame Anne-Louise Germiane Necker de Staël, daughter of the reforming finance minister of France. Married to the Swedish ambassador to France, she had been banished from Paris in 1803 for refusing to praise Napoleon in her writings. Now, trying to explain to her why he was attempting to keep the United States neutral in the Napoleonic wars, Jefferson wrote to his old friend, "If nations go to war for every degree of injury, there would never be peace on earth."[38]

Jefferson's erratic pacifism served the nation well for the first few years of his presidency. From 1801 to 1803, warfare ceased temporarily in Europe during the Peace of Amiens. Taking office at this very time, he had every reason to believe that his frugal fiscal and military policies would succeed. America's maritime commerce was booming, with exports nearly trebling between 1794 and 1801, largely as a result of the Jay Treaty with England, which he so despised. What Jefferson was unable to comprehend was that this was merely a function of continued war in Europe. The demand for American products in Britain dried up and American exports plummeted from $94 million in 1801 to $54 million in 1803, a 40 percent drop.

THE LOUISIANA PURCHASE, perhaps Jefferson's most lasting presidential contribution, doubled the territory of the United States. Ironically Napoleon, eager to close the sale in order to receive the purchase price of $15 million (60 million *livres*), could not wait to put it to work to build a navy that would enable him to realize his dream of invading England. He lost that navy in one day at the Battle of Trafalgar, a peerless moment for the Royal Navy but one that was to prove disastrous for Jefferson's policies and for the United States.

With no French navy to oppose it, the Royal Navy could spare enough ships to blockade the American coast and make virtually impossible any American shipments to French ports. With a diminished navy, Jefferson could do little more than brandish his gold-headed cane in the direction of London when the *Leander* lobbed the cannonball in New York harbor that decapitated John Pierce, the unfortunate helmsman of the sloop *Richard,* on a spring evening in 1806.

The practice of restricting trade on the seas was a measure that the British, as the preeminent naval power, had often used in the past to destroy an enemy's shipping. In defending the Orders in Council, the British pointed to the more devastating effects of Napoleon's Berlin Decree. In issuing the Orders, Prime Minister Spencer Perceval insisted that the British had no desire to stop all trade to the Continent but merely to recapture the lion's share from the predominant neutral trading nation, the United States. But in tightening its blockade of Napoleon-controlled Europe, the British were seizing all ships bound to or from the Continent and destroying or seizing neutral ships on the Baltic and North Seas, including many Russian vessels. In dealing with Americans, Britain gradually lessened the rigors of its blockade and lowered transit duties, and it issued thousands of licenses permitting trade with Europe to British subjects and European neutrals. In addition, the Orders in Council authorized shipment of goods manufactured or grown in the United States directly to European ports, in large part because American grain was feeding the British armies and navies fighting Napoleon. Many American ship owners winked at the British orders, so profitable was their trade with wartime Europe. They continued to ship goods not produced in the United States to the Continent by a variety of devices, including the carrying of dual papers and bribing of French officials. For its part, France ignored the licensing system and relaxed the Continental blockade from time to time whenever it served its purposes.

The two belligerent powers competed with each other in how much confusion they could create and how much American shipping they could seize. According to the U.S. Merchant Marine, Britain and France seized nearly 1,500 American ships between them from 1803 to 1812. Each country, in addition to damaging the economy of its adversary, attempted to coerce the neutral United States into accepting its own policies.

When the British Admiralty ignored American complaints over the *Leander* affair in 1806, Jefferson dispatched Monroe and Pinckney to London to seek a new Anglo-American treaty. The British agreed to allow trade with Caribbean islands as long as American ships paid a small transit duty during their U.S. stopover. In exchange, the United States pledged neutrality in the European war. But there was a catch. Napoleon had just promulgated the Berlin Decree, declaring a naval blockade of the British Isles that, since he lacked a navy to enforce it, existed only on paper. Thus Napoleon initiated the greatest commercial war of the era. Napoleon's declaration of a ban on trade with Britain included seizing all goods and ships, regardless of nationality, departing not only from British ports but also from those of its colonies—a large proportion of American trade was with European colonies in the Caribbean. France had essentially declared war on American trade with Britain. In revenge, the British demanded in a new Anglo-American agreement that England could retaliate if the United States honored the French blockade, which American merchantmen of course were not about to do. The British in their turn were outlawing all American trade with France. The combination of these British and French restrictions would essentially criminalize all neutral commerce, and one or the other of the European powers would now treat previously neutral American trade as contraband commerce.

Until this moment, Washington's declaration of American neutrality in 1793 had made it possible for U.S.-flagged vessels to dominate the shipping of goods between the warring European powers and their empires, particularly when carrying West Indies goods to Europe and European manufactures to the Western Hemisphere. In the fifteen years since the Napoleonic Wars broke out, the American carrying trade with both combatants had expanded fivefold.

In peacetime, while Americans were trading all over the globe, Britain boasted thousands of merchant vessels and warships that overwhelmed competition. While British and French commercial vessels were preoccupied by war and harassed by enemy navies, American merchant vessels, becoming more numerous than either warring power's merchant marines, took full advantage. But the definition of neutral versus contraband trade was creating increasing conflict. The United States maintained that neutral status meant that American ships by definition were carrying neutral goods and argued that even provisions and naval stores were not contraband. When the British objected that American ships were directly aiding France by shipping goods from French colonies to the Continent, American merchants began to import French goods to the U.S. ports and then re-export them as neutral goods. Many merchants manipulated paperwork, not even bothering to offload goods in U.S. ports before re-exporting them. To the British, this practice of affecting a "broken voyage," which had come to represent fully half of all American export trade, was little more than a form of laundering direct trade with the enemy. Suddenly, in 1805, the British High Court of Admiralty had ruled that landing goods and paying duties in the United States was no longer proof of importation.

As the Napoleonic Wars dragged on, the upstart United States found itself caught between European empires in a high-stakes trade war. The latest British restrictions on the re-export trade coupled with the absence of any clause banning impressment of American sailors cast a fresh pall over Anglo-American relations. Unless the British ceased what was in effect the imprisonment of Americans, all other British concessions seemed trifling. "Bad feeling between the governments," writes British economic historian Brian Arthur, "was further exacerbated by the impressment by the Royal Navy of apparently British seamen from American merchant ships at sea." Despite a capital sanction, desertion "had long been a major problem." The allegiance of British seamen found on neutral ships was, according to the Prince Regent, 'no optional duty which they can decline or resume at pleasure,' but 'began with their birth and can only terminate with their existence.'"[39]

Jefferson never quite forgave Monroe for returning from London with a treaty that not only ignored this key issue but agreed to continued British dictation of controls on American trade. He refused to submit the treaty to the Senate for ratification and refused to renegotiate it. From that moment, Anglo-American relations deteriorated. As historian Gordon Wood explains it,

> [i]t was not the actual number of seizures that most irritated Americans; rather it was the British presumption that His Majesty's government had the right to decide just what American trade should be permitted or not permitted. It seemed to reduce America once again to the status of a colonial dependent. This was the fundamental issue that underlay America's turbulent relationship with Britain through the entire period of the European wars.[40]

—— ∿ ——

SIX

"The Reign of Witches"

I n February 1807, Navy secretary Robert Smith sent orders to the officers of the thirty-eight-gun frigate *Chesapeake* to prepare to sail to the Mediterranean to relieve the frigate *Constitution*. After a two-year lull, Tripoli, ignoring the 1805 peace treaty, resumed seizing American ships and their crews for ransom, blindsiding Jefferson's policy of downsizing the navy. By the time Captain James Barron unsealed his orders to take over as commodore of a much-reduced Mediterranean squadron, the *Chesapeake* had wallowed for years in a long line of bare hulls moored near the Washington Navy Yard in the shallows of the Potomac's Eastern Branch.

In the four months required to restore the *Chesapeake* to seaworthiness, Barron, a veteran of five years on the Mediterranean station, lived comfortably at home in Hampton Roads, Virginia, while Master Commandant Charles Gordon readied the smallest of the United States' six frigates. After a final rush of boarding crew and supplies, the *Chesapeake* cast off, sharing the river with an armada of small boats fishing for shad, herring and sturgeon. The first sign that she was not quite ready for the long voyage came as she glided past Mount Vernon. Traditionally, to honor the memory of Washington, the *Chesapeake* was expected to fire a salute, but no one could find the sponges or the right shells to fit the guns.

On June 4 the *Chesapeake* threaded the shoals at Wolf Trap, left Windmill Point astern and dropped anchor in Hampton Roads. For two more weeks, Commodore Barron went ashore while his crew manhandled aboard eighteen-pound long guns and thirty-two-pound carronades and fitted them onto their carriages. It was not until the first fair wind of June 19 that the *Chesapeake* finally sailed.

A few miles to the east, a Royal Navy squadron composed of a fifty-gun frigate, a sixteen-gun sloop-of-war and three seventy-four-gun ships-of-the-line rode at anchor in Lynnhaven Bay off Norfolk, Virginia, where they had been stationed all winter, watching for French ships that had supposedly taken refuge higher up in Chesapeake Bay. For months British officers had walked the streets of Norfolk and Hampton, buying the squadron's provisions with none of the apparent tensions of the past year's *Leander* confrontation in New York City. Suddenly, everything changed. That spring, crewmembers deserted every ship in the squadron. As the waters grew warmer, British sailors, barred from shore leave, jumped overboard and swam or stole a ship's boat to reach land. Virginia authorities, restrained by state law from apprehending asylum seekers, refused to cooperate with the British, essentially protecting the deserters. Many of the well-seasoned British crewmen immediately signed up to man outbound American ships. "It was no secret that many British seamen—including both deserters and seamen who, though not deserters themselves, were liable to be pressed by virtue of their British birth—found their way onto American ships," attests naval historian Ian W. Toll. "They were lured by better pay, better working conditions, and the certainty they would be released from service at the end of a voyage. Once employed on an American vessel, they could pass themselves off as native-born Americans, often with the active collaboration of their officers and shipmates."[1]

According to Treasury Secretary Gallatin, there were more British seamen employed on American ships than Americans conscripted onto British warships. All native-born British seamen could be pressed into service, including any who had been naturalized in America. Most emigrant sailors didn't bother with the formalities of naturalization: they could obtain "protection certificates" from a magistrate attesting to their birth within the United States. British officials scoffed at such proof. The Admiralty had come to the conclusion that "the flagrant and undeniable abuses of the official documents of American citizenship have obliged their Lordships to look at all such documents with the utmost distrust." Investigating a sampling of 150 naval seamen based in New York City in 1808, Captain Isaac Chauncey ascertained that a minority were American born; 9 percent were naturalized and 49 percent were recent immigrants. Eighty of the foreign-born sailors came from Ireland; in all, 134 of the 150 sailors came from the British Isles.[2]

One reason British seamen deserted their ships to join American crews: their pay doubled. Captain John Rodgers reported in 1811:

> We never hear of English sailors deserting into the service of any other country than our own. Indeed, from our speaking the same language & possessing nearly the same habits, they are led to believe there is no actual crime attach'd to their exchange of slavery for freedom.[3]

According to records of natural-born Americans forcibly impressed by the Royal Navy who attempted to gain release through U.S. State Department channels, British officials turned aside American protests: Thomas Barclay, consul general in New York City, countered that "for every real American Citizen impressed aboard His Majesty's Ships of War, there are at least fifty of His Majesty's Subjects in the Service, civil and naval, of their states, furnished with certificates of American Citizenship."[4]

The underlying reason for Britain's insatiable need for more seamen was the rapid expansion of the Royal Navy. In 1792, at the outbreak of the twenty-three-year-long war with France, British fleets employed roughly 10,000 men; by 1812, that number had swollen to 140,000 aboard 900 ships on active duty. At the same time, America's merchant marine cargoes grew from 558,000 tons in 1802 to 981,000 tons in 1811, making it easily the largest of any neutral maritime power, its complement of crewmen mushrooming from fewer than 10,000 seamen in 1792—roughly equivalent to the Royal Navy—to 70,000 by 1812. The Royal Navy's fourteenfold expansion precipitated unprecedented desertion rates. In that interval, the British claimed that at least 20,000 English subjects fled to crew American merchant ships; Treasury Secretary Albert Gallatin placed the number closer to 9,000, roughly equivalent to the number of Americans taken off their ships and forcibly conscripted into British service.

Captain Decatur reported to a superior officer, "It is a well known fact, Sir, that a vast majority of our Seamen have, at some period of their lives, been impressed into the British service." C. S. Forester observed that "at least" half of the impressed sailors aboard a typical Royal Navy vessel between 1803 and 1812 would jump ship—and then have to be replaced by the press gang.[5]

On the night of March 7, a crewmember of the sixteen-gun sloop-of-war *Halifax* commandeered the ship's twelve-foot jolly boat and sailed ashore at Hampton Roads. He, along with three other men who had jumped ship from the frigate *Melampus*, asked directions to the U.S. Navy recruiting station in Norfolk. Using assumed names, the foursome signed on to the *Chesapeake*. Since this was the naval vessel of a nation at peace with Britain, they undoubtedly believed they did not have to fear the usual punishment for desertion, the near–death sentence of a flogging of five hundred lashes with a cat-o'-nine-tails, or hanging. Later that month, Captain James Townsend of the *Halifax* came face-to-face on a Norfolk street with two of the men who had stolen his ship's boat. He attempted to coax them to return to their ship voluntarily. One, Jenkin Ratford, a British-born tailor of breeches turned sailor, railed at his ex-commander, declaring, as the captain later reported, that "he would be damned if he should return to the ship; that he was in the Land of Liberty; and that he would do as he liked, and that I had no business with him."[6]

The British captain protested to Captain Decatur, commander of the Gosport navy yard, who said he had nothing to do with the *Chesapeake* and referred him to Commodore Barron, who in turn urged him to take up the matter with civilian officials. Townsend then lodged a protest with the British consul in Norfolk, who then referred it to the British ambassador in Washington, who lodged a formal protest with Secretary of State Madison, who in his turn declined to intervene on the grounds that there was no provision dealing with deserters in any Anglo-American treaty. Townsend then reported to Admiral Sir George Cranfield Berkeley, commander in chief of the British North Atlantic station in Halifax, Nova Scotia. No fewer than thirty-five British deserters had signed aboard the *Chesapeake,* he asserted, adding that several from the *Halifax* "were seen by me & several of the Officers . . . patrolling the Streets of Norfolk in triumph." Admiral Berkeley forwarded the report to London, seeking instructions. When he received no immediate reply, he wrote out a circular order to all ships' captains in the North Atlantic. They were "required and directed in case of meeting with the American frigate the <u>Chesapeake</u> at sea . . . to show to the Captain of her this Order; and to require to search his Ship for the deserters." The admiral dispatched his flagship, the fifty-two-gun frigate *Leopard*, with his orders. Stopping off several times along the way from Halifax to the Virginia Capes to impress sailors from American merchant ships, the *Leopard* dropped anchor in Lynnhaven Bay twelve days later.[7]

On the morning of June 22, 1807, the *Chesapeake*, with Commodore Barron nominally in command of a crew of 329 officers and seamen and fifty-two marines, weighed anchor and sailed from Hampton Roads. The vessel acted as her own supply ship for the long cruise, her gun deck littered with baggage, a large quantity of hastily stowed provisions, ships stores and extra ammunition. It was peacetime: her powder horns remained empty, her matches unlit. Crammed into every inch of the *Chesapeake* were casks of water and wine, a blacksmith's anvil and forge, a horse, the furniture of officers and passengers. Coils of anchor cable obstructed the gun deck, the hammocks of thirty-two men on the sick list slung between cannon. Barron, who had visited the ship only twice, obviously assumed he would have ample time to make everything shipshape. He now met the civilian passengers, including the wives of two officers, three children, two servants and ten Italian musicians who had performed with the Marine Band in Washington and now were going home.

By eight that morning, as the *Chesapeake* sailed past the anchored British squadron, Barron could make out signal flags flying from the seventy-four-gun *Bellona*, but he thought nothing of it. He rounded Cape Henry and headed due east toward the open ocean. By noon, deckhands were stowing the larboard anchor and "clearing Ship for Sea." Through his telescope, Barron could make out that it was the *Leopard* that had put to sea ahead of him and was acting oddly, standing off to the south, most of her sails furled. In midafternoon, the British frigate, three or four miles off, came around and sailed straight at the *Chesapeake*. As the *Leopard* closed, the *Chesapeake*'s officers noticed that her gun ports were open. Still, Barron remained unfazed: he had no reason to expect a hostile encounter. At 3:30 *Leopard*'s captain, Salusbury Pryce Humphreys, hailed Barron, asking permission to send an officer aboard the *Chesapeake*. Barron bellowed acquiescence through his speaking trumpet and hove to.[8]

When the *Leopard*'s boat came alongside, Lieutenant John Meade came aboard and announced he had written orders to muster the *Chesapeake*'s crew just as if he were inspecting a suspected smuggling ship. While Meade waited, Barron wrote his refusal to the *Leopard*'s captain: "I am also instructed never to permit the crew of any ship that I command to be mustered by any other but their own officers." As Meade returned to the *Leopard*, Barron turned to Captain Gordon. Since "their intentions appear serious," he was to quietly post the crew to quarters. As men rushed back and forth on the gun deck, they discovered there were no loaded powder horns or matches, nothing ready to fire a broadside. *Leopard*'s captain shouted, "Captain Barron, you must be aware of the necessity I am under of complying with the orders of my commander-in-chief." Barron pretended he couldn't hear him, shouting, "I do not understand what you say!" even as he gave the order to clear for action.[9]

At 4:30 the *Leopard* fired a warning shot across the *Chesapeake*'s bow. Barron ignored it. Then the *Leopard* let fly a broadside, her cannonballs mostly striking the *Chesapeake* amidships, showering her decks with splinters and shredding cordage. A large splinter sliced into Commodore Barron's leg. The ship's gunner was still below decks in the powder magazine, searching for powder horns. Without priming powder, the *Chesapeake* could not fire a response. The wounded Barron managed to climb atop a signal locker. He yelled that he wanted to discuss the deserters. Captain Humphreys ignored him and ordered a second broadside, showering the *Chesapeake*'s gunners with deadly splinters as they stood helplessly waiting for powder. "For God's sake, gentlemen, will nobody do his duty?" Barron cried, demanding of his sailing master, "Is it possible we can't get any guns to fire?"

By this time, twenty-one of *Leopard*'s cannonballs had crashed into the *Chesapeake*. Despairing, Barron sent an order to Captain Gordon: "For God's sake, fire one gun for the honour of the flag. I mean to strike." Lieutenant William Henry Allen, fetching a hot coal from the galley, touched the priming hole, firing an eighteen-pounder as Barron shouted, "Stop firing, stop firing. We have struck, we have struck." Only fifteen minutes after the *Leopard*'s warning shot, as the American flag slid down from the mizzen peak, the *Leopard* unleashed a third murderous broadside. Three American sailors lay dead; eighteen, counting Barron, were wounded. One died ashore a few days later.[10]

Within minutes, two boatloads of British officers and seamen boarded the stricken *Chesapeake* and demanded that her crew be mustered. From the lineup on deck, the officers mistakenly identified three Americans as British-born deserters: two of them—Daniel Martin from Massachusetts and William Ware from Maryland were, it would turn out, African American freedmen who had served, whether or not as conscripts, in the Royal Navy. John Strachan, of Frederick County, Maryland, may have been a volunteer. After a brief search, the British found Jenkin Ratford cowering in the coal hole. Manacled, the four prisoners were rowed back to the *Leopard* as Barron scratched an abject note to the *Leopard*'s captain, acknowledging that the *Chesapeake* was now legally his prize. Lieutenant Allen soon returned with Humphrey's reply: he had fulfilled his orders and was satisfied to return to the fleet in Halifax with his prisoners. A few minutes later, the *Leopard* sailed away. After the pumping of three feet of water from the hold and the sluicing of blood from the gun deck, a bandaged Barron gave the orders to get his captured ship underway in the *Leopard*'s wake. At noon of June 23, the disgraced American frigate dropped anchor amid British ships off Hampton Roads.

As news of the *Chesapeake*'s humiliation spread, outraged Americans protested in every city, clamoring for war. In Baltimore, a subscription drive produced enough money to build three sloops-of-war to be presented to the navy, and merchants laid the keels of their first three privateering ships. "But one feeling pervades the nation," reported one congressman. "All distinctions of Federalism and Democracy are banished." In a confrontation that constituted a serious escalation of the dispute between two sovereign nations over impressment, the *Leopard*'s commanders had done what no British Ministry or naval officer had ever succeeded in doing before: assert a right to impress from the crew of a vessel of a foreign navy.[11]

Refusing to fan the embers publicly even as he surreptitiously prepared for war, Jefferson ordered all British warships out of American waters and demanded an apology from the British. It did not come. At the same time, he tried to exploit what he saw as an opportunity to link the general problem of impressment with the egregious abuse of the practice in the *Chesapeake* affair, hoping to force the British to repudiate the odious practice as part of its settlement of the *Chesapeake* case. The British immediately foiled his stratagem by disavowing the *Leopard*'s conduct. On his annual vacation atop Monticello, Jefferson concluded that the British were not about to meet his demands for "reparation for the past, security for the future" against further attacks on American ships and continued impressment. He became reconciled to war with England and even began to think of fighting Napoleonic Spain.[12]

Even as he pondered this drastic step, Jefferson learned that, in September, a British fleet had besieged the Danish capital of Copenhagen. Denmark had remained neutral in Napoleon's war, but Napoleon's expected attack left open the possibility that he might be able to seize Denmark's ready-made fleet. The British issued an ultimatum that the Danish fleet must be turned over to Britain's custody. When the Danish crown prince refused, without the diplomatic nicety of a declaration of war the British fleet began shelling not just the fleet but populous neighborhoods as well. In three days, the bombardment killed an estimated 3,000 civilians before the Danish fleet surrendered. At the same time, at sea, the Royal Navy set about rounding up the Danish merchant marine, seizing some $10 million in property and eliminating a serious commercial rival.

IF JEFFERSON WAS not an outright imperialist, he certainly was an expansionist who considered it necessary and feasible to remove foreign powers from U.S. borders to provide security. He believed that Napoleon, blockaded on the European continent by the British navy, would be unable to defend his overseas empire against a massive American volunteer force allied with revolutionaries in a U.S.-led confederation of former Spanish colonies. To Madison, his secretary of state, he confided,

> I had rather have war against Spain than not, if we go to war against England. Our southern defensive force can take the Floridas, volunteers for a Mexican army will flock to our standard, and a rich pabulum will be offered to our privateers in their plunder of their commerce and coasts. Probably Cuba would add itself to our confederation.[13]

Jefferson's long-standing detestation of the British now seemed to ride the wave of American anger, at its highest point since the beginning of the Revolution. If he had long ago been a pacifist, now he was a ready proselyte for war:

> I never expected to be under the necessity of wishing success to Bonaparte. But the English being equally tyrannical by sea as he is on land, and that tyranny bearing on us in every point of either honor or interest, I say "down with England" and as for what Bonaparte is then to do to us, let us trust to the chapter of accidents. I cannot, with Anglomen, prefer a certain present evil to a future hypothetical one.[14]

Jefferson realized he had to keep the war spirit alive in America if he hoped his diplomacy to succeed.

The news soon arrived from Halifax that the four seamen seized from the *Chesapeake* had been court-martialed. Jenkin Ratford had been hanged from the yardarm of the *Halifax*, the ship he had fled. The other sailors were sentenced to floggings of five hundred lashes through the fleet, often a fatal punishment, but Admiral Berkeley commuted their sentences when he discovered that the two African Americans were freed slaves who had been impressed into service. They were instead imprisoned while arrangements were made for their exchange. One, William Ware, died in an English prison; five years later, the British finally repatriated Strachan and Martin, who promptly rejoined the crew of the *Chesapeake*.

Captain Barron's punishment, on the other hand, would drag on for years. On March 22, 1808, a court-martial aboard the *Chesapeake*, with Captain Decatur, Barron's former junior lieutenant in the Barbary Wars, presiding, convicted Barron of neglecting to clear his ship for action on the probability of an engagement. Suspended without pay, he returned from a self-imposed exile in Europe after the War of 1812 and sought a new posting, but Decatur blocked it. In 1820, the two fought a duel at Bladensburg, Maryland. Decatur's bullet struck Barron in the hip; Decatur, struck in the abdomen, died in agony in his house on Lafayette Square. Barron went on to act as superintendent of several navy yards until he died, the oldest senior captain in the Navy, at the age of eighty-two. Even the *Ches-*

apeake received a ritualized punishment: because it had been surrendered, it could neither give nor receive a salute ever again.

DELIVERING HIS 1807 annual message to Congress, Jefferson adopted a tone so stridently anti-British that Gallatin, reading the draft, considered it a manifesto against England that would certainly lead to war. Navy secretary Robert Smith, who still thought "peace is our favorite object," worried that Jefferson's rhetoric would incite a congressional declaration of war. Even Secretary of War Henry Dearborn questioned whether Jefferson wanted to threaten offensive actions against the British. But when Jefferson returned to Washington City, he discovered that the mood of Congress had once again shifted in the wake of news from Europe that, because Britain's allies Russia and Prussia had abandoned the war against France, the British might be ready to negotiate with the United States. Again shifting his ground, Jefferson wrote, "We are all pacifically inclined here." But no sooner had Jefferson become optimistic than he learned from Monroe in London that negotiations there had broken down. Jefferson's diplomatic initiative had failed. Disgusted, he wrote his son-in-law that it was now up to Congress whether there was to be "war, embargo or nothing."[15]

Although he made no recommendation to Congress at first, by December 18, 1807, Jefferson, writing to George C. Campbell of Tennessee and citing "the great and increasing danger with which our vessels, our seamen and merchandise are threatened on the high seas," proposed an embargo on the departure of all American vessels from U.S. ports.[16]

Jefferson had just learned that the new British prime minister, Spencer Perceval, had obtained an Order in Council requiring all naval officers to enforce impressment. Soon afterward, learning that Napoleon was blockading American as well as British ships, Perceval obtained an Order in Council prohibiting Americans to trade with ports from which British ships were excluded. Reportage of these latest coercions had already appeared in the Philadelphia *Aurora* by the time Jefferson submitted his request to Congress for an embargo. What anyone hoped to accomplish by boycotting all trade with the warring European powers was summed up by a Tennessee congressman trying to explain his affirmative vote to a constituent: "We may complain because we cannot sell for a good price our surplus provisions [but] they will <u>suffer</u> because they cannot procure a sufficient quantity of those articles to subsist upon—to support life."[17]

An American nonimportation act of 1806 had barely taken effect when Jefferson imposed the more drastic Embargo Act of 1807, which prohibited maritime commerce with foreign states. Jefferson believed he could coerce Britain and France into abandoning their arbitrary decrees without going to war. But the embargo did not, as Jefferson and Madison expected, bring England and France to their knees. Instead, within one year, it destroyed 80 percent of the United States' import-export trade and brought on the worst depression in the quarter century since the Revolution. The net tonnage of foreign vessels entering U.S. ports dropped by 50 percent from 1.2 million to 586,000 tons in 1808; from the record $144 million in 1807, the embargo slashed imports to $58 million—nearly 60 percent—in 1808.

The embargo hit hardest in maritime New England. In a pamphlet entitled *An Enquiry into the State of the Farm*, "A Cheshire Farmer" declared that "[t]en months of Embargo have driven from our country more of our mariners than we should have lost by three years of war. Seamen <u>cannot live</u> where they <u>cannot be employed</u>." Coastal communities suffered the most from the economic collapse. Yarmouth, Massachusetts, offered public assistance; Newburyport set up soup kitchens. In some areas of Maine one out of two men became unemployed. Even as Portland's poorhouse became overwhelmed by the needy, merchants lost fortunes and a bank failed. The town was forced to set up a soup kitchen in Market Square. The 98 percent drop-off—from $342,909 to $4,369—in customs collections that first year underscores the severe impact of the embargo on Maine's largest seaport. In Bath forty-three ships lay idle.

Virtually no one, from farmers to fishermen, escaped unscathed. The Wiscasset collector of customs had authorized sixty-seven cargoes to clear the port in 1807; only two in 1808. On treeless Nantucket, customers could not afford to purchase the rare shipment of cordwood from the mainland. In Marblehead, while eighty-seven fishing vessels rocked at their moorings, unemployed fishermen went on poor relief. In Rhode Island exports dropped off by 85 percent. As bitterness spread, little solace could be found from whisky distilled in Newburyport. Unable to export their wares, distillers stopped buying rye from farmers; unable to export salt pork to ship owners, farmers found their once-lucrative herds of swine had become grain-swilling liabilities.[18]

In town after town, parades and public ceremonies became protests; unemployed longshoremen, shipmasters, merchants and mechanics carried banners and sang songs denouncing the embargo, which they had quickly come to call the "O-Grab-me."

The effect on the British economy was not only negligible but British shippers actually gained from the removal of American competition by shifting their focus to South America as a fresh source of supplies. The French also used the embargo to their own advantage. Under the pretext of assisting the United States to enforce the law, Napoleon ordered the seizure of all American vessels entering the ports of France and Italy. He justified the confiscation of some $25 million in U.S. shipping and cargoes by accepting the embargo as effective and declaring that any American ship in those ports must obviously be British vessels using false papers.

Many Americans ignored the embargo, smuggling across the northern frontier to supply British bases in Canada and carrying on a wholesale illicit trade to the Caribbean and Europe that not even the seizure of nine hundred American ships by the British and French could completely stop.

At first, New Englanders and southerners trading with England and the Caribbean were thrown out of work. Many American ships at sea when the Embargo Act took effect remained in foreign waters and continued trading with foreign nations. The British government cooperated with American merchants who violated the law. But this still left wide open the lucrative overland, lake and river traffic between border states and contiguous British and Spanish territories. Here the lure that had attracted so many Americans to leave the more cosmopolitan East Coast and settle in the raw clearings and towns of the frontier was the opportunity to sell surplus crops and timber products for export to British and Spanish merchants and the quartermasters of voracious garrisons in St. Louis, St. Augustine, Montreal and Quebec. A hemorrhage of smuggled exports defied the embargo as the goods flowed north along Lake Champlain into Lower Canada: herds of cattle and pigs driven through Smuggler's Notch in Vermont fed British sailors and soldiers and fetched high prices paid in gold. In the Passamaquoddy Bay region where Maine (still part of Massachusetts) met British New Brunswick province, the demand for flour and grain in Europe generated a highly profitable black market. American merchants claimed they were shipping flour, corn, rice and rye for their own coastal trade, but little if any found its way to other American ports. In Canada, these crops brought in up to eight times their American market value.

The historian Benjamin Smith found that, in Passamaquoddy Bay, in a so-called Flour War,

> Borderland residents possessed an attitude that rejected the arbitrary authority of the state, an almost libertarian view that de-emphasized commercial restrictions and borders imposed by distant governments. Smuggling was the most obvious manifestation of this disregard for government interference in the economy. The more government forces attempted to halt unregulated trade, the more apparent it became to locals that the state was an unwelcome and alien force.[19]

Actively encouraging embargo busting, the British designated official "places of deposit." The Royal Navy sometimes actually escorted the smuggling vessels. Local fishermen used open boats of many kinds—rafts, canoes, skiffs, reach boats—to ferry goods to the New Brunswick shore. The goods were often transshipped from Boston on their way to Canada. The governor of Massachusetts, a Jeffersonian, facilitated the smuggling by issuing clearance papers to ships carrying "needed" flour to Maine coastal towns. Those towns flourished thanks to the influx of illicit supplies: Eastport, a major entrepôt for smuggled goods, drew merchants eager to cash in on the boom.[20]

Denouncing the smugglers as the "most worthless part of society," an embittered Jefferson, realizing he had failed to persuade Americans to comply with his Enlightenment theories of law and reason, invoked the coercive Enforcement Act of 1809, what the historian Peter Andreas characterizes as "the most draconian and coercive of the embargo laws." As outraged mobs revived Revolution-era protest songs and some editorial writers compared Jefferson to George III, "there was even talk of secession." In Providence, Rhode Island, Governor James Fenner received a credible threat on the life of any customs collector who attempted to enforce the act. When a customs collector did attempt to seize a smuggler's vessel, some three hundred rioters liberated the vessel. In Portland, Maine, an armed and disguised mob took possession of the wharves and loaded and sailed two smuggling vessels out of the harbor.

Jefferson's response to resistance and protest was military force. Embargo enforcement became the navy's main mission. The act called for arming thirty new federal gunboats and authorized Jefferson "to employ such part of the land or naval forces, or militia of the United States . . . for the purpose of preventing the illegal departure of any ship . . . or riotous assemblage of persons, resisting the custom-house officers." In a move reminiscent of his British predecessors, Jefferson fired customs collectors deemed too accommodating to smugglers and gave sweeping new search-and-seizure powers that did not require a court order.

This second phase of Jefferson's sanctions, a land embargo, aimed to close off all overland trade across American frontiers. In Vermont, at least one-third of all income depended on shipping fine white pine planks and white oak spars to Canada for shipbuilding as well as barrels of potash made from rendering timber scraps. Potash, vital to the British textile industry for cleaning and thickening wool, was also used in making soap, glass, sulphuric acid and gunpowder. Collector of Customs Jabez Penniman protested to Treasury Secretary Gallatin the "impossibility of executing" the new law "without military force." The ban commenced at the start of the spring season for transporting an estimated $400,000 in cargoes by rafts down the current of Lake Champlain to Canada.[21]

On May 8, 1808, Jefferson issued another, more pointed, proclamation, this one aimed at Vermont, until then the only Jeffersonian stronghold in New England. He warned Vermonters that any further trade with Lower Canada would be treated as an insurrection, as treason, to be quelled by force of arms. To put teeth into this decree, Vermont's Jeffersonian governor Israel Smith at first, in 1807, called up the Franklin County militia. In this county, closest to Canada, many of the conscripts, from hardscrabble farms, were themselves heavily involved in the illicit cross-border traffic. At Windmill Point, at the northern tip of Lake Champlain, Governor Smith posted militia to intercept the smugglers' enormous rafts and fast-running sloops that were slipping across the frontier on the strong current at night. Rotating the militia, the governor relieved the Franklin County militia and sent in 150 volunteers from Rutland County, his home district eighty-five miles south of the border. Militia and cavalry of the 2nd Vermont Brigade marched north on June 4, 1808, "to stop the potash and lumber rebellion on Lake Champlain."[22]

SOON THEY WERE on the lookout for one ship in particular, the *Black Snake*. Built as the Lake Champlain ferry between Charlotte, Vermont, and Essex, New York, this beamy forty-foot, shallow-draft, tar-blackened cutter was ideal for slipping in and out of shallow creeks and could carry one hundred 300-pound barrels of potash. The going price per barrel across the Canadian border, eight dollars in 1807, had soared to twenty-five dollars. In a cash-poor frontier economy, a smuggler could pocket between ten and twelve dollars in gold or silver coin for a single run; the captain of the *Black Snake*, Truman Mudgett, cleared six dollars a barrel or more. An informant tipped off officials at the Windmill Point, Vermont, customs house that Mudgett would pick up a cargo of potash on the Winooski River near Burlington.

On August 1, the *Fly,* a sleek, red-trimmed revenue cutter with a crew of fourteen militiamen commanded by Lieutenant Daniel Farrington, sailed out onto Lake Champlain to seize the *Black Snake*. As the *Fly* glided south past Grand Isle, another informant, waving a white handkerchief, flagged Harrington down and told him the names of the smugglers and exactly where Harrington could find the ship he sought.

Rowing up the serpentine Winooski in a small boat, Mudgett's gang pulled ashore at Joy's Landing on the outskirts of Burlington. They broke into the house of Magery Joy, a go-between for Burlington merchants supplying the contraband potash, and demanded food and rum. Each man carried a musket but little ammunition. For close-in fighting, they packed the *Snake* with fist-sized stones, three-foot clubs and homemade pikes. From a crewman's brother, they'd borrowed a large blunderbuss-like gun, variously called a puck gun or wall gun, and similar to weapons fired from the embrasures of French battlements. Nine feet, four inches long with an eight-foot-two-inch-long barrel and a one-and-a-half-inch bore, it weighed seventy-five pounds and was to be mounted in the *Black Snake*'s bow. Customarily reserved for killing large flocks of game birds with a single blast, it was primed with two handfuls of fine-ground gunpowder poured down the barrel accompanied by fifteen one-inch lead balls and a fistful of buckshot. By campfire light, the six smugglers awaited their cargo by sipping rum and molding bullets—1,100 of them.

The *Fly* wended up the Winooski and stopped to make camp for the night; a confederate of Mudgett who spotted Farrington's approach rowed rapidly ahead to warn the smugglers. Mudgett and his men moved their vessel farther upriver, concealing it in a dense stand of butternut trees behind an island near the foot of Winooski Falls. The next morning, August 3, with muskets loaded they marched along the riverbank and watched as the *Fly* approached. Lieutenant Farrington ordered his men to refrain from shooting once they had taken the smugglers' smaller boat in tow. As farmers ran to watch, the smugglers walked along the riverbank. When the *Fly* discovered *Black Snake*'s hiding place, Farrington and three soldiers prepared to board her.

From cover, a musket at his shoulder, Mudgett shouted, "I swear by God I will blow the first man's brains out who lays hands on her." Farrington and his men, ignoring him, clambered aboard the *Snake*, cut its mooring line and started to row the sloop to mid-river. A volley of shots came from the trees. Seventeen-year-old David Sheffield, who had impressed the other smugglers with his marksmanship as they tested their weapons the night before, allegedly fired one of the two shots that struck Private Ellis Drake in the head as he took the *Snake*'s rudder, killing him. Two bullets and two buckshot hit Lieutenant Farrington, one lead ball chipping off a piece of his forehead and falling in his hat. He survived. The other militiamen landed and prepared to return fire. As they stormed up the riverbank, Samuel Mott, evidently at the repeated demands of an older smuggler, Cyrus B. Dean, fired the oversized blunderbuss they had rested in the crotch of a tree. A cloud of lead shot cut down two more militiamen and Jonathan Ormsby, a forty-nine-year-old Revolutionary War militia captain who farmed the nearby Ethan Allen homestead. Ormsby had been barking unsolicited advice to Farrington's men. The two dead Rutland County militiamen became the first U.S. customs agents killed in the line of duty.[23]

Less than three weeks later, eight smugglers stood accused of murder and treason in a showcase trial. Potential jurors were accepted or rejected according to their party affiliations. In his closing argument, the state's Jeffersonian attorney, William Harrington, underscored the political nature of the trial: "The defense will say to you that the law laying an embargo has occasioned this unhappy affair. . . . It is painful to find that party spirit . . . has already assumed an alarming attitude."[24]

For three months after his conviction and sentence of death for instigating the firing on the *Black Snake*, Cyrus B. Dean waited anxiously for a presidential pardon, but no reprieve came. On November 11, 1808, Dean, who had urged Mott to fire, became the first Vermonter to be executed. An estimated 10,000 angry Vermonters followed the wagon taking him from the Burlington jail to the gallows, set up to overlook the scene of the shooting, and watched as an unrepentant Dean was hanged. That same autumn, thousands of Vermonters marched to the polls, defeated the Jeffersonian governor and replaced him with a Federalist. It was a vote for smuggling and against Jefferson and his detested embargo. A Vermont county changed its name from Jefferson to Washington. After the elections, the sentences of the two smugglers who had fired the fatal shots were commuted by the newly elected Federalist governor, Martin Chittenden. Truman Mudgett was released after a mistrial for treason.

Public demonstrations of outrage against the "dambargo" reached their peak in Baltimore when one ship's captain was pilloried for *not* smuggling. Daniel Carman had sailed his brig, the *Sophia,* from Rotterdam with a cargo of 720 gallons of Dutch gin. Stopped at sea by a British ship, he was ordered to England and required to pay a duty on each gallon of gin or face seizure of his entire cargo. Carman paid the levy and sailed home to Baltimore, where he was horrified to find himself the target of public wrath. For his acquiescence in paying "an infamous tribute," the town meeting condemned Carman's cargo.

In the gathering dusk of October 4, 1808, a giant parade wound its way up Hampstead Hill (now Patterson Park) on the city's eastern edge. Behind decorated barges filled with ships' captains, a trumpeter heralded the arrival of 1,300 horsemen, then 400 sailors waving the Stars and Stripes— and one carrying the white flag of surrender. Upward of 1,000 citizens filled the streets, singing "Yankee Doodle" as torches, lamps and candles illuminated the horsemen parading to an enormous homemade gallows. There, the barrels of the "tributary" gin hung surrounded by bundles of fagots. In what became known as the Gin Riot, a gigantic burst of fire consumed the barrels (which may or may not have been emptied) as the booming of cannon echoed through the night to the cheering of 15,000 Baltimoreans. That roughly 40 percent of the port's populace participated reflected the impact of the decline of the town's exports under the hated embargo.[25]

Jefferson blamed unpatriotic Americans, not himself, for the failure of his trade policies. At the outset, defending his embargo to all state governors, Jefferson had written, "While honest men were religiously observing it, the unprincipled along our sea-coast and our frontiers [have been] fraudulently evading it." But finding the law unenforceable, he was forced within a year to admit that "this embargo law is certainly the most embarrassing one we have ever had to execute." Increasingly disillusioned, Jefferson "did not expect a crop of so sudden and rank growth of fraud and open opposition by force."[26]

SEVEN

"Free Trade and Sailors' Rights"

By the time he sent his last annual message to Congress, Jefferson worried about the survival of his party, his failed embargo the main issue in the 1809 presidential election. He had long ago chosen the more popular Madison, his closest friend and the secretary of state, as his heir presumptive. Much of Madison's success as a national politician came from his marriage to a Quaker widow he met in Philadelphia in the wake of the worst yellow fever epidemic in American history.

In the spring of 1793, 2,000 French refugees fleeing a slave uprising in Santo Domingo arrived in the capital's crowded port, probably accompanied by mosquitoes that bore the yellow fever virus. In the city's swamps, the mosquitoes thrived and spread their virus, striking down in a single summer one-fifth of Philadelphia's 25,000 residents. Among the victims was a young Quaker lawyer named John Todd, who succumbed along with his father and his infant son William. He left behind a wife, Dolley Todd, and a five-year-old son also named John. Sadly, John Todd and his son William died on the same day that October, just as the first frost began to kill off the mosquitoes.

With five-year-old John, the widowed Dolley went to live with her widowed mother, who ran a boardinghouse for members of Congress. Dolley's striking beauty instantly attracted male attention. The unusually tall twenty-five-year-old stood five feet, eight inches; one commentator noted that she was "well proportioned," with an ample bosom, slender waist and a "mouth which was beautiful in shape and expression." Dolley had Philadelphia's bachelors, as they passed her in the streets, "in the pouts."[1]

One secret admirer was forty-three-year-old congressman James Madison, famous then for his role in drafting the Constitution and Bill of Rights. In a society where bachelors were suspect, Madison, an idealist in all things, would only marry for love. At five feet, six inches tall and a frail 140 pounds, he looked even smaller. The first time he had become infatuated—with fifteen-year-old Catherine Floyd, daughter of a Long Island congressman—his paramour broke their engagement by sending Madison a "letter of indifference" sealed with rye dough to signify her affection had soured. At forty, Madison had also become "fascinated" with a celebrated New York hostess, but she failed to reciprocate. When he first noticed Dolley, Madison asked his Princeton classmate, Senator Aaron Burr, habitué of Mrs. Payne's boardinghouse, to arrange an introduction. Pleading for help, Dolley dashed off a note to her best friend Eliza Collins: "Thou must come to me, Aaron Burr says that the great little Madison has asked him to bring him to see me this evening." Receiving him in a mulberry-colored satin gown, Dolley instantly entranced Madison.[2]

One of eight children, Dolley was born into two of Virginia's oldest white families, the Anglican Paynes and the Quaker Coleses. The Coleses lived in a colony where the Church of England was the sole sanctioned religion. Intolerant in their turn, the Quakers did not permit marriage to "strangers." Dolley's parents could not be married as Quakers until John Payne, born an Anglican, applied for membership in the Society of Friends. In 1765, as the first Stamp Act protests swept British America, John Payne and Mary Coles were formally admitted to the Cedar Creek Meeting in the Shenandoah Valley. Soon afterward, the Paynes migrated to Guilford, North Carolina. Land was cheap. Payne set up as a slave-owning planter and merchant. On May 20, 1768, the Paynes' third child, Dolley, was born.

But the Regulator uprising, a backcountry revolt against British taxation, made business impossible. Payne sold his land and moved to Winchester, Virginia. Dolley attended a Quaker school and, from her mother, learned to cook, sew and tend a garden. From her Anglican grandmother, she learned to appreciate fine food and fabrics. Grandmother Coles gave Quaker Dolley a golden brooch to wear hidden under her dress.

The Revolutionary War soon intruded. Hessian and British prisoners of war who surrendered after defeat at Saratoga trudged up the hill from their encampment to pay gold coins for Dolley's apple pies. At war's end, when Dolley was fifteen, Payne decided to free his slaves, sell his Virginia farm and move to Philadelphia to provide his children a Quaker education. He launched a laundry starch business. As he piled up debt, that business, too, failed, and the Quakers "read him out" of meeting. At his death, Dolley's mother turned her home into a boardinghouse for delegates to the Continental Congress. Tall, blue-eyed, raven-haired Dolley was her cook.[3]

WHEN MADISON'S FIRST term in Congress ended, he returned to Virginia and ran for his old seat in the Virginia House of Delegates. Low-key, patient and studious, he emerged as an expert on interstate affairs. Working long distance with Jefferson, who had taken Madison's seat in Congress, Madison shepherded legislation drafted by Jefferson. Their efforts blocked state support for churches. They also championed and won an early effort to bar slavery in federally owned territories ceded by individual states. Jefferson motioned to extend the ban to the original thirteen states, but it failed by a single vote when a delegate from New Jersey stayed in his boardinghouse with a cold.

By this time, post–Revolutionary War commerce, constrained by British embargoes of trading with her former American colonies, spurred political discontent. With public credit eroding, currency went into free fall after the loss of British and French gold. Amid widespread unemployment and uncontrolled land speculation, the Confederation teetered on the brink of financial collapse. Spiteful interstate rivalry spread: Connecticut exacted higher customs duties from Massachusetts than did Britain; New Jersey demanded customs duty on every boatload of firewood vital to fueling and heating New York City. Madison described North Carolina, trapped between Virginia and South Carolina, as a "patient bleeding from both arms."[4]

As chairman of Virginia's commerce committee, Madison sponsored a resolution to give Virginia and Maryland joint jurisdiction over the Potomac River to enable construction of a canal from the Chesapeake to

Pittsburgh, but Washington's pet project ran aground over division of tolls. At a private meeting at Mount Vernon, a handful of Virginia's leaders decided to summon delegates from each state to a convention on interstate trade at Annapolis in September 1786.

Madison had already abandoned hope that the Articles of Confederation could be revised sufficiently to resolve conflicting state laws. With Hamilton, he maneuvered delegates to summon a summer-long convention the next year. Madison brought to the Constitutional Convention in Philadelphia in 1787 a white paper entitled "Vices of the Political System of the United States." His self-assigned homework laid the groundwork for the U.S. Constitution. Enumerating the flaws of the Articles of Confederation, he recommended total abrogation, not amendment, and called for a new constitution to be ratified by state conventions, not by state legislatures. He argued vehemently for proportional representation in both houses of Congress; he championed a strong national government with a federal veto over state laws and a presidential veto over congressional legislation.

To secure state-by-state ratification, Madison joined Hamilton and John Jay in a nine-month newspaper campaign. Under the joint *nom de plume* "Publius," they coauthored *The Federalist Papers*. Their collaboration has been hailed as the greatest classic in the history of American political thought. At Virginia's rancorous convention, Madison resisted demands by promising amendments he himself would draft after he was elected to the First Congress.

LOVE STRUCK, MADISON MARRIED Dolley after a four-month courtship in an Anglican ceremony at his parents' home in Virginia on their anniversary. Jemmy, as she called him, was forty-three; Dolley, twenty-six. Philadelphia's Quakers promptly read Dolley out of meeting for marrying out. At Madison's urging, Dolley discarded plain Quaker dress. Wearing colorful gowns and elegant shoes imported from Paris, she presided over dinner parties and receptions, attended balls, played cards. The Madisons' townhouse in Society Hill became an oasis for political opponents. Once described as looking like a man on his way to a funeral, James began appearing in public with Dolley beside him. At dancing assemblies, he became graceful; at dinners, a lively conversationalist. When Madison went out on the stump, Dolley accompanied him, sitting in the front row. He was obviously proud of his "beloved"; she, devoted to her "darling little husband." From the first, Madison prized her political acumen.

Not everyone was so kind. Some deemed Madison "incapable of smiling. . . . A very Small thin Pale visag'd man of rather a sour reserved & forbidding countenance. . . . Being so low in stature he was in danger of being confounded with the plebeian crowds and was pushed and jostled about like a common citizen." And not everyone admired Dolley. "A fine, portly, buxom dame, who has a smile and a pleasant word for everybody," opined the writer Washington Irving, a New York Federalist, adding, "As to Jemmy Madison—Ah! Poor Jemmy!—he is but a withered little apple-John."[5]

As Jefferson's closest friend, campaign manager and secretary of state, Madison remained Jefferson's chief adviser. Along with the elimination of an oceangoing navy and the national debt, Madison's agenda included the abolition of the importation of slaves from Africa, neutrality in the Napoleonic Wars—and the disastrous Embargo Act. Not so visible were Dolley's contributions. When the Louisiana Purchase from Napoleon led to tension with Spain, the Spanish minister, Marqués de Casa Irujo, abruptly left Washington without bidding farewell to President Jefferson, a deliberate breach of protocol that might have damaged relations between the two countries. Dolley delegated her sister, Anna, to visit Irujo's wife, Sally McKean, an old Philadelphia friend, relaying private assurances that Madison himself could not officially proffer: "Remember me to McKeans & to Sally say a great deal for I feel a tenderness for her & her husband independent of circumstances."

Youthful secretary of legation Augustus Foster, nephew of future prime minister Lord Liverpool, described in his memoirs how Jefferson appeared to an English diplomat:

> He was a tall man with a very red freckled face and grey neglected hair, his manners good-natured, frank and rather friendly though he had somewhat of a cynical expression of countenance. He wore a blue coat, a thick grey-coloured hairy waistcoat with a red under-waistcoat lapped over it, green velveteen breeches with pearl buttons, yarn stockings and slippers down at the heel, his appearance being very much that of a tall large-boned farmer.[6]

And when a new British minister, Sir Anthony Merry, arrived shortly after Jefferson's reelection in 1804, the Anglophobic Jefferson received his credentials at the President's House in a dressing gown and slippers. He handed Merry a printed invitation to dinner. When Merry and his wife arrived for the dinner, Jefferson asked Dolley to take his arm, snubbing the ambassador's wife and leaving her to find a seat at the table. Merry deemed their treatment such an affront that it nearly rose to the gravity of a diplomatic incident.[7]

A more public slight infuriated envoy Merry. At a state dinner, he had to sit below the table salt with his wife, the diamond-bedecked Elizabeth Leathes Merry, where they were shunted when Jefferson entered escorting Dolley Madison on his arm. Foster later recited a litany of American indelicacies for a sympathetic home audience:

> Some of the most vulgar of the Democratic party took their cue from the style adopted at the Great House. In one way or the other, either by remarking on her dress or diamonds or by treading on her gown, wearied Mrs. Merry to such a degree that I have sometimes seen her on coming home burst into tears at having to live at such a place. . . . [8]

In letters home to his mother, the Duchess of Devonshire, Foster detailed the continuing erosion of Anglo-American relations, blaming them on office-seekers who came to British assemblies and emulated

> the systematic manners of Mr. Jefferson. . . . Among these was one of a stern, sour and Republican countenance who had been used to the best society, but who purposely came to the [diplomatic] parties in dirty boots, disordered hair and quite the reverse of what he knew to be the fashion in European capitals.[9]

Dolley quietly set about smoothing over the affair by adding Mrs. Merry to her intimate circle, but, after Mrs. Merry said she had written home that one of Dolley's dinners was "more like a harvest-home supper than the entertainment of a Secretary of State," Dolley read her a lesson from her American perspective: "[A]bundance was preferable to elegance."[10]

When the nation's capital moved to the raw District of Columbia in the spring of 1801, Madison occupied an office in the secretary of state's complex, the Six Buildings, at Pennsylvania Avenue and Twenty-Second Street; he and Dolley made their living quarters "above the store." Dolley quickly developed into the "Queen of Washington City." Not only did she preside over diplomatic dinners for her husband, she also acted as official hostess for the widower president. Her dinners featured American dishes whose recipes came from friends and relatives nationwide. Advised by a close friend, the wife of the French ambassador, she led fashion, introducing styles in dresses, hats and shoes from Paris, each new dress paired with ostrich plumes or feathery Birds of Paradise from her hallmark collection of "Dolley Madison turbans"—silk coiled upward, like a Turkish headdress. Eschewing wigs, she acquired a macaw and, in keeping with the style of Empire gown, revealed a cleavage. Not all of official Washington praised her taste: the Prussian wife of one British diplomat described Dolley as *"une bonne grosse femme de la classe bourgeoise"* ("a nice big woman of the merchant class.") The ambassador himself considered Dolley "fat and forty but not fair."[11]

Madison's announcement that he would run for president in 1808 blindsided Dolley. She had endured the loss of her mother, a sister and two nieces in only two years, and a depressed and physically ill Dolley withdrew deep into herself, issuing self-effacing disclaimers: "I am not much of a politician." In public, she remained Madison's running mate. In the nineteenth century, presidential candidates could not seem to be campaigning, could not even go out to dinners where congressmen could be present. Madison didn't have to: at Dolley's dinner parties, with Dolley presiding and politicking for him, James was free to talk to Senate caucus members and supporters.[12]

Nothing quite prepared the Madisons for the brutal name-calling of the 1808 campaign. Federalist newspapers called the author of the First Amendment a pygmy, an anchovy, a tortoise who lacked "amorous passion." The Georgetown *Federal Republican* ran a fake ad for a French book translated into English with a chapter entitled "Love and Smoke Cannot Be Concealed," which dealt with the intimate lives of a thinly disguised political couple, the oversexed, adulterous wife and the impotent husband. To quash rumors, the Madisons invited one of Dolley's supposed lovers to dine *en famille*.

Madison prevailed when the state caucuses cast their ballots, even though his own party contested his nomination in the congressional caucus. Southern "Old Republicans" nominated his longtime rival, James Monroe. The eastern wing, smarting under the embargo, nominated Jefferson's second-term vice president, George Clinton of New York. The Federalists chose Charles Cotesworth Pinckney of South Carolina and Rufus King, also a New Yorker. The tide of voters had shifted south and southwest, with more than a million Americans living west of the Appalachian Mountains, many of them cash-strapped farmers and frontiersmen favoring Jeffersonian small government, budget-slashing, no-tax policies.

Madison's only serious opponent appeared to be Monroe: they had once battled for the same seat in Congress. But Jefferson did not forget Monroe's failure to follow his instructions in negotiating with London three years earlier. When Jefferson reminded Monroe that Madison had long been his closest friend, Monroe withdrew his name from consideration. By this time, Madison had built up considerable support. Democratic-Republicans now included a newer business class, the owners of large and small estates, even tenant farmers. Madison, an erudite, unassuming political theorist, had ascended from Virginia assemblyman to third secretary of state. As far north as New York, once solidly Federalist workingmen had come to distrust Hamilton and his financial schemes and instead endorsed Jefferson's view of the Federalists as a party of speculators and men of property who cared only for protecting their own economic interests.

The election of 1808 hinged on populous Pennsylvania and New York, where Democratic-Republicans pitched their campaign to new Irish immigrant voters, and Federalists summoned up memories of pro-British Loyalists in the Revolution. As Federalists defended British policies, immigrant editors fanned anti-English hatred. One pro-Madison broadside exclaimed, "Every Shot's a Vote, and every Vote Kills a Tory! Do your Duty, Republicans, Let your exertions this day Put down the Kings and Tyrants of Britain." Both states went for Madison, giving him the election. In the Electoral College, Madison defeated Pinckney 122–47, with Clinton polling only six votes. In New England, the Federalists benefitted from anti-embargo sentiment and gained in the House, but fell short of a majority.

By Election Day, Dolley Madison was as popular as James Madison, so popular that James might never have become president without Dolley.

Pinckney, who had expected to defeat Madison handily, admitted to a friend after the election, "I was beaten by Mr. and Mrs. Madison. I might have had a better chance had I faced Mr. Madison alone." With no executive experience when he became president, he grew increasingly reliant on Dolley, his longest and most loyal collaborator. No president was ever better prepared for the office—for all it would be worth.[13]

PRESIDENT MADISON'S INAUGURATION occasioned the invention of a new Washington tradition: the inaugural ball. In the heat of the marshy capital city, a crowd surrounded Dolley at Long's Hotel. So stifling was the humidity that for some relief guests broke windows that would not open. John Quincy Adams wrote home to Massachusetts to assure his wife that he wasn't having any fun: "[T]he crowd there was excessive, the room suffocating and the entertainment bad."[14] Ex-president Jefferson, beaming broadly at his protégé's congratulations, soon left for the President's House—it would not be called the White House for another two years—which he still occupied. According to Margaret Bayard Smith, wife of the editor of the *Washington National Intelligencer*, the new president appeared exhausted and distracted. When she said she wished she had a chair to offer Madison, he replied, "I wish so, too." Only staying through dinner, the first couple left the guests to dance until midnight.[15]

Two days later, Madison summoned John Quincy Adams to an urgent meeting: he was appointing him the United States' first minister plenipotentiary to Russia. As the British tightened their blockade of Napoleon-controlled Europe, the Royal Navy was seizing any and all ships bound to or from the Continent. Adams was expected to provide copious intelligence on the war. The British had seized many Russian vessels. Czar Alexander I saw that his government and the Americans had common interests, and he invited them to establish diplomatic relations. Madison felt that the forty-one-year-old Adams was the best-qualified American for the post. The second president's son had spent half his life as a diplomat to the courts of Europe or in Congress, where he had distinguished himself for nonpartisan thinking.

AT TEN, ADAMS had accompanied his father to Paris for the negotiations leading to American independence. Adams attended schools in France and Holland and served as secretary to the American legation in St. Petersburg from 1781 to 1783. Graduating from Harvard College, he studied law but found the profession tedious. In 1794 Washington appointed him minister to The Hague and, during a visit to London, Adams met Louisa Catherine Johnson, daughter of the American consul. They married on July 26, 1797. London-born, educated in France and a talented musician, Louisa would greatly enhance the young diplomat's popularity. Appointed to Berlin, Adams and his bride remained there until his father's defeat in the 1800 presidential election. Attributing that defeat to factionalism, he nevertheless ran for the Massachusetts state senate as a Federalist. One year later he unsuccessfully stood for Congress. In 1803 Adams was selected by his legislative colleagues as a U.S. senator.

Adams's independence antagonized Federalist leaders. He approved Jefferson's landmark Louisiana Purchase and supported the president's attempts to uphold neutral rights. When he endorsed Republican resolutions protesting the British attack on the *Chesapeake* and then supported Jefferson's embargo, the Federalists disowned him. When the Massachusetts legislature met in special session to select his successor before his term expired, Adams resigned. His acceptance of Madison's appointment to St. Petersburg evoked severe criticism from Federalists, including his own parents. He received his commission from President Madison on July 4, 1809, with the Senate approving his nomination by a comfortable 19-7 margin.

He left behind his older sons, George and John, to be educated by their Aunt Elizabeth. With Louisa five months pregnant and breastfeeding Charles Francis, Adams embarked on the eighty-day voyage. The Adamses took along Louisa's flirtatious younger sister Kitty, Adams's nephew William Steuben Smith as his private secretary and two unofficial secretaries, Francis Calley Gray, the ship owner's son, and Alexander Everett, son of family friends. Nelson, a free black man from Trinidad, acted as John's valet.

Missing from the tableau were the ambassador's parents, John and Abigail. To Abigail, "the separation appeared like the last farewell." She sent the couple a heart-wrenching farewell message: "My dear children, I would not come to town today because I knew I should only add to yours and my own agony, my heart is with you, my prayers and blessings attend you."[16]

EIGHT

"War Now! War Always!"

Tecumseh had always known war. He was born in 1768 near present-day Springfield, Ohio, the same year that British Indian commissioner Sir William Johnson summoned leaders of the Six Nations Iroquois to a summer-long treaty conference at Fort Stanwix, New York. There the British, as usual, acquired vast areas of Indian lands, this time in western Pennsylvania and Kentucky. The Shawnees had no voice in the parley: their Iroquois overlords, subjects and allies of the British, spoke for them. Soon, settlers surged onto the lands south of the Ohio River. Before Tecumseh's birth, like other Shawnees, his parents had wandered for years, migrating north from the tribal lands of their cousins, the Creek, in Alabama. They were nudged along by British treaties through the Carolinas and up to Pennsylvania, where some fought against the British in the French and Indian War. When Tecumseh (which means "crouching panther") was six, William Murray, Lord Dunmore—an especially land-hungry royal governor of Virginia—led an army of 2,000 frontiersmen into modern-day Kentucky, the Shawnees' hunting preserve. Tecumseh's father, the war chief Puckeshinwa, and Tecumseh's oldest brother Cheeseekau fought ferociously at the head of outnumbered Shawnee and Mingo warriors at the Battle of Point Pleasant, in present-day West Virginia, until they were defeated.

In the Treaty of Camp Charlotte, principal chief Hokoleskwa, known by whites as Cornstalk, reluctantly accepted the Ohio River as the eastern boundary of Shawnee lands. Tecumseh's family deeply resented settlers who kept on coming. One settler came across Tecumseh's father when he was alone in the woods and shot him in the chest. He was dying when Tecumseh and his mother, Methoataske, found him.

At Fort Pitt in 1775 and 1776, in the first Indian treaties negotiated by the United States, elder Shawnee leaders labored to remain neutral in return for the promise of statehood when the war ended. More militant Shawnees, led by Blue Jacket, decided instead to seek British aid in reclaiming their lands. At nine, Tecumseh took part in his first battle; he was twelve when Colonel George Rogers Clark and 1,000 Virginia militiamen came to avenge an Indian raid into Kentucky. Crossing the Ohio, Clark and his men razed Tecumseh's birthplace, Old Piqua on the Scioto River, destroying the corn crop and shooting down Indians defending their wigwams. The Shawnees moved again, this time to the Maumee River, vowing resistance to further white settlement in the Old Northwest.

As a young man, Tecumseh befriended a family of white settlers and learned to read and write English. His facility with languages helped when he went on a mission with his brother Cheeseekau to support Cherokees attacking Nashville. He was able to translate interrogations of prisoners. It was on this foray that Tecumseh first distinguished himself in combat. Because of his prowess, the mantle of war chief of the Kispoko Shawnees passed to him at age twenty-four in 1792. In the Miami villages at the head of the Maumee, near present-day Fort Wayne, Shawnees and Delawares, displaced by Kentuckians, gathered. Brigadier General Josiah Harmar led almost 1,500 Kentucky militia in an attempt to burn the Indian villages; Miami chieftain Little Turtle ambushed and defeated them. In a second battle, Blue Jacket joined Little Turtle, nearly annihilating the Kentuckians as they fled. Alarmed, President Washington dispatched General Arthur St. Clair with reinforcements. As the general advanced toward the Miami towns, Little Turtle, Blue Jacket and fewer than 500 warriors killed 630 American soldiers, nearly two-thirds of St. Clair's force. Jolted, Washington sent a fresh army, commanded by "Mad Anthony" Wayne, who built frontier fortresses before marching northwest toward the Shawnees. Wayne's force, 3,000 strong, collided with Blue Jacket's Shawnees during tornado season in the Battle of Fallen Timbers. Tecumseh inspired many Shawnees that day as he fought hard against an overwhelming force before fleeing cavalry and bayonets.

The United States won a great deal of land that day. At the Treaty of Greenville, much that was sacred to the Shawnees passed into American hands, including most of Ohio and the sites of scores of cities, including Detroit, Toledo, Peoria and Chicago. Representatives of twelve tribes received promises of peace and handouts of money and goods amounting to about $20,000—between one and two cents an acre. Furious, Tecumseh refused to acknowledge the treaty. From experience, he couldn't believe that the whites would ever respect their own terms.

Tecumseh became heir to the defeated Blue Jacket; at twenty-six he was the head of a growing Indian confederacy. He moved his followers to the western fork of the White River, below present-day Anderson, Indiana. From there he spearheaded a reform movement to wean his people from European habits, including consumption of alcohol, and return them to native traditions. Tecumseh received aid from an unexpected source, his younger brother Tenskwatawa. Dissolute in youth, Tenskwatawa had drunk himself into a trance one night and awoke convinced that he had spoken with the Great Spirit and that he could stop drinking because he had encountered the "Master of Life." The radical change the Shawnees saw in him persuaded them that he had new spiritual powers, so much so that they started to call him "the Prophet."

The powerful new ideas of the brothers won over many young, strong and fierce warriors of the Sioux, Blackfeet, Arikara and Mandan tribes. Their zeal to rid themselves of tribesmen who had too easily cooperated with whites triggered a revolutionary purge, a massacre of natives by natives that Tecumseh stopped personally. He began to insist publicly on the difference between courage and brutality: winning had to do with honor.

When more tribes gave up on resisting the whites' incessant westward expansion, Tecumseh put his persuasive powers to work. He stressed the need for all tribes to unite against land cessions, contending that the Indians held land in common and that no individual or tribe had the right to cede territory without the consent of the others. Through the Great Lakes region, east to Tennessee, south to the Gulf Coast and Florida, he carried his message of abandoning tribal distinctions and consolidating forces against the encroachment of the U.S. government.

Like Cornstalk, Tecumseh had a talent for articulating what other Indians had once believed but had forgotten: "Sell a country. Why not sell the air, the clouds, and the great sea, as well as the earth? Did not the Great Spirit make them all for the use of his children?"[1]

Not all the tribes of the Old Northwest now sent representatives to treaty signings and cessions. As Tecumseh led them farther west, their discontent suited his plans to put himself at the head of an alliance of warriors from many tribes. He no longer wanted to be only a Shawnee leader but the leader of all Indians. He traveled from tribe to tribe on his messianic mission, and his fine features, light hazel eyes and superb physique helped the tall Shawnee create a strong visual impression. To address a crowd, he would often stand before it in only his moccasins and breech cloth, displaying his strength; his bearing and his eloquence riveting his audience's attention. With his powerful voice, he imparted a vision in which Indians would no longer see themselves as Creek or Sioux or Choctaws or Miamis separately but as Indians of the same race. The tribes he visited recognized the urgency of Tecumseh's new thinking. They knew that the United States was applying new ways of organizing lands for settlements. In particular, they were beginning to refer to the lands to the west of Ohio as Indiana.

During one of Tecumseh's recruiting missions, the Shawnees lost even more land through a treaty with General William Henry Harrison. In August 1810 Tecumseh and four hundred painted warriors paddled down the Wabash to Harrison's capital, the old French post at Vincennes, to complain about a recent sale by the Miamis to Harrison, who, acting as the government's agent, had purchased about 3 million acres on both banks of the Wabash. Refusing to sit on chairs set out for his entourage, Tecumseh sat on the ground with his warriors. He had come, he declared, to demand that the new Treaty of Fort Wayne be repealed.

By this time, settlers had already pushed the Indians all the way from the Atlantic coast and soon would force them into the Great Lakes. Tecumseh cataloged the whites' crimes against the Indians. Historian A. J.

Langluth recounts that he "acknowledged that he had threatened to kill
the chiefs who signed the treaty." In the coalition he was forming, village
chiefs had to turn over power to war chiefs. Tecumseh spoke English but
refused to use it; Harrison couldn't understand a word Tecumseh was saying. Through an interpreter, he told Tecumseh that "it was ridiculous to
claim that red men constituted one nation." Tecumseh rose and delivered
an impassioned argument, his tone so menacing that an American general on the scene sent orders to call out the guard. Soon, all the Indians
were on their feet, fingering their tomahawks and war clubs. As Harrison
struggled to get up out of his deep chair, he drew his officer's short sword,
and an army captain drew a knife. Tecumseh's warriors easily could have
slaughtered the small garrison and the town's unarmed civilians. After
minutes of tense, awkward silence, as the governor's guards ran up and
awaited orders to fire, Harrison asked the interpreter what Tecumseh was
saying. His answer: Tecumseh was telling his warriors "that everything
Harrison said was false." Harrison bristled and said he would listen to no
more. Tecumseh could leave safely, but he must leave the next day.

While Harrison summoned reinforcements, Tecumseh requested another meeting. He arrived along with chiefs from the Wyandot, Kickapoo, Potawatomi, Ottawas and Winnebagos who told Harrison they had
joined Tecumseh's confederacy. Tecumseh pledged that, if the Wabash
lands were returned to the tribes who had inhabited them, he would serve
the Americans as faithful allies; if not, they would join the British and he
would be forced to fight the Americans and would try to spare women and
children. Harrison promised to send Tecumseh's ultimatum to President
Madison, but he doubted the president would accede to his terms. Tecumseh's last words were direct and succinct: "Well, as the Great Chief is to
determine the matter I hope the Great Spirit will put sense enough in his
head to induce him to direct you to give up this land. It is true he is so far
off he will not be injured by the war. He may sit still in his town and drink
his wine, while you and I will have to fight it out."[2]

During the next year, Harrison repeatedly warned Tecumseh against
continuing to consolidate the Indians; Tecumseh countered that he was
only following the United States' example. In twenty years, the United
States had added four more states, Vermont, Kentucky, Tennessee and
Ohio. In July 1811 Tecumseh announced he was taking twenty braves to

spread his mission throughout the Illinois and Michigan territories, leaving his brother the Prophet in charge at his main settlement at Tippecanoe—with strict instructions to maintain peace. He asked that Harrison wait to settle the land sale until he returned. While Tecumseh was away, Harrison received a direct order from Secretary of War William Eustis: "I have been particularly instructed by the President to communicate to Your Excellency his earnest desire that peace may, if possible, be preserved with the Indians."[3]

But Harrison decided to press Tecumseh, to break up his concentration of followers by attacking Tippecanoe with 1,300 men, two-thirds of them mounted Kentucky and Indiana volunteer militia wearing blue coats and bearskin hats under the command of Joseph Hamilton Daviess, nephew of Alexander Hamilton. The rest were regulars, New Englanders from the 4th Infantry Regiment. A special edition of the Lexington, Kentucky, newspaper bannered the headline "War! War!" At the head of the column, riding a white horse, the slender, dark-eyed Harrison wore a calico hunting shirt trimmed with fringe and a beaver hat topped by an ostrich feather. Sallying forth from Vincennes, Harrison paused long enough to build a fort along the Wabash, naming it for himself. Harrison's force forded the Wabash ten miles from Tippecanoe. The next day, he marched eight miles, setting up camp on a blade-like peninsula of high ground enclosed on three sides by a marshy prairie. Under a white flag, Chief White Horse, one of Tecumseh's leaders, approached and requested a parley.

Before bedding down for the night, Harrison ordered his men to load their guns and affix bayonets. All night they could hear the sounds of Shawnee, Ottawa, Huron, Kickapoo, Chippewa and Potawatomi warriors as they danced, whipping themselves into a frenzy. Despite Tecumseh's injunction against fighting, the Prophet, urged on by two British officers, decided on a surprise predawn attack. After praying, singing and dancing, he told his warriors that he had cast a protective spell over them that would shield them from the white man's bullets, which would bounce off them like drops of rain.

Two hours before dawn on November 7, 1811, the Prophet and seven hundred braves, in groups of ten to twelve warriors, their faces painted black, surrounded the sleeping Harrison's camp. As they crawled toward Harrison's tent, one brushed against a sentinel, who fired a warning shot.

Letting out a terrifying war cry, the warriors fell upon the awakening soldiers, silhouetted against roaring campfires, with war clubs and British-
issued tomahawks. The Prophet evidently had instructed his warriors to
target Harrison's white horse. Unable to find his own horse, Harrison
grabbed a stray mount. As Harrison rode toward the line of fire, Colonel
Abraham Owen, a Kentuckian, was shot off his white horse. Daviess had
a white blanket on his horse: he, too, was killed. A private from Kentucky
recalled "the awful yell of the savages seeming rather the shriek of
despair. . . . [T]he tremendous roar of musquetry—the agonizing screams
of the wounded and dying, added to the shouts of the victors, mingling in
tumultuous uproar, formed a scene that can be better imagined than described."[4]

As it became light, Harrison was able to organize a flanking counterattack by his regulars and drove back the Indians. Most of the fighting
took place Indian-style from behind fallen logs, with one or two Indians
dropping at a time from the deadly accurate fire of the Kentuckians' rifles.
Running low on ammunition and unable to withstand the volleys of regulars firing cartridges charged with buckshot, the surviving Indians fled
into the forest. Mounted Kentucky dragoons raced after them as the infantry stopped to scalp and mutilate thirty-six Indian corpses they found
within their lines. Reaching Prophetstown, by now practically deserted,
they set fire to several houses where terrified natives huddled. Sparing the
one old woman too sick to flee, they looted the Indians' houses of anything
they could carry away and then burned them, putting to the torch 5,000
bushels of stored corn and beans. After pausing to disinter the bodies of
Tecumseh's dead followers and leaving them for the wolves, Harrison's
army returned to Vincennes.

In a jubilant dispatch to Washington, Harrison claimed a great victory.
He played down the fact that he had lost more men killed than the
Indians. Of 1,300 Americans, at least sixty-two men had died and 120
more had been wounded. Of the Indians, at least fifty died and eighty
were wounded. With his report, Harrison sent along two British muskets as proof that the British in Canada were arming and instigating
the attacks on white settlements; in actuality, the Indians had long bartered fur pelts for weapons.

When Tecumseh returned to the charred ruins of his capital, he grabbed his brother and shook him angrily: Why had the Prophet not followed his strict orders? And with that, Tecumseh banished his brother from the tribe. More calmly, he then sent a message to Harrison, assuring him that he would not lead a retaliatory attack. Tecumseh requested a personal meeting with President Madison in Washington to reestablish peace. A grateful Madison granted his request, but someone on the president's staff insisted that Tecumseh come without his usual entourage. By this time, Tecumseh had forged a confederacy that put some 5,000 warriors at his command—larger by half than the entire army of the United States, reduced to a mere 3,287 men by the budget-slashing Jefferson. The restrictions so offended him that he refused to make the trip. Instead, he called a council of chiefs of the confederated tribes along the Wabash and told them, "General Harrison made war on my people in my absence. It was the will of the Great Spirit that he should do so. We will not disturb them." But his tone was far less conciliatory when he met with British agents. They were not to judge the fighting abilities of his warriors by their poor performance at Tippecanoe.[5]

Canoeing once more to Fort Wayne, Tecumseh this time met not with Harrison but with the latest Indian agent, a man named Stickney, making it clear to him that he was still furious over Harrison's attack and his refusal to return the Indians' land. Even as messengers brought Harrison word that Americans were massing troops near the Canadian border, Tecumseh said he was about to travel to Fort Malden on Lake Michigan and needed arms to protect his people in his absence. When the Indian agent turned him down, Tecumseh warned him, "My British father will not deny me. To him I will go."[6]

Traveling to Machekethie, forty miles west of Fort Wayne, Tecumseh welcomed the Hurons, the newest members of his coalition, but upbraided the Potawatomi, whose attack on Americans in Illinois Territory had provoked the devastating attack on Prophetstown. He castigated the tribe for ignoring "our repeated counsel to them to remain quiet and live in peace with the Big Knives." When Tecumseh had returned from proselytizing among the Creek, he said,

> I found my Village reduced to ashes by the Big Knives. . . . Those I left at
> home were (I cannot call them men) a poor set of people, and their scuffle

with the Big Knives I compare to a struggle between little children who only scratch each other's faces. . . . [I]f they unprovokedly advance against us in a hostile manner, be assured we will defend ourselves like men— And if we hear of any of our people having been killed, we will immediately send to all the Nations on or towards the Mississippi, and all this Island will rise as one man.[7]

The outbreak of warfare in Indiana Territory late in November 1811 terrified Americans in the frontier settlements of the Old Northwest, the South and the Southwest, where some 50,000 Indians included roughly 10,000 warriors. The shocking news only intensified demands for war against England.

In maritime New England, where a series of embargoes and nonintercourse agreements had done the greatest economic damage, a rejuvenated Federalist Party loudly opposed the clamor for arms. In Washington City, the electrifying news arrived shortly after President Madison called the Twelfth Congress into emergency session to confront the decades-long crisis. "The people, the times and the government," as the Salem, Massachusetts, *Essex Register* put it, "all require DECISION."

Turmoil had immobilized the Eleventh Congress: in March 1811 Congressman John Wayles Eppes of Virginia wrote to his father-in-law, former president Jefferson, that "the rancor of party was revived with all its bitterness during the last session of Congress." The Federalist opposition was

[u]nited by no fixed principles or objects and destitute of everything like American feeling, so detestable a minority never existed in any country— Their whole political creed is contained in a single word "opposition"— They pursue it without regard to principle, to personal reputation or the best interests of their country.[8]

What would become known as the War Congress, the Twelfth Congress, assembling on November 4, 1811, included a fractious new element, a dozen bellicose patriots, some still in their twenties but all under forty and too young to remember the bloodshed of the last war with Britain. Their leader was Henry Clay of Kentucky, a fiery orator.

Growing up in Hanover County, Virginia, Clay, as a teenage boy, caught the eye of George Wythe, professor of law at the College of William and Mary, the teacher of Jefferson and John Marshall. Wythe retained Clay as his secretary. Under his tutelage, Clay studied law and attempted to translate Homer and Plutarch. Admitted to the bar at twenty, Clay moved to Kentucky, launched a lucrative law practice and married into the Bluegrass gentry.

Although Clay started as a Jeffersonian, his economic views aligned with the mercantile and banking theories of Hamilton. Elected at twenty-six to the Kentucky legislature, Clay, within three years, was appointed to an unexpired term in the Senate.

Running for the Senate in 1810, he railed against Britain's seizure of ships and sailors. While Clay's speeches brought him accolades, he found that the Senate was stodgy; he preferred the immediacy of the lower house. Returning to the Kentucky legislature, he became its speaker. In a landslide, he won a seat in the House. He now represented the most populous over-the-mountain state (400,000) at the very moment the emergency session commenced. On its first day, he was chosen Speaker of the House by a wide majority. The War Hawk faction believed he could lead them in forcing the government to declare war on Britain.

When rustic old John Randolph of Roanoke brought his dogs into the House to cement his authority, Clay ordered the sergeant at arms to remove the animals, something no Speaker had ever dared to do. Outside the House chamber, Clay's reputation as a party-loving, whiskey-drinking card player only enhanced his popularity; inside, Federalists wrote home, Clay presides "with dignity." Behind the scenes, he packed every key committee chair with War Hawks.[9]

On November 5, 1811, President Madison, in his annual address, accused Britain of "making war on our lawful commerce" and cited their "hostile inflexibility." Calling for war preparations, he urged Congress

[t]o put the nation into an armor and an attitude demanded by the crisis. . . . Our coasts and the mouths of our harbors have again witnessed scenes not less derogatory to the dearest of our national rights than vexatious to the regular course of our trade.

Madison flatly accused Britain of impressing American seamen, violating American waters, maintaining a "sweeping system" of illegal blockades, employing secret agents to subvert the Union and maliciously inciting the Indians of the Northwest Territory.[10]

He may have stopped short of recommending a declaration of war, but his listeners understood that the intent of his message was unambiguous: "We behold . . . on the side of Great Britain a state of war against the United States; and on the side of the United States, a state of peace towards Great Britain." He recommended enlarging the army, preparing the militia, finishing the U.S. Military Academy, stockpiling munitions, expanding the navy and increasing the tariff to encourage domestic trade and manufacturing. The Treasury bulged with an unprecedented $5 million surplus after a year of restocking the nation's shops and warehouses in a spree before the latest non-intercourse agreement took effect, but reduced customs duties and the costs of preparing for war would necessitate new taxes and loans.

Madison's sobering message drew accolades from critics usually at swords' points. John Adams opined that it did its author "great honor"; Jefferson termed it "most excellent, rational and dignified." Andrew Jackson exhorted his Tennessee militiamen to consider it "the pride and boast of every lover of his country to support the government in every measure it would take" to exact justice from England. The jubilant French minister Louis Sérurier reported to Paris that most Americans considered it "equivalent to a declaration of war on Great Britain," while worried British envoy Foster expedited a long-awaited agreement on reparations for the 1807 *Chesapeake* incident. At the same time, Foster predicted quite accurately that the British government would not concede that the French had actually revoked their blockading decrees and Britain would not revoke its Orders in Council until the United States persuaded France to admit British as well as American imports into Europe. Foster further cautioned that continued American sanctions on British imports would only bring British reprisals. When Madison told Foster he would gladly negotiate an agreement with France that would require "no sacrifice of principle" for Great Britain, Foster dashed off a dispatch to London explaining that, while Madison professed to "seize with avidity [any] pretext" to repair Anglo-American relations, the American president and Congress preferred to go to war rather than continue to endure the "present embar-rassments."[11]

To American envoy Joel Barlow in Paris, Madison sent a coded message on the dispatch sloop-of-war *Hornet* that he considered Britain's position "a fitter subject for ridicule than refutation." The United States would de-clare war on Britain unless "a change in the British system should arrest the career of arrests." Americans were equally disgusted with Napoleon's "crafty connivance and insatiate cupidity" as French privateers continued to seize or burn American ships at sea. A "hostile collision" could take place with either country or both. While Madison waited for the return of the *Hornet*, the United States would be preparing to fight in the spring of 1812.[12]

Although he had hoped for a fierier presidential address, Speaker Clay referred the president's written message to the Foreign Affairs Commit-tee, which he had packed with War Hawks. The committee, after confer-ring with Secretary of State Monroe, laid out a six-part plan endorsed by Madison. It would bring the army's ranks up to 10,000 regulars—its actual strength was one-third that number—plus 50,000 short-term volunteers. The proposal urged fitting out an enlarged navy and permitting the arming of merchant vessels. The House approved each measure by a wide margin, but only after spirited debate.

When one Federalist objected that the nation was ill prepared, War Hawk spokesman John C. Calhoun trumpeted, "So far from being unpre-pared, sir, I believe that in four weeks from the time that a declaration of war is heard on our frontier, the whole of Upper and a part of Lower Can-ada will be in our possession." John Randolph, sans his dogs, opposed making war only on England. After all, had not France seized American ships, crews and cargoes as well? In fact, only two years earlier Napoleon had rebuffed negotiations with then–U.S. minister to France John Arm-strong and instead had issued the Rambouillet Decree, authorizing the sei-zure and sale of all American property that had entered the Continent since May 20, 1809, the date Congress had enacted the Non-Intercourse Act. At the time, pressed on his reasoning, Napoleon had patronizingly told Armstrong that he was merely assisting in enforcing the American measure.[13]

For Henry Clay, there never had been any question whether the United

States should take on the British Empire. The Speaker of the House declaimed, "I would take the whole continent from them. I wish never to see a peace till we do." As the debate inside the House raged over which European superpower, or both, the United States should fight, two former presidents not known in recent years for congenial relations broke their long silence and wrote to each other. "As for France and England, with all their pre-eminence in science the one is a den of robbers, and the other of pirates," Jefferson wrote to John Adams.[14] Whether to enlarge the navy became the most contentious point of debate. In a dramatic renunciation of Jeffersonian thrift, Madison had called for constructing twelve 72-gun ships-of-the-line and ten new frigates, refitting the six existing frigates, further enlarging the Washington Navy Yard, the nation's largest, and stockpiling naval timber and supplies. Langdon Cheves, the Massachusetts Federalist chairing the Navy Committee, contended that, even if the Navy would still be minuscule compared with Britain's immense fleet, America's ships, with their well-trained crews and experienced officers, could defend her coasts and escort her merchantmen anywhere in the world. The debate exposed the gulf between representatives of landlocked western farmers and traditionally Federalist eastern mercantile and shipping interests. Many Democratic-Republicans were aghast once they learned from Gallatin what an enlarged navy could cost in new taxes and loans.

Of 213 members of the House, only 36 represented Federalists. All but two Federalists signed a petition penned by Josiah Quincy of Massachusetts. Entitled "Address of the Minority," Adams demanded how war upon the land could "protect commerce upon the ocean? . . . A war of invasion might invite a retort of invasion." Neither "any moral duty" nor "any political expediency" necessitated a war against Great Britain. Of the War Hawks, only Henry Clay advocated expanding the navy. The hated Orders in Council governing America's access to unrestricted use of the high seas could be combated only by sea power. The West's prosperity depended on exporting its surplus crops through New Orleans and it would take ships to keep that port open. A visionary Clay argued that "a navy will form a new bond of connection between the States, concentrating their hopes, their interest and their affections." But he did not prevail over budget-cutting congressmen. Confiding to Jefferson his disgust at the protracted deliberations, Madison wrote, "With a view to enable the Executive to step at once into Canada, they have provided after two months of delay, for a regular force requiring 12 to raise it." Jefferson responded, "That a body containing 100 lawyers in it, should direct the measures of a war is, I fear, impossible."[15]

As the drive to war seemed to stall, the political press entered the lists. In Philadelphia, John Binns, an Irish immigrant and staunch Democratic-Republican, editorialized, "The honor of the nation and that of the party are bound up together and both will be sacrificed if war be not declared." At least one erstwhile hawk flew from one side of the House chamber to the other and back. Hard-drinking Congressman Peter B. Porter represented New York's westernmost district on the frontier with British-fortified Upper Canada. Chair of the House Foreign Affairs Committee, Porter owned the leading mercantile and shipping business on Lake Erie. At first, he had urged the conquest of Canada; then, on April 19, 1812, he called it

[a]n act of madness fatal to the administration to declare war at this time when, so far from being in a situation to conduct offensive operations, we are completely exposed to attacks in every quarter.

Before the final vote for war, Porter shuffled home to Buffalo to take up his new and lucrative appointment as the quartermaster general of all New York militia. He also helped his brother win the contract for provisioning the garrisons at Detroit and Niagara. British envoy Foster commented, "Porter, after being for war, then against it, then for it and anew against it, set out at last for the frontiers of Canada with a commission for supplying the troops." As each controversial bill finally passed the House, the Senate concurred.[16]

Central to Madison's ability to gird for war was Swiss-born secretary of the treasury, Albert Gallatin. From a minor noble family in Geneva, he migrated to America during the Revolution with a keen sense he could make a fortune. Meeting Washington in western Pennsylvania shortly after the war, he became convinced there would soon be a land rush. Elected to three one-year terms in the Pennsylvania House of Representatives, he became a spokesman for small farmers.

Gallatin's brilliant reports established him as an authority on public finance, leading to his election to the Senate, where he immediately called for an investigation into Hamilton's management of the Treasury. When Federalists denied him his seat on the grounds that he had not been a citizen the required nine years, he joined the Democratic-Republican opposition, his critiques of the Adams administration's fiscal policy advancing him to the front rank beside Jefferson and Madison. Arguing the necessity of extinguishing the national debt, some of it left over from the Revolutionary War, he created the House's Ways and Means committee to monitor expenses.

As Jefferson's Treasury secretary, Gallatin reserved three-quarters of all government revenues every year to pay off the national debt even while paying for the Barbary War and the Louisiana Purchase. But Gallatin's financial program began to unravel when Britain closed Continental ports to neutral shipping. As American imports declined 80 percent, customs duties, the main source of federal revenue, plummeted, forcing Congress to raise taxes and increase government borrowing rather than reduce it. By 1812 the national debt was higher than ever.

When Gallatin unveiled for Congress the cost of arming the nation, he briefly chilled the feverish rush to war, but in February 1812 the Democratic-Republican press, its primary grievance against England being continuing impressment, initiated an incessant drumroll. At a time when most Americans took their political cues mainly from the printed press, Duane's *Aurora* unfurled, and four days a week the emotional banner of impressment waved on a masthead emblazoned with the number 6,257 (the figure Monroe had quoted to Baltimore journalist Henry Niles). Across the nation, other newspapers followed suit.

Between December 1811 and July 4, 1812, Congress passed 143 bills that, taken together, formed Madison's war program. Largely anticipating a land war, Congress raised the enlistment bounty from twelve to thirty-one dollars plus three months' pay and 160 acres of federal land to fill the ranks of a 10,000-man army. In addition, Congress provided for ultimately raising 25,000 more regulars and 50,000 one-year volunteers and, if needed, for calling out 100,000 militia for up to six months. At the time, there were 450,000 militia on the books of the fifteen states. At a time when Americans paid only one dollar per capita in federal taxes—compared with the equivalent of twenty-five dollars in England—the $1.9 million appropriation for ordnance seemed staggering. Gallatin, aware that Democratic-Republican electoral majorities had grown in inverse relation to taxes, proposed that Congress resort to loans instead of increasing internal taxes.

On paper, the House spent appropriations like sailors on shore leave. Only when John Quincy Adams called for building ten more frigates did other senators, especially southerners, yowl in protest: to build a larger navy would not only be too costly but would also invite a crushing contest with the British navy. "We cannot contend with Great Britain on the ocean," Adam Seybert of Pennsylvania contended, "but we can undermine our form of government by trying to do so." A larger navy would no doubt survive beyond the war, become a weapon in the hands of a dictator and, as well as endangering liberty, would drag the country into unnecessary wars. The proposal to build ten more frigates went down to a 3-1 defeat. Congress would only pay to refit the six existing frigates, spending $600,000 over the next three years to purchase ships' timbers and provide gunboats for the most exposed harbors. Finally, at Gallatin's behest, the House chopped in half the proposed $1 million appropriation he himself so recently had urged for improving coastal defenses.[17]

In March, House Speaker Henry Clay called for another short-term embargo intended to trigger a declaration of war unless the British rescinded their odious Orders in Council. In secret session, a bill to impose a new three-month embargo passed the House in three days. The Senate swiftly rubber-stamped it. The news leaked out even before the bill could be read out of committee. Frenzied merchants up and down the Atlantic coast crammed ships with goods and, sometimes within only two days after hearing the news, paying crews double their usual wages, ships' captains put out to sea before the embargo could take effect. Some 140 ships loaded with flour—destined for Spain and Portugal to feed the Duke of Wellington's armies in the Peninsular War against Napoleon's legions—cleared New York's harbor alone.

TIPPED OFF BY Gallatin, John Jacob Astor, well on his way to becoming the world's richest fur trader, was desperate to take pelts he had already purchased in Canada across the border. He sent off a courier to warn his Canadian partners that the declaration of war was imminent.

The son of a butcher, Astor, christened Johann Jacob Astor, was born in Walldorf, Germany, on the northern edge of the Black Forest. First working in a brother's flute factory in London, he learned English, anglicized his name and became a gifted salesman. At age twenty, he immigrated to the United States two months after the Treaty of Paris ended the American Revolution. Learning of the lucrative fur trade from fellow passengers during his crossing of the Atlantic, Astor brought with him a trunk full of flutes to sell, but in New York City he quickly found work in the butcher shop of another brother who had opened up a store in the Fly Market at the intersection of Maiden Lane and Pearl Street. John Jacob refused to cut meat; instead, he peddled cakes, cookies and rolls baked by one of his brother's friends.

Determined to learn the fur trade, he went to work beating furs to keep them free of moths for a Quaker merchant. At night, he combed the waterfront for cargoes of fur, using the profits from selling flutes until, in one year, he had accumulated a large enough quantity of pelts to justify sailing to London, where he sold them at a hefty profit. In 1785 he married Sarah Todd, whose dowry helped him to open an instrument shop at 81 Pearl Street and continue to invest in furs. By the late 1780s he was making risky backpacking trips through the backwoods of surrounding states as he dickered for furs to sell from his shop. Developing ties with merchants in Montreal, the hub of the North American fur trade, he made joint shipments to Europe while establishing trading posts in upstate New York.

For nearly two decades, as Americans competed with England on the high seas, Astor had been challenging British domination of the North American fur trade. His next bold step was to break into the fur business of the Great Lakes region based at Fort Michilimackinac on Mackinac Island, off the Upper Peninsula of Michigan. Forced to vacate the fort by the Jay Treaty, the British had moved their trading center to St. Joseph's, a Canadian island off the north shore of Lake Huron. Selling most of his furs in Europe, Astor bought the bulk of his Indian trade goods—blankets, coarse woolens, guns, tomahawks, powder and lead—in England, where they were cheaper and of better quality. To offset British competition, Astor formed a partnership with fur company investor William McGillivray, launching the South West Company as a hedge in case war closed off trade on one side of the border or the other.

Seeking to maintain friendly relations on both sides of the border, Astor, now a millionaire, was nonetheless so confident that there would be no war that, in late 1811, he offered the British a loan to help finance Canadian forces in Lower Canada. After each visit to Montreal, he reported to his close friend, Treasury Secretary Gallatin, on the size of the British armed forces. When the United States banned all trade with England and its territories that same month, the government prevented shipment of Indian trade goods manufactured in England from St. Joseph's Island in Canada to Michilimackinac. The shortage of goods angered the Indians and frustrated Astor, who considered the act unnecessary and futile. When he applied for a waiver, President Madison turned him down. Again appealing the ruling in June even as Congress debated the war resolution, he characterized his petition as a war measure on the grounds that the trade goods would be exchanged for furs that were dutiable and would therefore help the war effort. He was willing to sell the trade goods at St. Joseph's to the government if required. When Madison finally agreed, Gallatin ordered the customs officers at Michilimackinac and Detroit to receive Astor's goods. The transfer never took place, but, a few weeks later, worried that the outbreak of war would cost him the enormous trove of furs he had accumulated at Michilimackinac, Astor sent a courier west to alert his agents at his trading post there. Later he would be accused of deliberately warning the British; he argued that he was only trying to protect his furs.[18]

AFTER TIPPECANOE, WITH one in eight Americans living west of the Alleghenies, a wave of panic swept the frontier states and territories as settlers realized that, for years, Tecumseh had traveled widely to unite Indians into a powerful military alliance. Among his recruits, militant younger members of the Red Stick faction of the Creek nation were mesmerized by Tecumseh's blunt, fiery rhetoric. "Let the white race perish! War now! War always! War on the living! War on the dead!"[19]

Personifying the new westerners was Andrew Jackson, brigadier general of Tennessee's Second Division of militia. Standing ramrod straight at six-foot-two, Jackson's long face bore a saber scar inflicted during the Revolutionary War when, at fifteen, he refused to shine the boots of Tory Legion commander Colonel Banastre Tarleton. Jackson had lost two brothers in the war, one dying in combat, the other after being starved and refused medical treatment for a head wound as a prisoner of war. From childhood he had heard the harsh anti-English rhetoric of his Scots-Irish immigrant mother, whose father, she said, had fought the British in the Rising of 1745 before coming to America.

Exuding authority, Jackson had a vicious temper. He treated those who opposed him personally or in politics as enemies. Marrying into one of Tennessee's first families, he entered politics as the first United States attorney in Nashville, helped draw up Tennessee's constitution and soon became Tennessee's sole representative in the House. A maverick, he voted against paying tribute to Washington at the first president's farewell, objecting that the Jay Treaty with Britain stained the Republic's honor. When he was elected to the Senate, he arrived late for the session, taking his seat in Congress Hall in sweat-stained buckskins and with a rattlesnake skin pulled over his pigtail. Vice President Jefferson, presiding, wrote in his diary that night, "This is the new American!" Unhappy with the largely sedentary role of a senator, Jackson resigned and returned to his splendid plantation, the Hermitage, in South Carolina. Engaging in risky land speculation, he also traded provisions, tobacco, furs, lumber, horses, slaves and cotton down the Mississippi River to New Orleans.

Jackson's impassioned appeal to raise a volunteer army echoed the defiant frustration of many Americans after twenty years of provocations:

> Citizens! Your government has at last yielded to the impulse of the nation. Your impatience is no longer restrained. The hour of national vengeance is at hand. The eternal enemies of American prosperity are again to be taught to respect your rights. . . . War is on the point of breaking out between the united states and the King of Great Britain! And the martial hosts of America are summoned to the Tented Fields. . . . Shall we, who have clamored for war, now skulk into a corner the moment war is about to be declared? . . . Who are we? And for what are we going to fight? Are we the titled Slaves of George the third? The military conscripts of Napoleon the great? Or the frozen peasants of the Russian Czar?"[20]

Some 2,071 Tennessee frontiersmen eagerly answered his call.

ON MAY 19, 1812, the dispatch ship *Hornet* docked at New York City. The coded reports from American diplomats in England and France, summarizing developments in Europe up to mid-April, reached the nation's capital three days later. Madison, Monroe, Clay and the members of the House Committee on Foreign Affairs crowded into the small, sweltering anteroom of the two-and-a-half-story brick building on Pennsylvania Avenue, two hundred yards west of the White House, its low-ceilinged offices shared by the secretary of state, the secretary of war, the secretary of the navy and their handfuls of clerks. From Paris, the American minister, the poet Joel Barlow, reported that he had been discussing a new treaty of commerce with Napoleon's government. Giving assurances of relaxing the French Continental blockade of American trade, Napoleon had invited Barlow to travel with his suite to the general's winter headquarters in Poland to carry on further discussions. But Barlow could give no information about the way France would implement its existing decrees or when it might release or pay compensation for the American vessels it had seized.

The news from the American chargé d'affaires in London, Jonathan Russell, was hardly more reassuring. Against a backdrop of a serious recession, major protests were under way against the Orders in Council from Britain's manufacturing districts, where industrialists were attributing the recent downturn to American counterrestrictions on their trade. The manufacturing centers were largely unrepresented in Parliament and had little influence there. Russell held out almost no hope in April of any change in British policy from a largely anti-American cabinet.

Arriving in his carriage drawn by four matched white horses, the new British envoy, Augustus Foster, had been sent from London six months earlier in what at first had appeared to be an attempt to soften the tone, if not the content, of Britain's inflexible position on America's neutral trading rights. Now Foster informed the tense gathering that he had been given no authority to grant any serious new concessions. The Privy Council was willing to allow Americans a slightly larger share of the British-licensed trade passing through the British ports—after unloading and paying a 25 percent customs duty—to European ports. This totally disregarded the fact that Napoleon's agents confiscated any ship coming from Britain as if it actually were a British ship. As Foster must have known, Madison had never believed that neutrals should have to pay the British for a right to which they were already entitled under international law: the president considered this no concession whatsoever. Moreover, Foster warned, if the United States continued to flout the Orders in Council by trading directly with Napoleon on the Continent, the United States would run the risk of war with Britain.

Ten days later, on June 1, a resigned Madison sent a secret message to Congress, explaining that the British Ministry had stiffened rather than softened its demands. In his annual message to Congress, Madison wrote, "Our coasts and the mouths of our harbors have again witnessed scenes not less derogatory to the dearest of our national rights than vexations to the regular course of our trade." Although Madison avoided an open threat, he accused the British of impressing American seamen, violating American waters, maintaining a "sweeping system" of illegal blockades, employing secret agents to subvert the Union and maliciously influencing the Indians of the Northwest Territory.[21]

Speaker Clay referred Madison's message to the Committee on Foreign Affairs, where the War Hawks' spokesman, the beetle-browed thirty-year-old freshman representative John C. Calhoun of South Carolina, was allotted only two days to pen the committee's response to the president. "The mad ambition, the lust for power and commercial avarice of Great Britain have left to neutral nations an alternative only between the base surrender of their rights and a manly vindication of them," Calhoun wrote, concluding with an unmistakable plea for "an immediate appeal to arms":

> Our Citizens are wantonly snatched from their Country, and their families; deprived of their liberty and doomed to an ignominious and slavish bondage, compelled to fight the battles of a foreign Country and often to perish in them. . . . While this practice is continued, it is impossible for the United States to consider themselves an independent Nation.[22]

Madison, echoing his stance in *Federalist* number 46, called for a massive voluntary turnout of citizen-soldiers: "A well-regulated militia, composed of the body of the people, trained in arms, is the best, most natural defense of a free country." The House responded with unaccustomed alacrity, pushing through the declaration of war in only two days, by a 79-49 vote. The Senate took two weeks to deliberate.[23]

On June 17 the Senate finally put the question to a straight up-or-down vote: in the closest vote on any declaration of war in American history, the Senate voted 19-13 in favor of war, only 61 percent of the voting members supporting the authorization of a declaration of war against Britain. Most representatives and senators from Pennsylvania and the South and the West voted for war, while most from the North and the East voted against. The vote was so close that Foster, the British envoy, recorded in his diary on June 30 that he had an aide "make [Richard] Brent the old drunken Senator from Virginia" drunk every day so that he would not show up to cast a tie-breaking pro-war vote:

> In a very important stage of the bill the majority would have been against the party inclined to war [the War-Hawks as they were called] but that the debate was purposely prolonged in order to allow time for one very idle and drunken, and another very fat Senator to arrive, who were at some feast and had been sent for in a great hurry in order that they might turn the scale.[24]

Like the first war for American independence, the War of 1812, from the moment of its conception, was a bitter internal political struggle as well as a war against a foreign enemy. The breakdown of congressional voting proves beyond any doubt the political dimension of the decision to declare war: it followed party lines. Some 81 percent of Democratic-Republicans in both houses voted for war, 98-23. All thirty-nine Federalists voted against the war.

THAT EVENING, AS usual, Dolley Madison glided into what she called her "Wednesday drawing room" at the White House. Three large strategically placed mirrors played with the shimmering gaslight, amplifying the festive mood of the triumphant War Hawks. As the guests arrived, the president and first lady shook hands with them and congratulated them on the declaration of war. A New York Federalist journalist in the room thought the atmosphere "iniquitous," observing with disgust that "the President was all life and spirits." The first lady, as was her wont, paused with her protégé Speaker Clay. They had developed a close friendship; she even allowed Clay to help himself to a pinch of snuff from the elaborate little box she seemed always to carry decorously with her. If Dolley had any misgivings about the news leaking out of the day's meetings, she more than concealed them. British envoy Foster saw President Madison in a different light that night. To him, Madison appeared "ghastly pale" as they bowed three times to each other. Foster had learned to converse with the aristocrats and intellectuals of Europe—Goethe, Schiller, Madame de Staël—and on the eve of war he even managed to chatter to Madison about Napoleon's recent losses to the Duke of Wellington on the Iberian Peninsula.[25]

While keeping a careful diary of his years in America, Foster, in his official dispatches home, had misled his government about Madison's and the nation's determination to fight, always telling his government what he believed it wanted to hear. Since his arrival a year earlier, he had been downplaying the likelihood of war, characterizing the unrest as little more than the handiwork of malcontent Irish immigrants. When Duane's *Aurora* reported a tumultuous pro-war rally in Philadelphia, Foster reported to London that the crowd "amounted to but 2,000 persons principally composed of Irishmen of the lowest order, Negroes and boys." Duane was a special target: "The enmity of these Foreigners to Great Britain is kept alive by Duane, an Irishman . . . (he) is supposed to be in the French pay at Philadelphia."[26]

At Foster's return to America as British minister plenipotentiary during the *Leander* riots in New York City in 1807, a mob had threatened to hurl his carriage into the Hudson River. Since then, Foster had blamed much of the anti-British sentiment on Irish immigrants: "The ringleader on this occasion was, as might be expected, an Irish emigrant." He had special scorn for the ten naturalized Irish Democratic-Republicans sitting in the House of Representatives, calling them "a motley set of imported grumblers imported from Dublin." He characterized these "Irishmen, who live by agitation," as having "an immense influence over all the wild, unruly young adventurers of the western woods, especially the Democrats of the slave districts, who are of rather a rakish turn." Foster, who owned a string of racing horses, may have been aware that bluegrass Kentucky, represented by Henry Clay, had doubled in population, to more than 400,000, many of them Irish immigrants pushing west from the overcrowded sea-ports.[27]

Known to indulge his prejudice with a prank, Foster had learned that "plenty of sturgeon are caught at the little falls of the Potomac, a short dis-tance above Georgetown where the river becomes narrow and the scenery is very romantic; such abundance was there indeed of this fish that I de-termined to try if the roe might not be cured so as to afford caviar." Foster found his *maitre d'hotel* a copy of Ephraim Chambers's 1728 *Cyclopaedia*, which contained instructions "which he so successfully followed that I had some excellent caviar." Foster served it to members of Congress: "The pre-caution of telling them to taste a little first not having been observed, they took such quantities thinking it was black raspberry jam that the stock was soon exhausted. Very few of them liked it but spit it out very unceremoni-ously as a thing excessively nasty." Traveling widely along the Atlantic seacoast, Foster had never ventured west of the Alleghenies, but he none-theless had formed firm opinions that he transmitted home to England:

> I have not been in the west, but I conceive that little can be said of a coun-try so lately settled and where the houses with few exceptions are built of logs, a great part of the active population being composed of refugees from society or of people who have emigrated from Europe. . . . Who can describe the manners or the institutions of such a motley race, some liv-ing in harmony together, others carrying the vices of civilized life into forests and morasses while calling themselves a young people?

Completely underestimating the determination of many Americans to take on his arrogant countrymen again, Foster scoffed at Henry Clay's overt hawkishness as nothing more than drollery. Clay and his friends al-ways talked of war "as necessary to America as a duel is to a young officer to prevent his being bullied and elbowed in society."

As soon as the Senate narrowly voted for war, a stunned Foster rode over to the White House to implore President Madison to suspend hostili-ties until he could report to London and seek the government's reaction. Madison turned him down. Secretary of State Monroe then summoned the chagrined Foster to the State Department where, in an awkward scene over a pot of tea, Monroe spelled out the American demands for a return to peace: complete repeal of the 1807 Orders in Council and cessation of impressment of Americans from her merchant ships. Britain must also sign a treaty containing a definition of blockades similar to one it had negotiated with Russia in 1801 that had relaxed its notions about policing neutral trade. The timeless British practice of impressment must be abolished by a mutual agreement, written into both British and American law, that the two nations would no longer employ each other's citizens in their merchant marines. Americans already serving in the British Navy were to be released from service; compensation was to be paid for seized ships and cargoes. Although Madison would later maintain that he offered the British government "reasonable terms," nothing Foster could say would sway either Madison or Monroe. Indeed, as war would commence immediately, Foster would not be able to wait in America for further instructions from London. He would have to leave; he would have to sell his prized string of racehorses at a loss.

As a shaken Foster made arrangements to shutter the British legation and sail back to England, the *Washington National Intelligencer* on June 23 reported the assassination of Prime Minister Perceval. It would be weeks more before Foster could learn the assassin's motivation, but he could surmise that the act might bring about a dramatic change in England's policy toward America. Rushing back to the White House, Foster again asked Madison for an armistice while he elicited his government's response to the war declaration. Foster contended that a new cabinet very likely would soften relations with the United States. But Madison again refused him. Foster later wrote of his frustration at Madison's intransigence:

> As our Councils appeared likely to become weaker the American Cabinet felt stronger, and had a disposition to bully. They now insisted on the impressment question as the main point at issue and declared that a modification or even a repeal of the Orders in Council would not suffice without a final settlement of the questions of impressment and blockade; and, as the Congress were separating, the Government declared they had no power during the recess to do more than listen to our proposals.[28]

Even though President Madison would not agree to an armistice, he approved keeping open diplomatic channels. British legation secretary

Anthony St. John Baker could remain in Washington while American chargé d'affaires Russell would remain in London, and British packet boats could pass freely under flags of truce. Foster carried with him a coded message from Madison to Russell containing the president's terms for an end to hostilities that Russell was to present to the new foreign secretary, Lord Castlereagh. Later that day, Foster left in his carriage for New York City, where he boarded the fast sloop-of-war *Colibri* and sailed to the British North American Station's headquarters at Halifax. In his haste, the flustered emissary forgot to send word to Sir George Prevost, governor-general of Canada, that the two neighbors were now at war.

On the morning of June 19, 1812, President Madison signed the act of Congress declaring that the United States, after a decade of frustrating diplomacy, was now officially at war with England. Attorney General Richard Rush reported the day's events to his father, Dr. Benjamin Rush, in Philadelphia: "He visited in person—a thing never known before—all the offices of the departments of war and of the navy, stimulating everything in a manner worthy of a little commander-in-chief, with his little round hat and huge cockade." The president's pep talk was then dutifully reported in the *National Intelligencer*, which was sent in mail pouches to newspapers throughout the nation.[29]

On the very day that Britain's minister plenipotentiary left Washington, at Whitehall Palace in London, a new prime minister, Lord Liverpool, Foster's uncle by marriage, won the approval of the king's Privy Council to repeal the 1807 Orders in Council that had provoked the five-year crisis, its ruinous embargoes and ship confiscations. In the absence of modern communications, the action that could have averted the War of 1812 would not be known in Canada for another month, in Washington for nearly six weeks. A seismic reversal of British policy in London was, as Foster had predicted, the first result of the assassination on May 11 of Prime Minister Perceval, shot in the chest by an aggrieved petitioner at point-blank range as the PM stepped from a parliamentary debate at Westminster Hall. Perceval had been unyielding in his opposition to rescinding the orders because he believed they were protecting British trade with her colonies and with the Continent and because he considered the United States as Britain's primary commercial rival. Reacting quickly, Jonathan Russell, unbeknownst to Madison, had proposed an armistice in exchange for Britain's renunciation of impressment and the Orders in Council.

The aged King George III suffered from a rare blood disease called porphyria. As it worsened, his son, the future George IV, assumed his duties as prince regent, arousing a momentary hope in Washington. The prince had at first supported Perceval's anti-American agenda but more recently had grown closer to the Whig faction in Parliament, which favored a more amicable relation with the United States. Presiding at Carlton House and taking an active role in the Privy Council proceedings, the regent also made no secret of his growing disapproval of the policies of Perceval, a Tory. It had been Perceval's last set of instructions to his envoy Foster, arriving after a month on the Atlantic on the dispatch corvette *Hornet*, that had dashed Madison's last hope for a substantial change of policy in London that would avert war. Madison's message to the new prime minister did not reach London until hostilities had broken out on the Canadian border.

Russell delivered the decoded dispatch to foreign minister Castlereagh on August 24, but the new British administration had not waited for it: fully a month earlier, the British ten-gun brig *Bloodhound* had arrived at Annapolis, Maryland, with official word that the Orders in Council had been withdrawn and were suspended as of August 1. Lord Liverpool, worried about having to reinforce Canada and fight on a second war front even as Napoleon's threat to Europe daily grew more dire, sent word through Halifax that he, too, wanted an armistice. Madison again refused: he had sent his terms to London and the British would have to accede to them before he would consider any armistice. Madison feared that the British were stalling while they reinforced Canada. Only a few days after Russell, in London, presented Madison's terms to Castlereagh, he received their rejection out of hand. Castlereagh wrote to Russell, "No [British] administration could expect to remain in power that should consent to renounce the right of impressment. . . ." His response removed any lingering doubt that the principal, ineluctable issue dividing the two nations remained impressment.[30]

Madison still was waiting to learn the outcome of a second secret diplomatic initiative. He had instructed the American envoy in Paris, Joel Barlow—often preoccupied with haunting the stylish boutiques of Paris for the latest fashions to ship to the first lady—to press Napoleon to rescind his blockading Berlin and Milan Decrees, themselves retaliation for Britain's Orders in Council. By this time, the French had seized some 519 American ships, surpassing the toll of 389 captured by Britain. Madison clung to the hope that Napoleon would compensate Americans for their losses. (The United States finally received compensation twenty years later.) In April, American chargé d'affaires Russell, in London, had received assurances from the British colonial secretary that if Napoleon yielded first, Britain would soften its sanctions on American trade.

When he had decamped from Paris to his winter quarters in Poland, Napoleon had invited Barlow to follow him and meet to sign a treaty. Receiving the British offer from Russell just before joining Napoleon's court, Barlow was able in May to forward a document to Russell in London assuring the British that Napoleon would release the United States from enforcement of the Berlin and Milan Decrees. Traveling with Napoleon's legions as the emperor unleashed his invasion of Russia, an exhausted Barlow contracted pneumonia and died in Żarnowiec, Poland, in December 1812. Whether he was able to wring from a distracted Napoleon a commitment to release American ships he held or to compensate American ship owners was vital intelligence buried with Barlow in Poland.

Madison had known since receiving intelligence from John Quincy Adams in St. Petersburg in October 1811 that all Europe expected Napoleon to launch a massive invasion of Russia in the summer campaigning season of 1812. Napoleon was marshaling some 600,000 troops, the largest army in history, on the Russian border to punish his former ally, Czar Alexander I, for abandoning the Continental System. Russia's defection from Napoleon's camp promised to bolster the British-led alliance that was still struggling after two decades to prevent France from achieving total dominance over Europe. Once again, Russian wheat and timber were being shipped to the British Isles to feed and keep afloat the British army and navy. But the new British cabinet was well aware that its armies in Spain and Portugal, where Wellington was tying down 250,000 French troops, depended on grain shipments from the United States. The new cabinet assembled by the prince regent also realized that it would be virtually impossible to spare troops from its Iberian army to reinforce the anemic garrisons in Canada.

While it was incomprehensible to the new British prime minister, Lord Liverpool, that the Americans seriously intended to make war on the mighty British Empire merely over its Orders in Council, he persuaded the Privy Council to accept Napoleon's concessions. It voted on June 23, 1812—three days after Madison signed the declaration of war and the same day that Foster was asked to leave the United States—to repeal the 1807 Orders in Council. It would take nearly a month, however, before a British dispatch ship could whisk the requisite documents to Halifax. By that time, Foster was no longer in North America to receive them and sail to Washington to deliver them.

When Foster finally did arrive in England after a two-month ocean voyage, Foreign Secretary Castlereagh chided him for leaving Halifax instead of waiting there for proposals of peace to carry back to Madison. The next morning, at an audience at Carlton House, the punctilious prince regent seemed less interested in intelligence that Foster might be bringing him from America than in upbraiding the envoy for appearing at the meeting in his dress uniform when the prince regent was receiving him informally, in a dressing gown. A few days later in Parliament, the hapless Foster found he was being blamed for not correctly appraising the seriousness of America's determination or officially apprising Britain that its recent colonies were once again prepared to go to war over such trivialities as free trade and sailors' rights.

Amused by the peccadilloes of a people he considered in every way his inferiors and only listening to antiwar Federalists, Augustus Foster was unable to interpret for his diplomatic superiors the full ramifications of the changing mood of America. He had completely missed the point that an unnecessary war was breaking out for which neither side was prepared. For their part, obsessed by the hypnotic megalomaniacal maneuverings of Napoleon, the distracted British Ministry had once again proven its capacity for underestimating the frustration and fury of its American relations. It would be August 12 before Madison learned officially of Britain's volte-face: by that time, heavy fighting had broken out all along the Canadian-American frontier. Madison immediately canceled an armistice agreement signed by Dearborn and Prevost, and due to take effect September 10. One month later, Britain officially authorized reprisals against the United States.

So distracted had President Madison been by his diplomatic tête-à-tête with Foster that he hadn't noticed—if he ever even heard of it—a portentous episode on the Tennessee frontier and the call for swift action it provoked in Andrew Jackson, the forty-five-year-old general in the Tennessee militia. Jackson wrote to Governor Willie Blount on June 5 to report a massacre of women and children by the Red Stick Creek in Georgia. Three weeks earlier, five Red Sticks had invaded the homes of two settlers, Jesse Manley and John Crawley. They murdered and scalped Manley's wife and five children before killing a neighbor's teenage boy and kidnapping Mrs. Crawley. Jackson, who had raised a 1,200-man brigade of mounted Tennessee militia, was writing to Governor Blount for permission to retaliate, pointing out that the general in charge of Georgia's militia had been nearby with 500 men when the attack took place and had done nothing to prevent or avenge it. Jackson insisted, "This cruel outrage must not go unrevenged. The assassins of Women and Children must be punished."

> Now Sir the object of <u>Tecumpsies</u> [*sic*] visit to the creek nation is unfolding to us. That Incendiary, the emissary of the <u>Prophet</u>, who is himself the tool of England, has caused our frontier to be stained with blood, and our peaceful citizens to fly in terror from the once happy abodes.

Jackson assured Governor Blount that he could muster 2,500 men "ready on the first signal to visit the Creek towns."

> The sooner we strike, the less resistance we shall have to overcome; and a terrible vengeance inflicted at once upon one tribe may have its effect upon all others. Even the wretches upon the Wabash might take some warning from such a lesson.

In response, Blount urged Jackson to restrain his men while he sought the approval of the War Department in Washington. If Madison ever received the message, he was too preoccupied to respond.[31]

NINE

"A Mere Matter of Marching"

During the agonizing weeks that Congress debated in secret declaring war, a conflict of another kind raged the length of America, nowhere more intensely than in Baltimore, Maryland. The Chesapeake Bay port city, which stood to gain from what promised to become a privateering bonanza at sea, clamored for war. Baltimore had rapidly grown to become America's third-largest city, its population of 41,000 including thousands of Irish refugees, many of them unemployed, bitter and chafing to fight the British. Throughout the embargo years, its Democratic-Republican and Federalist presses hurled vitriol at each other. One outspoken Federalist who vehemently opposed Madison's plan to declare war had been one of Washington's boldest generals in the Revolution: Henry "Light Horse Harry" Lee.

Scion of one of Virginia's leading families, Lee, like Madison, matriculated at the College of New Jersey (now Princeton). Excelling in debating, he planned to study law in England, but the growing resistance movement drew him to join the Revolutionary army. Commissioned a captain, Lee rebuffed Washington's summons to become his aide-de-camp, preferring the cut-and-thrust of cavalry. The Continental Congress gave him command of the First Continental Light Dragoons. Promoted to major, he formed an independent corps of cavalry and infantry known as Lee's Legion, earning the sobriquet "Light Horse Harry" when, at a low point in the war, he caught off guard a British outpost at Paulus Hook, New Jersey, taking 158 prisoners. Promoted to lieutenant colonel, he shielded the retreat of Nathanael Greene's Southern Army, clashing repeatedly with Tarleton's Legion. In one subterfuge, Lee's legionnaires rode alongside three hundred Loyalist militiamen who mistook him for a British officer. His men killed one hundred of them, wounding most of the rest. Detached to raid Loyalist posts in Georgia, Lee captured four enemy forts, saving Greene's army from certain rout.

The war hero married twice: first his second cousin, Matilda, heiress of Stratford Hall, who bore him four children; second, the land-rich heiress Anne Hill Carter, who gave him five more children. Elected to the House of Burgesses, he became a delegate to the Continental Congress, serving three years. In Virginia's turbulent ratification convention, he argued in favor of the federal Constitution. Three times elected governor, he sometimes opposed Washington's policies but, like the first president, dreaded party politics. Washington considered him to lead an army against Indians in the Ohio country but instead decided on Anthony Wayne, fearing senior officers wouldn't serve under a colonel. During the Whiskey Rebellion on the Pennsylvania frontier, Washington appointed Lee to lead a 15,000-man militia force that overawed the tax resisters, who surrendered without a shot. Again, when the Quasi War with France loomed, Washington appointed Lee a major general. Elected to Congress, Lee wrote the congressional resolution of honor when Washington died, coining the famous epitaph: "First in war, first in peace, and first in the hearts of his countrymen."[1]

Bankrupt after running through two fortunes, Lee wrote his memoirs to appease his many creditors but nonetheless landed in debtors' prison for a mortifying year. Jefferson, overlooking Lee's Federalist politics, rescued him, appointing him, during the Embargo crisis, to reorganize Virginia's militia. At the onset of war in 1812, Lee pleaded unsuccessfully with Madison to restore his rank—and salary—as major general. He then moved his family to a modest house in Alexandria before riding off to Baltimore to put his memoirs through the press, arriving June 22, just four days after the United States went to war.

At news that Madison had signed the declaration, jubilant Baltimoreans, many of them Irish immigrants who had fled persecution, others
unemployed sailors and waterfront workers left jobless by embargoes,
vented their enthusiasm by attacking the printing office of the leading Federalist newspaper, the *Federal Republican*. Its coeditor, Alexander Contee
Hanson Jr., had repeatedly editorialized against Jeffersonian policies. Hanson, a lieutenant in the Maryland militia, had been cashiered by Jeffersonian officers who claimed that one editorial was "mutinous and highly
reproachful to the President." As war approached, rumors swirled in
Baltimore's taverns and coffeehouses that, if Hanson did not change
the paper's tone, he would be shut down and tarred and feathered.

Hanson counterattacked editorially: he would not be cowed into supporting a war he considered unjust and unwise. War would put the Constitution and all civil rights to sleep. Those who commenced it would
become dictators and despots, the people their slaves. Two days after Madison signed the declaration of war, Hanson came out against it. Labeling
the war "unnecessary" and "inexpedient," he vowed to oppose it by "every
constitutional argument and every legal means."[2]

The next evening, at beer gardens on Fell's Point, plans to destroy the
Federalist newspaper building took shape. Several hundred Irish, German
and native-born laborers marched to Gay Street and surrounded the newspaper office. A French apothecary named Philip Lewis seemed to be the
leader of thirty to forty of them. Cheered on by the crowd, they attached
blocks and tackles and ropes to the frame building and pulled it down.
City officials, virtually dragged to the scene by Federalists and either too
terrified or approving the mob action, refused to call out the militia. As
he later testified, when Mayor Edward Johnson approached Lewis at the
scene, the apothecary told him, "Mr. Johnson, I know you very well, nobody wants to hurt you: but the laws of the land must sleep, and the laws
of nature and reason must prevail; that house is the Temple of Infamy, it is
supported with English gold, and it must and shall come down to the
ground!"[3]

The mayor and his entourage walked away as the mob destroyed the
printing press and scattered the fonts in the street. At exactly this moment,
General Lee arrived. Outraged, he declared his determination to support
his old friend Hanson. Lee had long known Hanson as an outspoken Fed-

eralist but regarded him as an educated and wealthy planter, like Lee a member of one of the nation's most distinguished families. One Hanson had signed the Declaration of Independence; another, John Hanson, was the first president under the Articles of Confederation. Yet another had served as Maryland's governor during the Revolution, in which two Hansons had died in battle; yet another was a member of the First Congress. Nevertheless, by June 21, 1812, most Baltimoreans considered anyone who opposed this second war against Britain a Tory siding with the English, a traitor.

Escaping to Georgetown, Hanson printed the paper there for the next month and delivered it by mail to subscribers in Baltimore. He rode the countryside with a young actor, John Howard Payne (who would later compose "Home, Sweet Home"), raising funds to reopen. Amid the war fever of that summer, Protestant and Catholic began to attack each other.

The publisher of the Federalist paper, James Lingan, another decorated Revolutionary War general, came forward and arranged to lease a stout three-story brick building at 45 Charles Street. On July 25, he supervised installation of a new printing press as scores of Federalists came by to welcome him. Many sons of Maryland's leading Federalist families gathered around Lee and Lingan, volunteering to stay and guard Hanson, believing he was striking a blow for freedom of the press. The Federalists put Lee in charge of defensive preparations. "Hanson and his friends believed that if they stood firm, a mob composed of riffraff and the dregs of society would not dare to confront men of their social position," argues Gilje.[4]

But the mood in Baltimore in June 1812 was closer to the French Revolution than it was to the American Revolution of 1776. On the morning of July 27, the *Federal Republican* appeared, its new address boldly emblazoned on its masthead above an editorial decrying the citizenry's resort to violence. Characterizing the city's leading Democratic-Republican politician, Revolutionary War general and U.S. senator Samuel Smith, as a "monster" who was following orders from "his superiors" in a "desperate attempt to intimidate and overawe the minority" and "to destroy the freedom of speech and of the press," Hanson castigated him for "corruption, profligacy and [a] jacobinical heart."

That evening, hundreds of men and boys appeared on East Charles Street and taunted the two dozen armed Federalists inside, pelting the building with stones until they had smashed all the windows, shutters and sashes. Calls from the house to disperse drew a shout of "Fire, fire, you damned Tories. Fire! We are not afraid of you!"[5]

At about 10 p.m., at a signal from General Lee, several Federalists leaned out of windows and fired a volley of blanks. In the street, a doctor named Thaddeus Gale shouted, "That ball was aimed at me—the Tories ought to be hanged upon this tree." The crowd scattered; then, quickly reappearing, they rushed the building. As they reached the front doorway, the Federalists lowered their muskets and fired again, this time using live ammunition, killing a shopkeeper. They continued firing as the crowd retreated, wounding several more. The siege lasted all night. Five hours later the city magistrates finally signed an order calling out the city's troop of cavalry.

Shortly before dawn, as John Stricker, the militia's commander, made a half-hearted attempt to negotiate a truce, a cannon appeared from a nearby alley, aimed at the house. Thomas Wilson, the editor of the rival *Baltimore Sun*, declared he wouldn't give up the attack on the Federalists "until he had off their damned heads." Encouraging the mob to fire, he cried, "We must have blood for blood! We will not be satisfied till we put them to death." By now, the crowd had swollen beyond 2,000. Over Hanson's protests, General Lee accepted Stricker's offer to escort the Federalists to the local jail for their protection. While the crowd ransacked the press building, a hollow square of militia, hard-pressed to hold off the milling, screaming mob, escorted the Federalists to the lightly guarded county jail a mile away, where they spent a sleepless night huddled in an empty cell.

The next night, as darkness descended, forty dockworkers from Fell's Point returned to the county jail. Swarming through heavy wooden doors suspiciously left unlocked, they brushed the mayor and the magistrates aside, tearing open the cells and searching them by torchlight. In a melee of shoving, punching and pushing, half the Federalists managed to escape. In what an investigating committee for the Maryland House of Delegates later described as a "scene of horror and murder," the mob pulled down the jailhouse. The rioters stripped the Federalists, severely beating them as they dragged nine of them outside, including Hanson,

Lee and Lingan. Women screamed, "Kill the Tories, kill the Tories," and the crowd broke into an old Revolutionary War song:

> We'll feather and tar every damned British Tory,
> And that is the way for American glory.

The militia officers stood by, disinclined to dampen their patriotic ardor.[6]

Over the next three hours, in a frenzy of bloodletting, the rioters beset their Federalist prisoners, repeatedly clubbing and beating them, slashing and stabbing with penknives and dripping hot candlewax into their eyes to determine whether they were still alive. Pleading for his life, the elderly General Lingan reminded his tormenters that he had suffered for his country in the Revolutionary War, that he had a large family depending on him. Cries of "Tory! Tory!" drowned out his pleas as he was repeatedly stabbed in the chest. He died several hours later, the first casualty of the War of 1812.

Finally, a sympathetic doctor convinced the crowd he needed the bodies for his dissection studies, but by then eleven other Federalists, including General Lee, had suffered severe injuries. Printer Hanson sustained internal injuries, a broken nose and finger, cuts on the head, hands and back and spinal damage. Escaping only by playing dead, he never recovered completely but ran successfully for Congress the next year. A Federalist hero, he served for five years until he died at thirty-three. His brother-in-law Daniel Murray tried to play dead, but a stick jammed down his throat gave him away. He, too, was severely beaten but survived.

John Thomson, a large man, was stripped and, after being coated with tar and feathers, dumped into a cart and stabbed with old swords as he was dragged around the city. Members of the mob took turns torturing him: one attempted to break his legs with an iron bar, others pitched flaming tar and feathers over him; one man tried to gouge out his eyes. The crowd threatened to hang Thomson, already severely burned, unless he gave them the names of everyone in the defenders' house.

Lee suffered severe internal and head injuries, his face so slashed and bruised by repeated blows that it remained swollen and blackened for several months. A friend described Lee's face as "black as a negro, his head cut to pieces." His once-eloquent speech impaired and halting for the rest of his life, Lee, barely recognizable, went home to Alexandria more dead than alive. The fifty-four-year-old general remained a permanent invalid. Attempting to recover his health and unwilling to stay in America, he sailed to Barbados in the British West Indies, out of reach of political opponents, creditors and family. One of his sons, the future Confederate general Robert E. Lee, was six when he last saw his father.[7]

In the first month of the War of 1812, American democracy failed. The only blood spilled was American.

As early as the arrival in Washington of the alarming news of the bloody battle at Tippecanoe on the long Indiana Territory frontier with Canada, Americans had taken it for granted that any war effort must be directed mainly against vast, underpopulated, fur-rich Canada. The United States' lack of a significant navy ruled out invasion of any other British territory. In what would perforce be a land war, the regular U.S. Army boasted only about 3,000 officers and men—a third of its authorized strength—but the Republic possessed an overwhelming numerical superiority of nearly fifteen to one over Canada, whose 400,000 males contrasted with 6 million free white men in the United States. If only they could be mobilized, organized and motivated, every advantage seemed to be with the Americans. The mother country, Great Britain, had far larger naval and land forces, an operational fleet of 623 vessels—including 120 ships-of-the-line—and a battle-seasoned standing army of 250,000 men, but it could muster only 5,600 regulars in all of Upper Canada (today's Ontario Province), Lower Canada (Quebec) and the Maritime Provinces. Nonetheless, British officers had faith in their Canadian provincial militia and navy, totaling 86,000 men. With Napoleon's vast armies engaging 98 percent of its armed forces, Britain could not afford to spare to replenish its garrisons in North America.

The first public hints of an American war strategy had appeared in the administration's newspaper, the *Washington National Intelligencer*, fully six months before the declaration of war. "It would be the duty of the government of the United States to lose no time in reducing the whole [of Canada] above Quebec," the paper declared. This would require roughly

20,000 men, "two thirds of whom would be volunteers and one third regulars." Their efforts should be aimed at three targets, "principally to the
region of Montreal, [to] the outlet of [Lake] Ontario and across the Niagara river." It would not be necessary to attack the citadel at Quebec (where
the American invasion of 1775 had foundered), even if most of the 7,000
British regulars in Canada defended it, because its garrison would be cut
off from the rest of Canada while Americans carried out their other objectives and could reduce the walled fortress with a "regular siege." The
primary target should be Upper Canada, where 1,200 British regulars were
spread thinly over an 800-mile-long frontier. Of the 77,000 white inhabitants of Upper Canada, three-fifths had been born in the United States,
their loyalties not yet tested.[8]

To organize a new American army, Madison, who had no experience
of command and had never fought in one, had to appoint its officers. As
Congressman Richard Rush of Pennsylvania pointed out, there was "a real
dearth of capable military men in the country." Jefferson's political purge
had drained the pool of officers' talent. The U.S. Military Academy at West
Point had graduated only eighty-nine fledgling officers by 1812. Most of the
officers with any military experience had served during the American
Revolution and were too old for rigorous frontier warfare.

Madison preferred to rely on loyal Jeffersonians to help him choose his
officers. Between December 1811 and April 1812, Madison and Secretary of
War Eustis churned through piles of letters of recommendation from state
congressional delegates and applications for commissions, some of them
memorable. One correspondent who signed himself "No Trimmer" wrote
to President Madison on April 14 that the Federalist congressman Robert
LeRoy Livingston, known as Crazy Bob, would make "a most excellent
Lieut. Colonel . . . if throwing Decanters and glasses were to be the weapons used."[9]

That summer, Madison offered commissions to some 1,100 officers, of
which 15 percent declined. According to Madison scholar J.C.A. Stagg,
the ranks above major were filled from the legal, mercantile and political
elite on the state and local levels, while men from agrarian backgrounds,
farmers and planters, were significantly underrepresented. "A smaller sub-
set of the higher officers, fewer than twenty percent of the total, came
from the broad middling spectrum of American society, including such

groups as artisans, manufacturers, and merchants." On average, they were in their late thirties to mid-forties when they entered the officer corps. Some 8 percent of them would resign their commissions after brief tours of duty. Many of the junior officers were "the younger sons of prominent and well-connected families in their localities who had yet to settle on a profession."[10]

Recruiting to fill the enlisted ranks went slowly, despite few restrictions. Recruits had only to be white male citizens, free of serious health problems and between eighteen and forty-five years of age. After the first year of the war, the citizenship requirement seems to have been ignored. Of the new recruits, 87 percent were native-born Americans, including a small number of free-born African Americans; the remainder were immigrants, most of them Irish. A lively controversy persists among scholars of the period over the proportion and motives of Irish immigrants who signed up for the army. Many historians hold that revenge against the English, especially over their brutal, recent repression of the 1798 rebellion, was a powerful motivator, while Stagg insists this is fallacious. Both camps seem to overlook the possibility that far more Irish preferred to join the crews of the approximately 2,000 privateering ships that, in addition to plaguing British shipping, offered considerable emoluments for each sailor's share of prize money received for capturing British ships and selling them and their cargo at auction, vastly more than they could make in the army.

The average age of all army volunteers was twenty-seven, but among farm-born recruits it was five years younger, suggesting, as Stagg points out, that these did not yet own their land and could not expect to inherit much but were attracted to military service by land bounties. Minors younger than twenty-one and apprentices needed the written consent of their parents, guardians or masters to enlist. On joining, they received a sixteen-dollar cash bounty, a full set of clothes and pay of five dollars per month; they would receive 160 acres of land upon honorable discharge, a major inducement. The recruitment effort proved somewhat less than a success, as only 14,000 new recruits joined up in the first year.

How to pay for the war was the vexatious task facing Secretary of the Treasury Gallatin. As military expenses mushroomed, he could expect the British naval blockade to slash tariff revenues, still the government's main source of income. The year before the war started, the Democratic-Republican-controlled Congress had refused to re-charter the Bank of the United States, the source of loans for the past twenty years to fund the government's operations, including war. The national bank's opponents charged that too much of the bank's bonds were held in England. Bank restrictions on lending were crippling boom-era venture capitalists; they preferred state banks that would enable an expansion of credit. In New York alone, the state legislature had chartered ten new banks in two years, including the Federalists' Bank of America and the Democratic-Republicans' City Bank of New York.

To add to Gallatin's catalog of worries, customs duties already lagged behind expenditures, necessitating taking on small loans to make scheduled repayments. Because of the widening war in Europe, foreign loans were no longer available. Gallatin would have to turn to private capitalists for large federal loans. When he submitted his proposed $26 million war budget for 1812, Gallatin asked Congress to double customs duties, revive the old duty on imported salt and authorize a $10 million loan. After the initial shock wore off, Congress approved an $11 million loan but at 6 percent interest, which Gallatin knew would be too low to attract investors. He floated the loan in April, but by the end of June, after the war had begun, only $6 million had been taken, leaving the government with a projected $10 million shortfall. Congress again saw fit to double the customs duties and sold Treasury notes against expected, but now far from predictable, future revenues.

From the rolls of aging veterans, William Hull was among the first officers plucked by Madison. A lieutenant colonel in the Revolutionary War, he had failed at land speculations in New England. Appointed by Jefferson as military governor of Michigan Territory, he quarreled with other officials and forced native tribes to cede more land. Lobbying in Washington against Secretary of War Eustis's plan to invade Canada from Lake Champlain, he complained about the administration's failure to build naval vessels on the Great Lakes. Instead, Eustis placed him at the head of a small army to defend Michigan territory and to prepare to invade Upper Canada without a navy. Tecumseh's threat to the region's security induced Madison to commission Hull brigadier general over the "North Western Army," on paper an army of 2,000 men. Made up of regulars and volunteers from Ohio, they were to reinforce Detroit and "secure the peace of the country." Hull's force was to be the largest assembled since the end of the Revolutionary War.

Nearly six months before he declared war, Madison had already nominated sixty-year-old Henry Dearborn of Massachusetts as the highest-ranking major general in the Army, charging him with formulating a comprehensive war strategy. A junior officer in the Revolution, Dearborn made the epic march to Quebec with Benedict Arnold, only to be captured. Following his exchange, he again served under Arnold at Saratoga, ending the war as deputy quartermaster general. Serving briefly as secretary of war under Jefferson, he prospered as a land speculator while U.S. marshal for Maine. Dearborn helped Jefferson purge Federalist officers from the Army. He modernized the army's weaponry and centralized its command structure and supply systems, at the same time negotiating major land cessions from the Indians. Jefferson further rewarded his loyal Dearborn by appointing him collector of the port of Boston, one of the most lucrative federal posts. As war loomed, Madison commissioned Dearborn senior major general and commander of the sprawling Northeast Theater, which stretched from the Niagara River to New England's seacoast.

Dearborn's strategy retained Madison's objective of seizing the region between Montreal and Lake Ontario by attacking across the Niagara peninsula. But Quartermaster General Porter, who had sizable business interests that he wanted to protect from British counterattack, persuaded Dearborn to alter the plan, thereby disallowing incursions across the Niagara River into Canada. Dearborn preferred incursions into New Brunswick province, which would prompt the British to withdraw their forces to defend Halifax; meanwhile, he protected his own business interests in Maine in the bargain. He overlooked the fact that New Englanders, having paid disproportionately in the French and Indian Wars and in the Revolution, balked at contributing their sons to the army for another invasion of Canada. They still believed that they should rely on their militia, not the regular army, for defense against the British. Dearborn never thought of defense.

From the outset, internal struggles over command and conflicts of interest plagued the American war effort. Dearborn, looking far older than his sixty years, weighed 250 pounds and had to be pulled on a trolley to mount his horse. After serving as secretary of war, he had trouble accepting orders from current secretary of war Eustis. Dearborn, called "Granny" by his men, a veteran Washington lobbyist, now found himself in Boston surrounded by manufacturers' agents trying to sell him equipment, uniforms, provisions and war matériel. He also attracted would-be officers, making it his first duty to form "a list of nominations of officers for several states." Colonel Winfield Scott, a young regular army officer observing the process, described the applicants as "swaggerers, dependents, decayed gentlemen and others fit for nothing else." Scott's opinion of Dearborn, his future commanding general, was little higher: "Old, vain, respectable and incapable." As Dearborn burned through hundreds of thousands of dollars outfitting an army, he was reluctant to delegate authority to subordinates. Officers could not spend more than fifty dollars without his written approval. At remote camps and bases, requisitions for rations and medical supplies had to pass over primitive roads in both directions.[11]

Conflicts of another kind soon surfaced. When fur merchant John Jacob Astor learned from his close friend Secretary of the Treasury Gallatin that war was imminent, he immediately dispatched a mounted courier, James Vosburgh, to the New York–Canadian frontier to warn his Canadian partners to send south across the border large quantities of furs, including a shipment of wolf furs for which he had already paid, before they could be seized by the British government as prizes of war. Avoiding Fort Niagara, Vosburgh crossed instead to Queenston, in Upper Canada, and delivered his message to Thomas Clark, one of Astor's Canadian partners. In addition to being a prominent merchant, he was also a crown magistrate. Clark performed his duty as a loyal British subject and immediately informed the forty-two-year-old Brigadier General Isaac Brock, the lieutenant governor of Upper Canada.

After sending Vosburgh, Astor obtained a letter from Gallatin to the Treasury secretary's friend, Peter Sailly, collector of customs at Plattsburgh, New York, twenty miles south of the border, instructing him how to handle Astor as he brought his furs and other property across. Astor, traveling from Washington by carriage, canoe and sloop, personally carried the letter to Plattsburgh by July 2, barely two weeks after the declaration

of war. While his agent, Auguste l'Herbette, hurried to Montreal to obtain a passport—the round trip took just four days—Astor left for Canada. Sailly would write to Gallatin that he doubted the British government
in Canada would allow Astor to bring out his furs but, if it did, he would
see to it that there was no obstruction at the border. All that Sailly asked
was that Astor give him advance notice of any shipment and "surrender"
it to him temporarily. He would place the furs in storage on the New
York side. Then Astor or his agent would present him with a legal claim
to the pelts, pay a small "administrative" fee, and Sailly would release
them.

Astor next arranged for another old friend, Pliny Moore, an innkeeper,
to "lodge the information in time" with Sailly. Moore expected no payment for his services or for forwarding Astor's letters to Canada, but from
time to time Astor sent him gifts of cigars or books for his wife and
daughters. On July 9, within a week of arriving on the frontier, Astor
asked Moore to notify Sailly of the first shipment. Across the border from
his Canadian partners came twenty-seven bales of furs, some 2,693 skins,
mostly wolf. Over Lake Champlain to Burlington, Vermont, the bundles
sped to tavern owner Gideon King—known as the Admiral of the Lake
because he controlled virtually all of its shipping and docks—then on to
New York City, where they were placed in storage under the watchful eye of
Deputy Customs Collector Benjamin Graves until Astor could personally
claim them.[12]

Returning to New York City, Astor fretted about furs he'd left behind
in Canada. On November 3, nearly five months into the war, Astor wrote
Moore to notify Sailly that l'Herbette was bringing across another large
shipment to store temporarily in Plattsburgh. An even larger trove of pelts
soon arrived at the border, where Sailly impounded 20,380 marten, 46 bear,
18,000 muskrat, 525 fisher, 6,021 otter, 3,389 mink, 2,048 fox, 271 cat and
6 wolf skins, estimated to be worth $50,000. Disregarding Astor's instruc-
tions, Sailly sent the shipment on to New York escorted by a customs inspector. Three months later, in February 1813, Astor's agent l'Herbette
was back in Canada to fetch 5,214 pounds of dressed beaver coating, 4,517
mink, 32 beaver, 102 otter, 35 fisher, 60 lynx, 5 fox, 9 wolf, 6 deer and 1,490
muskrat, again accompanied to New York City by a customs inspector.
More than a year into the war, as fierce fighting flared on three Canadian

fronts, Astor would send his nephew George to Montreal. This time, 221 bales, 9 puncheons and 1 barrel of skins came over the border. Sailly, by now suspected of taking bribes, received five hundred dollars "in lew of any claim" and released all the furs to young Astor.[13]

Astor did not allow politics to interfere with business: he remained a staunchly pro-war Democratic-Republican. Indeed, profitable trading with the enemy may have contributed to the ability of America's first multimillionaire to provide massive loans to the American government, without which Madison's war efforts arguably would have collapsed. For the moment, General Brock, a twenty-five-year British army veteran who had fought in India, promptly seized all American visitors and goods on the Canadian side. Astor's courier, Vosburgh, returned to the American side to an angry reception at Fort Niagara, where he was accused of being a courier for the British minister Augustus Foster and jailed. Eventually he would escape trial, since it was not a crime to pass commercial information. He was no more guilty of treason than Astor, who would, like many American merchants again and again in the next three years, put loyalty to profits ahead of any qualm about allegiance to the United States.

DEPRIVING THE AMERICANS of any advantage of first declaring war, General Brock turned Astor's self-serving intelligence to Britain's military advantage. His orders dictated a defensive strategy to minimize British forces needed in North America. Governor-General Sir George Prevost was keeping most of these forces close to him at the fortress city of Quebec, the capital of British North America. Prevost believed his best strategy was to divide Americans. A British offensive would discredit the Federalist, pro-English opposition party in the northern United States and unite Americans against England. Brock, with only 1,200 British troops to protect Upper Canada's 80,000 settlers, saw little hope of defending the vast province—today's Ontario—without the help of a large number of Indians. He doubted, he told Prevost, that he could rely on many settlers for defense, so strong was pro-American sentiment running: "My situation is most critical, not from anything the enemy can do, but from the disposition of the people—the population, believe me—is essentially bad—a full belief possesses them all that this Province must inevitably succumb—this prepossession is fatal to every exertion."

After learning of the American declaration of war, Prevost wrote pointedly to Brock "to avoid every measure which can have the least tendency to unite the people of America, [because] whilst disunion prevails among them, their attempts on British American Provinces will be feeble." But Brock, ordered to refrain from attacking the undermanned, dilapidated American ruins of Fort Niagara, decided to finesse his orders. He told himself his orders didn't apply farther to the west. He passed along a suggestion to Captain Charles Roberts, in command of a small garrison at Fort St. Joseph.[14]

Only a few American forts defended the entire Northwest frontier. Little defense existed west of the Maumee River, which flowed northeast 175 miles from Fort Wayne to Toledo at the western end of Lake Erie, or west of the Wabash River, which flowed southwest 475 miles from Fort Recovery, Ohio, through Indiana to the Ohio River. Only small contingents of U.S. Army regulars, from 50 to 120 men, garrisoned Detroit, Fort Wayne, Fort Harrison (Terre Haute), Fort Dearborn (Chicago) and Fort Michilimackinac.

Virtually no American navy existed on the Great Lakes. Madison seemed to have no inkling how crucial the ability to move troops was. The only American warships were the six-gun *Adams,* a twelve-year-old, barely serviceable army transport based at Detroit, and the sixteen-gun brig *Oneida* at Oswego on Lake Ontario, stationed there to enforce Jefferson's embargo. By contrast, the Canadian Provincial Marine boasted the sixteen-gun *Queen Charlotte,* the twelve-gun *Hunter* and the twelve-gun *Lady Prevost* on Lake Erie and the twenty-two-gun *Royal George,* the eighteen-gun *Earl of Moira,* the fourteen-gun armed schooner *Duke of Gloucester* and the newly launched eighteen-gun *Prince Regent* on Lake Ontario. Controlling the lakes, the British were able to use a workhorse armada of 190 bateaux—flat-bottomed river craft from twenty-four to forty feet long—to ferry men, guns and supplies between Montreal and Fort Malden, their bastion at Amherstburg, five miles from the mouth of the Detroit River.

The narrow Straits of Mackinac link Lake Huron and Lake Michigan. Fifty miles to the east, the St. Mary's River dumps the overflow from Lake Superior into Lake Huron. The British had clung to their control of this strategic intersection of waterways and the fur trade with surrounding

Indian tribes from a small fort on Mackinac Island, at the eastern end of the straits, until, by the terms of the Jay Treaty of 1795, they were forced to turn the strongpoint over to the Americans and establish a new fort on St. Joseph's Island in Upper Canada, near the mouth of the St. Mary's River. When Brock heard that war had been declared, he sent canoes racing westward to notify British outposts. At Fort St. Joseph, Captain Roberts recognized the strategic importance of Brock's intelligence and rapidly organized an attack on Fort Mackinac.

Seizing John Jacob Astor's eighty-six-ton fur-trading brig *Caledonia*, Roberts hauled aboard two brass six-pounders. On July 12, with forty-five British Regulars and two hundred Canadian militia—many of them fur traders—Roberts embarked for Mackinac Island, forty miles to the west, in small boats accompanied by four hundred Indians—Sioux, Chippewas, Winnebagos, Menominees and Ottawas—in war canoes. Early on the morning of July 17, Roberts's forces landed on the island, taking the small American garrison completely by surprise. Lieutenant Porter Hanks awoke to see cannon pointing toward him from a hill overlooking the fort. In the darkness, the British and Indians had surrounded the fort. Captain Hanks and the sixty-one-man garrison of U.S. Army regulars now received their first hint that they were at war. The British commander understood that his best weapon was the Americans' terror of scalping. At his signal, his Indian allies revealed themselves and, as one American soldier would never forget, "discharged their pieces in the air & kept up a most hideous yelling." Captain Roberts warned Captain Hanks that if he did not surrender, Roberts would set the fort afire and "that if a single Indian should be killed before the Fort, it would be impossible to protect [the Americans] from their fury & thirst for blood."[15]

Unprepared to defend his post and fearing that resistance would only provoke a massacre, Hanks surrendered the key to the entire Upper Midwest—the fort, along with four privately owned schooners—without firing a single shot. Paroling the Americans, Roberts packed them off to Detroit on two vessels. Inside the fort, the British discovered great bundles of furs, stored for eventual shipment by Astor's South West Company. Later, Astor arranged with his old friend Governor-General Prevost to send a ship to retrieve his goods. But the United States, despite determined efforts, could not retake the strategic fort until the war's end. The signal

British victory persuaded Tecumseh and thousands of his Indian confederates to cast their lot with the British.

While Brock rushed timely intelligence west to Roberts, Dearborn, still ensconced in Boston, delayed the coordinated three-pronged invasion of Canada that was to guarantee a swift victory and a short war. Querulous, obese and sluggish, Dearborn was anything but an inspiring leader. As the nation girded for war, he made excuses to Dolley Madison, who passed them along to the president: "Genl. Dearborn has had a fall which, tho not serious, confines him to his house." Convalescing ever so slowly, Dearborn was nonetheless busy, indulging his fantasy that a Federalist plot was afoot. His friend, Elbridge Gerry, had told Dearborn that the Federalists were planning the "secession of the Northern states and the erection over them of a Hanoverian monarchy. . . . If we do not kill them, they will kill us. . . . By war, we should be purified, as by fire."[16]

In frustration, Secretary of State Monroe wrote Dearborn, imploring him to drag himself out of bed, leave Boston and its partisan warfare, hurry to Albany and launch the invasion. "The blow must be struck," Monroe wrote. "Congress must not meet without a victory to announce them." Unmoved, Dearborn wrote back that he first had to make sure that New England was safeguarded in case the Federalists "effect a serious and open revolt."[17]

When Dearborn finally arrived in the Hudson Valley more than two weeks after the fall of Fort Mackinac, he encamped at Greenbush, near Albany. He probably learned about the debacle in Michigan from Colonel Edward Baynes, the British adjutant general in Canada, who arrived under a flag of truce. Prevost had just learned from London that the Privy Council had rescinded the inflammatory 1807 Orders in Council. On his own initiative, without awaiting instructions from London, Prevost proposed an armistice, allowing both sides to exchange diplomatic messages. Prevost wanted time to ascertain whether the British policy reversal could still avert war. Dearborn could not have known that behind the seeming British change of heart was the fact that, at that very moment, Napoleon was unleashing his long-expected invasion of Britain's ally, Russia, with an enormous army of 600,000 men. Britain could ill afford a war on another front that would drain their forces from the Continent. Unwilling and ill prepared to invade Canada, Dearborn took it upon himself to sign an armistice agreement on August 9 without forwarding it to Washington, apparently expecting Madison's concurrence.

Dearborn then sent a courier to western New York to General Van Rensselaer, who was preparing to cross over to attack Upper Canada along the Niagara frontier. Dearborn did not deem it necessary to extend the same courtesy to his perceived rival for command of American forces, General Hull. Dearborn would later assert that he was unsure his jurisdiction extended as far west as Detroit.

By this time, the military governor of Michigan had already crossed his Rubicon, the Detroit River. Leaving Washington early in April, Hull raised 1,200 Ohio militiamen, organizing them into three regiments—each one commanded by a Madison appointee with no military experience—to augment the 400 regulars of the 4th Infantry, veterans of Tippecanoe. From the outset, Hull's force, the largest military force so far assembled on either side, was hampered by tensions between militia and regular officers who bickered over precedence in rank, and these strains were exacerbated by a shared disbelief in their leader's capabilities.

At fifty-nine and considered far too old for the rigors of a frontier command, Hull also suffered from the aftereffects of a stroke he had concealed from Madison. One officer characterized Hull as a "short, silver-haired, corpulent, good natured old gentleman who bore the marks of good eating and drinking." Before leaving Cincinnati, with his regiments drawn up on parade for a full-dress review, Hull lost control of his horse, his stirrups, his hat and his balance, and he clutched at the horse's mane as it bolted across the front of his army.

Mustering his inexperienced, undisciplined troops, Hull further inspired them with a slurred speech. They were about to march "through a wilderness memorable for savage barbarity" and would tread "ground stained with the blood of your fellow-citizens" as they slogged west toward Detroit. Originally, Hull planned to follow a water route—up the Auglaize River to Fort Defiance, then along the Maumee River to Miami of the Rapids and the northwestern shore of Lake Erie—but water levels were too low for loaded boats. Instead, he gathered his forces at Dayton and marched them to Urbana. From there, his troops hacked a two-hundred-mile road through dense forest, creeks and swamps, building blockhouses along the way. By garrisoning soldiers as he went, he steadily weakened his main force.[18]

Heavy rains and the necessity of traversing the vast mosquito- and blackfly-infested Black Swamp slowed the makeshift army's progress. On June 26, Hull received orders from Secretary of War Eustis, dated June 18, urging him to hurry along to Detroit but not mentioning that war had been declared that day. To expedite his march, Hull chartered the *Cuyahoga* packet boat and placed aboard her most of his heavy baggage, sick soldiers and personal papers, including his secret orders. Two weeks later, as the schooner's unsuspecting American captain attempted to sail past Fort Malden, the Provincial Marine's twelve-gun *Hunter* easily captured her. Lieutenant Colonel Thomas Bligh St. George, in command, realized the importance of Hull's documents and rushed them to General Brock, who now knew not only the American strategy and Hull's detailed plans but also the low morale of his officers, revealed in undelivered letters home.

After a six-week slog from Cincinnati, Hull's exhausted army reached Detroit. The muddy, palisaded frontier town consisted of 150 houses, its waterfront lined with pelt-crammed warehouses employing most of the 770 civilians protected by 120 regulars. Fort Detroit scowled down on the ramshackle settlement from the brow of a hill.

On July 12, Hull ordered a small detachment to cross the Detroit River, setting in motion the first American incursion into Canada of the war. Colonel Lewis Cass, leading the understrength 3rd Ohio Regiment, quickly established a beachhead, occupying the village of Sandwich (now Windsor) without resistance. Its inhabitants fled. Cass, a classmate of Daniel Webster at Phillips Exeter Academy, had moved at age eighteen to Ohio to clerk in the law office of the governor and subsequently entered politics. Jefferson rewarded Cass's staunch support of the Democratic-Republicans by appointing him the U.S. marshal for Ohio. He had no previous combat experience. Once inside Canada, the enterprising Cass, receiving no further orders from Hull, marched on, winning two skirmishes and seizing a key bridge, bringing his regiment within four miles of Fort Malden, the target of the entire campaign.

By this time Hull, still unaware of the armistice, had every reason to believe that Dearborn had already launched his attack on Lower Canada and, marching toward Montreal, would have drawn off considerable British strength, making reinforcement of Fort Malden impossible. Hull did not know that the expected diversionary attack in his favor had been delayed. Dearborn had not bothered to inform Hull of the armistice he had signed. Dearborn had unwittingly given Brock time to rush reinforcements west to face Hull.

On July 13 Hull issued a proclamation promising to liberate Canadians from English "tyranny" if they stayed at home and did not take up arms with the British and their Indian allies: "Raise not your hands against your brethren. Many of your Fathers fought for the freedom & Independence we now enjoy. . . . You will be emancipated from Tyranny and oppression and restored to the dignified station of freemen."[19]

Hull failed to mention that if they were later captured by the British, they would be hanged as deserters as well as traitors to their new land. His vainglorious proclamation succeeded in weakening British defenders by persuading five hundred Canadian militia, many of them recent immigrants from the United States, to desert. The province had been settled by Loyalist refugees after the American Revolution, but by 1812 roughly 60 percent of the settlers had emigrated from New York, where land had become far more expensive. After a recent visit to the region, Mayor DeWitt Clinton of New York City had reported that "[a] great majority of the people prefer the American government, and on the firing of the first gun would unite their destinies with ours. . . . The Irish and emigrants from the United States are opposed to the Scotch, who have monopolized the government."[20]

The American force by now outnumbered the British two to one, yet Hull did little more than fortify a camp on Canadian soil; he issued no further orders, nor did he drill his men, or practice with his two cannon on the pretext of waiting for more supplies from Ohio. The supply train was still forty miles away at the Maumee River, being harassed by Tecumseh's warriors. Fearing that more and more Indians were joining the British and that he would soon be surrounded, Hull talked of abandoning Detroit and retreating to the Maumee. Astounded, Colonel Cass warned Hull that if he did retreat, all the Ohio militiamen would go home.

Finally receiving official notice of a state of war, Hull also learned that Dearborn had postponed the American attack farther to the east. Hull dispatched fully one-third of his 1,800 effectives, including 200 regulars with cavalry and artillery support to escort the vital supply train into Detroit. Fourteen miles south of Detroit, at the Indian village of Maguaga, a mixed force of 250 British regulars, Canadian militia and Tecumseh's Indians had attacked and routed the relief column, leaving 17 soldiers dead and scalped. The battered relief force managed to drive the British and Indians back across the river to Canada, but then it retreated to Detroit without linking up with the detachment Hull had sent toward Ohio to fetch the supplies. Panicking, Hull ordered Cass and his Ohioans back across the river to protect Detroit, disregarding Cass's warning that if he did retreat, the Ohio militia would go home.

As his officers threatened to mutiny, Hull sent his more outspoken critics to rendezvous with the supply column. No sooner had he seen off the troublesome Ohioans than he learned that Brock, reinforced, was approaching Fort Malden. Hull called his men back. "Instead of having an energetic commander," complained Colonel Cass, "we have a weak old man."[21]

During the brief American incursion into Canada, Hull, angry at the British for seizing his personal property and papers, allowed his troops to loot Sandwich. Tearing down fences and cutting down fruit trees to build barracks and campfires, some of his mounted troops plundered sheep, blankets, flour and boats. In the process, Hull gave Brock the propaganda weapon he needed to galvanize support among wavering Canadians against the invaders.

Deciding to cast his lot with Brock, Tecumseh now persuaded the Wyandot, southern neighbors of Detroit, to abandon their neutrality and withdraw their families and cattle at night to the Canadian side of the river. Severing Hull's supply line to Ohio on August 5, Tecumseh, in an ambush, routed the convoy's American guards, killing seventeen and staking them to the ground beside long poles from which their scalps fluttered in the breeze.

When Lieutenant Hanks arrived and confirmed the capitulation of Fort Mackinac, Hull panicked. Without calling the requisite council of war to consult with his officers or advising his detachments in the field, Hull and the main American force crossed back over the river on the night of August 7 and crowded into the stockade at Detroit, abandoning the erstwhile Canadian militiamen. "We have wholly left the Canadian shore and have abandoned the miserable inhabitants who depended on our will and power to protect them, to their fate," reported Colonel Cass.[22]

By his brief, inept incursion into Canada, Hull made it possible for Brock to ignore instructions from Prevost to remain on the defensive and to take advantage of Hull's intercepted plans. In mailbags seized by Tecumseh's warriors, Brock read again how demoralized the American officers had become. Now that the grain harvest was finished and the farmers had brought in their crops, Brock had no trouble recruiting stoutly Loyalist volunteers from York and Newark (present-day Niagara-on-the-lake) who resented their former countrymen's plundering. In early August, Brock led them west in open boats along the north shore of Lake Erie to Amherstburg. Under cover of a bombardment from ships and gunboats, Brock crossed into the United States just south of Detroit with 1,925 men, including 600 of Tecumseh's warriors.

Inside overcrowded Detroit, many of Hull's 2,500-man force had become ill and unfit for duty. As Indians began raiding farms around the fort, 600 Michigan volunteers slipped away to defend their homes. Hull could not stop worrying about the women and children, his daughter and his grandchildren among them, and the thought that they would be scalped if he held out.

On August 15 Brock ordered the Provincial Marine's *Hunter* and *Queen Charlotte* upriver directly in front of the fort. Shore batteries Brock had placed at Sandwich, directly opposite Detroit, opened fire; Hull's thirty-three iron and brass artillery pieces responded. In the ensuing artillery duel, shells rained down on Detroit. Panic-stricken civilians—and General Hull—sought shelter. One cannonball scored a direct hit on the officers' mess, dismembering three men and cutting in half Lieutenant Porter Hanks, ending his ordeal of awaiting court martial for surrendering Fort Mackinac. An officer's wife, Lydia Bacon, wrote in her journal that "bombs, shells & balls were flying in all directions." The barrage completely unnerved Hull, one officer recalled. "His lips [were] quivering, the tobacco juice running from the sides of his mouth upon the frills of his shirt." Unable to rally his troops, Hull crouched in a bomb shelter, drinking heavily.[23]

Under cover of the shelling, Tecumseh and his warriors silently crossed the river at night. Before dawn, Brock and 750 regulars also made the crossing, bringing five fieldpieces with them. By now investing the fortified town, Brock was rendering irrelevant Prevost's order not to provoke a confrontation. Moreover, he had no express authority to invade the United States. And it is arguable whether he was unaware of an armistice.

Collaborating in a ruse suggested by Tecumseh, Brock now arranged for an Indian scout to be captured by the Americans, planting the false information that 5,000 Indians were on their way from the lakes to the north to reinforce Tecumseh. To make the lie credible, Tecumseh went with his men into the nearby woods and marched them single file past a small convoy of Americans under Captain Henry Brush. Then Tecumseh took his warriors back through the woods and marched them by a second time, then a third. The trick worked. Hull believed that Brock's reinforcements had arrived.

Informed that Brock was landing just south of Detroit, Hull made no effort to oppose him. He simply ordered his men to stay inside the fort. Later that day, Brock sent a courier with a letter under flag of truce to summon Hull to surrender: "It is far from my intention to join in a war of extermination, but you must be aware, that the numerous body of Indians who have attached themselves to my troops, will be beyond control the moment the contest commences." Huddling in a corner, Hull seemed transfixed by the vision of his daughter and granddaughters "bleeding under the Tomahawk of a Savage."[24]

As if he needed to intimidate Hull further, Brock paraded Tecumseh's hallooing warriors, stripped and painted, "some covered with vermillion, others with blue clay, and still others tattooed in black and white from head to foot," around the stockade. One observer noted that "the terrific din was increased by the howls of the savages." French Canadians in the Detroit militia fled to join Brock rather than face the Indians. As Brock's forces advanced closer to the fort's gates, Hull ordered his gunners to hold their fire and hoist a white flag over the fort. Without consulting his officers, Hull accepted Brock's terms, surrendering the entire Army of the North West, including the five hundred men in detachments miles away, and all of Michigan Territory.[25]

By daring and bluff, Brock had scored an important victory. In the ensuing pandemonium, neither side could quite comprehend that the largest American army in the field, some 2,500 regulars and militiamen, had capitulated to an inferior force made up mostly of militia, sailors, Indians and fewer than four hundred regulars. In the confusion, jubilant Indians

rode through the streets in captured carriages and on stolen horses, hallooing and shouting all the next day as they broke into houses and plundered them. Hull would later plead at his court-martial that he was short
of ammunition and had enough provisions for only a few days, but Brock
inventoried 5,000 pounds of gunpowder, enough rations for the whole
populace and garrison for more than a month, 2,500 muskets and thirty-
three cannon that had been seized by the Americans from the British
in the Revolutionary War. The victors renamed the *Adams*, a six-gun brig
they found tied up at the waterfront, the *Detroit*. Of the troops Hull surrendered, Brock paroled the Michigan militia and sent home the 1,600
Ohio volunteers, but he shipped Hull, his officers and 582 regulars off to
prison in Quebec. Triumphant, Brock now had the weapons he needed to
defend Upper Canada.

PRESIDENT MADISON AND Dolley were driving home for summer vacation on their plantation in Orange County, Virginia, escaping the stifling
heat and humidity of Washington, when a courier overtook them with a
message from the secretary of war, informing Madison of the fall of Detroit. In the midst of a contested presidential election, Madison knew the
political ramifications of Hull's capitulation. Turning around and returning to the White House, he and his aides orchestrated a campaign of placing the blame solely on Hull. When Colonel Cass sent him a report of
Hull's surrender, it appeared in full in the *National Intelligencer*. Jefferson
joined the chorus of condemnation: "The treachery of Hull, like that of
Arnold, cannot be a matter of blame to our government." Monroe characterized Hull as "weak, indecisive, and pusillanimous."[26]

The collapse of the western American army left the northern army,
clustered at Burlington, Vermont, and Plattsburgh, New York, on opposite shores of Lake Champlain forty miles south of the border, as the only
barrier to a British counterattack. Intended for a swift advance into Quebec Province and on to Montreal before winter, they remained woefully
unprepared. Governor Daniel Tompkins of New York blamed Secretary of
War Eustis for the slow pace of events in this theater of war. On September 9, Tompkins sent a courier from Albany to Washington to complain
to Eustis that the northern army had received very little money and had
already run through it:

Of the 50,000 dollars which were sent to me from your Department, 42,500 have been paid by the District Paymaster and a large sum beyond the balance has been advanced to the Quartermaster General of the State and this State and his deputies for Barracks, Camp equipage and other articles of the frontier militia . . . and to the Commanding Officers. . . . Volunteers have received an advance of two months' pay and Sixteen dollars on Account of cloathing. That part of the detachment of 100,000 men ordered into service after the declaration are in great need of pay and indeed suffering for it. . . . The militia of Plattsburg have as yet received nothing.[27]

After a brief confinement in Canada, Hull received an officer's parole of honor from Prevost, allowing him to return to the United States so long as he did not fight again until he was formally exchanged for a British captive of equal rank. On September 13 Hull reached the American camp at Plattsburgh en route to Washington and his attempt to exculpate his disastrous command. Militia officer Calvin Everest, after listening to Hull's lament, wrote to his friend, Daniel Russel. He described Hull's arrival "from Montreal on Saturday last with his aidecamp [sic] and three soldiers that are out on parole of honor." Recounting his version of events to anyone who would listen, Hull

state[s] that he lost two hundred and fifty Men in the Engagement and all Communication was cut off and his provisions and ammunition quite Exhausted and Surrounded by three times his Numbers and no practicability of obtaining reinforcements his troops Naked for Clothing destitute of Money He must have Surrendered or Suffered his whole Army to be Massacred by the Savages his militia were Suffered to return home by Swearing not to take up arms during the war. Seven hundred of his Regular troops remain Prisoners of War in Montreal.[28]

Hull was to be court-martialed, but he was not put on trial until the beginning of 1814. Dearborn, the very man who had failed to inform Hull of the armistice, chaired the court-martial. Accused of treason by a young prosecuting judge advocate, Martin Van Buren, Hull was convicted, after a three-month trial, of cowardice and neglect of duty and condemned to death by firing squad. Hull became the only American general ever sentenced to death. President Madison commuted the sentence and cashiered Hull from the army.

In his own defense, Hull blamed the debacle on Dearborn for having failed to draw off the British by simultaneously attacking in the East, instead allowing them to concentrate their forces against him. Dearborn recommended clemency to Madison because of Hull's advanced age and exemplary Revolutionary War service. Neither the court-martial nor Madison accepted Hull's defense—that he was trying to save the lives of women and children.

When news of Hull's capitulation reached London, William Franklin, the illegitimate son of Benjamin Franklin, gathered up his papers and ventured out into the cold dampness. At eighty-one and suffering from angina pectoris, the last royal governor of New Jersey and president of the Board of Associated Loyalists had left America with the defeated British army. Before the Revolution, he and his father had organized a land company that would have given the Franklins, leading Philadelphia merchants and several members of Parliament a grant of roughly 20 million acres loosely coinciding with the modern American Midwest. They expected to become fabulously wealthy when the American Revolution ended, but the 1783 Treaty of Paris, primarily negotiated by Benjamin Franklin, subsumed the lands in the independent United States. They became known as the Old Northwest.

Now that Britain had recaptured much of this land, William Franklin's expectations matched those of thousands of other Loyalists who had fled into exile in Canada, England and Bermuda. They now expected the British government to restore to them their pre-Revolutionary wealth and status. The octogenarian ex-governor had never doubted that he would someday, at last, receive his share of the Illinois Company charter lands, roughly 222,000 acres. Ignoring the cold, his health and his wife, Governor Franklin, as he was still known in London, set off as fast as he could to the American consulate to present his papers and to make a sworn deposition.

He must have been happy, feeling vindicated that events seemed to be proving that he had, after all, chosen the victorious side in the protracted American Revolution. Soon, he was certain, he would be justly rewarded for the thirty-six years of suffering and ostracism since his arrest by New Jersey revolutionaries as his father had stood by. He had insisted on upholding his oath of office, conferred on him personally by King George III, to serve loyally, as his coat of arms pledged, "for king and country."

A few weeks later, felled by pneumonia, William Franklin died.[29]

BEFORE HE SURRENDERED Detroit, Hull ordered Fort Dearborn in Chicago evacuated because, after the fall of Fort Mackinac, he considered its defense impossible. Situated on the bank of the Chicago River and garrisoned by sixty-five regulars and militia under the command of Captain Nathan Heald, the well-stocked fort also housed nine women and eighteen children. Guarded by two blockhouses, it was more a trading post for merchants, who traveled in schooners from Lake Erie through Lakes Huron and Michigan, then a military stronghold. Almost everyone opposed leaving, but Captain Heald was determined to carry out Hull's order. Pouring the fort's liquor supply into the river and destroying surplus arms and ammunition, he led the march out of the fort, supposedly under the protection of five hundred Potawatomi, on August 15, the day of the British attack on Detroit.

By now the Indians were aware of British victory at Michilimackinac. Two miles south of the fort, after surrender terms had been worked out, four hundred hostile Potawatomi and Winnebagos attacked the column, killing twenty-six regulars, all the militia, two women and twelve children—fifty evacuees in all. Blackbird, the Potawatomi chief, protected the survivors. Some later escaped, and British officers who burned Fort Dearborn ransomed a few others. The massacre, occurring two days after the fall of Detroit and soon after the fall of Fort Mackinac, persuaded the Indians of the Upper Mississippi and Missouri regions to join the swelling ranks of the alliance between Tecumseh and the British.

IN THE FIRST season of frontier warfare, Americans learned of only one success: by the twenty-eight-year-old Virginia-born Zachary Taylor, a cousin of President Madison and a veteran of Indian warfare. Short, barrel-chested and gray-eyed, Taylor had trailed along with Harrison on the Prophetstown attack and was left behind with only fifty men to hold Fort Harrison. With his company of militia and a few civilians, he had held out during a relentless three-day attack by Tecumseh and four hundred warriors in early September. Tecumseh knew the fort all too well from confrontations with Harrison but not well enough to pry out young Taylor. One of Tecumseh's few defeats became the first of many victories for the future Mexican War hero and twelfth president—and the first American triumph on land of the War of 1812. Taylor's victory offered small consolation for American defeats in the first season of war. The fall of Detroit, the most important post west of the Alleghenies along with Forts Dearborn and Mackinac, left the entire Old Northwest exposed to enemy attack.

As soon as he could reinforce his namesake fort, Harrison, prudently deciding not to try to retake Detroit at once, made it his base from which, in the autumn, he raided and destroyed Indian villages and provisions. Madison wanted to replace Harrison with a regular army officer, General James Winchester, but frontier leaders preferred the hero of Tippecanoe, and Kentucky promoted Harrison to major general of its militia. Finally, under intense political pressure, Secretary of War Eustis gave Harrison command over the entire western theater. He spent that autumn building up an army and consuming money and supplies at an astonishing rate, intending to eliminate all hostile Indians from the region and retake Detroit, but an early winter interfered with his plans.

HARRISON COULD NOT expect any reinforcements from the East. All available American forces had massed on the Canadian frontier for a major assault across the Niagara River into Canada. Secretary of War Eustis had decided to allow the Democratic-Republican governor of New York, Daniel D. Tompkins, to decide who should take charge of the offensive since it was based on New York soil. A Jeffersonian career politician, Tompkins had toured the state's fortifications and knew that Buffalo and the Niagara frontier were especially vulnerable to British attack. Hoping to win over other wealthy Federalists, he placed the militia under the command of Major General Stephen Van Rensselaer, a wealthy Federalist with no military experience. He was to share his command with a regular army officer, General Alexander Smyth, an armchair general who had written a pamphlet on field maneuvering but also lacked actual combat experience and refused to accept Van Rensselaer's authority.

By October, Van Rensselaer had amassed 6,000 troops at Lewistown, New York, who faced 2,000 British across the fast-moving Niagara River. Van Rensselaer's plan was to take the Queenston Heights on the Canadian peninsula while Smyth made a diversionary assault on Fort George, six miles to the north. Smyth refused to cooperate. Even without Smyth, Van Rensselaer decided to make his amphibious attack on October 11, but an army officer disappeared down the river with all the oars.

At 3 a.m. on October 13 the advance force of three hundred militia under Colonel Solomon Van Rensselaer and three hundred regulars under Lieutenant Colonel John Chrystie pushed off in the dark in thirteen boats. Three boats, including Chrystie's, ran afoul of swirling eddies and were carried downstream. The British, on a cliff overhanging the river, heard the Americans coming and opened fire from several directions. Captain James Dennis's grenadiers scaled halfway down the steep cliff, firing with deadly accuracy. Six bullets struck Colonel Van Rensselaer, leaving him unconscious. The two hundred Americans who had made their way ashore sent the boats back for reinforcements and sought cover. Taking charge, Captain John E. Wool, himself shot in the thigh, led his militia company off the riverbank and up to the base of Queenston Heights. One of his men, Lieutenant John Gansevoort, knew of a rarely used fisherman's path leading up the steep escarpment. Leaving a hundred of his men to distract Dennis's grenadiers, Wool led 240 men up three-hundred-foot cliffs to the edge of Queenston, where the British had positioned an eighteen-pounder.

Taken completely by surprise, General Brock had instead expected the Americans to attack Fort George. He raced the six miles to Queenston on his black horse and made his way directly to the artillery battery, arriving at dawn to see Wool and his men storming the battery, forcing the artillerists to spike the gun and flee. At once, Brock regrouped his troops and ordered them to retake the gun. After Wool beat back two charges, Brock, a tall officer in a red tunic, was shot in the chest and died instantly. His demoralized troops retreated upriver.

As Wool and other wounded Americans were ferried back over the river, Lieutenant Colonel Winfield Scott took command and awaited reinforcements. But the sight of so many bloodied men was too much for the New York militia. They refused to cross the river, refused to fight on foreign soil. After Scott and his men fended off Indians for an hour, a British counterattack organized by Major General Roger Sheaffe finally drove the men back down the escarpment to the river's edge. There they were forced to surrender in sight of Van Rensselaer's army, and they were transported to Quebec as prisoners of war. The second American attempt to take Canada had failed dismally.

What was to have been the most important element of the American campaign of 1812 was the invasion of Lower Canada—today's Quebec Province—and capture of Montreal. In September, substantial numbers of regulars began to arrive in Plattsburgh and Burlington, the advance bases straddling Lake Champlain. They were put under the command of Brigadier General Joseph Bloomfield, another fifty-nine-year-old veteran of the Revolutionary War, who had held no rank above major. A Federalist and two-term governor of New Jersey, he had been rewarded by Madison with high rank to win federal support. Most of his command obligations would trickle down to his adjutant general, Colonel Zebulon Pike, head of the newly created 15th Regiment. Pike's troops carried the latest infantry weapons: their rifles were accurate at up to three hundred yards, more than thrice the effective range of even the most modern muskets developed at the Harpers Ferry, Virginia, armory. Each weapon had its drawbacks. A rifle took longer to load, at best thirty seconds, an eternity when facing a bayonet charge; the musket could be reloaded and fired in twenty seconds but was usually only fired in volleys at close range.

Pike's appearance on the northern front, leading six hundred regulars in an overland march from Albany, buoyed the morale of his men. Recruiting for service along the lakes had lagged, owing to the region's reputation for deadly "lake fever"—malaria—outbreaks every summer. Soon, however, volunteers began to arrive at Plattsburgh from New York and Vermont. Born in New Jersey into a military family, Pike had grown up on the Ohio frontier. Enlisting in the army at fifteen, he had served under General Anthony Wayne. By the time he became Dearborn's second in command, he was already famous for leading two expeditions of exploration through the Louisiana Purchase lands. In 1805 he received a commission in the Corps of Discovery to find the source of the Mississippi. Leaving St. Louis with twenty soldiers on a keelboat, he reached Little Falls, Minnesota, before camping for the winter. Turning back from his original assignment—the source of the river in Lake Itaska would not be discovered until

1820—Pike negotiated a treaty with the Sioux to acquire the site of present-day Minneapolis-St. Paul. In 1806, trekking to Colorado, he attempted to climb the peak now bearing his name. After exploring the headwaters of the Arkansas River, he next went on to the Rio Grande, where he built a log fort. There, Spanish authorities seized him as a spy and, after holding him briefly, released him. Nevertheless, promoted to lieutenant colonel, he trained the troops that had destroyed Tippecanoe.

Not until mid-November, the start of winter in the north country, did Dearborn take command of his 8,000-man army, the largest to take the field since the Revolutionary War, to begin the attack on Montreal. The ever-dilatory Dearborn arrived after Bloomfield had already issued the marching orders: "The US Troops & all the Vermont Militia will be at Champlain on Sunday the 17th & on the 18th Enter Canada." All tents and baggage were to be left in the two border towns. With six days' rations, the troops were to march north with only "what they carry on their backs."[30]

Teams of oxen had no sooner dragged the artillery to the border at Champlain when, again, New York militia refused to cross it, insisting that they were obligated only to fight on American soil. Few Canadians and even fewer British soldiers could be found. The palpable enemy was the advancing season. Dr. William Beaumont, surgeon of the 6th Regiment, described the Americans as "destitute of covering save a Blanket or two . . . lying upon the cold, wet ground, with only a fire before their tents, for two, three or four weeks."[31]

Dearborn finally sent a detachment of regulars five miles into Canada under Colonel Pike. They skirmished inconclusively with the British at the fork of the Richelieu and LaColle Rivers, shooting at each other in the dark. After a foot of wet, heavy snow fell on his troops, Dearborn decided to abandon the attack, ordering the entire army to retreat, intact. He turned over to Colonel Pike the task of building a sprawling cantonment of log cabins just south of Plattsburgh at the mouth of the Saranac River to shelter 4,000 men; an equal number were to be ferried across Lake Champlain to temporary barracks on a five-acre bluff in Burlington.

News of the aborted American invasion stunned Secretary of the Treasury Gallatin: "The series of misfortunes exceeds all anticipations made even by those who had least confidence in our inexperienced officers and undisciplined men." The Federalist press was less understanding: one Vermont editorialist fumed that the "blustering, bullying, mountain laboring campaign" ended in "an unbroken series of disaster, defeat, disgrace, and ruin and death."

In August, urging rejection of the armistice and peace negotiations, the Philadelphia *Aurora* had printed the supremely confident Jefferson's prediction of swift annexation of Canada. "The acquisition of Canada this year, as far as the neighborhood of Quebec, will be a mere matter of marching," the former president wrote to editor Duane, "and will give us experience for the attack of Halifax the next, and the final expulsion of England from the American continent." The nation's most influential newspaper now blamed Jefferson and his party's pinchpenny policies for the debacle: "The degraded state in which the military institutions have been retained comes now upon us with a dismal sentence of retribution." Back in August, three weeks after the fall of Detroit, President Madison had received from Britain official confirmation that the 1807 Orders in Council had finally been rescinded; with it came an offer to discuss a speedy end to hostilities. Had not the cause of the war vanished? No, argued Madison. There remained what he now insisted was the greatest cause of antipathy between the two nations. Until Britain abandoned its predatory practice of impressing Americans from American merchant ships, virtually shanghaiing them into brutal lifelong penury far from America on the king's ships, the war would go on. Receiving the armistice document Dearborn had signed, Madison rejected it outright.[32]

————— ∾ —————

TEN

"Purified as by Fire"

As reports of the dismal failure of Madison's Canadian strategy rever-
berated from the Midwest to Washington and to Europe, the president
had to seek reelection. He faced a formidable challenge from DeWitt Clinton, nephew of his own vice president, George Clinton. After graduating
from Columbia College and studying law, Clinton had served as private
secretary to his uncle, the longest-tenured governor in the United States.
Plunging into upstate New York real estate speculation and canal projects,
he married a wealthy Quaker heiress and entered politics.

Handsome and over six feet tall, Clinton handily won election to the
state assembly and, only a year later and still in his twenties, to the state
senate. As leader of the powerful state Council of Appointment, he dispensed patronage to as many as 15,000 jobseekers. Appointed to the U.S.
Senate, one year later he became mayor of New York, the nation's largest
city (population 85,000 by 1808), the busiest port and largest source of customs duties. Democratizing the city's politics, he introduced the secret
ballot, broadening the franchise to include renters.[1]

Clinton balanced his sympathy for destitute Irish immigrants with
concern for commercial interests suffering under Jefferson's embargo. Still

considered a Democratic-Republican, Clinton decided to oppose Madison's pro-war policies, holding himself out as the candidate of peace and prosperity. As bad news flooded in from the Midwest, the war became the central campaign issue. Many Federalists supported Clinton because they believed he would fight more effectively than Madison. Gouverneur Morris, his campaign manager, presented Clinton as the only hope for the maritime states to escape commercial ruin by the British navy. At one rally Morris even urged the northern states to secede from the Union if Madison were reelected. An experienced politician, he talked in antiwar regions of negotiating a settlement with England; in pro-war areas, he advocated a quick and decisive victory, leading one observer to comment, "In the West he was a friend of war . . . in the East, a friend of peace."[2]

When Vice President Clinton died in April, Madison chose firebrand Elbridge Gerry of Massachusetts as his running mate. Gerry delivered sorely needed electoral votes from Federalist New England and added incendiary rhetoric to the campaign. To the president, he wrote, "We should be purified, as by Fire."[3]

In New England's Federalist stronghold, the declaration of war provoked sharp remonstrance. Governor Caleb Strong of Massachusetts issued a proclamation declaring a public day of fasting, humiliation and prayer in answer to "Mr. Madison's War." Flags flew at half-mast and memorials from numerous towns appeared at the statehouse and in newspapers. The Massachusetts House of Representatives condemned the war by a margin of two to one. In an "Address to the People," it denounced war "against the nation from which we are descended." The assembly ruled against supporting volunteers "except for defensive war." When Dearborn urged Governor Strong to forward Massachusetts' militia, Strong flatly refused, taking the position that only he had the power to determine when an emergency warranted putting the state's militia under federal authority; since the Constitution limited such an emergency to a foreign invasion or domestic insurrection, Massachusetts' militia would be used only inside the commonwealth and under his direction.[4]

After the shocking news of Detroit's surrender, Connecticut's Assembly also condemned the war. Federalist governor Roger Griswold refused to furnish militia on the same grounds as Massachusetts. In New Hampshire, the Rockingham memorial, drafted by Daniel Webster, protested "hasty, rash, and ruinous measures" and made thinly veiled hints of seceding from the Union.[5]

When the Electoral College tallied the election results on December 3, 1812, five western states unsurprisingly had given all their votes to Madison, but he received only 90 votes from the original thirteen states. Clinton carried New York, New Jersey, Maryland and all of New England except Vermont. Apart from Pennsylvania and Vermont, no northern state favored the president's reelection. In a vote essentially for or against continuing the war, Clinton carried all the commercial centers while the once virtually defunct Federalists doubled their numbers in Congress. Madison won by the smallest margin of any Democratic-Republican. What saved the election for Madison was the one heartening piece of news that came in an otherwise disastrous first year of war.

If Madison had only antediluvian, inept former Revolutionary War army officers to command his inexperienced militias and anemic regiments of regulars, he had his choice of highly skilled, combat-seasoned young officers to lead seasoned professional sailors in what remained of the downsized U.S. Navy. After a dozen years of Democratic-Republican budget slashing and aversion to imposing taxes to defend its shore and merchant fleet, the United States had only sixteen ships in active service. Of these, the largest were five 44-gun and one 38-gun frigates, the rest sloops, brigs and other unrated vessels. The bulk of the Jefferson-era navy were sixty-four unseaworthy sloop- or schooner-rigged armed gunboats with one or two 24- or 32-pound long guns, little more than harbor patrol boats.

Of 651 battle-ready British warships, observed naval historian Ian Toll, "175 were ships-of-the-line, mounting at least 64 guns on two covered decks, any one of them able to overpower the largest American ship." While the Royal Navy's assets were spread around the world, guarding its imperial convoys and blockading French ports, even the relatively small North American station in the summer of 1812 boasted a 70-gun battleship, nine 38-gun frigates and twenty-seven unrated warships—and this was *before* reinforcements began to arrive from England in the autumn of 1812.

As if British numerical superiority were not enough of an advantage,

Americans had a hard time imagining themselves challenging absolute British rule of the waves. What Toll calls the "almost supernatural aura of invincibility" that the British exuded for the more than two centuries since they defeated the Spanish Armada in 1588 had become even stronger since Nelson's utter destruction of the combined French and Spanish fleets in a single day at Trafalgar in 1805.[6]

It was a closely guarded secret that the British Ministry had decided to maintain only a modest presence in North American waters. Napoleon was rebuilding his navy in the Mediterranean. The Royal Navy could spare no more ships to fight the Americans. In response to American demands for an alteration to Britain's policies of impressment, blockade and confiscation, the *London Evening Star* declared that England would never compromise its "proud preeminence which the blood and treasure of her sons have obtained for her among the nations, by a piece of striped bunting flying at the mastheads of a few fir-built frigates, manned by a handful of bastards and outlaws."[7]

Madison, his cabinet and leaders of Congress all feared the loss of their handful of fighting ships in a single engagement with the Royal Navy. Madison had bent to the argument that the American squadron—it certainly could not be called a fleet—should be kept safely in port. When they heard this argument, two senior naval captains confronted Secretary of the Navy Paul Hamilton—a bibulous rice planter and former governor of South Carolina—in his office in Washington. Hamilton confirmed that he planned to move all frigates into New York harbor and moor them as fixed artillery batteries to protect the nation's busiest port. Incredulous, Captains William Bainbridge and Charles Stewart, both veterans of the Barbary Wars, went down the street to the White House where they urged the president to send the frigates to sea. As Stewart recounted the meeting years later, they won Madison over. "It is victories we want," said Madison. "If you give us [victories] and lose your ships afterwards, they can be replaced."[8]

Bainbridge and Stewart argued that the frigates should be deployed as commerce-raiders. But where and how? As single ships or as squadrons? Close to American shores or to English shores? To protect American shipping or to attack British convoys? As late as May, the navy secretary was scribbling notes to two other captains, John Rodgers in New York and

Stephen Decatur in Norfolk, asking their advice. Rodgers advocated dispatching a squadron to English waters to disrupt commerce and to draw off Royal Navy ships from attacking American vessels. Decatur, famous for his daring raid on Tripoli, proposed dispatching individual or paired frigates for lengthy cruises to attack British convoys.

Madison's closest adviser, Treasury Secretary Gallatin, worried about the fates of hundreds of merchant vessels already at sea whose captains were unaware that war had been declared. He wanted the frigates to guard the sea lanes approaching America's ports. He estimated that the value of incoming cargoes for the first month of the war would be between $1 million and $1.5 million per week, their customs duties vital for funding the war budget.

After the captains' letters sat unanswered for two weeks on the indecisive Hamilton's desk, Madison and his cabinet voted to gather the entire navy at New York, home port to most of the homeward-bound merchantmen under the command of Rodgers, who would be the commodore of the squadron. The other ships, based in Norfolk and Washington, D.C., were to sail at once to join Rodgers. But by June 21, three days after the war declaration, Hamilton had not yet sent cruising orders. After Gallatin complained to Madison that "not one day longer ought to be lost," the cabinet convened on June 22 and decided the issue. Express riders pelted off with orders. Rodgers was to divide the navy into two squadrons, to cruise off New York and Norfolk.[9]

Rodgers had not waited for orders. He had heard that an annual British convoy of some 110 ships laden with an estimated $12 million in cargo was about to sail from Jamaica to England. On June 20, still without orders from Washington, Rodgers learned from General Bloomfield that war had been declared. Early the next morning, he ordered a signal gun fired from the *President*, warning all officers and men to repair to their ships. As the entire crew mustered on the frigate's weather deck, Rodgers addressed them:

> Now lads, we have got something to do that will shake the rust from our
> jackets. War is declared! We shall have another dash at our old enemies.
> It is the very thing you have long wanted. The rascals have been bullying
> over us these ten years, and I am glad the time has come at last when we

can have satisfaction. If there are any among you who are unwilling to risk your lives with me, say so, and you shall be paid off and discharged. I'll have no skulkers on board my ship, by God.[10]

Among the crew cheering at Rodgers's words that morning were many Americans, some of them naturalized: of these, many were Irish immigrants. Among the American born, several were free African Americans: about one in five crewmen on American ships was a freed black.

At 10 a.m., Rodgers weighed anchor. *President* and the sloop-of-war *Hornet* dropped down the Upper Bay, passing through the Narrows to the Lower Bay and on to Sandy Hook to await the three warships sailing up from Norfolk under Decatur's command. Rodgers still had not received his orders from Washington and, in an act tantamount to insubordination, had decided to sail without them.

At dawn on June 23, one hundred miles south of Nantucket, *President*'s lookout sighted a sail. Rodgers gave the signal to chase and cleared for action as the *Belvidera,* a smaller and lighter frigate whose captain and crew were unaware they were at war, hoisted her British colors.

At 4:20 p.m. Rodgers, personally touching a slow match to the priming hole of a bow-mounted chase gun, fired the first naval shot of the War of 1812. Before the first ball found its mark, four British stern-mounted guns responded. As *President* overtook *Belvidera*, her volleys struck the British ship's rudder, crashed into the captain's cabin and dented a chase gun, killing one seaman and severely wounding several others.

Ten minutes into the sea fight, with the *President* the sure winner, one of the loaded chase guns on her main deck exploded, tearing a gaping hole in the forecastle, killing or maiming fifteen men and breaking Rodgers's leg. While the surviving crew removed the dead and wounded and Rodgers waited for the rest of his ships to come up, the British frigate sailed out of range, reaching Halifax on July 1, where her captain informed the British command they were at war.

At the Washington Navy Yard, Isaac Hull, the short, thick-set, deeply bronzed captain of the *Constitution*—and nephew of General Hull of Detroit—had been refitting his ship all spring. Commandeering black spruce logs from Maine, he had the hull recaulked, masts stripped, planking replaced and more sails added. The bottom, sheathed with Paul Revere's copper, needed only minor patching. After fifteen years at sea, *Constitution* was in exceptional condition. On July 19 the 204-foot-long frigate threaded the Potomac as Hull read the declaration of war to the huzzaing crew.

Two days after Hull finally received Hamilton's written orders to sail to New York and join Rodgers's squadron, the *Constitution* hoisted anchor, clearing the Virginia Capes and heading out to sea. Slowed by light headwinds and an adverse current, Hull hugged the Maryland and Delaware coasts. On July 17, just north of present-day Atlantic City, the *Constitution*'s lookout spied the sails of five large ships, the exact number in Rodgers's squadron in roughly the position he expected to find it. At four o'clock, Hull gave the order to tack and head for the nearest sail. But shortly after dark, when he hoisted signal lanterns, no signal came back. Something was wrong. At eleven, Hull gave the order to make sail away, to windward. All of the ship's crewmen remained at their battle stations, wide awake, all night.

At first light, Hull was horrified to see he was sailing in the middle of an entire British squadron. Four frigates—the 36-gun *Belvidera*, the 38-gun *Shannon*, the 38-gun *Guerriere*, the 32-gun *Aeolus*—and the 64-gun ship-of-the-line *Africa*, had raced down from Halifax. With them was the 14-gun American brig *Nautilus*, which the British squadron had captured the day before. As the British ships "came up very fast," Hull was certain, he wrote to the Secretary of the Navy the next day, that there was "little chance of escaping from them." He "cleared Ship for Action, being determined that they should not get her, without resistance on our part." By eight that evening, "four of the Enemy's Ships [were] nearly within Gun Shot. . . . It soon appeared that we must be taken." This Hull was determined not to surrender.[11]

But then the wind died. It became virtually impossible for him to outrun the lighter British frigates. Skeptical, he listened to his young sailing master, First Lieutenant Charles Morris, and allowed him to attempt a maneuver called "kedging," usually used only in shallow harbors and rivers—the British could later label it a "Yankee trick." Taking soundings, Morris had discovered that the *Constitution* was in relatively shallow water—144 feet.

After attaching lightweight kedge anchors to hastily spliced hawsers three and four hundred feet long until they had lines stretching nearly half a mile, sailors hauled hard on the oars, pulling a launch and a cutter ahead and dropping small anchors, four hundred and seven hundred pounds. All hands on deck took turns pushing around the wooden spokes on the two capstans, literally pulling the ship along until it was directly over an anchor. Repeating the backbreaking exercise day and night, an anchor was always being rowed ahead. When the faintest breeze blew up, Hull ordered the ship's fire engine to play water from her pumps onto her sails—wetting them to hold the wind from the royals down. Adding and subtracting new sails as the wind came and went, Hull also lightened the vessel, pumping 2,300 barrels of drinking water over the side. Meanwhile, he shifted long guns to the stern, firing them to keep his pursuers at bay. Even when the British imitated his maneuver, they hesitated to come too close to him: the American guns had a longer range. Two British frigates attempted to pull abreast to unleash a broadside; the *Constitution* raked them. When *Belvidera* opened fire, her shots fell short even as the *Constitution*'s found their mark; when *Guerriere* pulled close enough to let loose a broadside, her balls fell short and she dropped out of range.

By dawn of the third day, *Constitution* had pulled twelve miles ahead of the three British ships that the lookout could still make out from the mainmast head. After a fifty-seven-hour chase, British commodore Philip B. V. Broke finally broke off the chase and headed northward. Hull would later recount, "We soon found that we left the Enemy very fast." Lieutenant Morris, whose maneuver had saved the ship, was modest as he shared the credit: "Our escape must depend on our superiority of sailing, which we had no reason to hope nor expect." Amos Evans, the ship's surgeon, described the mood of apprehension that helped to drive the men beyond any normal definition of human endurance: "We had many times given over all expectations of making our escape, & had it not been for uncommon exertion we must inevitably have fallen a prey to the superiority of an enemy."[12]

Even the disappointed British commodore tipped his bicorne:

On the 17, 18, and 19 we had an anxious [chase] after an American frigate supposed to be the <u>Constitution</u>, but she escaped by very superior sailing, tho' the Frigates under my Orders are remarkably fast ships.[13]

By this time, Hull knew he had missed his rendezvous with Rodgers's squadron. In fact, Rodgers's orders would never have reached him even if he had waited for them: they were aboard the dispatch brig *Nautilus* when she was captured by Commodore Broke and had been destroyed by the brig's captain. Hull decided to bypass New York and put into Boston, the *Constitution*'s home port, to restock provisions, then return to sea quickly to avoid being trapped in port. The sea lanes were already crowded with ships that had been at sea when war broke out and were rushing home before being ensnared in the expected British blockade. When the winds died, the *Constitution* had to be towed into port—to a hero's welcome. The newspapers had reported her capture.

Anxious at every lost day, Hull knew he should not sail independently without fresh orders. While still sailing north, he had hailed the *Diana*, a merchant vessel bound for Baltimore, giving her captain a message for Secretary Hamilton, requesting that new orders be rushed to him in Boston. After six days in port, Hull wrote again to Hamilton: he had "determined to run out," deciding to sail on the west wind on Sunday morning, August 2. Waiting just beyond Boston Light, he sent the ship's launch ashore to the post office one more time, "having great hopes" that the mail "may bring me letters from you. If she does not I shall indeed be at a loss how to proceed, and shall take responsibility on myself."[14]

Hull may have fathomed from conversations at the Boston Navy Yard, where Bainbridge was the superintendent, that if he remained in port, he might not like the letter from Washington. Hull's intuition proved correct. On July 28 Navy Secretary Hamilton had written, "On the arrival of the Constitution in port, I have ordered Commodore Bainbridge to take command of her." Bainbridge, an astute politician with seniority over Hull, would have taken command of the *Constitution* away from Hull if he had not dallied in Washington. By the time Hamilton's order finally reached Boston, the *Constitution* had sailed.[15]

Hoping to intercept British shipping, Hull followed the New England coast northeast to the Bay of Fundy and then toward Cape Race off Newfoundland's southern tip, where he hoped to intercept British convoys en route to Halifax and Quebec. On August 15 his lookouts spied five sails; Hull, thinking he had found a prize convoy, pursued. Upon seeing him, the ships scattered. Chasing ships to fight day after day, Hull finally overtook an American ship being sailed by a British prize crew: he learned that he had narrowly missed Broke's squadron, which was trying to intercept Rodgers's squadron before it could catch the coveted Jamaica convoy. At night on the eighteenth, he overtook an American privateer, the *Decatur* out of Newburyport, Massachusetts, which was fleeing homeward after capturing nine British merchantmen. Turning south, Hull spied a British frigate. He instantly recognized the *Guerriere*, one of the frigates that had chased him a month earlier off the New Jersey coast, and she was not running away from a fight. Her skipper, the twenty-eight-year-old James Dacres, scion of a family of admirals, was confident his ship would easily take the slightly larger American vessel. The *Constitution*, rated at 44 guns but mounting 55, had a crew of 456 men; the 38-gun *Guerriere* was carrying 49 guns and had a complement of only 272, not counting the American prisoners. More striking was the disparity in armaments: with thirty long-range guns on her main deck, *Constitution* carried two long 18-pounders at her bow and twenty-four 32-pound carronades—small, lightweight cannon with wide, short barrels that could hurl large-caliber shells at short range. The *Guerriere*, with thirty 18-pounders, sixteen 32-pound carronades, two long 12s and a 12-pound howitzer, could project 550 pounds of iron in a broadside in contrast to 762 pounds from the American ship. Their differences in size and firepower didn't faze Dacres. So confident was he of an easy victory that he allowed ten impressed American seamen to go belowdecks so that they would not have to kill their countrymen.

Clearing for action in midafternoon, Hull steered straight for the *Guerriere*. A marine drummer beat the call to quarters, and the crew, giving three cheers, raced to battle stations. Moses Smith, a crewman, remembered, "The word had passed like lightning from man to man . . . and all came flocking up like pigeons." Hull walked calmly among his men, telling them, "Men, now do your duty. Your officers cannot have entire command over you now. Each man must do all in his power for his country." As the *Constitution* continued to race through the running swells toward the *Guerriere*, Dacres ordered a broadside: the shells fell short. Bringing the larboard guns to bear, he ordered another broadside: again and again, cannonballs struck and bounced harmlessly off the *Constitution*'s thick oak hull. At that moment, she earned her enduring sobriquet, *Old Ironsides*.[16]

As Dacres failed to gain the weather gauge, Hull drove his ship closer, narrowing the distance between them to ten yards until he came "less than Pistol Shot" away. There he fired a crushing broadside, then another and another, his 24-pounders, double-charged with round and grape shot, battering *Guerriere*, whose 18-pounders were no match. After fifteen minutes of point-blank punishment, the English vessel's mizzenmast went overboard, its rigging, still attached to the ship, acting as an anchor, making steering impossible. Hull, meanwhile, turned hard to port and crossed *Guerriere*'s bow, raking her decks with cannonballs and grapeshot. Coming back across, *Constitution* unleashed yet another broadside with her port guns. As the two broadsides ripped apart *Guerriere*'s sails and rigging, *Constitution*'s sharpshooters fired down at officers and crew on the littered and bloody deck. Dacre's ship would no longer answer her helm. Out of control and drifting, her bowsprit and jibboom came across *Constitution*'s quarterdeck and grew entangled in the American ship's mizzen rigging, the two ships trapped in a lethal embrace. Trumpeters summoned the boarding parties. As Lieutenant Morris tried to fasten the two ships together, a musket ball struck him in the chest and hurled him to the deck: somehow, he got up. The captain of the marines, Lieutenant William Bush, waiting for the order to board, jumped up on the taffrail, taking Morris's place: "one musket shot entered his face & passed into his brains." American musketry cut down all of the British ship's officers: Dacres suffered a severe wound in the back from a marine sharpshooter.

The British attempt to board failed: the seas were too rough. Suddenly, inexplicably, the two ships separated. Hull resumed pounding the stricken *Guerriere* at close range for several minutes more until her foremast went over the side, taking the collapsed mainmast overboard, dragging down with them the jibboom and every spar. The *Guerriere*, "having got into the trough of the Sea," Dacres later testified, "she lay there." Another officer testified, "She rolled so much . . . the Shot and Shot Boxes on the Quarter Deck were flying from side to side." While the dismasted ship wallowed helpless, her surviving crew labored on, clearing the decks, preparing to fight on. Hull stood off while his men repaired the damage to the *Constitution*. But the sea was spewing through the *Guerriere*'s gun ports and the scores of gaping holes shot through her. Realizing his ship was doomed, the wounded Dacres huddled briefly with his officers: no more lives could be wasted. Firing one cannon to leeward, he indicated he was surrendering. He could not strike his colors: they had gone over the side, still attached to the masts. Hull would later claim the engagement had lasted only thirty-five minutes; others said he went on pounding the British frigate, detested for its many insulting searches and seizures in American waters, for fully four hours as it became dark. In the end, the British had lost fifteen men, with sixty-three wounded and twenty-four presumably swept overboard with the masts. Hull had lost seven, with seven wounded.[17]

Hull had wanted to sail the *Guerriere* into Boston harbor as his prize, but daylight revealed gruesome carnage. He noted in his logbook, "pieces of skulls, brains, legs, arms & blood Lay in every direction amid the groanes of the wounded." Hull ordered the wounded rowed over to the *Constitution* and her hard-pressed surgeons. Then he ordered the stricken hulk set afire. After witnessing the explosion, the great fireball, the shower of shards of iron and splintered timber and burning rigging rain down around him, the ship's surgeon Amos Evans wrote to Commodore Bainbridge, "She blew up presenting a sight the most incomparably grand and magnificent I have ever experienced, no painter, no poet, or historian could give on canvas or paper any description that could do justice to the Scene."[18]

Sailing back to Boston after a voyage that had taken six weeks of elusive navigating, Hull encountered Rodgers and his squadron off Nantasket Roads, returning with nine small merchant ships they had captured during their fruitless search for the Jamaica convoy. On August 30 *Old Ironsides* entered Boston harbor first, with Rodgers trailing him in the *President* with the three other frigates and a brig strung out behind him, to a tremendous reception. The shore batteries fired one thunderous salute after another that punctuated the cheering of the crowds on the wharves, the rooftops and all the other ships in the harbor. "Boston was wild with fervor at the triumph of her favorite frigate," wrote one celebrant. "Partisan politics and hatred of the war were thrown aside in the general rejoicing." In nearby Marblehead, home of some eighty of the ship's complement, the townspeople took credit for the good tidings: "So large a proportion of the crew of the victorious frigate were citizens of the town, it was considered almost a local victory." In Washington, Congress voted Hull a gold medal.[19]

Skeptical until then about the need for the war, Bostonian Thomas

McClure excitedly sent by messenger to his brother at Dartmouth College in Hanover, New Hampshire, a copy of the September 30 *Boston Gazette*:

> Containing an acct. of Capt. Hull's taking & destroying a British frigate Hull has done himself lasting honour in this capture by his masterly maneuvering & fighting he arrived in the <u>Constitution</u> here yesterday morning & this day [Commodore] Rodgers with his fleet got safe in 5 sail they all came up together making a fine show the Town is very lively this day joy on every countenance. . . .
>
> Rogers it is said lost a leg in the engagement with the <u>Belvidera</u> the belief is he did himself no honour in that engagement for being superior & having other vessels with him ought to have taken her and shall know more about it soon, some make no scruple to say R. ought to be shott, others that he ought to be broken, not so Hull he is highly applauded. . . . The joy is much greater as it was feared Rogers' fleet would never get back, almost all the U.S. navy are here with the <u>Chesapeake</u> repairing 7 sail—The Town needed something to enliven it it had become very dull especially about the wharves. . . . [20]

The view from Washington was quite the opposite. Navy Secretary Hamilton showered laurels on Marylander Rodgers for diverting the British fleet long enough for 250 American merchantmen to get safely into Boston and 266 more into New York. In his annual message to Congress, President Madison expressed his satisfaction that the customs duty-paying merchant ships had made it home safely, "having been much favored in it by the course pursued by a squadron of our frigates under the command of Commodore Rodgers." But it was Captain Hull who received the laurels from an incredulous *Times* of London. His victory over *Guerriere* had "spread a degree of gloom through the town, which it was painful to observe." There could not have been "any calamity of twenty times its amount that might have been attended with more serious consequences." It was also calamitous for British ship owners, sending insurances rates at Lloyds to new heights. [21]

At his subsequent court-martial in London, the mortified Captain Dacres—who would be exonerated—noted that half the crew of the *Constitution* consisted of skilled English sailors and that the enemy ship was larger and more heavily armed, able to project heavier shot from a longer range. Both of Dacres's assertions were true. Vessel for vessel, American ships carried more firepower than their classifications, but Dacres made no allowance for the marksmanship or the motivation of the sailors. Many of them had jumped British ships for better pay and living conditions—they could never forget their harsh treatment or the simple fact that they would be hanged as deserters if they were ever captured.

The ultimate victor of the sea fight was Madison. Coming hard on the heels of gloomy news from the West, Hull's victory bolstered the nation's sagging morale, convincing many Americans for the first time that they could win in a war against the mighty Royal Navy. It also wiped away any question of the future direction of the navy: single ships would roam the seas, their experienced commanders seeking targets of opportunity and forcing British convoys, not American ports, onto the defensive. In the waning months of 1812, more good news seemed to come with each month. On October 17 the 18-gun sloop-of-war *Wasp*, Captain Jacob Jones commanding, defeated the 16-gun British brig *Frolic* six hundred miles off the Virginia coast: U.S. losses, five killed, five wounded; British, seventeen killed, forty-five wounded. A week later, the 44-gun frigate *United States*, Captain Decatur commanding, subdued the 38-gun British frigate *Macedonian* off the Madeira Islands, bringing her home to New London, Connecticut, as a prize. On December 29, *Constitution*, under its new commander, Captain Bainbridge, destroyed the 49-gun British frigate *Java* in a duel off the Brazilian coast. American casualties, nine killed, twenty-five wounded; British losses, sixty dead, more than one hundred wounded.[22]

As NAPOLEON'S LEGIONS menaced Russia and guerrilla warfare engulfed the Iberian Peninsula, the new British Ministry decided to devote more assets to a serious second front in America while continuing to offer armistice and negotiation. On September 30, Vice Admiral John Borlase Warren—victor over the French invasion fleet during the Irish Rebellion of 1798—sent under flag of truce another peace feeler into the Chesapeake. But Madison suspected that the British were only stalling for time to send reinforcements, and he rejected it. The olive branch arrived tied to a sword in a secret order to Warren from Sir John Croker, secretary of the Admiralty

Board, dated November 27. In the event the Americans rejected Britain's offer of a cessation of hostilities, Warren was to institute a blockade, destroy the American navy and return any extra ships-of-the-line to England to blockade France. With the order came reinforcements to Halifax, bringing the number of ships at Warren's disposal to ninety, including ten ships-of-the-line, thirty frigates and fifty sloops-of-war. Madison notified Warren that the British would have to suspend their policy of impressment before he would talk further. Warren retracted the olive branch, announcing that the day after Christmas, the Royal Navy would blockade the Delaware and Chesapeake Bays to cut off commerce from two of America's major ports, Philadelphia and Baltimore.

Warren's second in command, Rear Admiral Sir George Cockburn, had already sailed from Bermuda with a reinforcing squadron to commence raids along the Atlantic and Gulf coasts. In February 1813, Warren, arriving at Lynnhaven Bay aboard his flagship *San Domingo*, formally declared the blockade, then sailed for warmer waters off Bermuda. He left five frigates for Cockburn to augment his blockading squadron: four 74-gun ships-of-the-line, two additional frigates, a sloop-of-war and a schooner, their combined firepower greater than that of the entire U.S. navy. In the first eight months of the war, Warren's fleet had already captured 120 American prize ships, netting the admiral, from his three-twentieths share of their sale at auction, 15,238 pounds, 16 shillings and 2 pence, about $1 million in 2017 American currency.[23]

Considering Britain's aura of invincibility banished, thousands of Americans now drew upon their maritime heritage. Experienced mariners and efficient crewmen decided to seek a profitable if dangerous role in the war. Fitting out armed merchant ships, they obtained as their commission letters of marque from President Madison and set to sea to punish the British for years of arrogance, abuse and the seizure of hundreds of ships. American privateering vessels—the militia of the seas—would devastate British shipping, forcing the Royal Navy to trim its sails and tie down scores of men-of-war to provide protection to convoys. Of the 500 British merchantmen captured in the first six months of the war, American privateers captured 450; in the next two years, American privateersmen would take 1,175 British merchant vessels as prizes, in addition to the 254 captured by U.S. Navy vessels. Taken mostly along the Atlantic coast of Canada and the Caribbean and sailed into Atlantic ports, they were auctioned off along with their contents, the proceeds shared among investors, captains and crews, creating new fortunes overnight. Sailing out of Bristol, Rhode Island, the *Yankee* captured eight British vessels that fetched $300,000 at auction, a figure far surpassed by the *Rossie*, sailing out of Baltimore under the command of Captain Joshua Barney. Eighteen vessels netted Barney, his backers and his crews a staggering $1.5 million. Captured British prizes would fetch nearly $40 million—at least $4 billion in 2017 dollars—at auction in the next two years. Many of the captured ships, rearmed and filled with eager recruits, would soon sail again, seeking more prizes, even more profits, the taxes they paid outfitting and training an equally unsuccessful volunteer army.[24]

Yet a small number of thrilling American ship-to-ship victories at sea occurred independent of any policy directives from Washington and, in fact, in spite of them. Madison launched the war with no naval policy and he seemed especially unaware of the importance of the Great Lakes to his Canadian invasion plan. The British could provide small naval and merchant vessels to support their troop movements on the lakes and the rivers linking them. At his eventual court-martial, William Hull pointed out the impossibility of his mission without naval support.

In September 1812, Navy secretary Hamilton ordered Commodore Isaac Chauncey, a forty-year-old veteran in command of the New York Navy Yard, to "assume command of the naval force on Lakes Erie and Ontario, and to use every exertion to obtain control of them this fall." Chauncey, taking whatever men and matériel he had at hand, was to hurry west and base himself at Sackets Harbor, a tiny hamlet beside a superb natural harbor on the New York shore of Lake Ontario. There he was to build naval vessels or buy, convert and arm any merchant ships he could commandeer. With 170 sailors and marines from the *Constitution*, 140 shipwrights and joiners and their tools and one hundred cannon of various sizes, Chauncey made a slow six-hundred-mile journey—against the Hudson River current, up the Mohawk River to Oswego, then along Lake Ontario's south shore to Sackets Harbor, much of the way traversing hostile Indian country. Iron, cordage and shot would have to be hauled overland from Pittsburgh.

Hamilton next commissioned an experienced Great Lakes mariner, Daniel Dobbins, as Chauncey's sailing master and dispatched two experienced young lieutenants, Oliver Hazard Perry and Thomas Macdonough, to assist him. Perry, twenty-eight, in command of the gunboats at Newport, had pleaded for a more challenging post. Macdonough, also twenty-eight, commander of gunboats at Portland, Maine, was a veteran of the Barbary Wars who had boarded the *Philadelphia* at Decatur's side. Secretary Hamilton ordered Macdonough to take control of Lake Champlain and support Dearborn's dilatory Quebec invasion.

Perry, son of a Continental navy captain, had enlisted as a midshipman at fourteen, serving under most of the navy's distinguished captains. Having the patronage of Commodore Rodgers when war came, he received promotion to master and commander, a step between lieutenant and captain, along with his posting to Sackets Harbor. Chauncey was delighted when he heard Perry was considering the posting. "You are the very person that I want for a particular service, in which you may gain Reputation for yourself and honor for your country." Now Chauncey could devote himself solely to Lake Ontario and turn over Lake Erie to Perry. On the Canadian side, General Brock, writing two days before his death at Queenston Heights, had urged British officials to take seriously Chauncey's challenge: "The enemy is making every exertion to gain a naval Superiority on both Lakes which if they accomplish I do not see how we can retain the Country."[25]

On Lake Ontario, Commodore Chauncey assembled a scratch fleet in only five weeks after arriving in Sackets Harbor. He was now able to chase pursuing British warships back to Fort Erie. But the northern climate soon cut into the time and materials needed to build ships. Chauncey's regulars diverted piles of planks to build themselves cabins where they could huddle through four months of harsh winds and blizzards, waiting for the pack ice of winter to melt into a spring season for war. For the boat builders, there would be no rest.[26]

In his annual message to Congress, President Madison put the best face he could on the first five months of war. He pointed first to America's good harvest and the "unusual degree of health dispensed to its inhabitants." When he got around to the war, he conceded that the loss of Detroit and the Midwest was "painful" and the failure of the invasion of Canada "deeply to be lamented." Praising his naval officers for "an auspicious triumph," he condemned the British for enlisting Indians—"that wretched portion of the human race." With rhetoric characteristic of such addresses, he promised a more "vigorous prosecution" of the war, including higher pay for enlisted men and an enlarged navy. He did not say where he would get the money.[27]

Before planning the 1813 campaign, Madison believed that he had to reshuffle his cabinet to reflect political realities. Adhering to his self-imposed requirement of simultaneously rewarding service in the long-ago Revolutionary War and more recently in Democratic-Republican politics, he ousted his secretaries of war and the navy and made appointments that only complicated the command structure. To replace Navy secretary Hamilton, in a bid for Federalist support, Madison named William Jones, who had twice been wounded in the Continental army, twice captured as a privateer and then had joined the Continental navy as a junior officer. After a single term as a congressman representing South Carolina, Jones had grown rich as a merchant in Philadelphia, his profitable ventures including the opium trade with China.

Ousting the feckless Secretary of War Eustis, Madison appointed the contentious John Armstrong. One of the anonymous authors of the infamous Newburgh Addresses—protests over back pay owed officers by the impecunious Continental Congress—Armstrong had been humiliated when Washington discovered the incipient plot. The discovery of Armstrong's involvement ended his political career in Pennsylvania and he moved to New York, marrying into the wealthy Livingston clan. Supported by his wife's estates, Armstrong accepted appointment as American minister to Paris, where he served for six frustrating years.

Both of Madison's new cabinet appointments foreshadowed worsening problems with the chain of command in the field. But Madison did not leave it to his new secretaries of war and the navy to plan the overall strategy for the coming campaign: he left that to Monroe, his secretary of state. A former intelligence officer in the Revolution, Monroe aspired to become a field general. Instead, he was to share strategy-making decisions with Treasury Secretary Gallatin, whose eye never left the bottom line. Both men realized that they could not follow the offensive-only strategy that had failed so dismally in 1812.

It was Gallatin's suggestion, seconded by Monroe, to first overhaul the army's administrative structure. Nine military districts would each possess its own body of regulars and a commanding officer with a competent staff to coordinate defensive measures with each state's governor and militia. Requiring at least 10,000 troops, Gallatin's plan left few for Monroe's ambitious proposal for an offensive war. Monroe fantasized not only about recapturing Detroit and the Northwest territories lost to the British but also, in a single year, conquering and occupying all of Canada, in addition to seizing East Florida on the pretext that the Spanish regency was allowing its British ally to use it as a base for attacking southern states. Monroe proposed raising an army of 20,000 one-year volunteers from states bordering Canada. Gallatin dismissed the proposal, saying it would destroy the public credit and require high taxes, an anathema to Madisonian politicians. Monroe lowered his sights to filling up the existing regiments to a strength of 20,000 regulars. This measure passed Congress in January, along with a pay increase from five to eight dollars a month for enlisted men, augmented by a doubling of signing bounties and land grants.

Armstrong, the new secretary of war, believed it was a waste of money to prepare defenses for such cities as Washington. Neglecting the professional training of officers at the recently formed U.S. Military Academy at West Point, he had enshrined Revolutionary War–vintage memories of militia victories over British regulars—unable to grasp that there were far fewer embattled farmers who would willingly take down the old family firelock and march off to smite the invader.

Bibulous former navy secretary Hamilton had proven oblivious of the need to greatly expand naval forces on the Great Lakes. The Senate had slashed the naval appropriation to a mere $2.5 million, the cost of only ten vessels. Jones's navy would concentrate on commerce raiding by frigates, with gunboats to protect ports. Once again, Jones's appointment aligned with Madison's overall strategy of employing militia rather than professional soldiers and to conduct war solely on the offensive.

Gallatin had every reason for apprehension over the exploding costs of the war. He would have to find $20 million more in revenues than he had expected for the year, even without expanding the army or navy, as the threatened British coastal blockade endangered the vital import trade. Gallatin's brilliant attempt to finance the war without imposing direct taxes had revealed cracks in the solidly pro-war Democratic-Republican majority in Congress. After Great Britain repealed the Orders in Council, imports to America driven by pent-up demand for British goods had flooded the nation's ports. Believing that British relaxation of sanctions would avert war, shippers had ignored the lingering U.S. nonimportation ban of 1811 on trade with Britain, ratified *before* the Privy Council had acted. Legally, their cargoes were forfeited to the government, a step that could embitter merchants and bankers vital to Gallatin's bond-selling strategy. But to waive the penalties would create enormous profits. Gallatin proposed a doubling of the import duties on the illicit goods while requiring the importers to lend the government one-third the value of their cargoes. The $10 million thus raised would reduce the amount he still needed to slightly less than the 1812 level.

To Gallatin's disgust, the Democratic-Republicans in Congress bickered over his proposal and failed to cobble together a majority for either remitting the fines or enforcing them. Consequently, the Senate could reach accord only on remitting the penalties altogether. A minority of Democratic-Republicans joined the Federalist minority, and the penalties were waived entirely. This left Gallatin with the task of hurriedly raising an unprecedented $21 million for the war. When he floated a $16 million loan in February, one measure of the war's growing unpopularity was that the Treasury could borrow only $3.75 million, less than one-fourth the required amount. Gallatin had the unenviable task of informing Madison that the government had only enough reserves left for one month and that military operations might have to be suspended for the year.

Privately Gallatin approached his friend, financier and fur trader Astor, once again, feeling him out on the possibility of forming a consortium of investors to lend the government $10 million. But Astor told Gallatin that the 6 percent interest yield was not palatable and that the loans would be considered too risky because the prospects for winning the war seemed so slender. The government's best approach would be to reestablish the national bank and then borrow from it. The Madison administration and the Democratic-Republican majority in Congress had blocked the renewal of the charter of the first Federalist-founded Bank of the United States, created by Hamilton in 1790, only the year before.

ON FEBRUARY 5, 1813, his third day in office, Secretary of War Armstrong took over planning the 1813 campaign. Aware that the Northern Army was ill equipped and unready for a spring offensive, Armstrong settled on a less ambitious strategy: attack the key British naval base at Kingston, Ontario, followed by assaults on York (today's Toronto), the provincial capital of Upper Canada, and Fort George to win naval control of Lake Ontario and sever communications by water between Upper and Lower Canada.

Armstrong ordered Dearborn to muster 4,000 men at Sackets Harbor to attack Kingston, while the 3,000 troops based at Buffalo were to attack York and seize the Niagara peninsula. Armstrong's directive bounced back. Dearborn and Chauncey contended that Kingston was just too heavily defended. Instead, they proposed taking York and Fort George before the British stronghold of Kingston, with Dearborn's forces to be drawn from New England, Pennsylvania and Maryland. As soon as the ice broke up on Lake Ontario, the Americans launched their second invasion of Canada on April 23.

What proved to be the tipping point in the Democratic-Republicans' favor was the arrival in Washington in February 1813 of an offer from Czar Alexander I of Russia to act as broker in a mediation between the United States and Britain. The message from American envoy John Quincy Adams, sent off by courier ship from St. Petersburg in September 1812, had taken five months to reach Madison. The czar, facing a massive invasion by Napoleon, had no desire to see his British ally remove troops from Europe to fight the Americans. Moreover, after years of difficulties with France and Britain over neutral trading rights, the czar sympathized with the Americans, a major trading partner. Adams had worked carefully to cultivate relations with the extroverted czar, the favorite grandson of Catherine the Great.

As Adams noted in his diary, he had learned of the declaration of war only a full two months after the congressional vote, and then only from an aging New York newspaper. No official notification had arrived from Secretary of State Monroe. Another month passed, and on September 6,

Adams received an invitation to tea from the celebrated Madame de Staël, who was visiting the court of the czar on the way to her husband's home in Stockholm. In the ninth year of her exile from France, the most famous woman of letters on the Continent was traveling through eastern Europe when she invited Adams to call on her at the Hôtel de l'Europe.[28]

Adams's discreet notes mask the fact that his father, as a peace negotiator in Paris during the American Revolution, and her father, Jacques Necker, prime mover of financial reform under the late king Louis XVI, were open admirers of each other's work. Among her *salonistes* in Paris were the Prince de Talleyrand, who had once paid court to President Adams in exile in Philadelphia, and Adams's envoy to France, Gouverneur Morris, a major New York landowner. She had invited Adams to her hotel in St. Petersburg, he noted in his diary, for discussion "concerning something relative to America":

> She has lands in the State of New York, upon Lake Ontario, and stocks in the United States funds, and she wished to enquire how she could continue to receive her interest in England while there is war between the United States and Great Britain.[29]

Adams knew none of the other invited guests: "To every soul in the room I was a total stranger." To his surprise, among them was the newly arrived British ambassador, Lord Cathcart. There could not have been a more awkward moment. Since Adams had not yet received official notification of the declaration of hostilities between the two countries, he could only make small talk with Cathcart; he was not free to discuss politics. He certainly knew about His Lordship, commanding officer of a British legion of dragoons in the American Revolution who had risen to the rank of full general in the Napoleonic Wars. After serving as commander in chief of the British army in Ireland, he had led the expedition that had shelled and seized the neutral port of Copenhagen, Denmark, entrepôt for many blockade-running American merchant ships, along with Denmark's own neutral fleet.[30]

As Adams entered Madame de Staël's hotel suite, she was "in a very animated conversation with Lord Cathcart, and expressing in warm terms her admiration of the English nation as the preservers of social order and the saviors of Europe." Some of her comments were more biting: "She also complimented his Lordship very highly upon his exploit in Copenhagen."

At this, Adams recorded, "My Lord looked a little awkward. . . . [T]o the personal tribute offered to himself, he made no answer." But he replied at length "to the besmearing of his nation," protesting that it "felt itself bound by moral obligations." Adams "thought of the moral obligations of the Copenhagen expedition, and of the American Revolutionary War . . . Lord Cathcart had his share in both."

Madame de Staël eventually "had leisure for some conversation with me," Adams noted. She wanted to discuss the war, but privately. Chiding Adams for not having called on her sooner, she said that she did not have time at the moment—she was going out for dinner—but desired him to call again the next morning. When Adams returned the next day, they enjoyed a "second long conversation." She was "one of the highest enthusiasts for the English cause," but mostly because of her "personal resentment against Bonaparte. . . . He will not let her live in peace anywhere, merely because she had not praised him in her works."[31]

That same day, as Madame de Staël left St. Petersburg to travel to Stockholm, Napoleon's Grande Armée, reduced to 130,000 men, faced the one-eyed general Mikhail Kutuzov and 121,000 Russians at Borodino on the high road to Moscow. In a series of massive frontal attacks, Napoleon attempted to crush the Russian line, but the Russians held. As his force wore down the Russians, Napoleon, tired and ill, failed to throw in the 18,000 elite troops of his Imperial Guard. One French observer, Armand de Caulaincourt, remembered,

> The Russians showed the utmost tenacity: their fieldworks and the ground they were forced to yield were given up without disorder. Their ranks did not break; pounded by the artillery, sabered by the cavalry, forced back at bayonet-point by our infantry, their somewhat immobile masses met defeat bravely, and only gave way slowly before the fury of our attacks. Never had ground been attacked with more fury and skill or more stubbornly defended.[32]

The casualties at Borodino amounted to a staggering 28,000 French and 42,000 Russians. The Russian army slipped away, leaving Napoleon a technical battlefield victor, but Napoleon, with scarcely 100,000 of the 600,000 men he had led into Russia—the rest of his army strung out over hundreds of miles—could not go on. Entering an undefended Moscow, the Grande Armée wanted only food and sleep. It would get neither.

As the French historian Marie-Pierre Rey describes it,

> Suddenly a gigantic fire burst out in several points of the city on the night of September 15–16. The majority of houses, churches and storerooms were made of wood, and because the water pumps had been evacuated from the city by the governor-general, Count Rostopchin, the fire quickly spread and would last three days. . . . There is little doubt about his responsibility for the fire.[33]

In her memoirs, Natalia Rostopchin, the count's daughter and the sister of the Countess of Segur, attested that, at a secret meeting at her father's house the night before the fires broke out, the chief of police and several of his assistants received from the count precise instructions which buildings were to be burned. The fiery glow of the ancient capital city soon contrasted with the biting cold of an early and intense Russian winter—and Kutuzov's army was growing every day with fresh recruits.

Hundreds of miles to the north at his diplomatic post in St. Petersburg, John Quincy Adams observed all around him preparations for a last-ditch defensive war. By mid-September the nobles were to give up one in every ten of their serfs to the army: "I saw many of them this morning," Adams wrote one week later, "just in from the country, with the one-horse wagons, and the families of the recruits taking leave of them." His own coachman was conscripted; at the last moment before he was marched off to the front, twenty-five rubles to the correct official brought him back.[34]

Amid the kaleidoscopic European alliances, Adams, in his fourth year in St. Petersburg, had emerged as dean of foreign diplomats, the only emissary who had not fled the imperial palace when Napoleon's legions swarmed across the Niemen on June 26—one week after the American declaration of war against Britain and three days after Parliament had rescinded its troublesome Orders in Council. During his years in St. Petersburg, Adams had been able to win major trade concessions from a Russia starved for American goods because of Napoleon's continental blockade. He had even been able to persuade the czar to intercede with the Danes to release some of the impounded American ships.

The scholarly, stocky, unassuming forty-six-year-old Adams seemed able to open doors at the highest level, in part because of his relationship with Alexander. Adams was more than once observed conversing with the czar, sometimes during long walks; sometimes along the broad, tree-lined road to Czarskoye Selo, the czar's country residence; sometimes as they rode together along the Marble Quay beside the Neva River. Studying Adams closely, Alexander observed that, even on a Russian winter's day, while he wore a heavy greatcoat and a tall fur hat, the Bostonian wore no gloves. The czar seemed insatiably curious, in both their official and unofficial meetings, to learn more about the United States. Were not many immigrants coming to America? From what lands? And what languages did they speak? When they spoke in Congress, could they understand one another? From their first meeting in 1809, when Adams had presented his credentials in French at the imperial palace, the czar had praised the United States' "system" as "wise and just" and criticized the "obstinate adherence of England to a system of maritime pretensions which was neither liberal nor just."[35]

Louisa Adams was the only diplomat's wife remaining in St. Petersburg, and she became a court favorite. This required altering lifelong habits: now she must rise late, attend teas and lavish dinners, parties and balls that began at eleven o'clock at night and lasted often until four in the morning with three hundred other courtiers. From among them, the czar often invited Louisa to be his dancing partner as her husband, wearing the requisite wig, waited to take his turn. The American couple could find little peace in their rented quarters, where fourteen servants and their hungry families had attached themselves and helped themselves to whatever they thought they were entitled. The strain had proven too great for Louisa: in mid-July 1810, she had miscarried. By that November, she was pregnant again. That child, a daughter also named Louisa, born in August 1811, died eleven months later and was buried in St. Petersburg.

On September 21, 1812, with Napoleon's victorious army in Moscow, a courier called at the American Ministry, a corner house fronting the Moika River, to summon Adams to a rare evening meeting at the home of the minister of foreign affairs, Count Nikolai Rumiantsev. Returning late that night, Adams wrote in his diary what Rumiantsev had told him: that he had been summoned by the czar's express command, that the czar, who was still in the field with his troops near Moscow, had sent an urgent message with an aide, and that he was expecting a prompt reply. The czar had made a recent alliance with Britain. Adams's conversation that night took place shortly after the British shipped Russia 100,000 desperately needed .75-caliber muskets to seal their new alliance. Rumiantsev, Adams noted, was "much concerned and disappointed" that "having made peace and re-established relations" with Britain, "the whole benefit" was being "lost by the new war that had arisen between the United States and England." The czar thought he had detected "various indications that there was, on both sides, a reluctance at engaging and prosecuting this war."

It had occurred to the emperor, Rumiantsev related, "that perhaps an amicable arrangement of the differences" could be accomplished by "indirect rather than direct negotiation." Was Adams aware of any obstacle on the part of the United States to the czar's offering to mediate? Pointing out that he still had not officially received the declaration of war from Washington, Adams assured Rumiantsev that, in his opinion, America was acting with "extreme reluctance," and that he was "not aware of any obstacle" that would disincline his government to accept the czar's offer. Adams agreed to transmit the czar's offer to mediate: it took six months to reach Washington.[36]

NOT LONG AFTER she returned to Stockholm in the autumn of 1812, Madame de Staël wrote to her old friend, former president Jefferson, a letter that stunned him. In strong language, she excoriated the United States for declaring war on Britain, the nation that had for a decade resisted the ambition of her tormenter, Napoleon, as his armies marched across Europe and invaded the Middle East and the Caribbean, placing himself and his family on thrones in forty-four palaces in his quest to make himself the emperor of a "universal monarchy." In a blistering rebuke, she warned Jefferson that

[t]he greatest misfortune which would come to the American people in the present war would be to do real damage to their enemies, for then the English would no longer be in a condition to serve you as a bulwark against the despotism of the Emperor of France, or rather of Europe. . . . When he shall have overthrown the liberty of England it will be yours that he will attack next.[37]

When Madison received the Russian offer, he accepted it before he took the time to ascertain whether the British government concurred. Meanwhile, Napoleon had abandoned Moscow and ordered a retreat from Russia. On the march into Russia, thousands of men had died of dysentery from eating raw meat and drinking marsh water; now, even more froze to death as they limped homeward. Napoleon, sometimes alone on a single sled, hurtled along his humiliating path back to Paris while 40,000 more of his men succumbed to Cossacks, winter and wolves.

OVER DINNER ONE night in St. Petersburg, shortly after news arrived of another American army lost to the British and their Canadian allies, Count Rumiantsev confessed to Adams that he was mystified by the Americans' abject military performance. "In a tone of pleasantry," Adams noted, the imperial chancellor asked "how happens it that you are constantly beating at sea the English, who beat all the rest of the world, and that on land, where you ought to be the strongest, the English do what they please?"[38]

NAPOLEON'S COLLAPSE IN Russia had made his retreat from Moscow an American tragedy, portending a British onslaught by veteran troops freed from battling the French. In his May 24, 1813, message to a special session of Congress, Madison spelled out the nation's predicament. With customs duties slashed 60 percent by the British blockade, the Treasury was nearly empty. All the Atlantic coastline but New England had been sealed off by the Royal Navy—except, that is, for illicit trading with the enemy welcomed and actively encouraged by the hungry blockaders themselves and Wellington's armies in Spain and Portugal, who had become dependent on smuggled American wheat. (Smugglers and ship's captains could purchase a license to trade with the enemy at any British consulate for $5,000.)

After an initial heady season of one-on-one single-ship victories, all but two U.S. frigates were bottled up in American harbors and did not dare venture out to sea for fear of capture by patrolling British squadrons. The introduction of unpopular internal taxes appeared unavoidable. With recruiting drying up as the news of military failures arrived from the north and west, even a whisper about conscription was considered political suicide. Increasingly leaders of both parties in Washington, even the chief War Hawk Henry Clay, doubting the wisdom of protracting the agony if honorable peace terms could be obtained, were coming to favor an early end to the war.

WHEN THE CZAR's offer to mediate finally arrived in Washington, Madison hurriedly selected a delegation of peace commissioners. As its ministers plenipotentiary, he selected Adams and the Swiss-born Gallatin, who was intimately familiar with European trade, politics and diplomacy. In an attempt at political balance, Madison chose Federalist James A. Bayard of Delaware, whose break with his party had helped to end the 1800 Electoral College deadlock. Madison counted on Bayard to be more sympathetic to the British viewpoint on impressment. Gallatin took along his seventeen-year-old son James as his secretary and recruited three attachés. They included John Payne Todd, the wastrel twenty-one-year-old son of Dolley Madison, and future vice president George M. Dallas of Philadelphia, descendant by marriage of Benjamin Franklin. With passports issued by British Admiral Cochrane, Bayard, Gallatin and their entourage sailed on May 9, 1813, to rendezvous with Adams and the British negotiators in St. Petersburg.

Until this juncture, Jefferson, as a former president, had made it his policy to avoid making public his personal opinions on how best his friend Madison should conduct the war. Jefferson's attitude toward Britain had become increasingly more sclerotic over the years since he had last corresponded with Madame de Staël in July 1807 at the height of national outrage over the Chesapeake Affair. Back in June 1812, as unemployed Americans indignantly rushed to join the army, Jefferson had predicted that the conquest of Canada would be "a mere matter of marching." But less than a year later, when a courier from Washington pelted up Monticello, Jefferson had abandoned his pacifism along with his optimism.

A British armada had invaded the undefended Chesapeake. On May 2, Jefferson set aside his self-imposed neutrality for an hour. Taking up his quill, he drafted a lengthy anonymous reply to Madame de Staël:

> The dangers of the sea are now so great, and the possibilities of interception by sea and land such, that I shall subscribe no name to this letter. You will know from whom it comes, by its reference to the date and place of yours . . .

Jefferson took pains to persuade his old friend that America's animus toward Britain did not imply friendship for France under Napoleon. "It is by millions that Napoleon destroys the poor." The self-styled French emperor had emerged from the French Revolution as

> [t]he greatest of the destroyers of the human race. What year of his military life has not consigned a million of human beings to death, to poverty and wretchedness! What field in Europe may not raise a monument [to] the murders, the burnings, the desolations, the famines and miseries it has witnessed from him.

At the same time, Britain had produced "a tyrant as unprincipled and as overwhelming":

> Not in the poor maniac George, but in his government and nation. Buonaparte [sic] will die, and his tyrannies with him. But a nation never dies. The English government and its piratical principles and practices, have no fixed term of duration.

The United States had suffered the seizure of "one thousand ships" and "more than six thousand of our citizens" before "we concluded that the war she had been for years waging against us, might as well become a war of both sides." In making a detailed bill of particular injustices carried out by the British before the declaration of war, Jefferson insisted that "the object of England is the <u>permanent dominion of the ocean</u>, and <u>the mono-poly of the trade of the world</u>."[39]

MADISON'S, AND THE nation's, euphoria at the prospect of peace faded in the harsh summer light of 1813. Viscount Castlereagh, the British foreign minister, flatly rejected the Russian offer of mediation. He feared that trade ties between Russia and America and their agreement on the rights of neutral nations at sea would weigh in America's favor. Once more, Madison's administration suffered an embarrassing setback. But as the fighting in Europe continued unabated, Castlereagh reconsidered. While he wouldn't accept an intermediary, he opened the door to direct negotiations between the two combatants. He proposed that peace talks take place either in Gothenberg, Sweden, or in London.

Reshuffling the peace commission, Madison retained Adams, Gallatin and Bayard but added Henry Clay, despite his total lack of diplomatic experience. Resigning as Speaker of the House, Clay received a thunderous endorsement, a congressional resolution passing by a 149-9 vote. Madison also nominated Jonathan Russell, charge d'affairs in London and his nominee as minister to Sweden, since he believed the talks would take place in Gothenberg.

Meeting with Secretary of State Monroe on January 28, 1814, Clay received the delegates' instructions. One issue was to be nonnegotiable: impressment of American sailors must end. In exchange, Madison would bar all British seamen from American ships and surrender British deserters. In compensation for British-inspired Indian depredations, the British must cease the attacks and cede a negotiable amount of land, with the annexation of all Canada by the United States a possibility. If the British refused to make amends, they would lose treaty rights to trade in the states. In addition, American naval power on the Great Lakes was to remain unrestricted. By February 25 all the delegates and their functionaries were ready to sail to Sweden. After a miserable forty-eight-day winter crossing of the North Atlantic, they reached the ice-bound city of Gothenberg on April 13.

Clay and Russell had expected to be greeted by Adams, Gallatin and Bayard, but Adams would not leave St. Petersburg for two more weeks, and Gallatin and Bayard wrote that they were in London. The first round of negotiating turned to the location of the negotiations. Bayard and Galla-tin found Sweden unacceptable, even if it had been Madison's choice, no doubt influenced by Jefferson and Madame de Staël. Gallatin preferred London, close to Castlereagh, but Clay refused: "I shall not consent to go to London," he declared. The British were bent on "the chastisement of America"; in a letter to Gallatin he objected to what would be seen as "fur-ther condescension" for the peace talks to take place at the seat of the Brit-ish government, "especially when we have yet to see the example in British history of that haughty people having been conciliated by the condescen-sion of their enemy." To avoid damaging relations with Russia and Swe-den, Russell took on the task of making it appear that it was the British who had insisted on a change of venue; Bayard urged that they move the proceedings to a town in "friendly" Holland. Finally, it was Castlereagh who broke the impasse: the British would consent to the neutral medieval Flemish city of Ghent (in present-day Belgium). Gallatin and Bayard ac-cepted and informed the others.[40]

James Madison by John Vanderlyn. *White House Art Collection*

Dolley Madison by Gilbert Stuart. *White House Art Collection*

Constitution outruns a British squadron, July, 1812, by Anton Otto Fischer.

U.S. Naval Historical Center

Battle of Lake Erie, September 10, 1813. *U.S. Navy*

Battle of the Thames with death of Tecumseh, October 5, 1813. *Library of Congress*

Admiral George Cockburn
with Washington, D.C.
burning in the background.
Royal Museum Greenwich

Macdonough aboard the *Saratoga* during the Battle of Lake Champlain, September 11, 1814. *Library of Congress*

The Battle of Lake Champlain viewed from Plattsburgh, New York.
Library of Congress

Thomas Macdonough by Gilbert Stuart. *National Gallery of Art*

Signing of the Treaty of Ghent on Christmas Eve, 1814, by Amédeé Forestier.
Center, from left to right: Lord Gambier, John Quincy Adams and Henry Goulburn.
Smithsonian American Art Museum, Washington, D.C.

ELEVEN

"Father, Listen to Your Children"

On the northwestern frontier, 1813 began as the previous year had ended: with an unnecessary American defeat hard on the heels of even more bungling in Washington, D.C. With the Great Lakes, all of Michigan and the northern Ohio frontier settlements exposed to British and Indian raids by the surrenders of Detroit and Chicago, Secretary of War Eustis needed to appoint a dynamic new commander of all forces in the Old Northwest to replace Hull and calm the terrified frontier. Instead, he appointed a Tennessee planter, James Winchester, who had never served above the rank of captain in the Revolution. As brigadier general in the regular army, he would be superseded by the popular veteran military governor, William Henry Harrison. Winchester was to have raised 1,200 militia and marched to reinforce Hull in Detroit, but he arrived there too late. By this time, the alarmed Kentucky legislature, at the bidding of Clay, had appointed Harrison major general and commander of the Kentucky militia.

When Winchester eventually arrived at Fort Wayne, the officers he found there faced a conundrum: could a regular army brigadier general outrank a militia major general? After mulling the question with his staff officers, Harrison yielded to Winchester, but not before he had appealed over Secretary of War Eustis's head to President Madison. Winchester remained in command only six days before a letter came from Madison, turning over the command to Harrison.

Building up a huge army, Harrison ordered massive amounts of supplies—one order was for 1 million rations—and paid prices far above market rates, if nothing else reviving the region's economy and making the war popular. But he was literally stuck in mud and short on supplies, which were maddeningly slow to arrive, the sodden, unpaved roads impassable for artillery and supply wagons. Harrison was about to furlough his men to their warm homes until spring when news of the American rout at Queenston Heights reached Washington. Eustis fired off fresh orders: Harrison was to keep his forces intact, no matter the conditions. By Christmas, up to three hundred men had become seriously ill, as Private Elias Darnell wrote in his diary, from being "exposed to the cold ground and deprived of every nourishment. . . . The camp has become a loathsome place."[1]

At last convinced that he was ready to unleash a counteroffensive to sweep the Indians from the region and to retake Detroit, Harrison turned over his left flank to Winchester and ordered him to march to Fort Defiance (present-day Defiance, Ohio), secure it and await further orders. But, disregarding Harrison's command, Winchester moved his camp several times in the next three months as winter and disease, including typhoid fever, worsened. Finally in late December Winchester received clothing and two days' rations, along with fresh orders to rendezvous with Harrison's main force at the Miami River rapids. On Christmas Day, as the weather turned bitter cold and a heavy snow fell, Winchester and his men marched off. On the third day, he received countermanding orders from Harrison to turn back. Tecumseh and his Indians were pursuing him. When, finally, after a horrendously cold eighteen-day march, Winchester and his frostbitten men finally reached the Maumee rapids, he set his sick and wounded to work building a new fort, naming it for himself. There, at Fort Winchester, sixty miles north of Harrison's main encampment, the men rested.

Winchester's officers were restless. They insisted that they had heard credible reports from settlers that the Indians were about to attack Frenchtown (now Monroe, Michigan). What they probably heard was that the hamlet offered warm cottages and abundant food. They finally persuaded Winchester to act. He sent two messages, one to Sandusky for militia reinforcements, the other to Harrison that he was going to attack French-town on his own initiative. By the time the courier returned with Harrison's denial of permission, Winchester had already marched. When Harrison learned that his order had not been acknowledged, he set off after Winchester through a winter storm, followed by two regiments and artillery, which often became sunk in snow drifts. Leaving his army behind, Harrison rode on alone.

Winchester had sent his best troops, 550 regulars under Lieutenant Colonel William Lewis, ahead to Frenchtown. They formed a line of battle on January 18, 1813, on slippery river ice and scaled the riverbank to the village, where street fighting seesawed for three hours. Finally, the Canadians withdrew two miles into the forest. Two days later, Winchester and the rest of his troops arrived in time to feast and enjoy the hospitality of the grateful villagers. Harrison sent word ahead that he would arrive in two more days with the rest of his command. Winchester hadn't been so comfortable since he had left his plantation. He believed that the British never fought in the winter. His position seemed secure, with breast-high ramparts on three sides. But he had stationed his regulars too far out on his right flank, and they were staying indoors on a bitter cold night.

At four o'clock on the morning of January 22, in the first battle of the new year, three British 3-pounders and three small howitzers mounted on skids opened fire as six hundred redcoats and five hundred Indians swarmed into the village. Half-dressed Americans stumbled out into the darkened streets, their muskets unloaded. Their officers, who had scattered them, grabbed any soldier running by and ordered him to the log barricade as the mounted Indians rode around its flank. Disorganized militia clotted in the center of the village while the regulars, driven by the British, fled down the Raisin River bank. Without weapons, they slithered across the ice as screaming Indians clubbed, tomahawked and scalped them. Indians on horseback rode past them and ambushed them as the regulars tried to form a defensive line. An Indian chief captured the half-dressed Winchester, stripped him, took his uniform coat for himself and, after painting the shivering Winchester's body, led him to the British commander, Colonel Henry Procter.

For the first time, Winchester learned that some militia led by Major George Madison of Kentucky had managed to form a stronghold in the town. Procter urged Winchester to surrender before the Indians went on killing. He accepted Winchester's two conditions: that his men be considered prisoners of war, assuring them of humane treatment, and that Procter control his Indian auxiliaries. Major Madison and his men surrendered under a white flag. But Procter couldn't control his victorious Indians. By the next morning, drunken Indians, celebrating their victory, had killed and scalped sixty more men, among them most of the wounded. Any of the other prisoners able to walk trudged off to Canada under Indian guard to join the growing number of prisoners of war. Of Winchester's 1,200-man command, three hundred were killed and nearly nine hundred captured. Only thirty-seven escaped to rejoin Harrison. When the news of the latest military fiasco spread, the massacre gave the Americans a battle cry: "Remember the Raisin!"

In the frontier settlements, men wore black armbands and women wore black widow's dresses to church.

In October 1812, as fighting on the Niagara frontier had intensified, a premature attempt had miscarried to capture two vessels of the Canadian Provincial Marine and sail them past the British forts on the Niagara River and into Lake Erie. The only American warship on the Great Lakes as the year 1813 opened was a three-year-old brig, the *Oneida*, moored at Sackets Harbor. Perry set to work laying the keel for a larger vessel, the corvette *Madison*. Commodore Chauncey was under pressure from Navy secretary William Jones; in turn, he pressed Perry to have the *Madison* under sail before the lake froze over:

> It is impossible to attach too much significance to our Naval operations on the Lakes—the success of the ensuing campaign will depend absolutely upon our superiority on all the lakes—& every effort & resource must be directed to that object and would be important to the success of Major General Harrison's campaign.[2]

Jones backhandedly was informing Chauncey that President Madison had taken priority of command away from Dearborn and given it to Harrison. The newly appointed major general was to raise a force and build a fleet that would enable him not only to retake Detroit but to carry out Hull's botched mission of invading Canada. Jones also informed Chauncey that it was Perry who, to support Harrison, would be placed in command of the Lake Erie naval campaign, not his superior Chauncey.

Brushing aside Jones's instructions, Chauncey only informed Perry that they were to shift their operations to Lake Erie. By the time Chauncey stored his cannon in Buffalo and shifted his headquarters to their new base at Erie, Pennsylvania, despite ten days of slogging through "very deep" snow, the first of an eventual workforce of two hundred master ship-builders had arrived from New York City. One of them, Noah Brown, and navy sailing master Dobbins, an experienced lake mariner, selected the peninsula of Presque Isle, which provided a protected harbor surrounded by forests of oak ideal for making ships' ribs and planking.

In New York City, at their shipyard at the foot of Jefferson Street, Noah and Adam Brown had built John Jacob Astor's outsized cargo ship *Beaver*, the equal of any merchant ship afloat, for the China trade. Between the wars, the Browns built or refitted schooners and whaling ships, frigates, brigs and gunboats for the Navy. Throughout the War of 1812 they would build many of the fastest privateering ships that made New York City the prime port for the activity, accounting for some seven hundred captures in two years.

On Lake Erie, Noah Brown laid out a shipyard, blockhouse, guard-house, cookhouse with bunks for all his men, an eighty-foot-long black-smithy and an office to share with Commodore Perry. Brown's younger brother, Adam, remained in the city, recruiting skilled shipwrights and forwarding supplies. By late February, crews were laying the oaken keels for two brigs. "Nearly everything else had to be imported from distant cities," writes historian Ron Soodalter.

Rope, sails and other nautical staples came out of Philadelphia, while the Pittsburgh forge supplied cannon and balls, anchors, bolts, chains and other iron products, floated up the Allegheny River and French Creek to Meadville, then hauled to Erie by a Conestoga freight wagon over forty-one miles of rough road. An American army officer had described the passage as "little more than an Indian trail."[3]

As late as March 1813, the United States had no ships on Lake Erie.

Perry and Brown had only a little more than three months to build a lake fleet strong enough for the impending spring campaign. The Provincial Marine dominated Lake Erie with half a dozen well-constructed ships: the *Queen Charlotte,* the *Hunter,* the *Provost,* the *Nancy,* the *Caledonia*—the merchant vessel of John Jacob Astor seized at Michilimackinac—and the *Detroit,* captured at Hull's surrender. Together, they mounted seventy cannon. With the enemy marooned by winter on the north shore of the lake, the Americans set to work mass-producing small, shallow draft boats that could navigate Lake Erie's tricky sandbars and shoals and converting and arming vessels Perry found on the lake into fore-and-aft schooners. By mid-June, the last lake ice melted, Perry had his squadron ready to sail: twin twenty-gun brigs *Niagara* and *Lawrence,* the latter Perry's flag-ship, the fast-sailing schooner *Ariel* and three seaworthy gunboats, *Porcu-pine, Scorpion* and *Tigress.*

AFTER SO MANY casualties, so much sickness and so much melting away of militia over the winter of 1812–13, General Harrison, now commander of the Army of the West, could only depend on some eight hundred regulars, far too few to carry on his campaign to retake Detroit and barely enough to finish constructing Fort Meigs, a vast log-and-dirt stronghold encompassing ten acres with fifteen-foot-high wooden walls reinforced by eight substantial blockhouses. Perched on high ground commanding the Maumee rapids, the river guarding its north side while steep ravines made approach from any other direction difficult, it was well situated to protect the gateway to northern Ohio. In order to raise enough troops to invade Canada, Harrison rode off to Cincinnati, believing that mud season would make a British attack on the new fortress impossible.

On the contrary, British general Procter felt that a well-timed attack on American positions south of Lake Erie would deter any new American offensive against Canada. Harrison returned from the west with three hundred fresh troops and, trailing them, a brigade of 1,500 Kentucky militia. Among all the frontier states and territories, Kentucky, the most militant, was providing the most fighters. Pennsylvania's militiamen, closer at hand, refused to leave their own state to help their next-door neighbors in Ohio. Harrison and his fresh recruits arrived at Fort Meigs (Perrysburg) in late April, just as Procter arrived at the mouth of the Maumee with a Provincial Marine flotilla that put ashore 1,000 regulars and Canadian militia and some 1,200 of Tecumseh's warriors, the largest force of Indians ever assembled for battle.

Ignoring the explicit written instructions of Governor-General Prevost to remain on the defensive, Procter was leading the first British invasion of the United States since the American Revolution. It had taken several days for hundreds of Procter's troops to drag eleven heavy guns captured at Detroit—two 24-pounders, each weighing a ton, and nine 6-pounder field guns—through the spring quagmire and into positions in two batteries on either side of the river. On May 1, 1813, Procter's artillery, reinforced by 9-pounders on his ships, opened fire.

Harrison braced his men with stirring rhetoric:

> Can the citizens of a free country, who have taken up arms to defend its rights, think of submitting to an army composed of mercenary soldiers, reluctant Canadians goaded to the field by the bayonet, and of the wretched naked savages? . . . To your posts then, fellow citizens, and remember that the eyes of your country are upon you.[4]

Harrison succeeded in getting a messenger through British lines to tell Brigadier General Green Clay of Kentucky to divide his force, half the Kentuckians to be sent in boats to hem in the British guns from the rear, the other half to breach the Indian lines and get into the fort. For four days, the fort fended off the British siege. It slowly dawned on the British commander that capturing the stronghold would not be as easy as he had expected. Tecumseh had decided to concentrate his forces on taking the fort and left the shoreline undefended. When eight hundred Kentuckians under Colonel William Dudley arrived, Harrison ordered them to storm the battery on the north shore. As Kentucky horsemen closed in from behind, they charged the Indians, who panicked and fled into the woods. The Kentuckians chased them, some pausing long enough to take Indian scalps. But a combined British and Indian counterattack shattered the militia force, killing or wounding three hundred militiamen and capturing the rest. The British victory proved illusory. They could not sustain the siege, their cannonballs sucked harmlessly into a twelve-foot-high earthen embankment protecting the fort.

Tecumseh had managed to reorganize his warriors in the British rear near a holding area for American prisoners. There, the Indians were dragging away the prisoners one by one and forcing them to run a gauntlet where the warriors clubbed them to death. After his warriors had murdered twenty prisoners, Tecumseh rode up and ordered them to stop.

When Harrison still refused to surrender and instead continued to fight off the British, after two more days Procter had to abandon the siege. The British invader had become caught between two foes. The Indians, slipping away, carried off with them supplies to feed their families; the disheartened Canadian militia, half of Procter's remaining force, petitioned to go home to plant their crops.

Three months later, the Canadians were ready to fight again. Explaining that he had received intelligence from his spies that Harrison had left the fort, Tecumseh persuaded Procter to make a second assault on Fort Meigs. In fact, Harrison had shifted his headquarters to Cleveland, closer to the naval shipyards at Erie, where Commander Perry's new fleet was now ready to support Harrison's invasion of Canada. In the three months since the last siege, Harrison had left Kentucky colonel Clay in command at Fort Meigs, charging him with building what would be named Fort Stephenson as a supply base for the Canadian invasion. Tecumseh persuaded Procter to rely on a ruse to draw Clay out of Fort Meigs. Staging a mock battle a mile from the fort, Procter's force would pretend to be an American relief column trapped by British regulars. But Clay refused the bait, and again the British invasion collapsed. For the Americans, it was a bloodless victory of profound importance: Procter never heeded Tecumseh again.

Nonetheless refusing to abandon his mission to prevent the Americans from retaking Detroit, Procter returned in August to attempt another amphibious attack. This time his target was newly constructed Fort Stephenson, crammed with food, powder and shot. With only 160 regulars, Major George Croghan, defying Harrison's order to destroy the supplies and burn the fort if he was attacked, held off Procter's superior forces until reinforcements arrived. The fort's thick log-and-mud walls absorbed the shells of the six-pounder fieldpieces Procter's gunners were able to haul

within range—which in turn were within range of the best Kentucky riflemen. Once again, Procter and Tecumseh backed away.

IGNORING SECRETARY OF War Armstrong's directives, Chauncey and
Dearborn feared that the British base at Kingston was already too strong
and that the British ships and troops there were about to mount an attack
on Sackets Harbor. To be sure, the British had moved eighteen cannon
from Montreal, where they obviously were not immediately needed, to
Kingston, where they had assembled a force of 1,900 British regulars, militia and Indians. Instead, the American commanders decided to attack
the less well-defended targets of York and Fort George.

Acknowledging the British threat, Dearborn had ordered Colonel Pike
to make a grueling midwinter march across New York State with eight
hundred regulars to reinforce Sackets Harbor. Pike had sent press gangs
through the countryside, looking for horses, sleighs and snowshoes. He immediately sent ahead four hundred men with a howitzer and a three-
pounder on sleighs; he would forward the other four hundred soldiers with
ten more artillery pieces as soon as he could gather 150 sleighs, enough
ammunition and sufficient grain for the men and the horses that pulled
them. On March 3, 1813, Pike left Plattsburgh with one-third of his men on
snowshoes or on sleighs. Many still had to march but, as a severe late-season
storm dumped heavy, wet snow three feet deep, some of those who insisted
on riding the sleighs froze to death instead of getting off to walk. To prepare
his ragtag troops for the impending invasion, Pike took advantage of the
thick lake ice. As the days of spring lengthened, he drilled his men in maneuver up to six hours a day on the brilliant surface of Black River Bay.

By mid-March, Pike had requisitioned a farrier, a hundred pairs of pistols, 333 swords, two 12-pounders and all the stores from Plattsburgh. He
could see signs that spring and the probability of a British attack were approaching. Several horses had plunged through the thinning ice. Learning that he had been promoted to brigadier general, Pike ordered another
brigade to march from Plattsburgh to Sackets Harbor "without unnecessary delay with arms & accoutrements." He was moving with alacrity, a
concept unknown to Dearborn, because he expected massive British reinforcements from Europe with the spring, as many as 20,000 regulars to
Montreal alone.[5]

Traveling from Washington to Albany in midwinter, Secretary of War Armstrong conferred with Dearborn on a Canadian strategy even as Governor-General Prevost traveled up the frozen St. Lawrence to inspect garrisons and fortifications in Upper Canada, bringing with him only a few small detachments of reinforcements. Dearborn told Armstrong that both he and Chauncey believed that Prevost's arrival augured an imminent attack on Sackets Harbor. Chauncey had a second reason for ignoring Armstrong. He had learned that construction of the thirty-gun frigate, the *Sir Isaac Brock*, and two brigs were nearing completion at the shipyard at York (today's Toronto), the provincial capital of Upper Canada. To buttress his argument, Dearborn lied to Armstrong that 6,000 or more British regulars now defended Kingston. In fact, when Prevost had returned to Quebec, deserters and pro-American Canadian civilians had reported to Dearborn that the true size of Kingston's garrison of regulars was merely one-tenth that number and 1,400 militia. Dearborn did not pass along to Armstrong these latest revised estimates. Even with the arrival of Pike's two brigades, due to sickness and exposure the number of effective American troops at Sackets Harbor had fallen far short of the 7,000 men Armstrong believed necessary to attack heavily defended Kingston. Dearborn's concealment of this vital intelligence effectively reversed Armstrong's entire strategy—approved by President Madison and the cabinet—for the 1813 campaign.

By late April, the ice had melted on Lake Ontario, providing an opening for the Americans to take the offensive. Ice still had not broken up on the St. Lawrence River, paralyzing travel and making it virtually impossible for British troops in Montreal to reinforce garrisons in Upper Canada. Seizing this advantage, some 1,800 American troops clambered aboard the new lake squadron on April 25. Fourteen warships, including a ship-rigged corvette, a brig, twelve fore-and-aft-rigged lake schooners and a host of smaller boats set sail from Sackets Harbor for a stormy passage to York, appearing off the provincial capital of Upper Canada late the next day.

While Commodore Chauncey tried to guide his ships and his guns from a bobbing rowboat, Dearborn, still the overall army commander, preferred to remain aboard the *Madison* throughout the battle, busying himself with paperwork and pleading a medley of ailments. He delegated the field command to Pike. To prepare for the attack at dawn the next day, Pike issued explicit orders to his troops. Any man who quit his post would be instantly put to death. The bayonet was to be used in preference to the bullet. Plunderers of private property would be shot.

York was a prosperous town of solid lakefront houses, unprepossessing provincial government buildings and the ample taverns where legislators hobnobbed. Its populace of about seven hundred included aging Loyalist Americans who had fled across the border from the United States at the end of the Revolution intermixed with new immigrants seeking land that sold for a fraction of the cost of New York real estate. Benedict Arnold's family had taken refuge in York. Arnold's sister, Hannah, and three children from his first marriage had fled to the 13,400-acre grant of land he had received for his service against the French in the Caribbean in the early years of the Napoleonic Wars.

Considering that it was the provincial capital of Upper Canada, a shipbuilding center and the supply base of the Provincial Marine, York was surprisingly ill defended. West of the town, the Government House Battery mounted only two 12-pounder guns. Even farther west, on the edge of a deep ravine bordered by dense forest, was the smaller Western Battery, armed with two ancient eighteen-pounders. One, a Simcoe long gun cast in England as long ago as the 1650s for Oliver Cromwell's artillery, had been disabled, its trunnions broken off so that it could only be mounted in a wooden cradle that made it impossible to raise or lower and useless except for firing straight ahead. Through their field glasses, the American commanders could espy, also to the west of the stockaded town, four unfinished batteries lining the shore. In various stages of completion, they were shaped from mounds of earth lined with timbers and faced with sod. To the east, a sprawling wooden stockade, stretching down to the shoreline, housed a two-story blockhouse and some twenty public buildings. Government House, with the royal standard flapping above it to signal that the province's royal governor, Major General Sir Roger Sheaffe, was in residence, perched on a rise. Sheaffe, who had reluctantly succeeded to command at the death of Brock at Queenston, had just arrived in York. He commanded four companies of regulars—roughly three hundred men—drawn from the Royal Newfoundland Regiment of Fencibles, the Glengarry Light Infantry Regiment of Fencibles and the grenadier company of the elite 8th Regiment of Foot. When he ordered the provincial militia to turn out, only three hundred reported for duty. In addition, Sheaffe could muster about one hundred neighboring Ojibway, Mississauga and Chippewa Indians.

In the first combined army-navy amphibious operation in American history, Chauncey's schooners raked the beachhead at seven o'clock the morning of April 27, just before the first unit of three hundred American troops, a company of the 1st U.S. Regiment of Rifles led by the stocky Major Benjamin Forsyth, vaulted over the gunwales of the handful of bateaux. They sloshed ashore through bone-chilling water near the ruins of Fort Rouille, three miles west of the town. The British commander had time only to dispatch Captain Neal McNeale and the grenadiers of the 8th and thirty Indians under the command of Major James Givins to dash along the shore firing their muskets at the invaders in their landing craft.

Quickly moving off the beach and disappearing into the woods, the North Carolinian sharpshooters, armed with Harpers Ferry rifles, spread out to engage the Indians, slowly outflanking them. Killing or wounding ten warriors, including two tribal leaders, they drove the Indians back toward the old fort. Sheaffe ordered a company of the Glengarry Light Infantry to reinforce the Indians, but following the instructions of the provincial adjutant general, Aeneas Shaw, they became lost in the dense woods.

The second wave of Americans, Pike's 15th Regiment, carried off course by the wind and the current, attempted to land four hundred yards west of the beachhead. A storm of bullets from the shore killed three officers and wounded three enlisted men. Captain John Hoppock was fatally wounded in the thigh as the second boat scraped ashore. On the quarterdeck of the flagship *Madison*, General Pike, seeing that the British musket fire from a bluff was pinning down the landings, became impatient. Declaring to an aide, "By God, I can't stand here any longer," he jumped into a boat to take personal command of the operation. Pike's earlier order that the Fifteenth were not to load their rifles but were to charge with lowered bayonets and pikes was causing the delay in landing more troops.[6]

As Pike led three bright-green-uniformed platoons of the 15th up from the beachhead, Captain McNeale's British grenadiers became trapped between two attacking forces. Firing a volley that killed Lieutenant Moses

Bloomfield and five other Americans, the grenadiers then charged with the bayonet. Pike's men reciprocated, driving the grenadiers back with heavy casualties. Of eighty-nine grenadiers who went into battle that morning, only eight would survive. By now, attacking from the west, the North Carolina riflemen of the 1st Regiment were pursuing the retreating Indians back through the British ranks. The American sharpshooters, targeting the grenadiers' red uniforms, shot their commander, Captain McNeale, through the head. His sergeant major, Robert Beveridge, attempting to regroup his men, was next to fall dead. York magistrate and clerk of the Provincial Assembly Donald McLean, so keen to volunteer for the fight, also fell and died.

Supported by two 6-pounders firing in tandem, Pike personally led the assault on the redoubt of the Western Battery, decimating what remained of the 8th Regiment's grenadiers and the Newfoundland Fencibles. The British were attempting to rally when a British gunner, dragging a lighted match behind him toward a cannon, touched it to the battery's portable magazine, a chest filled with cartridges. The explosion killed a score of the British. Demoralized, the surviving British fell back to a ravine north of the fort, attempting to link up with provincial militia. All the while, in a bobbing boat, Commodore Chauncey personally directed bombardment of the fort and its Government House battery with twenty-four- and thirty-two-pound shells.

Conceding defeat, Governor-General Sheaffe decided to conserve his remaining regulars and retreat the 150 miles to the main British base at Kingston. Giving orders to leave behind the wounded, Sheaffe took all the medical supplies with him. Jettisoning packs, weapons and heavy outerwear, his men streamed out of York. To slow down their pursuers, Sheaffe ordered his men to destroy the wooden bridge over the Don River to the east of the town. Leaving the royal ensign flying, he abandoned the town's citizens, including any women and children who hadn't already fled, instructing provincial officials and senior militia officers to remain behind and make the best surrender terms they could. Finally, he commanded the sixty-year-old deputy quartermaster general, Captain Tito Le Lièvre of the Royal Newfoundland Regiment, to burn the two unfinished warships on the ways in the dockyard, the sloop-of-war *Sir Isaac Brock* and the brig *Duke of Gloucester*, and then blow up the province's grand magazine.

A militia surgeon, Doctor Amasa Trowbridge, who tended the wounded, later described the ammunition magazine and its lethal contents:

> Their principal magazine [was] about Thirty feet [in size], with solid mason work and stone, 30 feet deep in the earth and [with] an entrance at the bottom from the lake. Over this stood a large stone building with apparatus for elevating military stores from the bottoms; different apartments were formed and arranged for the reception of military and naval stores. . . . There were five hundred barrels of powder on the first floor and the other rooms [were] filled with fixed ammunition and the stone Arsenal above well-filled with the same material. All of an explosive character.

The magazine contained "close to 30,000 pounds of highly inflammable powder alone," calculates Canadian military historian Robert Malcomsen. "Its destructive potential was enormous."[7]

It was early afternoon before Pike was able to bring up the bulk of his troops and heavier guns to silence the fire from the Government House Battery and prepare to lead a decisive assault on York's remaining gun emplacement. Selecting a tree stump from which he could view the continuing artillery fire, Pike, surrounded by his staff, interrogated a prisoner, inquiring how many redcoats still defended the fort. Meanwhile, reaching the underground powder magazine two hundred yards away, Captain LeFievre and two assistants had broken open barrels of gunpowder, laid a trail out of the tunnel and struck flints to it.

When the magazine exploded, three hundred battle-weary American soldiers were still standing in formation, leaning against their weapons. "The explosion was tremendous," testified one eyewitness. "The column was raked from front to rear." As many as 263 Americans—and forty British prisoners—were killed or maimed. Patrick Finan Jr., the thirteen-year-old son of the quartermaster of the 8th Regiment, had fled the town with his mother but then had slipped away from her to see the battle. Fifteen years later, he recounted that he

> [w]as proceeding towards the garrison when the explosion took place. I heard the report, and felt a tremendous motion in the earth, resembling the shock of an earthquake; and looking towards the spot I saw an im-

mense cloud ascend into the air. . . . At first it was a great confused mass
of smoke, timber, men, earth . . . but as it rose, in a majestic manner, it
assumed the shape of a vast balloon. When the whole mass . . . became
spent, [it] fell from the cloud.

Struck by a falling boulder that crushed his spine, Zebulon Pike collapsed, gasping, mortally wounded. While subordinate officers tried to
conceal his condition from the men, just as Pike was lifted onto a makeshift stretcher a round of huzzas went up from the troops. He asked a sergeant the reason for the cheering. The royal standard had come down and
the stars and stripes gone up, the stretcher-bearer told him. In agony as he
was rowed first over the choppy water to a schooner and then transferred
to the *Madison*, with the folded British royal standard as his pillow, Pike
succumbed. Amasa Trowbridge remembered that he and his fellow surgeons "cut & slashed for 48 hours, without food or sleep," wading "in
blood, cutting off arms, legs and trepanning [boring holes in] heads." Of
the men of the 6th Infantry standing close to Pike, thirteen men were
killed outright and 104 wounded; thirteen artillerymen died and eighty-
three were wounded.[8]

In the first American military victory of the war, the British casualty
toll at York was a staggering 475, including a dozen native warriors, 274
militia and volunteers and 166 regulars, more than half of the town's defenders. It far exceeded the Americans' 308 killed or wounded, including
the 263 victims of the explosion. But it was the death of Zebulon Pike, a
famous explorer and promising commander, that triggered an aftermath
that would render the American military success a pyrrhic victory. Without Pike's restraining influence, American sailors and soldiers ignored his
explicit order to spare private property and eagerly imbibed the contents
of the town's taverns, resulting in a binge of vandalizing and looting. First
ransacking the ornate legislative chamber of Government House, the ine-
briated sailors discovered what they later claimed was a scalp "suspended
near the Speaker's chair, in company with the Mace & other Emblems of
Royalty." Infuriated, they set fire to the government buildings. They would
proudly present the mace to General Dearborn, who sent it off to Washington, along with Dearborn and Chauncey's official report. The two commanders officially reported that the "scalp" constituted proof that the

British government was colluding in bloody Indian raids. The province's royal insignia, taken from the podium, was sent as a trophy to the United States Naval Academy in Annapolis. After 121 years, President Franklin Delano Roosevelt would return the mace to Canada in 1934 as a goodwill gesture.[9]

In Governor-General Sheaffe's absence, provincial and town officials negotiated terms of surrender with American officers, who agreed to protect private property and parole the local militiamen. In return, the Canadians agreed to surrender all government and military property. But then Dearborn dragged his feet for an entire day: he considered the burning of the sloop-of-war a violation of the surrender terms. He maintained that the ship and the fort had been destroyed after negotiations for surrender had already begun. By the morning of April 28, Dearborn still had not ratified the terms of capitulation and refused to leave the *Madison*.

After sacking government buildings and vandalizing the government printing office—destroying its press and scattering the type in the harbor—during the two nights while Dearborn mulled the surrender terms, his soldiers and sailors systematically ransacked empty houses, devoting special attention to the home of Major Givins, head of the Indian Department. They plundered silver and gold altar pieces in St. Mary's Anglican church, stripped the town's subscription library, even hauled away York's fire engines to an uncertain fate. Provincial militia leader William Allan would report, "Few houses in the town escaped a minute search by two or three parties, under the pretext of looking for public property. Many have been pillaged and some have had everything taken." Sheriff John Beikie reported that "those who abandoned their Houses found nothing but the bare walls at their return."[10]

Forsyth's riflemen had been assigned to guard the town's private property, but an American naval officer recorded in his journal that

> [s]ome of them have had handkerchiefs full, and have made several hundred dollars in one battle. They have mashed up, between two stones, some of the most elegant Silver embost urns, turines and plate of every discription to get them in their napsacks. The officers generally attempt to prevent it; but Forsyth is a perfect savage himself. He, it is said, encourages it.[11]

Either unable or unwilling to rein in their personnel, Dearborn and Chauncey gave the orders to burn the fortifications, barracks and storehouses, writes historian Alan Taylor, although they would later deny having given orders for any building to be destroyed. Before sailing away, Chauncey carried off a large quantity of naval stores intended for Captain Barclay's Lake Erie squadron. The weeklong foray crippled one of the two British naval bases on Lake Ontario and evened the balance of power on the lake, in addition to hampering British operations on Lake Erie.

The lawless aftermath of the Battle of York set a disastrous precedent and would have far-reaching consequences. The mistreatment of the homes and property of private citizens, many of whom had previously been unwilling to commit to the British cause, coupled with the burning of government buildings—a new and inflammatory incident in the annals of American warfare—and combined with the pilfering of British royal symbols led to a stiffening of Canadian resistance and invited retribution.

While Chauncey sailed away with his fleet and most of the garrison of Sackets Harbor to attack Fort George at the western end of Lake Ontario, the British commanders at Kingston, bent on retaliation for the sacking of York, decided to attack the most important American post on the lake. On May 29, 1813, Prevost and Sir James Yeo, the new British naval commander of Lake Ontario, sailed into the deep-water harbor and landed an assault force of nearly nine hundred regulars, their flat-bottomed landing craft scraping ashore on Sandy Horse Island, west of the fort and connected to the mainland by shallows. In tight regimental formation, the redcoats fixed bayonets and splashed through the cold water as their fleet's cannon pounded the hastily formed American defensive line. Chauncey had left behind seven hundred raw New York militiamen under the command of Brigadier General Jacob Brown to guard the beachhead along with 750 regulars. As the British charged east toward them, the sight of their bayonets terrified the militiamen, five hundred of whom fled. Brown managed to rally two hundred of his men and, joining with the regulars, conducted a fighting retreat.

From their strong defensive works and deep surrounding forest cover, the regulars poured into the redcoats' ranks such accurate fire that it unnerved Prevost. So heavy was the Americans' fire that a British soldier would write, "I do not exaggerate when I tell you that shot, both grape and musket, flew like hail." An unfavorable wind also prevented the British ships from keeping up effective covering fire. Believing that the weather was unlikely to improve his naval support and might well endanger his escape, Prevost ordered the two-thirds of his force still able to retreat to slog back to Horse Island and board landing craft to take them back to their ships. While the Americans had suffered one hundred casualties, the British decided to abandon the attack and sail back to their base at Kingston. The Americans failed to pursue them. A few minutes before the British withdrawal, Colonel Electus Backus, commander of the American regulars, was fatally shot. Brown was able to rally enough of his men to give them—and himself—disproportionate praise in the report that he, as the surviving commander, wrote and sent to Washington, netting him promotion to general in the regular army.[12]

The attack on Sackets Harbor might have been counted as a signal American victory if a nervous U.S. naval lieutenant in charge of guarding the dockyard and the large quantity of supplies in its warehouses had not become confused when several men told him that defeat was imminent. To prevent their capture by the enemy, he set afire the warehouses, the barracks and two ships under construction. Dockworkers rushed to save the severely damaged warship on the stocks, the *General Pike*; it would later join Chauncey's fleet. As the British sailed away, they could see the Americans' warehouses engulfed in flames, the plumes of smoke rising from the ashes of all that was left of the plunder of York. There had been no clear winner. Brown had sacrificed three hundred men, but a greater defeat was Chauncey's loss of fighting spirit. He would never again cooperate in a joint expedition with the army.

WHEN THE BRITISH finally vacated their lake forts inside the United States under the Jay Treaty, they left behind Fort Niagara, the most important of their posts on the Great Lakes. To maintain their dominance of the region, they erected the formidable Fort George, built upstream from their pre-treaty position on the west bank of the fast-moving Niagara River and on higher ground to the river's west. The log-and-palisade fort was made of a dozen earthen bastions and ravelins, with barracks and the headquarters of the British on the Niagara frontier. American officers, dining with their British counterparts in the fort when they first heard news of the war, finished their meal and were escorted across the river. Infrequently, the cannon of the two strongholds blasted away ineffectually at each other, their artillery rounds either falling short or doing little damage. The exception had been on October 13, 1812, when British ships fired hot shot that set buildings on fire, including a direct hit on the powder magazine containing eight hundred barrels of gunpowder, but a small party of engineers had torn off the metal roof and quickly doused the burning timbers with buckets of water.

In May 1813, Chauncey and Dearborn, sailing from Sackets Harbor, were ready with nearly 5,000 men to launch the largest amphibious attack to date against Fort George. Colonel Winfield Scott, captured hero of the Battle of Queenston who had recently been exchanged and promoted to command the 2nd Regiment of Artillery, received from the inert Dearborn the task of coordinating the attack with Commodore Perry. They mapped out the routes of the landing craft and the best positions for naval vessels to deliver effective covering fire. On the morning of May 27, Scott was in the lead boat coming ashore in the first wave, behind him more than 180 small craft crowded with soldiers supported by sixteen larger ships firing a steady tattoo at the British shore batteries.

As musket balls splashed around him, Scott landed and raced to the top of a twelve-foot embankment to face a Canadian soldier pointing his bayonet at him. Losing his footing, Scott slid down, then rallied his men and charged again. In desperate hand-to-hand fighting, Scott held his beachhead until the next wave came ashore and helped him push back the outnumbered British defenders. The British retreated and reformed in a battle line in a meadow, holding their ground until they were nearly all killed or wounded. When the British commander, Brigadier General John Vincent, ordered the fort abandoned, Scott led the pursuit. The first man into the fort, Scott snuffed out a burning trail of gunpowder leading to the powder magazine and tore down the fort's colors. For the first time employing Indians—Buffalo Creek Senecas and Onondagas led by Chief Red Jacket of the Wolf tribe of the Seneca nation—in combat, the American invaders killed, wounded or captured nearly half of Fort George's 1,400 defenders, forcing the British to retreat fully 30 miles west to their provincial headquarters at Burlington Heights.

Repairing the fort, Dearborn intended to use it as the bridgehead for another incursion into Canada. He sent Brigadier General William Winder, nephew of the governor of Maryland and a military neophyte, with eight hundred men to pursue the retreating British army. Winder had been captured in Canada when he wandered away from his troops and had spent a year as a prisoner of war in Quebec. Brigadier General John Chandler, also lacking combat experience, joined him with five hundred reinforcements. They overtook the British outside the walls of Burlington Heights but hesitated, deciding to pull back to Stoney Creek to plan their offensive.

Their military experience apparently didn't include properly protecting a camp. The British brigadier John Vincent decided not to wait for the two American generals to counterattack. With reinforcements rushed from Montreal, he moved close to the Americans and, armed with the countersign for the American sentries, infiltrated the American camp before dawn on June 6. During the chaotic fighting, both American generals became separated from their men and, stumbling into the British lines, were captured.

Undaunted though bedridden, Dearborn decided to extend the American perimeter around Fort George by mounting a surprise attack on a small British force at Beaver Dams, an outpost of the British base at Burlington Heights garrisoned by only a company of regulars and 450 Indians. Dearborn chose Lieutenant General Charles G. Boerstler of the 14th Infantry Regiment to lead 484 men, including an artillery company and twenty dragoons, to make a surprise attack. Marching out of Fort George, Boerstler failed to scout the route and also failed to keep secret his destination from townspeople he encountered. Reaching Queenston around midnight, he talked about his plans within earshot of the wife of a Canadian militiaman wounded there in the last American assault on the town, in October 1812.

Laura Ingersoll Secord was born in Massachusetts to Loyalist parents who had migrated to Queenston, Upper Canada, with their children at the end of the Revolution. She married James B. Secord, a sergeant in the First Lincoln Militia. In the first American invasion, he helped carry the body of General Brock from the field of battle before he was seriously wounded by a musket ball. Laura Secord fled the town as "the cannon balls were flying around" her. She returned after the battle and found her wounded husband, bringing him home to recover. She discovered that her home had been plundered and her possessions destroyed.

Six months later, on June 21, 1813, she learned—how, she never said—the plan of the American commander to make a surprise attack on the British post at Beaver Dams, twelve miles southwest of Queenston. To get through the ten-mile cordon of American guards around the town, she "left early in the morning, walked nineteen miles" over "a rough and difficult part of the country." By moonlight, she stumbled "terrified" into an Indian camp. Persuading a chief to take her to Lieutenant James Fitzgibbons, the British officer in charge at Beaver Dams, she outlined in detail the American plan. The young lieutenant had time to arrange his Indians in a wooded area near Beaver Dams.[13]

Leaving Queenston on the morning of June 24, Boerstler again failed to scout his front or his flanks. He was well into the woods when the Indians struck, taking his men entirely by surprise. Boerstler, wounded, took refuge in a supply wagon while his men fought so tenaciously that most of the Indians withdrew. His men had battled their way out of the trap and into the open and were about to escape when a British lieutenant approached Boerstler waving a white flag. He demanded that the Americans surrender. He told Boerstler that 1,500 redcoats and 700 Indians were only minutes away and would surround the Americans, and then he would not be able to restrain the Indians. Boerstler hesitated but then asked for terms: protection from the Indians, the right of officers to keep their sidearms, the paroling of militia. Fitzgibbons agreed. Only after the Americans surrendered their weapons did Boerstler discover the ruse. He had surrendered his superior force to one half its number! The Indians, returning, set about killing and scalping the wounded.

Boerstler's blunder had major ramifications. The British increased pressure on Fort George and began to raid American positions across the Niagara River. When word of the latest debacle reached Washington, Secretary of War Armstrong finally had to relieve the listless Dearborn of his command. And Canada now had its symbol of heroic resistance to American expansionism: forty years later, Laura Secord would write of her epic experience in a Toronto newspaper, concluding her account by saying simply, "I returned home the next day exhausted." A popular brand of chocolate candy now memorializes her name.[14]

EACH TIME THE Americans tried to break out of the defensive perimeter they had set up around Fort George, they had to retreat back into it. In effect, the 250 Americans left behind to maintain an American toehold on the Canadian side of the Niagara River found themselves besieged all summer. Guarding the American lines had been left to the Indians, but they soon became disgruntled when one American general after another failed to keep his promises to pay them. Protesting to the Indian agent Erastus Granger, Chief Red Jacket complained, "We think we are trifled with. We were promised that all horses and cattle should be free plunder. We took horses; we had to give them up. We have been deceived. . . . We want you to state this to the president." Calling unsuccessfully for an Indian conference in Washington, Red Jacket argued that Madison should welcome an Indian alliance:

> Let us unite, and in one season more we will drive the red coats from this island. They are foreigners. This country belongs to us and the United States. We do not fight for conquest, but we fight for our rights—for our lands—for our country. We trust that you will make our request known to the President and that we shall not be deceived.[15]

As a Canadian winter closed in, New York militia brigadier general George McClure was left to hold Fort George and its environs with his skeleton force, while the bulk of the Americans sailed back to Sackets Harbor with Harrison. McClure and his men had already plundered and burned a swath to Queenston after their rebuff at Beaver Dams. On December 10, 1813, McClure received intelligence that a major British force was approaching, and he ordered Fort George abandoned. He burned all but the ramshackle outbuildings of Butler Barracks and then torched the nearby town of Newark (present-day Niagara-on-the-Lake), its 150 dwellings the homes of many of the British soldiers and their families. Driving women and children, the elderly and the ill out into a cold, stormy night, he triggered a midwinter backlash of bloody reprisals by British forces. When McClure disavowed the attack in a letter to Prevost, the royal governor-general issued an angry proclamation. The American forces at Fort George, he countered,

[u]nder various pretences burned and destroyed the farm houses and buildings of many of the respectable and peaceable inhabitants. . . . The troops of a nation calling itself civilized and Christian had wantonly and without the shadow of the pretext forced 400 helpless women and children to quit their dwellings and to be mournful spectators of the conflagration and total destruction of all that belonged to them.[16]

Prevost's widely publicized reaction to the Newark raid would come to haunt Americans in the year ahead.

Arrival in the East of news of Harrison's brilliant victory in Ohio and the capture of Fort George on Lake Ontario did little to dispel the gloom cast over the nation by a totally avoidable naval disaster off Massachusetts at exactly the same time. On June 1, off Boston harbor, the luckless *Chesapeake*, defeated by the British *Leopard* and forced to capitulate in the impressment crisis off Virginia six years earlier, in an unprecedented act again struck its color, this time after a brutal fifteen-minute engagement with the British frigate *Shannon*. The fifty-gun *Chesapeake* had been considered disgraced and to be shunned by navy officers. Following its first defeat, after it was handed back by the largesse of its British captor, it had been barred from giving or receiving salutes as a mark of its disgrace.

As the British extended their blockade of American ports, the *Chesapeake* became bottled up in Boston harbor. The ill-starred frigate's crew welcomed a new skipper, Captain James Lawrence, on board. Lawrence had a reputation as a capable, brave and resourceful, if sometimes rash, officer. He had trouble recruiting a crew: most of the ship's original complement had resigned after their enlistments expired, as much from superstition as the lure of enrichment as privateersmen. Lawrence fleshed out his crew with English and Portuguese sailors and a handful from the *Constitution*, which idled nearby. Only one officer, a third lieutenant, had sailed on the ship before; most of the officers and crew were new and unfamiliar with it.

For eighteen months, the fifty-two-gun British frigate *Shannon* had patrolled the Atlantic coast. After his first encounter with the American frigate *President* a year earlier, *Shannon*'s captain Philip Bowes Vere Broke had daily drilled his crew in gunnery practice, concentrating especially on firing all guns on one target area. At his own expense, Broke had fitted the guns with dispart sights—a gunsight set at the middle of the cannon for point-blank firing—and gunners' quadrants. He had developed a ballistics pendulum for regulating a gun's position during horizontal firing. Broke was proud that he had made his ship far superior in gunnery to most British ships. In most other ways, the two ships were evenly matched: the *Chesapeake* could hurl 542 pounds of lead in a broadside, the *Shannon*, 550; *Chesapeake*'s crew numbered 379, *Shannon*'s, 330.

In his letters home to his wife on their Surrey estate, Broke showed his aristocratic scorn for the Americans, calling them variously "savages," "reptiles" and "animals." He decried the "bitterness and rancour with which the Americans have made war upon us." He had been mortified when Rodgers and the *President* had slipped out of Boston harbor in a fog only three weeks earlier. Just three days before the *Chesapeake* sailed out to meet him, he wrote that Boston harbor "still contains another wild beast; if all the nobler prey elude us, we much chace the vermin."[17]

There was something medieval about their encounter. Broke hurled a challenge like a gauntlet at Lawrence: come out and fight in the name of honor. Lawrence, a fifteen-year navy veteran, had risen from midshipman and was unimpressed by the Royal Navy. He had served in the Quasi-War in the Caribbean, in the Barbary Wars in the Mediterranean and as second in command to Decatur in the daring raid into Tripoli harbor. He had sailed with Commodore Rodgers in the prior faceoff with Broke. Only four months earlier, as commander of the *Hornet*, he had in a matter of weeks captured a gold-laden British brig and sunk a second brig. As his reward he was promoted to captain and given command of the *Chesapeake*.

Under pressure from Navy secretary Jones to refit quickly and get back out to sea, two weeks after coming aboard and without time to train his crew, in a replay of the 1807 debacle Lawrence sailed out of Boston harbor to accept Broke's challenge at high noon on June 1. All Boston tensed, aware that Broke had brazenly come into the harbor with the *Shannon*, showing her Union Jack and taunting Lawrence by heaving to and firing a single cannon to punctuate his challenge before sailing back out to sea. Crowds gathered with a sea view as the *Chesapeake* led a parade of small boats from her mooring at President's Roads.

Their duel took place eighteen miles off the Boston Light. On a line between Cape Cod and Cape Ann, the *Shannon* hove to and waited for the *Chesapeake*. Broke had time to carefully instruct his assembled crew: "Don't try to dismast her. Fire into her quarters; maindeck to maindeck; quarterdeck to quarterdeck. Kill the men and the ship is yours.... Don't hit them about the head, for they have steel caps on, but give it them through the body."[18]

Lawrence sailed the *Chesapeake* right up to the *Shannon*, taking a parallel course only fifty yards to windward. The first British broadside swept the *Chesapeake*'s decks with grape and canister shot, decapitating the sailing master and cutting down the helmsman and fourth lieutenant, hitting some one hundred of the 150 men on the top deck. A second helmsman ran to the wheel; he was instantly shot dead. Captain Lawrence, in his full dress uniform, with tall cocked hat, high-collared coat with epaulets and gold lace shimmering in the bright afternoon sun, took a musket ball in the thigh. A shot from a nine-pounder splintered the wheel. With no helm, her foretopsail, jib and headsails shot away, the *Chesapeake* surged ahead out of control. The *Shannon*'s gunners emptied three broadsides into her in six minutes before the American ship was out of range, turning into the wind, exposed to more of the *Shannon*'s broadsides. Another musket ball struck Lawrence, this time in the groin, mortally wounding him; all around him on the quarterdeck, his men, every single one, were struck down by grapeshot. As Lawrence was carried below, most of his other officers, including his first lieutenant and captain of marines, also were cut down. Helpless, the *Chesapeake* backed around and, stern first, struck the *Shannon* amidships. Captain Broke bellowed for the boarding party to follow him. Brandishing a heavy Scottish broadsword, he bounded onto the *Chesapeake*. When her chaplain fired at him and missed, Broke hacked off the clergyman's arm. Broke reached the *Chesapeake*'s forecastle just as Second Lieutenant George Budd rallied a few men: one American sailor smote Broke in the head with his musket; a second swung his cutlass down at Broke's head, slicing off his scalp and cutting open his skull. A British sailor ran the man through. With both captains felled, the fight was over. Herding some surviving Americans belowdecks, British sailors fired down into them; others shot Americans on the decks or threw them overboard. Fully half of the Americans and a quarter of the British had died or been severely wounded in only fifteen minutes.

As he was carried below, James Lawrence achieved immortality by giving his last command: "Don't give up the ship. Fight her till she sinks." For a second time, the *Chesapeake* had struck her colors to become the first and only American frigate defeated in the War of 1812. A week later, the *Shannon* led the *Chesapeake*, her prize, into Halifax harbor. Lawrence was buried in Halifax with full military honors. Broke lay motionless for a week, unable to speak. He never fully recovered, retiring to his country seat with his £3,000 prize money.[19]

In London, two days after announcing the victory in the House of Commons, Sir John Croker, the secretary of the Admiralty, sent a confidential directive to his station commanders that henceforth there was to be no single-ship combat with "the larger class of American Ships." In Washington, Navy secretary Jones also issued a new order to his captains: "You are also strictly prohibited from giving or receiving a Challenge to, or from, an Enemy's Vessel." Repaired at Halifax, the *Chesapeake* ironically served the Royal Navy with distinction. Sailing to England at war's end, she was eventually broken up and her timbers used to build a mill at Wickham. Known as the Chesapeake Mill, it still stands.[20]

Lawrence's vain run accompanied a tightening of the British blockade that all but eliminated the American navy's action on the open sea. As the British allocated more Royal Navy ships to blockade duty on their North American station, fewer American warships could slip past them. Rodgers's escape with the *President* from Boston just before the destruction of the *Chesapeake* was the last successful sortie by a frigate from that port. Four months later, when Decatur sailed from Boston on the *United States* in October 1812, he intended to raid British commerce off the Canary Islands. Encountering the thirty-eight-gun frigate *Macedonian*, in what was to be the last two-frigate duel of the war, he pounded the British vessel into a wreck in forty-five minutes, but, instead of sinking her, he chose to return with his prize in tow, entering New London victorious on December 4. The $30,000 prize money made him rich, but when he tried to sail again in May 1813 with the *United States*, the refurbished *Macedonian* and the *Hornet*, he failed to elude British blockading squadrons off Long Island and at Sandy Hook. Putting in temporarily at New London rather than chance an encounter with a far superior force, he waited for an opportunity to escape, but the British immediately set up a strong blockade there, too. Idled for a year, Decatur's ships eventually were stripped and mothballed on the Thames River until the war was over.

BY MIDSUMMER OF 1813, as Perry prepared to confront the British challenge on Lake Erie, he was ready to transport Harrison's army in a joint operation to take control of the northwestern theater, but Harrison was nowhere near ready. He could barely muster 2,500 regulars, little more than a third of the force Secretary Armstrong intended for the campaign. Resorting to a call-up of militia was expensive and politically sensitive. First Harrison approached Representative Richard M. Johnson of Kentucky, who once before had raised 1,200 mounted infantrymen and now was willing to attach them to the Northwest Army. To make up the force of 7,000 that the War Department allowed, Harrison then called on the governors of Ohio and Kentucky for volunteers. Ohio provided very few men: Governor Return J. Meigs could not agree to Harrison's terms for pay. But Kentucky's governor, the sixty-three-year-old Isaac Shelby, hero of the Battle of King's Mountain in the Revolutionary War, personally pledged to lead his men and arrived at Harrison's headquarters with 3,500 undisciplined troops. President Madison, vacationing at Montpelier, worried when he heard of the number of volunteers about to drain the nation's fragile finances. He urged Harrison to calm his nerves and assuage congressional critics by providing him with some conspicuous successes.

TO WIN THE war in the Northwest, both sides knew they must control Lake Erie. By the end of July, Commodore Perry had assembled a sizable fleet of brigs and gunboats at Presque Isle, where a British squadron under Captain Robert Heriot Barclay, a veteran of Trafalgar, was attempting to bottle them up. Faced with shortages of supplies, Barclay had to abandon the blockade and return to his base at Amherstburg. British reluctance to attack Presque Isle—Procter believed he lacked enough men, guns and supplies to destroy the American base—allowed Perry time to build and launch one ship after another throughout the spring and summer. By midsummer, his shipyard had produced a pair of twenty-gun brigs, *Lawrence* (to honor its fallen namesake) and *Niagara*, plus four gunboats—*Ariel*, *Porcupine*, *Tigress* and *Scorpion*—a small brig captured from the British, and three merchantmen converted into armed schooners, their rigging re-sembling modern fore-and-aft sailboats.

During July Barclay's squadron established a blockade outside the Presque Isle harbor. By the end of the month, however, supply shortages forced Barclay to return to Amherstburg. While Barclay's ships still were patrolling nearby, Perry decided to break out of the blockade, but his two new twenty-gun brigs—each carronade weighed a ton—drew only two feet more water than covered the treacherous bar at the harbor's mouth.

To get the new brigs over the bar, Perry had to lighten the ships. He ordered their guns taken off. His men quickly built camels—hollow cases of wood constructed in two halves that embraced the keel of the ship and held on to the ship from both sides. The camels were filled with water and sunk, holding each ship in a firm grip. When the water was pumped out, the vessel gradually rose. The process was repeated again and again until each ship had passed over the bar into open water. As Perry carried out this delicate maneuver, Barclay's squadron appeared a mile offshore. Au-daciously, Perry sent two smaller ships sailing straight at the British ships, their long guns blazing away, creating the impression that the entire American squadron was already in open water. Barclay shrugged them off and sailed away.

But Barclay no longer had a choice: Perry had cut off supplies for Detroit and Amherstburg. For more than a month, Barclay avoided battle, stalling until a new nineteen-gun sloop-of-war, the *Detroit*, could be com-pleted. Finally ready for battle, he set a course directly for the new Amer-ican base at Put-in-Bay, on Ohio's South Bass Island. Perry had a slight advantage in number of vessels, nine ships to Barclay's six, and a far greater one in firepower, 1,528 pounds of shot to Barclay's 883.

At daylight on September 10, 1813, Perry's lookouts sighted the sails of Barclay's fleet. From the flagship *Lawrence* Perry signaled his other ships to move out into the bay and close with the enemy. From her mainmast the *Lawrence* flew a pennant with Captain Lawrence's dying words, "Don't give up the ship," making her a conspicuous target for the long guns of the entire British fleet. The two fleets maneuvered for a while, each trying to gain the weather gauge—the wind at their backs enabling greater maneuverability—especially important to Perry, whose ships had wide-mouthed carronades firing up to thirty-two-pound timber-shattering shells but with a shorter effective range. To win, Perry had to get in close, within hailing distance of the enemy's ships.[21]

By 11:45 the flotillas were lined up directly opposite each other. In a five-hour battle, British long guns concentrated their fire on Perry's flagship. In close, Perry engaged in a deadly two-hour duel with the two largest British ships, firing from both sides simultaneously. Her sister ship, the *Niagara*, had fallen far behind and could not help her. Soon the *Lawrence* was smashed to deadly impaling splinters, four out of every five of her crew members dead or wounded. When the last cannon no longer had a gun crew to fire it, Perry called down into the four-foot-high wardroom where kneeling surgeons were shearing off shattered limbs and applying tourniquets to ninety-six of the wounded. Perry shouted over the din of cannon fire, moaning and screaming, "Can any of the wounded pull a rope?"[22]

Lowered over the side, Perry jumped into a lifeboat and rowed through murderous fire from British sharpshooters to the as-yet-unscathed *Niagara* and transferred his flag to her. Now the fourteen upright crew members of the *Lawrence* could strike her colors and surrender her battered hulk to the British. But Barclay had scant cause to celebrate what appeared to be a British victory. The Americans had mauled all of his ships, their decks were awash with blood and Barclay was badly wounded. Worse, he had lost the use of his two largest vessels, the *Queen Charlotte* and the newly launched *Detroit*, which had collided with each other when they attempted to change course. Aboard the *Niagara*, Perry ordered his surviving ships to renew the battle, and he sailed right into the center of the British line. Turning the tide of battle by 3 p.m., he forced all six of Barclay's ships to strike their colors. Later that day, on the back of a used envelope, Perry scratched out a message and sent it ashore to an anxious General Harrison: "We have met the enemy and they are ours: Two Ships, two Brigs, one Schooner, and one Sloop."[23]

In one of the bloodiest naval engagements of the war, Perry's decisive victory on Lake Erie ensured American control and left British forces in the western Great Lakes region cut off from supplies. Fort Detroit, Fort Malden and the main British naval base at Amherstburg became untenable.

With captured and repaired British ships augmenting his fleet, Perry now transported Harrison and his army as he captured all three British strongholds. In the Old Northwest, the British would never fully recover from Barclay's defeat.

If Madison and his cabinet seemed incapable of grasping the strategic significance of Perry's victory on Lake Erie, the British forces facing the American army and navy had little doubt that the Americans were now winning the war in the West. As Harrison's army boarded Perry's ships in the early autumn, Procter, promoted after his victory at the River Raisin, believed he had no alternative but to abandon Detroit as well as strategic Fort Malden and retreat east toward British headquarters at Burlington Heights. Although he still had a strong force of at least 1,000 of Tecumseh's Indians, Procter could see that some of them, principally the Chippewas, Wyandot and Ottawas, were slipping away. At Amherstburg, the main British and Indian base in the region, Procter still did not confide his plans to Tecumseh by late August. The Shawnee leader, already so thoroughly disgusted with Procter's habit of retreating in the face of the enemy that he privately called him "a miserable old squaw," assembled his followers and vehemently rebuked Procter in a speech:

> Father, listen to your children! You have them now all before you! Listen! You told us . . . to bring forward our families to this place; and we did so; and you promised to take care of them, and that they should want for nothing, while the men would go and fight the enemy. . . . [W]e are much astonished to see our father tying up everything and preparing to run away. . . . [W]e, therefore, wish to remain here, and fight our enemy. . . . [W]e now see our British father preparing to march out of his garrison. Father! You have got the arms and ammunition which our great father sent for his red children. . . . [G]ive them to us. . . . We are determined to defend our lands, and if it be his will we wish to leave our bones upon them.[24]

John Richardson, a sixteen-year-old volunteer in the British 41st Regiment, watched enthralled as the great warrior inspired the British soldiers as well as his own followers:

Habited in a close leather dress, his athletic proportions were admirably delineated, while a large plume of a white ostrich feathers, by which he was generally distinguished, overshadow[ed] his brow. . . .

Writing thirty years later, Richardson could not forget his admiration for Tecumseh, "whose gallant and impetuous spirit could ill brook the idea of retiring before his enemies."[25]

Procter assured Tecumseh that he would halt his retreat at Moravian-town on the Thames River, closer to the British provincial stronghold of Burlington Heights where he would receive reinforcements. Young Richardson remembered that Procter then gave orders to burn all the supplies and munitions from Amherstburg and Detroit they could not carry across the river.

The troops were immediately employed in razing the fortifications, and committing such stores as it was found impossible to remove to the flames, kindled in the various public buildings; and the ports of Detroit and Amherstburg for some days previous to our departure presented a scene of cruel desolation.[26]

Tecumseh could foresee what would happen next. As he prepared his warriors to follow Procter up the Thames River in retreat, he told them, "We are now going to follow the British, and I feel certain we shall never return." He knew that without the British to feed the warriors and their families—the British had only recently been providing meals and weapons for 16,000 Indians—they could not fight on. Thousands had already slipped away, until only 1,000 warriors remained as the British column abandoned the twin forts on September 27; they guarded crammed baggage wagons as they retreated along the north shore of Lake Erie. Critically short of rations and slowed further by women and children, Procter could march only a few miles a day. He paused at Thamesville, seventy miles east of Detroit.[27]

On October 2, Harrison and 5,000 fresh troops, arriving from Fort Meigs, disembarked from Perry's ships on the bank of the Detroit River. With a force made up largely of Kentucky volunteers, he soon was trampling on Procter's heels. Procter argued that he needed to join up with

British forces at the head of Lake Ontario, but Tecumseh refused to go any farther. On October 5, 1813, outnumbered more than two to one even with Tecumseh's warriors, Procter chose to make his stand near Moraviantown on a swampy, forested battleground at a sweeping bend of the Thames River. Making no effort to fortify his position, he ordered eight hundred redcoats and militia into the woods, with Tecumseh and his warriors to his right and the river road, defended by a single cannon, on his left. Harrison sounded the bugles for the attack before Procter could get off more than a single shot from his solitary six-pounder. The redcoats only had time to fire a volley before Harrison ordered his 1,200 mounted Kentucky riflemen to charge the center of the British line. The English quickly broke ranks as the Kentuckians rode right through them, sending them running in all directions. Procter, "mounted on an excellent charger, and accompanied by his personal staff, sought safety in flight at the very commencement of the action." Only fifty British troops escaped; the rest, some six hundred redcoats and militia, surrendered.[28]

Regrouping his horsemen for a second charge, Harrison sent them galloping and hallooing off after Tecumseh's Indians. But Tecumseh did not replicate Procter's cowardice. Taking a position on the British right flank, Tecumseh and his warriors resisted the American attack, repulsing the Kentuckians with deadly accurate rifle fire. What happened next has been the source of speculation for the past two hundred years. One version, depicted on many canvases, shows Tecumseh cut down by rifle fire as he tried to lead a counterattack. According to historian Reginald Horsman, "The most accepted version at the time was that Tecumseh had been shot by the commander of the Kentucky mounted militia, Col. Richard M. Johnson. The assumption that Johnson had shot Tecumseh helped the Kentuckian in his subsequent political career." (Johnson won election as vice president in Andrew Jackson's second term.)

Other scholars maintain that Tecumseh was last seen fighting most of the day in the forest, inspiring his fighters as he roared and swung his tomahawk and that, by the end of the day, severely wounded and with blood streaming from his mouth and wounds, he stopped—and vanished. The next morning, according to this version, Harrison's men felt disappointed, mystified and even afraid when they could not find his body.

Horsman, noting that there never was any proof of what happened to

Tecumseh's body, points out that the "U.S. troops mutilated many of the Indian dead after the engagement, and it is possible that one of these bodies was that of Tecumseh." One persistent, if ghoulish, legend is that the Kentuckians cut off swatches of Tecumseh's hair, clothing and skin to take home as souvenirs, a grisly practice that had also taken place after the Revolutionary War campaign against the Iroquois.[29]

Years after the Battle of the Thames, some white settlers still believed that Tecumseh roamed the woods; some of his devout followers believed that he had ascended into the sky after they carried their wounded leader away into the woods, along with his dream of a lasting Indian confederacy that would save their lands from the white man's insatiable westward expansion. The Battle of the Thames, which also decided the fate of the once-powerful British-Indian alliance in Upper Canada and the Old Northwest, had lasted only forty-five minutes.

WITH ONLY PRIMITIVE overland communications between eastern seaboard states and the northwestern war zone and no effective mail, most Americans remained starved for accurate news. Many relied on letters carried by troops traveling to and from the front.

One frustrated citizen of Lancaster, New Hampshire, resorted to sending a long, wax-sealed letter along with a neighbor, a young ensign heading west to join the 11th Rifle Regiment at Sackets Harbor. To his friend, Captain John W. Weeks, Edward Lyman groused that

> [w]e have fresh news daily from the [North West] army, at one time we heard of the defeat of all the forces in a battle, <u>thousands killed and thousands taken</u>, at another, that, [& in the same contest] our army had made a noble conquest, Canada was taken, etc, etc news of all sorts & sizes ready to accommodate the wishes of anyone—Dearbourne [*sic*] Is dead, the next day he resigned & finally we have concluded that he has been somewhat sick at the stomach from some cause or other. . . .

But Lyman's complaint went deeper:

> We, as a nation, are in a most deplorable condition, suffering all the miseries of (shall I say offensive) war, divided in sentiment as to the justice of

our cause; many, very many of the most wealthy and influential with-
holding their aid, and discouraging others from engaging in the 'bloody
contest'—The [North East] states, opposed to it in <u>every</u> shape. . . . Are we
not to expect something more serious to befall our country. . . . Is it possible that we will 'succeed' in the attempt? Have we not everything to fear
& but little to expect? . . . It does really appear that <u>patriotic fire</u> does not
warm the heart of the nation now, as in the former contest, when Washington directed the destinies of our country.[30]

If a nation's success is measured by the government's balance sheet,
the year 1813 was discouraging indeed. Despite a doubling of customs
rates, customs receipts were down 76.5 percent from 1812, 65 percent from
1811. In Maryland the British blockade cut off Baltimore and Annapolis:
revenues of $1.8 million in 1812 had shriveled 90 percent to $182,000; Philadelphia's plummeted from $2.4 million to $311,000 in 1813, an 85 percent
plunge. In all, the war had cost double the customs receipts.

TWELVE

"You Shall Now Feel the Effects of War"

L ittle more than a month before Tecumseh's death in battle, the crown fire of Indian resistance had flared far to the south among the Creek Indians, his mother's tribe. Long-simmering tensions within tribal councils in the Gulf borderlands had been ignited by his proselytizing missions. In recruiting Creek to join his confederacy, Tecumseh had polarized the tribe. The Red Sticks, named for the color of the sticks they carried to proclaim their disapproval of European ways, joined Tecumseh's crusade against further accommodation of land-hungry whites spreading through major portions of Alabama, Georgia and Mississippi territories. Creek elders favored cooperation with the U.S. government and had adopted the white lifestyle. Their lands, once rich in game, now supported only agriculture, and many Creek, intermarrying with Europeans, owned slaves.

The rift among the Creek had grown into a full-blown civil war. Red Sticks led by Little Warrior of Wewocau on the Coosa River had joined Tecumseh in Canada. Returning home in the spring of 1813, they attacked isolated white settlements abutting Creek territory. When Indian agent Benjamin Hawkins demanded that the Creek National Council hand Little Warrior and his followers over for punishment, tribal leaders agreed but then ordered the militants hunted down and executed. Intent on revenge,

Red Stick leader Peter McQueen and his band journeyed to Pensacola, where the Spanish colonial governor gave them powder and shot.

In July 1813 Secretary of War Armstrong directed the governors of Tennessee and Georgia to raise 1,500 troops each to suppress the Red Stick uprising. As McQueen and his warriors returned home, the Mississippi territorial militia, assuming that the Indians intended to wage war against the United States, attacked the band at Burnt Corn Creek. The whites' attack failed, only succeeding in boosting Red Stick recruiting until their ranks swelled to 8,000 warriors. What had been a civil war among the Creek now became a Red Stick war against the United States.

In Alabama, frightened settlers as well as peaceable Creek crowded into fortified towns and blockhouses along the frontier. McQueen's adherents considered the militia attack unprovoked and set out to avenge it by attacking forts in southern Alabama, selecting Fort Mims as their first target. Named after mixed-blood Creek Samuel Mims, the fort sheltered an agglomeration of 120 Mississippi militia, about 180 white, Creek and mixed-blood men, women and children and an undetermined number of black slaves. The mixed-blood Red Stick leader William Weatherford (Red Eagle) organized the attack.

The day before the assault, two slave boys ran into the fort and reported that they had seen a large number of war-painted Indians. Militia major Daniel Beasley sent out a few scouts, who found nothing, and Beasley ordered the boys flogged for lying. On August 30, during the noon meal, the Red Sticks, led by McQueen, attacked, running through the fort's open gates. Sentries shot a few warriors while Beasley, reportedly drunk, struggled to close the gates until he was shot. Firing through the fort's portholes, cut only four feet above the ground, the Red Sticks triggered a panic. As 750 warriors surged in and started to set fires, the inhabitants took shelter in two buildings so crowded the settlers had no room to load and fire their muskets.

Only six men survived by cutting their way out of the fort while the Red Sticks, enraged by the deaths of one hundred warriors during the attack, slaughtered more than five hundred men, women and children in the bloodiest massacre in American history. All along the southern frontier, especially in Tennessee where large numbers of settlers answered Andrew Jackson's call to arms, states mobilized their militias.

HARRISON'S LONG-RUNNING VENDETTA with Tecumseh had ended with a decisive outcome, the only successful facet of the grand American strategy to wrest Canada away from the British. While Harrison and Perry celebrated their victory, Secretary of War Armstrong called on the talents of a former colleague from the Revolutionary War, Major General James Wilkinson, to conquer Lower Canada, today's Quebec Province.

The ranking general when the War of 1812 broke out, Wilkinson had earned a reputation of never having won a battle or lost a court-martial. Ingratiating himself with Horatio Gates, Wilkinson had carried news of victory at Saratoga to the Continental Congress, which commissioned the messenger a brigadier general at age twenty. He then participated in the Conway Cabal, a failed plot to depose Washington as commander in chief. Discovered but not punished, Wilkinson took refuge in a noncombat role on the Board of War. But, as clothier general, he was forced to resign after discovery of financial irregularities. Moving to Kentucky after the Revolution, he swore allegiance to Spain, receiving an annual pension of $2,000 in exchange for a promise to help it to gain possession of Kentucky. Rejoining the army as Wayne's second in command, he fought at the Battle of Fallen Timbers even as he received large sums for providing intelligence to the Spanish. Taking command of New Orleans as military governor of Louisiana Territory, a court-martial acquitted him of negligence after 1,000 troops succumbed to disease. For his alleged secret dealings with Mexico, Madison ordered him court-martialed in 1811 but he was acquitted for lack of evidence.

Placed in command of the Seventh Military District with his headquarters in New Orleans, Wilkinson quarreled with militia officers, especially with Jackson. For the only time in his life, he moved quickly to seize Spanish Florida west of the Perdido River and occupied Mobile, Alabama, on April 15. Promoted to major general in command of the Ninth Military District—including Vermont and parts of New York and Pennsylvania—to organize the summer invasion of Canada, he slowly made his way to Sackets Harbor, not arriving until mid-August.

To launch his grand plan to conquer Upper Canada, Armstrong traveled from Washington with Major General Wade Hampton, a martinet from South Carolina who hated Wilkinson. Soon, all three generals were quarreling in public. One staff officer trying to render Armstrong's plan on paper—to take Fort Malden, then Montreal, then Kingston—labeled its objectives as "impenetrable."[1]

As the summer of 1813 brought the war to fever pitch in the nation's north and contention to new heights in a divided Congress, another kind of fever felled its president. Given to worry and depression and already frail at one hundred pounds, the sixty-two year old Madison contracted a near-fatal bout of malaria, endemic in sultry, miasmic Washington. Unforgivingly strident New York Federalist congressman Thomas P. Grosvenor prayed for a speedy end to the president's life so that he could "soon appear at the bar of Immortal Justice" and be judged for his "bloody crime"—the war. Major John Lovett could not wait to hear the death knells of Madison *and* his vice president, the sixty-nine-year-old "scant-patterned skeleton of a French Barber," as the *Georgetown Federal Republican* referred to Elbridge Gerry.[2]

On June 28, Monroe wrote to Jefferson at Monticello that the Senate, led by newly elected New Hampshire Federalist Daniel Webster, was capitalizing on Madison's absence by blocking his diplomatic appointments of Jonathan Russell to Sweden and Albert Gallatin to the peace talks in Russia. The Federalists insisted that Gallatin could not serve as Secretary of the Treasury while on a diplomatic mission. "The object is to usurp the Executive power in the hands of a faction in the Senate," Monroe told Jefferson. "These men have begun, to make calculations & plans, founded on the presum'd death of the President & Vice-President." Monroe characterized Madison's illness as "remittent." The fever "has perhaps never left him, even for an hour. . . . This I think is the 15th day." Three attending physicians "think he will recover." Monroe had just heard that Madison had enjoyed "a good night, & is in a state to take the bark, which indeed he has done on his best day, for nearly a week."[3]

EVERY TIME THE Americans tried to break out of their bastion at Fort George on the Niagara River, they had to retreat into its defensive perimeter. In effect, the Americans found themselves besieged all summer. Scott had been left to hold the fort with a skeleton force while the bulk of the American forces sailed back to Sackets Harbor. As summer vanished and the weather worsened, many of the men Wilkinson was assembling fell ill after eating bread baked from contaminated flour and drinking polluted lake water. Their commander took to his sickbed "with a giddy head and trembling hand." By the first week of October, he was still debating with Armstrong the relative merits of attacking Kingston or Montreal. While they argued, the British moved 1,500 regulars from Montreal to Kingston, eliminating that possibility.[4]

Before heading back to Washington, Armstrong ordered Wilkinson, who had already started boarding men and supplies on Chauncey's transports, to sail down the St. Lawrence and attack Montreal. Aware that to bypass Kingston would only guarantee his failure, Wilkinson became convinced that Armstrong was trying to humiliate him. Acknowledging that he had lost the season, Wilkinson sent orders to Plattsburgh to prepare winter quarters for his troops.

At the same time, the duplicitous Wilkinson agreed to carry out Armstrong's directive. On October 21, he boarded his 8,000 troops and twenty-four guns on Chauncey's ships and, with more than 150 gunboats and transports, sailed to Grenadier Island at the entrance to the St. Lawrence River. During the two-week passage, gale-force winds and heavy sleet scattered the flotilla and ruined most of its supplies. As Wilkinson entered the river on November 5, Armstrong departed for Albany, where, on November 15, he announced that he was sure the American army had already taken Montreal.

Bypassing Kingston, Wilkinson slipped past Fort Wellington without being fired on by the heavy British guns. Disembarking his soldiers above Ogdensburg, New York, the fleet had ghosted past the fortress in the night, the soldiers marching downriver to reboard. Meanwhile, Wilkinson, pronouncing himself ill again, medicated himself with ample doses of whiskey and opium-based laudanum, leading his officers to note that he became "very merry, and sung, and repeated his stories."[5]

For Wilkinson's amphibious force to continue the expedition, they still would have to travel 150 miles down the St. Lawrence through five major rapids with only enough supplies to last fifteen days. Worse, Chauncey failed to interdict a flotilla of British sloops and gunboats from getting behind the Americans, forcing them to fight rearguard actions even as they tried to advance. Unfazed, Wilkinson sent orders to Hampton to meet him in two days at St. Regis to coordinate their assault on Montreal.

But Wilkinson had not left enough time for Hampton to link up with Wilkinson's army. Ignoring Armstrong's order not to attack until he connected with Wilkinson for a two-pronged attack, Hampton marched his troops north from Burlington around Cumberland Head and crossed the border to Four Corners on the Châteauguay River. There, a well-trained force of 1,600 volunteer light infantry, the Canadien Voltigeurs under the command of Lieutenant Colonel Charles-Michel d'Irumberry de Salaberry, defeated Hampton's ill-trained army. Thus repulsed, Hampton was not eager to follow Armstrong's order, received after the engagement, to go into winter quarters inside the Canadian border. Instead, he retreated to Plattsburgh, as far as he could get from Wilkinson. Pleading lack of supplies, he left his nemesis to continue his quixotic invasion at his own risk. And then Hampton resigned.

Despite the imminent onset of Canadian winter, Wilkinson still expected to conquer Montreal. He crossed the St. Lawrence just above the treacherous Long Sault rapids and, on November 11, detached 2,500 regulars to march upriver in a snowstorm and confront the British force following him. He found the British spread out on the north shore of the river over the snow-covered fields of a farmer named John Crysler. Outnumbered more than two to one, the British commander had placed his men in marshes and forest to protect them. The better-disciplined mixed force of British redcoats, Canadian volunteers and Iroquois concentrated accurate musket and cannon fire, hurling back one American assault after another. The demoralized Americans boarded their transports and fled back to the American side of the river. British casualties, some two hundred, paled beside Wilkinson's 450 men lost, though each side suffered 20 percent casualties. But the battle represented a turning point in Canadian history, with British and French Canadian troops cooperating as equals.

Proclaiming victory, Wilkinson sent orders to Brigadier General Jacob Brown of New York to retreat with the brigade he had sent ahead east to clear the road to Montreal. Learning that Hampton had refused his order to join him and, short of men and supplies, Wilkinson decided to abandon the Montreal campaign and went into winter camp at French Mills, just south of the border.

With the second failure of an invasion of Canada, the United States may have lost any real hope it had to win the war. And Canadians, at first noncommittal toward risking active engagement in the War of 1812 but now infuriated by the wanton destruction of border towns like York, gained a new spirit of nationalism. At Crysler's Farm, for the first time British, French Canadian and Native American forces fought side by side to repel a common invading army—and won.

ALONG LAKE CHAMPLAIN, the watery highway between New York and Canada, most of the traffic by the end of 1813 was one way. American smugglers were growing rich supplying the British Army in Canada while the American militia continually ran short of provisions. Cattle and goods were smuggled across the border from Vermont, usually at night; rafts made of timbers and spars floated down the lake to the British Navy shipyard at Isle-aux-Noix. At American encampments at French Mills, Major General George Izard had reported to General Benjamin Mooers on September 5 that a Canadian agent was openly contracting for American army supplies and that a cattle drive from Cornwall, Vermont, halfway down the lake, had just passed through:

> The host of smuglars that huver on our lines is beyond description. Since the first of August to this date there has been from the best calculation more than sixty yoak [sic] of oxen besides other beef cattle drove to Canada.[6]

Master and commander Thomas Macdonough, arriving at his base at Burlington, had found only three sloops used to ferry army supplies across the lake and two leaking gunboats. Ordered to assert American control of the vital lake, he built up a small squadron in Shelburne Bay. He added eleven guns to each sloop—*President, Eagle* and *Growler*—and decided that the best use for these single-mast vessels, larger than anything the British could muster, would be to break up smuggling. But he could never obtain enough trained sailors: "There are no men to get here and soldiers are miserable creatures on shipboard. . . . I very much fear that unless I get the above [ordinary] seamen and not soldiers, there will be a dark spot in our Navy."[7]

As he feared, disaster struck in June 1813. The *President* ran aground near Plattsburgh and remained out of action for weeks. When Macdonough sent a gunboat under a midshipman's command into the Bay, a gust of wind capsized it; the crew clung to it in icy waters for hours until the *Eagle* could rescue them. Laying up his near-useless gunboats, he transferred their crews to *Growler* and *Eagle* and sent them north with orders to patrol the American side of the border and interdict British gunboats being used to escort smugglers' vessels.

The very next day, Lieutenant Sidney Smith on the *Growler* couldn't resist following the British gunboats across the border and signaled the *Eagle* to follow him. As they entered the Richelieu River, the wind died. They became trapped under heavy artillery fire from both shores, from British row galleys and two bateaux filled with redcoats. Trying to tack and run, the two American sloops came too close inshore. In a four-hour engagement, after many men were wounded and others fled, a twenty-four-pound shot hit the *Eagle* below the waterline. She sank in shallow water. The *Growler*, its forestay and main boom shot away, ran aground and Smith surrendered. The British had taken nearly one hundred prisoners and two sloops—and control of Lake Champlain.

LAUNCHING A COORDINATED campaign of retaliation against villages on the American shore of the Niagara, on the night of December 18, 1813, 550 British infantrymen commanded by Colonel John Murray slipped quietly across the south end of the river in boats they had secretly dragged overland. Landing south of Fort Niagara, they crept through the dark toward the thinly garrisoned fort, surprising American pickets playing cards at a local tavern and forcing them at bayonet point to reveal the fort's password. The British advance guard was able to cross the fort's drawbridge unmolested and, once inside, began slaughtering the sleeping garrison with bayonets. When some defenders barricaded themselves in the massive South Redoubt, Murray ordered his troops to rush the bastion and offer no mercy: they bayonetted some eighty Americans before the remaining three hundred surrendered.

With retaken Fort Niagara as his base, Lieutenant General Gordon Drummond, commander of all British forces in Upper Canada, expanded the series of retaliatory raids. He detached Brigadier General Phineas Riall with five hundred regulars and five hundred Seneca to cross the northern end of the river and, in retaliation for the American destruction of Newark, destroyed Lewiston, which had served as the headquarters for the 1812 American attack on Queenston.

As the British approached the town, most of its citizens were asleep. Militia posted outside the village fled without warning the townspeople. Three of Riall's Indian auxiliaries surprised Mrs. Solomon Gillette as she milked her cows. With her ten-year-old son, she ran home to safeguard three younger children. With her children in tow, she was unable to stop Indians who shot and scalped her seven-year-old son. On the other side of town, her captured husband watched helplessly as Indians shot and scalped their nineteen-year-old son. Unchecked by the British commander, Indians killed ten civilians, scalping nine and decapitating the other. As a handful of New York militia arrived to shield the survivors' escape, Riall ordered Lewiston burned, then moved on to sack and obliterate all the other villages on the American shore. The war had entered a new and more savage stage where women and children were not spared from the escalating cycle of atrocity, revenge and reprisal.

In the dying days of 1813 Riall led a mixed force of two hundred British soldiers with eight hundred militia and Indians in attacks on the neighboring villages of Black Rock and Buffalo. More than 2,000 New York militia and a handful of Iroquois warriors turned out to defend Black Rock, but they were no match for Riall's well-disciplined regulars and the Indians fled at the first shots. Only one house in Black Rock, sheltering women and children, survived Riall's torches.

The first American raid on Canadian soil, the humiliating capture of two brigs right under the guns of Fort Erie, had come from Buffalo. While many of Buffalo's four hundred settlers now managed to escape to nearby farms and into snow-covered forests, some refused to leave. Forty-two-year-old Sarah Lovejoy, trying to defend her home, argued with Indians and was stabbed to death on her doorstep. When the British troops left in the afternoon, Ebenezer Walden and women who were Lovejoy's neighbors carried her body into the house and placed it on her bed. When the British completed their systematic sacking and burning of Buffalo the next day, her house burned with her body in it.

Margaret St. John had already lost her husband and son in battle. She sent her younger children to safety and appealed personally to the British commanding officer. He posted a guard at her door, and her house was the only building in Buffalo spared by the British. St. John thus virtually saved Buffalo's survivors single-handedly from starvation through the bitter winter, feeding and sheltering many homeless villagers until they could rebuild. In all, the British incinerated five New York towns: Lewiston, Manchester, Tuscarora, Black Rock and Buffalo. As the year 1813 ended, the war on the northwestern frontier had degenerated into a cruel, inconclusive hit-and-run, torch-for-torch stalemate, establishing unsettling precedents that had given neither side a decisive advantage.

WHEN CONGRESS HAD offered signing bonuses for one-year enlistees in June 1812, hundreds of men from Virginia and Maryland signed up and marched off to invade Canada. So tranquil at first was the Chesapeake Bay region that, in July, the captain of the seized British schooner *Whiting* pleaded that he was unaware that there was a war. He was allowed to quit United States waters with all possible speed. Shortly afterward, Parliament authorized reprisals, worrying about the American troop buildup on the Canadian front.

In an attempt to draw off American forces from the northern frontier, Admiral John Borlase Warren, newly appointed commander of the North American Station, ordered raids against seaport towns along the Atlantic and Gulf coasts from New York to New Orleans. Warren arrived at Lynnhaven Bay aboard his flagship *San Domingo* and, on a cold and blustery February 5, 1813, issued a formal declaration of blockade of all ports and harbors on the Chesapeake. His second in command, Rear Admiral George Cockburn, arrived four weeks later aboard the seventy-four-gun *Marlborough*. In addition to the ships already anchored at Lynnhaven Bay, Cockburn would have at his disposal four seventy-fours, seven frigates, a sloop-of-war and a schooner. As he sailed from Bermuda, he expected to find when he arrived a 2,300-man expeditionary force, including two battalions of royal marines, each with 842 men and a company of artillery, a detachment of three hundred regular infantry, and two "Independent Companies of Foreigners," made up of three hundred French prisoners of war who, in exchange for their freedom, had enlisted to fight for England as "Chasseurs Brittaniques (British Hunters)."

Cockburn's instructions, written by Admiral Viscount Robert Saunders Dundas Melville and forwarded to him from London by Admiral Warren, were to "effect a diversion" that would siphon off American troops from the expected summer invasion of Canada. Cockburn's expedition-ary force was to capture and burn naval or military stores around Chesa-peake Bay, extract ransoms from civilians who wanted to protect their property from destruction and generally to "harass the Enemy by differ-ent attacks." Cockburn and his commanders were forbidden to foment a general slave uprising but were authorized to enlist and promise to safe-guard the freedom of any "Individual Negroes" who offered to assist the British cause.[8]

The British squadron immediately set sail to block the only access from the Chesapeake to the sea. Its first quarry, the frigate *Constellation*, had set sail from Annapolis, Maryland, on February 1 as the ice began to break up, heading for Hampton Roads and the open sea. As the frigate ap-proached the capes at the entrance to the Atlantic, she encountered two of Cockburn's ships-of-the-line, a brig and a schooner just entering the bay. The *Constellation*'s captain, Charles Stewart, decided to make a run for Norfolk, but the wind was flat calm. He ordered his boats lowered to kedge the frigate to safety. But the tide was going out. The *Constellation* soon stuck fast in mudflats at the mouth of the James River. Stewart lightened the ship by dumping drinking water and cargo as the British, facing a con-trary wind, waited nearby.

By early evening, as the returning tide raised the ship off the flats, her boats towed her to safety under the guns of Fort Norfolk. Later that night, the British squadron sailed down to Lynnhaven Bay and anchored, seal-ing off the *Constellation* from the Atlantic. She would spend the duration of the war bottled up in the Elizabeth River.

Within days, Cockburn's Royal Navy squadron began to capture pri-vateers heading home to Baltimore with their booty, quickly scooping up four schooners, each armed with six to twelve guns. Manning them, Cockburn sent them sailing into narrow inlets, where they seized an-other thirty-six prizes. The rear admiral bore the most reviled name in America in the War of 1812. In Lowland Scots, it is pronounced "Coe-burn;" but after two years of the havoc Cockburn wreaked wherever he went, Americans pronounced it phonetically. "There breathes not in any quarter of the globe a more savage monster than this same British Admiral," bristled the *Boston Gazette*. "He is a disgrace to England and to human nature."[9]

Second son of a Scottish baronet, Cockburn went to sea as a midshipman at nine, moving up to lieutenant by age twenty-one. Commanding the frigate *Minerve*, he fought French privateers in the Mediterranean, capturing many prizes. Lord Nelson, admiring the ruthless, dashing young officer, gave him a gold-hilted sword. Fighting in the Indian Ocean, in the Caribbean and off the coast of Spain, he rose to the rank of rear admiral by the time the United States declared war on England. Sent to Halifax as second in command of the North American Station, he found orders waiting for him from Warren to sail with a squadron to the Chesapeake. En route, he peeled off ships to harass American ports, including Philadelphia. Cockburn brushed aside Warren's instructions: "You must be content with blockading its [the Chesapeake Bay's] entrance & sending in occasionally your cruisers for the purpose of harassing & annoyance."[10]

In March, after three unsuccessful waterborne attempts to capture the trapped *Constellation*, Admiral Warren in his flagship led the entire fleet north into the bay. He dropped anchor off Annapolis and threatened Baltimore. Cockburn, in *Marlborough*, led 450 Royal Marines up the bay. His squadron included the frigate *Maidstone*, the brigs *Fantome* and *Mohawk* and three tenders.

As his ships tacked up the choppy bay, Cockburn spread panic in his wake. Along the western shore, he overtook a wagon train stacked with books and official records hauling Maryland's state papers from Annapolis to the supposed safety of Upper Marlboro, the county seat of Prince George's County. Cockburn spared it: for now, he was aiming for more lucrative targets. Transferring to the shallower draught *Maidstone*, he sailed to the very top of the bay. At dawn on April 29, 150 Royal Marines rowed toward the sleeping village of Frenchtown in the darkness; fifteen militiamen fired their cannon from behind a log battery and fled. Spiking the guns, the marines set fire to boats at the wharves and warehouses containing a vital $30,000 in government supplies.

Raiding the tributaries of the Chesapeake, Cockburn led his marauders into the mouth of the Elk River. The marines rowed on; rounding a bend in the river, they encountered heavy cannon fire from two earthen forts. Two hundred Elkton residents had subscribed the funds to build the makeshift defenses, Forts Frederick and Defiance, and stretched two heavy chains across the river. Repelled by heavy fire, the Royal Marines retreated to seek an easier target.

One of Cockburn's captains would later attempt to explain that there was more than pecuniary gain intended by his raids:

> The more you ruin in a war, the more you hurt the nation at large. . . .
> The hue and cry always was—'Respect private property, pay for what you take but take care to take all you can' and under this wholesome legislation we burnt and destroyed right and left.[11]

For all its numerical superiority, the British blockade, extending from the northern approaches of Long Island to all American "ports, harbours, bays, creeks, rivers, inlets, outlets, islands and sea-coasts" to the south, failed to seal off America's porous ports. In the summer of 1813 Rodgers escaped from Boston harbor in the *President* and sailed to England's home waters. Capturing and burning prizes all the way to Bergen, Norway, the *President* eluded British warships in a three-day chase before turning to intercept British merchantmen entering the Irish Sea. Returning safely to American waters. Rodgers ran straight through the British blockade into Newport after destroying a dozen enemy ships and tying up twenty-five British men-of-war, including six seventy-fours and ten frigates deployed by Warren between the Grand Banks off Newfoundland to the Chesapeake to intercept him. As a final insult on the way into Newport, Rodgers captured Warren's personal tender, the schooner *High Flyer*, snaring the admiral's signal book before its captain could destroy it and leaving Warren to lament his failure "to intercept his return" to the British Admiralty: "I am sure that every captain was anxiously vigilant to fall in with him."[12]

Sometimes personal motives of revenge outweighed the national interest in Cockburn's raids. Moving past the wide, open mouth of the Susquehanna River in April, Cockburn's ships drew the ineffectual fire of the guns of the small town of Havre de Grace, which proudly hoisted its flag. Writing to Admiral Warren, Cockburn quipped that the gunfire "of course gave to the Place an Importance which I had not before attached to it."[13]

On May 2, 1813, Cockburn personally led an attack by nineteen row barges carrying four hundred British troops. He had carefully sounded the river and knew that his assault craft could not get close enough to the shore before being detected, so he had sent 150 men ashore the night before the attack. They attacked at dawn and quickly silenced the shore battery. Townspeople awoke to the roar of cannon and the shrieking of Congreve rockets. Cockburn relied on these new and wildly inaccurate weapons to terrify Americans. Propelled by black powder and armed with solid shot, shrapnel or exploding warheads of twelve to forty-two pounds, they hissed and whizzed along arcing trajectories over a two-mile range. Sometimes gyrating unpredictably, they could reverse course, sending their firing crews scampering for cover. Only three Americans—including one Havre de Grace militiaman—and one British artilleryman were killed by these rockets in the entire war, but Cockburn considered them indispensable weapons.[14]

As half-naked women and children screamed through the streets, British marines turned the guns of the town's twin forts on the village. The militia fled almost as hastily as it had assembled, but, as Cockburn reported, they turned to aim "a teasing and irritating fire from behind their Houses, Walls, Trees, etc.," before fleeing into the woods pursued by fifty British marines.[15]

When all resistance ceased, the British marched into the square, split up into platoons and plundered the abandoned town. Sparing a few nearby houses at the tearful requests of women crowded inside St. John's Episcopal Church, Cockburn sarcastically reported how his raiders "shew[ed] their respect for religion" by "magnanimously attack[ing] the church windows with brick-bats and stones, and demolishing them." Cockburn had one particular target in his sights. Sion Hill was the home of Commodore John Rodgers, who only recently had harassed British home waters before embarrassing the English blockaders off Newport. Cockburn's visit to Havre de Grace demonstrated his capacity for vengefully personalizing his campaign of terror, as he then demonstrated at Rodgers's house. While Mrs. Rodgers managed to persuade her husband's enemy to spare the house, Cockburn did not extend his courtesy to Rodgers's personal property: he commandeered Rodgers's desk, his pianoforte and a carriage. Sir David Milne, a British admiral commanding a ship-of-the-line on the American station, wrote that he had heard that Rodgers's pianoforte was in the house of a fellow officer in Bermuda and Cockburn "was riding in his, the Commodore's, carriage at Halifax," adding, "This is not the way to conquer America."[16]

Cockburn and his laden troops returned to their boats leaving sixty burning buildings, two-thirds of Havre de Grace. Three militiamen lay dead, including the one disintegrated by a Congreve rocket. Cockburn had raised the level of destruction higher. Moving on quickly, the raiders burned the warehouse at Bell's Susquehanna Ferry, then glided across the Susquehanna to destroy the Principio Iron Furnace and cannon foundry. After spiking forty-five heavy guns, including twenty-eight 32-pounders destined for the American navy, they burned the century-old works, for the first time inflicting measurable damage on the American war effort.

Commodore Rodgers later learned of the raid on his hometown. On May 28 he had chased, boarded and then released an American ship bound from New York to Lisbon. From her captain he obtained a copy of a newspaper with an account of Havre de Grace's sacking. There was no other reason for the attack, Rodgers contended, by "the Mild, the Philanthropic, the Eloquent, the Seasoned, & the Brave Right Honourable Admiral Sir John Borlase Warren, Knight Baronite &c. &c. &c.," than "because it gave Birth to a Captain of the American Navy."[17]

IN JUNE, AS Admiral Warren sailed north to Halifax with forty prizes in tow, he shrugged off the latest instructions from London to extend the blockade to all ports south of Rhode Island, including the Mississippi. "We do not intend this to be a mere paper blockade," Lord Melville had written, "but as a complete stop to all trade & intercourse by Sea with those Ports." He told Warren that "if you find this cannot be done without abandoning for a time the interruption which you appear to be giving to the internal navigation of the Chesapeake, the latter object must be given up." Warren and Cockburn appeared to the Admiralty to be losing the big picture. "You must be content with blockading its entrance & sending in occasionally your cruisers for the purpose of harassing & annoyance." But Warren and Cockburn continued to ignore what London considered the higher priority of crippling American trade.[18]

On June 19 Warren returned from Halifax with an even more disproportionate naval force and the promised 2,000 soldiers and marines from

Bermuda. He now had assembled at Hampton Roads an armada of eight ships-of-the-line, twelve frigates, eight smaller men-of-war and assorted tenders and transports—70 percent of the entire Royal Navy ships assigned to the North American Station—to capture the *Constellation*! The vexsome American frigate had taken refuge behind a thrown-together floating battery of thirty-four guns on Craney Island at the mouth of Norfolk's harbor, and a line of ships' hulks sunk in the channel to block the entrance to the Elizabeth River.

On June 21 twenty British ships sailed to the mouth of the Nansemond River, just west of Norfolk. American forces on Craney Island had been reinforced with two 24-pounders and one 18-pounder manned by 150 sailors from the *Constellation*, along with 400 men from the Virginia militia and the Portsmouth Artillery Company. The British, planning a two-pronged attack, deposited a flanking force of 2,500 marines and infantry on the mainland west of the island before fifty barges, the main force, rowed straight toward the island from the Hampton Roads side. In the lead boat of the amphibious charge was Captain John Hanchett, skipper of the ship-of-the-line *Diadem* and purportedly an illegitimate son of King George III. He had volunteered for the command. Sitting beside the brass three-pounder in the bow of *Centipede*, Admiral Warren's personal bright-green twenty-four-oar barge, Hanchett held an umbrella over his head to block the searing summer sun.[19]

As Congreve rockets rained on Craney Island, the American gunners held their fire until the British flotilla was in easy range. A hailstorm of round shot, canister and grapeshot ripped into *Centipede*, one cannonball hulling her, another shearing off the legs of a French mercenary; Hanchett received a serious gunshot wound in the thigh. Along with the admiral's barge, four other barges ran aground on the shoals shielding the island only one hundred yards from the American battery. *Constellation*'s officers "fired their 18-pounder more like riflemen than Artillerists," reported Captain John Cassin, commanding officer at Norfolk naval base. "I never saw such shooting and seriously believe they saved the Island yesterday."[20]

A British sailor used a boathook to take a sounding and found only three feet of slime under the boats. Hanchett ordered the retreat. American militiamen waded out and seized sixty prisoners while forty deserters ran toward the American lines. In all, seventy-one British attackers were killed without firing one shot. The only American casualty was a Quaker who volunteered to watch the ammunition tent on the island and absent-mindedly lit his pipe, setting off a blast that terrified Norfolk. British lieutenant colonel Charles Napier wrote in his journal that "[o]ur attack on Craney Island was silly," adding that he thought the fault lay with "one simple cause—there were three commanders." He thought the fiasco revealed British overconfidence: "We despise the Yankee too much."[21]

Stubbornly seeking revenge for their humiliation, the British commanders ordered an attack four days later on nearby Hampton, a town of 1,000 with no military targets. Under Cockburn's command, the British brushed aside a few hundred Virginia militia and began their pillaging, stealing the church's silver, tearing down the sails of windmills, ransacking every house. Green-uniformed French chasseurs shot and killed an old man in his bed, stripped another and stabbed him with their bayonets, then dragged off several women and raped them. One woman remembered seeing British red uniforms and hearing correct English among the six soldiers who gang-raped her.

After American protests, the British officer in charge that day reported to Warren that the "Two Independent Companies of Foreigners" were shipped off to Halifax as punishment for "their brutal Treatment of several Peaceful Inhabitants." That no officer was held responsible disgusted Lieutenant Colonel Napier: "Every horror was committed with impunity, rape, murder, pillage, and not a man was punished!"[22]

In an escalating cycle of violence and reprisal, the war entered a more brutal phase. Raid upon relentless raid followed all through the summer of 1813, most of them unopposed as the helpless locals could only stand by while their livestock, produce, possessions and slaves were taken away. The British grew bolder, attacking Woodland Point on the Potomac River. A group of 140 militia, unarmed or with little ammunition, fought off a nighttime raid, aided by Secretary of State Monroe, who rode to reinforce them with a troop of cavalry from Washington. From bases at Point Lookout and Kent Island, some 2,000 British raided farms and seized ships, especially targeting towns that built privateering vessels.

On August 10, from Kent Island, Cockburn launched a raid on the eastern shore, sending a dozen war barges up the Miles River to St. Michael's, known to have constructed at least four successful privateers. As they overran the town battery in the darkness, its defenders got off a few rounds that awakened the townspeople. When the militia poured in, the British withdrew but not before their sloop-of-war *Conflict* fired its cannon at nearby homes. Three nights later, he struck due east, targeting a militia encampment at Queenston.

There, Colonel Sir Thomas Sidney Beckwith landed with two hundred men and two cannons; a battalion of marines rowed on, missing their designated landing. In the darkness, twenty American pickets fired on Beckwith's troops, the flash of their muskets in the dark panicking the British who began shooting each other. In what became known as the Battle of Slippery Hill, the commander of the Queen Anne's County militia compounded the chaos: when he heard that the marines had landed, he ordered his men to escape. The British regrouped and sacked the town.

Once more, as a blisteringly hot August ended, the British struck St. Michael's, sixty barges disgorging 2,100 men. Splitting their force, three hundred attacked a militia camp while the rest marched toward the boat-building center. A mile from town, the main British force ran into five hundred militia supported by cavalry and artillery. After the first few volleys, the largest battle on the eastern shore ended with the British retreating to their boats.

After a ten-day visit to St. George's Island, during which they cut down all the large oaks suitable for shipbuilding, burned all the houses and took away 170 slaves—Cockburn's commandos wrapped up their season of terror on the Chesapeake and, leaving a small blockading force at the mouth of the Bay, boarded ship for the balmier climes of Bermuda for the winter. Cockburn sent off to Halifax another seventy-two merchant ships he had seized in only four months. He left behind angry Americans whose government seemed to be doing nothing to prevent a reoccurrence in the spring of 1814.

As the second year of the war ended, the British strategy of economic strangulation made it increasingly difficult for the United States to carry out offensive warfare. Still bemired in a land war in Europe, the British relied on the Royal Navy to cut off the flow of the American government's principal source of revenue, customs duties, gradually tightening its blockade of the Atlantic seaports. Madison's sporadic imposition of embargoes only deepened the federal deficit.[23]

Even as Gallatin relayed the grim news to Madison, the British were deploying more warships to extend the blockade south to the Mississippi delta and north to New York City, the nation's most populous seaport, from which came fully one-fourth of its customs revenue.[24]

The unpredictability of revenue collection made preparing an accurate federal budget virtually impossible. Based on 1811 figures of $8.2 million in customs duties plus revenues from sale of federal lands and other fees, Gallatin had projected that $9.7 million would be available in 1812 for the war effort, but expenditures of $20.3 million quickly outran income, creating a $10.5 million deficit. To help close the gap, the government for the first time issued treasury notes, $5 million in $100 notes. Not intended to circulate as currency, they could be used to pay customs duties, taxes or to buy public lands.

But even this popular measure could not staunch the hemorrhage of red ink: Gallatin's forecast of $17 million in federal revenues available for the war in 1813 fell far short of the actual cost of $36 million. Faced with a $10.5 million debt from 1812 and a $19 million deficit in 1813, Congress deviated from its policy of issuing government bonds at face value and instead offered $16 million in bonds at 7 percent with discounts of 25 percent to major investors such as John Jacob Astor. By the end of 1813, even though Congress had doubled the rate of customs duties, collections were down by 76.5 percent from the start of the war. Because the Democratic-Republican-dominated Congress had refused to renew the charter of the First Bank of the United States when it expired in 1811, bankers were increasingly wary of the government's ability to meet interest payments. Indeed, as 1814 began, American investors had so little confidence in their government's liquidity that they began to withdraw their gold and silver deposits from banks in Boston and New York and send them to Canada to buy British bonds and commercial paper.[25]

As 1813 ended, the British, employing 106 warships on the North American station, had bottled up all U.S. Navy warships in American harbors, had captured fifteen warships of more than twenty guns and preyed at will on American merchant shipping, capturing 209 merchant ships. Yet the British Navy was unable to stop the unofficial American navy, its privateers, as they outmaneuvered larger British men-of-war and carried on a campaign of commerce raiding against Britain's merchant marine. Some

125 privateering vessels operated out of Baltimore alone. From Halifax on December 30, 1813, Admiral Warren wrote to John Croker, secretary of the Admiralty in London,

> Several large Clipper Schooners of from two to three hundred Tons, strongly manned and armed have run thro' the Blockade in the Chesapeak, in spite of every endeavor and the most vigilant attention of our Ships to prevent their getting out, nor can anything stop these Vessels escaping to Sea in dark Nights & Strong Winds.

Brazenly forming convoys, the Baltimore privateers, Warren reported, sometimes escaped from the Chesapeake in squadrons. To First Lord of the Admiralty Robert Melville, Warren was sorry to report "that the American Small Vessels, notwithstanding the Vigilance of the Blockading Squadron; from the severity of the weather and in the Dark Snowy nights Do get out, & and it is almost impossible to prevent it."[26]

With all navy ships along the Atlantic coast bottled up by the British blockade and a second season of American attempts at invading Canada outright and costly failures, public support for continuing the war ebbed, especially in New England. In New Hampshire the Reverend Andrew Mack, a schoolmaster at Gilmanton Academy, sat down on the evening of January 9, 1814, and sharpened his quill. To his friend Samuel Fletcher in Concord, he wrote that he was stretching his brain "to find any argument" to affirm that "the campaign of 1813 has been properly conducted. The land war was [no] better but disgrace."[27]

THIRTEEN

"Destroy and Lay Waste"

Several months after the British cabinet rejected Czar Alexander's offer to mediate a settlement between the United States and Britain, Russia's trading partners, Britain's foreign secretary Viscount Castlereagh suddenly decided, after conferring with the prime minister, Lord Liverpool, that negotiations with the United States were necessary, if not opportune. By early 1814, as the dreary war in Europe dragged on with no diminution in sight and the American war turned into a stalemate, it was clear that the two conflicts were becoming an unsupportable burden. Castlereagh, nonetheless, would brook no intermediary. Negotiations must be direct, between his government and the United States, either in London or Gothenburg, Sweden. He rightly comprehended that Russia and the United States might find common interests and act in "concert" at Britain's expense.

When Castlereagh's counterproposal reached Madison in January 1814, the president accepted it, but, as he informed Congress, only on condition that fighting continue until the ratification of an actual treaty. Madison was not as optimistic as he had once been, especially since Castlereagh had declared in writing that any solution would have to concede "the maritime rights of the British Empire." Madison's chief concern remained the impressment of American sailors.

After a seven-week winter voyage aboard the twenty-eight-gun corvette *John Adams*, Clay, Russell and their staffs reached Gothenburg on
April 13, 1814. Gallatin and Bayard joined them a week later with "bad
News." After defeat at Leipzig, Napoleon, on the defensive, had been
forced to fall back to France. The Allies, Britain, Austria and Russia, had
invaded France from the south and east and, on March 31, Russians had
occupied Paris. Twelve days later, Napoleon had abdicated uncondition-
ally at Fontainebleau. Peace had suddenly descended on the European
world, leaving the United States to fight the triumphant British alone.[1]

The collapse of Napoleon's Continental System of blockade and embargo freed Britain to trade openly with Europe. The United States must
do likewise, especially if it wanted European nations to defy the British
blockade and trade with the United States. When he learned the news,
Navy secretary Jones, in a memorandum to Madison, insisted that the
United States abandon its attempts to conquer Canada, go on the defensive by land and, resuming direct trade with Europe, concentrate on waging a naval war against Britain. At least, Jones contended, this would
produce desperately needed customs duties. Unable to deny Jones's logic,
Madison called on Congress to repeal its latest ninety-day embargo on importation. To his surprise, a new alliance of Federalists and discontented
Democratic-Republicans supported him.

In an about-face, Madison proposed an armistice to stop the fighting
before the peace talks, but Admiral Cochrane could see no advantage in
easing his campaign of intimidation. On the contrary, Cochrane, sensing
new American vulnerability, pressed his advantage by extending the naval blockade to include New England. Now, the entire American coast
from the Gulf of Maine to the Gulf of Mexico lay under siege by the Royal
Navy. Additionally, to the horror of slave owners, Cochrane issued a proclamation inviting free and enslaved blacks "to emigrate from the United
States" and either enlist in British naval and land forces or relocate to
other British possessions as "FREE Settlers." His proclamation banished
any lingering fantasy in Washington that, the balance of power in Europe
having shifted in their favor, the British were ready to scale back their
American offensives on land and sea.[2]

FROM SOARING PRIDE at seeing *Old Ironsides* and the American flotilla glide triumphantly into Boston harbor in September 1812, Thomas Mc-Clure had by April 1813, little more than six months later, slid into gloom at the retrograde course of the war. Even as Napoleon capitulated in France, McClure wrote again to his brother David in East Windsor, Connecticut, on April 12:

> This war, this wicked because unnecessary war, is ruining many & injuring all except a few & and those not the best character. . . . My business is cut off now almost intirely since the cruisers have come into our Bay and take the Coasters. The only way now for the eastern people to get Bread stuff which they are suffering for is cut off. . . . They are nearly in a state of starvation. . . . The communication with C[onnecticu]t is cut off. . . .
>
> There is now two British frigates in sight & while I am writing this they are chasing in a large ship & I hear the guns it is feared she will not get in & there is the other cruising ship in the bay cutting off all our trade & taking vessels there is now 4 of our frigates in here. . . .
>
> It is really melancholy to view the long wharf & other places that used to be alive with business now still & dead wearing the appearance of the Sabbath almost. Madison has much to answer for enmeshing us in this war there is an increasing opposition to it. Mad. is in a bad box & he will find it now difficult to get out.[3]

ALONG THE CANADIAN front, British counterattacks became more determined as massive reinforcements crossed the Atlantic, propelled by an angry tailwind of public opinion. Many British wanted to punish the Americans for their perceived backstabbing, as their declaration of war occurred at the exact moment that Napoleon was invading Russia. "Chastise the savages," the *Times* of London editorialized, "for such they are, in a much a truer sense than the followers of Tecumseh or the Prophet." Meanwhile, the British Ministry launched a combined sea-and-land onslaught along the Great Lakes and the Atlantic and Gulf coasts. The new offensive aimed to secure the safety of Canada from further American invasion and to occupy as much American territory as possible for leverage in the peace negotiations—once John Bull had given Brother Jonathan a thorough drubbing.[4]

On June 3 Lord Bathurst, secretary of state for war and the colonies, in a letter marked "secret," outlined a strategy of a considerable "augmentation of the Army in Canada" to Prevost in Quebec. Four regiments had already sailed from Spithead, Cork and Bordeaux; twelve of the Duke of Wellington's best regiments from Spain were en route with three companies of artillery. In all, 10,000 veterans were bound for Canada. Six more regiments were being detached from the Gironde and the Mediterranean for "offensive operations on the Frontier" and for "a direct operation against the Enemy's Coast." In all, Prevost was to expect 14,000 troops.

The new forces' prime objective would be to defend Canada, specifically Fort Niagara, but then they were ordered to carry out "the entire destruction of Sackets Harbour and the Naval Establishments on Lake Erie and Lake Champlain," reoccupy "Detroit and the Michigan Country" and return it to the Indians. Prevost was to extend Canadian territory by seizing Lake Champlain, shifting the Canadian border more than one hundred miles farther south. And he was to occupy Maine north of the Penobscot River "to secure an uninterrupted intercourse between Halifax and Quebec."[5]

A FRESH SHOCK had come at Castlereagh's insistence on direct negotiations. Madison's peace commissioners had converged on Sweden only to learn that the British deemed this site unsuitable. The British had given the Americans the choice of London or a city in the Netherlands. Adams had refused to negotiate in London. The British Cabinet had settled on Ghent, in present-day Belgium, medieval capital of Flanders.

On June 13, 1814, on the eve of sailing across the English Channel, Gallatin, who had been gathering intelligence in London from his financial connections, sent a disquieting diplomatic analysis to Secretary of State Monroe. Gallatin's principal contact in London was Member of Parliament Alexander Baring, partner in a leading international bank. Married to Philadelphian Anne Louisa Bingham, daughter of the wealthiest Philadelphia merchant, Baring handled the peace commission's finances and was in an ideal position to learn details of the Ministry's plan. He told his friend Gallatin of a recent conversation with Castlereagh. "They mean to inflict on America a chastisement that will teach her that war is not to be declared against Great Britain with impunity," Gallatin warned Monroe. "This is a very general sentiment in the nation." Baring informed Gallatin that he had heard that Admiral Warren had told an acquaintance that the new instructions given to Admiral Cochrane, his successor on the North American Station, were very different from the olive-branch-and-sword directives he had received at the start of the war "and that he apprehended that very serious injury would be inflicted on America."

If it is a given that diplomats also act as spies, then Gallatin was a master. His intelligence was breathtakingly accurate: the British would land 15,000 to 20,000 men, he warned his superiors in Washington. "I think it probable that Washington and New York are the places the capture of which would most gratify the enemy, and that Norfolk, Baltimore, and the collected manufacturing establishments of the Brandywine and Rhode Island also are in danger." British objectives everywhere would include "the destruction of all public naval magazines and arsenals, and of all the shipping, whether public or private." Americans must expect to pay ransom, endure plundering "and whatever marks of a predatory warfare must be expected."

Gallatin suspected that the ultimate British intention would be "to sever the Union" and "demand a cession of territory," most likely New York, and to cripple the naval and commercial resources as well as the growing manufactures of the United States." The Americans could expect no help from Europe: "Europe wants peace." Most Europeans cared little about America's neutral rights: "America cannot, by a continuance of the war, compel Great Britain to yield any of the maritime points in dispute." The "most favorable terms of peace that can be expected are the status ante bellum." Madison's greater goals, to end impressment and blockade, "will ultimately be attained" but at a more propitious moment, "provided you can stand the shock of this campaign, and provided the people will remain and show themselves united."

Gallatin warned Monroe that, as he sailed to Ghent, he considered peace improbable "before the conclusion of this year's campaign. This nation and government will be tired of a war without object, and which must become unpopular when the passions of the day will have subsided and the country sees clearly that America asks nothing from Great Britain."

And then Gallatin sailed with Russell to join Clay and Bayard in Ghent; Adams was on his arduous way from Russia in a lumbering six-horse carriage.

Even with passage on a fast courier ship carrying it across the Atlantic, Gallatin's message did not arrive on Monroe's desk until August 5, some fifty-four days later, underscoring the American envoys' disadvantage. Because of their strategic choice of Ghent, the British could send messages to London virtually overnight, take action and provide answers in a matter of days. In Washington, several days after Monroe sent Gallatin's gloomy message over to the White House, Madison, canceling his usual summer visit away from the District, decided to call a special session of Congress to ponder the nation's deteriorating condition.[6]

Most of the news reaching Madison was bound to dishearten him. The nation's economy was in tatters. Unemployment was running high. Consumer prices were soaring, in part because New England's ports, left open for nearly two years by British blockaders who had sold illegal licenses to American ships' captains eager to sell the enemy provision, were now closed. Isaac Hull, captain of the *Constitution* bottled up in Boston harbor, expressed his frustration at the practice in a letter to the customs collector of the port of Boston. The navy schooner *Enterprise* "has this moment sent in a Privateer Prize," he wrote to Henry A. S. Dearborn.

> In her Logbook I find the following remarks, on the 13th August: "At 11 brought to and boarded the American Schooner Fox from Boston Bound to St. Johns [New Brunswick] with a License: ordered her to proceed on being loaded with Flour and Bread." What can be done with such scoundrels? Would you see who she belongs to & where she cleared for?[7]

But now the ports of New England, too, slammed shut. Neutral ships, especially from Sweden, Portugal and Spain, had kept dockyards, shipyards and warehouses thriving, in part because British strategists hope to widen the region's disaffection with "Mister Madison's War." Yet trade had declined markedly. Inverted tar buckets mounted on the mastheads of idled ships to discourage rotting became known as "Madison's nightcaps." While shipments of grain to Canada for re-export to British forces remained brisk, the traditional "broken voyage" re-export of West Indian

"DESTROY AND LAY WASTE"   *305*

goods in New England's ships was down by 95 percent since 1811. According to British naval historian Brian Arthur, by December 1813

> Boston harbor held ninety-one ships, two barks, 109 brigs and forty-three
> schooners, totaling 245 vessels excluding coasters [attributable] to the lack
> of employment. From December 1 to December 24, forty-four vessels were
> cleared from Boston for abroad, only five of which were American.

Evidently, by the end of 1813, even where neutral vessels were still allowed and the cargoes in them paid some customs duties, the United States was not paying for its war by taxing trade.[8]

When the first blockading British man-of-war appeared off Block Island, a dozen local fishing boats followed it into the anchorage. Benjamin Sprague's boat got closest, and he quoted the officer a price of "twenty cents apiece" for his fish. Sending up his whole catch, Sprague, pocketing hard money, moved aside and told the next fisherman what price he'd gotten. Arriving home, he told his wife he wanted to press his good fortune. He gathered some chickens, ducks, beans and a mug of half-watered rum and returned to the ship. The officers touched their hats in recognition and asked, "What's in that jug?" They sent Sprague to the ship's steward with instructions to let each man have a drink. That evening, the officers invited Sprague aboard for dinner and asked him to try their rum: didn't he think it was better? Returning again and again, Sprague soon had sold the British every drop of rum he could find.

Provisioning the British was no laughing matter to forty American prisoners of war aboard the man-of-war *Albion*, lying at anchor in the Elizabeth Islands at New Year's when a man "habitted as a Quaker" arrived with a boatload of fresh beef for sale. Several prisoners recognized the purveyor, called him a traitor and threatened that they would see him punished when they were exchanged. The Quaker appealed to the ship's captain, who ordered the men who had made the threat put in irons; weeks later, he released the prisoners on a far distant shore. Two other Quakers, John and Ebenezer Hussey of Berwick, Maine, weren't so fortunate. When they couldn't sell the thirteen scrawniest of the fifty cattle they had herded from town to town in Maine, they fobbed them off on less-selective British officers at Provincetown. Arriving home in January, they were arrested by federal officers and charged with "high treason, in giving aid and comfort to the enemies of the United States." Imprisoned for four months, they were released after a grand jury failed to uncover sufficient evidence or witnesses to hold them.[9]

As the British tightened their vise, they began to coerce coastal towns into supplying them. In January the British warship *Nimrod* chased a coastal schooner full of provisions onto a reef off Falmouth, Massachusetts. When they tried to seize it, local militia poured musket fire into three British barges sent to offload the provisions. Under a flag of truce, Captain Nathaniel Mitchell demanded Falmouth pay tribute of a Nantucket packet sloop and the town's two brass cannon. The militia captain John Crocker refused. The British officer gave them one hour to comply. As the militia evacuated the sick, the women and the children, Mitchell ordered his thirty-two-pounders to open fire. Eight shells passed through Crocker's house, more through his outbuildings and his salt works. In all, some three hundred shells hit the town, striking thirty buildings but hurting no one. This first raid on a coastal town sent a chill of foreboding through New England. Massachusetts was finally willing to appeal to Washington for federal weapons: the penny-pinching Secretary of War Armstrong reluctantly sent along 1,500 muskets to defend the entire state.

After British dispensation of New England from the blockade for nearly two years, its imposition caught many ships' captains unawares. According to Eleanor Roosevelt, Warren Delano—maternal great-grandfather of President Franklin Delano Roosevelt—sailed one such merchant ship out of New Bedford, Massachusetts, early in 1814 to neutral Sweden. On its homeward journey, the ship was captured by the British and taken to Halifax, where, along with its cargo, it was auctioned off as a prize of war and the proceeds divided among its captors—this was the fate of about 2,500 ships in Delano's lifetime. He and his men were later released. While he was away, the British, intensifying their campaign of coastal terrorizing and looting, attacked his hometown of Fairhaven, which was protected by a Revolutionary War–era fort mounting a dozen cannon. Mrs. Delano was able to spirit away their sons—including FDR's grandfather—to safety up the Acushnet River. The British abandoned the attack after they mistook the blast of a postman's horn for a bugle, assuming it prefigured a of the synchronized landings planned by the British along the Gulf Coast to support their Indian allies not only saved Jackson's army but also blocked, at least temporarily, British capture of New Orleans and the lower Mississippi valley. Moving his army to an old French fort at the juncture of the Coosa and the Tallapoosa Rivers, he renamed it Fort Jackson. Five months later, he imposed a treaty cession on the broken Creek nation that added to the United States some 23 million acres of land—half of all the Creek homeland—which make up three-fifths of the state of Alabama and one-fifth of Georgia. Madison rewarded Jackson by promoting him to major general in the U.S. Army and conferring on him the command of the new Seventh Military District, including Tennessee, Louisiana and the Mississippi Territory.

Far to the north on the Canadian front, all through the winter of 1813–14, sickness, including smallpox and dysentery, ravaged the army's northern encampments, depleting the ranks of the nation's meager military forces. At French Mills, New York, the blockhouse of Fort Covington soon overflowed with the sick and the wounded from Wilkinson's feckless foray into Quebec Province. Thousands of men suffered for twelve days in open boats on the St. Lawrence. Most of the sick, too weak to build huts, had to live in tents and shanties. One-third of Wilkinson's army was too sick at any one time for duty. Wilkinson himself was not exempt: eight men had to carry him to a mansion in Malone, eighteen miles from the sight of his army's suffering.

But the sick soon followed him, 250 of them filling an arsenal, an academy and private homes. In December, in one unit of 160 men, seventy-five were sick: thirty-nine had diarrhea and dysentery, eighteen pneumonia and six typhus, and twelve suffered from paralysis. Secretary of War Armstrong finally ordered pestiferous French Mills abandoned and half the troops moved to Sackets Harbor, half to Plattsburgh. The sick and wounded were taken across frozen Lake Champlain to Burlington. The 450 sickest men, including Wilkinson, went on sleighs. Twenty were left behind and taken prisoner by the British; six died during the fifty-mile trip.

At Burlington, they found a new hospital, "a new heaven and a new earth," according to one doctor who accompanied Wilkinson's wounded. Hundreds of soldiers from the 4,000-man garrison were transferred to the University of Vermont's hilltop building—the largest building in the

charge by a considerable force. At least that's the way they tell the story around Buzzards Bay.[10]

AS STILL-SMOLDERING EMBERS of a forest fire thought to have been extinguished can leap great distances and rekindle, so too did sparks of the War of 1812 flare up far from the fixed positions where most forces were concentrated. The death of Tecumseh in Canada fomented even greater determination among young militant Creek in faraway Alabama to fight the ever-encroaching white society. In return, frontiersmen flocked to the standard of Andrew Jackson after he received permission from Governor Blount of Tennessee to avenge the massacre at Fort Mims.

Speeding his army deep into Creek country, Jackson drove his mounted Tennessee volunteers an incredible thirty miles a day, halting at the southern tip of the Tennessee River only long enough to construct Fort Deposit as a supply depot. Pushing on to the Coosa River, he cut a road over the mountains and established a base at Fort Strother, near Ten Islands, within striking distance of the Red Sticks' encampment thirteen miles to the east at Tallushatchee. With 1,000 unruly Tennessee men, Jackson surrounded the village on November 3, 1813, and systematically slaughtered most of the warriors. Tennessee congressman David Crockett described the carnage succinctly: "We shot them like dogs." After ordering the town burned, Jackson moved on to Talladega, where the Tennesseans killed another three hundred Red Sticks even as many more fled.

As the year 1814 began, volunteer Samuel E. Snow had a moment to write home:

> Dear Wife,
> We have been on the trail of the red devils for three days but our scouts report they have disappeared and we start back tomorrow—rations getting short. The Creeks true to tradition vanished after their killing and Major Conn says it is useless to go farther. We have looked on sad sights. God grant I won't see much more. The fiends butchered a woman and two small children we found two days ago. Also buried five men horribly mutilated and scalped. Old Hickory is the boy for the reds and a day of settlement is at hand.[11]

Forced to return to Fort Strother to resupply, Jackson appealed repeatedly to Governor Blount for reinforcements even as many of his sixty-day volunteers deserted and went home. By February 1814 he had finally received permission to raise more volunteers and to attack the Red Sticks. On March 14 he was ready to march again, this time with 3,300 troops—nearly three times his earlier strength—including 2,000 infantry, six hundred of them regulars, seven hundred cavalry and mounted riflemen and six hundred friendly Indians, mostly Cherokees but some one hundred Creek as well.

To avoid a reoccurrence of mass desertions and to set an example of stern discipline, before he marched, Jackson court-martialed an eighteen-year-old recruit named John Wood who had rudely refused to carry out an order. Convicted of insubordination and mutiny, young Wood was sentenced to death. Jackson refused to overturn the verdict or commute the sentence. Before the youth faced the firing squad, Jackson wrote to him, "An army cannot exist where order & subordination are wholly disregarded."[12]

After the execution, the first for a crime other than desertion since the American Revolution, Jackson marched straight toward entrenched Red Stick fortifications at Horseshoe Bend, a heavily wooded peninsula enclosed by the twisting course of the Tallapoosa River. Indian breastworks made of horizontally stacked timbers and tree trunks crossed its 350-yard neck, leaving only a single entrance. Cut into the curved, zigzagging breastworks at five to eight feet high was a double row of portholes, which afforded a deadly crossfire on attackers with no possibility of return enfilading fire. Inside the fort, the prophet Monahee, the principal chief, had gathered warriors from the towns of Oakfuskee, New Youka, the Fish Ponds and Eufala. Menewa (Great Warrior), a mixed-blood, commanded.

Arriving the morning of March 27, Jackson deployed his artillery, one 6-pounder and one 3-pounder, on a rise facing the barricade. In a letter to Secretary Armstrong, Jackson later wrote that he admired the Indians' defenses in "a place well-formed by Nature for defense & rendered more secure by Art." To his wife Rachel he wrote, "They had possessed themselves of one of the most military sites, I Ever saw, which they had as strongly fortified with logs, across the neck of a bend." Inside their fort, the Indians began screaming defiance and beating their war drums. At ten thirty,

Jackson's guns opened fire. "I endeavoured to levell the works with my cannon, but in vain—The balls passed thro the works without shaking the wall."

Jackson had posted General John Coffee across the river with his cavalry and Creek auxiliaries to cut off the possibility of retreat. Suddenly, without orders or warning, the hundred friendly Creek and their Cherokee allies crossed the river in canoes with 150 horsemen and, setting fire with brush to buildings along the shore, attacked the Red Sticks from the rear. The fight behind the breastworks raged for two hours before Jackson, fearing Coffee's force was "about to be overpowered" as he told Rachel, "ordered the charge and carried the works, by storm." Under a murderous rain of arrows and bullets, his troops rushed the barricade. Major Lemuel P. Montgomery of the 39th Regiment reached the breastwork first: leaping to its top, he yelled for his men to follow him, but the Indians' yelling drowned him out. A bullet struck him in the head and, as he fell to the ground, Ensign Sam Houston vaulted onto the wall and yelled for his men to follow. An arrow pierced his thigh, but Houston, followed by a large number of regulars, jumped into the compound. Within minutes, the rest of the army scaled the ramparts and captured the fortifications, driving back the Red Sticks as the friendly Indians continued their attack from the rear.

Unable to escape, the Red Sticks tried to hide in thick underbrush but were quickly flushed out and shot at close range. For the next five hours, as the army burned the village, "the firing and the slaughter continued until it was suspended by the darkness of the night," Jackson reported to Rachel. "It was dark before we finished killing them." Jackson conceded that "the carnage was dreadfull." Tallying the dead, Jackson told her, "I have no doubt but at least Eight hundred and fifty were slain." He recounted that twenty-six whites died and 107 were wounded. He did not mention his dead and wounded Indian allies. Only nineteen Red Sticks escaped; Jackson took three hundred warriors and fifty-seven women and children as his prisoners. As a souvenir, he took away for his little son, Andrew, "a warriors bow & quiver."[13]

Some 3,000 Red Sticks, about 15 percent of the Creek population, had been killed in a matter of weeks and numerous Creek villages and their food supplies destroyed. The extirpation of the Red Stick Creek on the eve

state—to make room for the sick and wounded crowding into the five-acre lakeside cluster of army barracks. College officials, faced with plummeting enrollment, willingly dismissed faculty and students and rented the campus to the U. S. government for $5,000. There, Dr. James Mann instituted hygienic practices that made it the cleanest hospital in the North: whitewashing walls with lime and water, scattering a fresh coat of sand on the floors every morning, removing and cleaning bunks and burning and replacing sacks of straw after each change of patient. Still, the number of sick troops multiplied. By March 1814, in forty wards staffed by eight surgeons and surgeons' mates, 931 sick men had been admitted and twenty-nine of them had died. Between January and April, ninety-five men succumbed. As smallpox ravaged the base, wagons hauled patients to quarantine in rural farmhouses, and those who died were buried in mass graves.[14]

The desertion rate soared as dispirited men went home or fled into Canada. In 1813 thirty-two soldiers had been shot for desertion; more than four times that number faced firing squads that same year. Corrupt officers at French Mills continued to carry the dead and the deserters on their rosters, pocketing their pay. Recruitment had fallen off drastically because of the government's inability to continue to pay enlistment bounties. After two seasons of military failures, few citizens were willing to die for their country or even serve under such primitive conditions and harsh discipline. "Something must be done and done speedily," Secretary of the Navy Jones said, "or we shall have an opportunity of trying the experiment of maintaining an army and navy and carrying on a vigorous war without money."[15]

There was so little money in the Treasury that the navy secretary was reduced to writing out all orders and letters himself: his budget did not allow him to employ two part-time clerks. The State Department wasn't even able to pay its stationery bill. When the Treasury could not pay a Pennsylvania foundry its bill for procuring the metal to strike new coins, the foundry refused to extend the government further credit. There would be no pennies in 1815.

The mere fact that the British had offered to negotiate and that Madison had accepted their arrangements had given fresh hope to many in Congress that another season of war and its appropriations might be avoidable, a line of thinking encouraged by the projected costs. In mid-January 1814 acting Treasury secretary Jones estimated that the total costs for the army and navy in 1814 would be $45 million, an increase of more than half over 1813 expenditures. Anticipated revenues would cover only the salaries of government workers and loan interest. Most of the needed revenue would have to come from an unprecedented loan of $30 million.[16]

Compounding the government's problem had been the Royal Navy's exemption of Federalist New England from its blockade through 1812 and 1813. This had drawn most of the nation's hard money into banks in the Northeast, especially Boston, discouraging investors farther south from subscribing to government bonds. In 1814 John Jacob Astor declined to subscribe unless Congress resuscitated the Bank of the United States. Astor would then borrow from the revived bank, but not before.

Talk of disunion continued to spread after the news hit home that Napoleon's surrender had cleared the path for the British to carry on a total war of economic blockade and military devastation against New England. Many Yankees had survived so long only by trading with the enemy. Before the year 1814 was over, the 7,000 citizens of treeless Nantucket, thirty-five miles from the mainland and dependent on it for firewood and food, was facing starvation. Their whaling and fishing fleets moldering at their moorings, Nantucket's selectmen decided they must negotiate a separate peace rather than face another winter of privation.

Carrying a petition to Captain Robert Barrie of the blockade ship *Dragon,* they declared the island "in a state of starvation." Barrie forwarded the petition to a suspicious Admiral Cochrane. Barrie was to ascertain the veracity of the islanders' claims:

> The request they make to carry on their Fishery cannot be complied with, but if they actually are in the distressed state they represent, permission may be granted them to import from the Continent supplies of food provided they will declare themselves neutral and deliver up such Artillery, Guns & Ammunition as may be on the Island and submit to His Majesty's Ships getting from them whatever refreshments the Islands will afford . . .

After further negotiations, the Islanders at a town meeting on August 23 declared the island neutral and free of United States jurisdiction.

Pledging "not to take up arms against Great Britain," they agreed to sur-render their weapons and "make no opposition against any British Vessel Coming into this harbor to Refresh." They also voted to stop paying direct federal taxes. Cochrane, ever eager to drive a wedge between New En-glanders and the U.S. government, lifted the blockade on the island, promised to release Nantucket privateers held at the notorious Dartmoor prison in England and agreed to allow Nantucket vessels to resume fishing and trading for food and fuel on the mainland.[17]

But as the blockade continued to tighten all along the Atlantic sea-board, the alarmed citizens of Block Island were forced to endure unac-customed indignities. As early as June 1, 1813, the captain of the *Ramilies* had reported from his station offshore that he received "plenty of wood and [live]stock from [Block Island] and we also get our linen washed there. . . . The inhabitants are very much alarmed . . . but as long as they supply us we shall be very civil to them." As their part of the exchange, the British promised the islanders exemption from raids.[18]

ALARMED BY GALLATIN's analysis of the changed attitudes in Europe, Madison created the Tenth Military District, with 3,000 regular troops to be transferred from the Canadian front and 10,000 to 12,000 volun-teers called up from neighboring states to defend the District of Colum-bia, northern Virginia and all of Maryland, including Baltimore and Annapolis.

At a cabinet meeting at the White House on July 1, 1814, Madison ar-gued that recent dramatic shifts in the balance of power in Europe had transformed the prospects in America. He warned "unequivocally" that Washington offered "the most inviting object of a speedy attack."

But Madison was alone. Secretary of War Armstrong laughed at the possibility of a British attack. The adopted New Yorker with landed inter-ests in the Hudson Valley argued that New York was a more likely target. Navy secretary Jones later recalled, "I was not equally impressed with the apprehension of immediate danger." Secretary of State Monroe, a Revolu-tionary War colonel, also seriously doubted that the British had the logis-tical capacity to mount such an ambitious attack.[19]

The ramifications in North America of Napoleon's capitulation hit home as thousands of Wellington's veterans boarded ships in France to reinforce British posts on the Niagara frontier and around Lakes Erie and Ontario. Prevost and his generals expected to be able to make short work of the militia they had so easily routed only months before. By this time, however, American regulars were undergoing advanced training by the newly promoted Brigadier General Winfield Scott at America's first boot camp. Physically imposing at six feet, five inches—nearly a foot taller than many of his troops—the broad-shouldered Scott had inspired courage in the chaotic Battle of Queenston even as he was forced to surrender. Later, as colonel of the 2nd Artillery Regiment, he had planned the joint army-navy attack on Fort George with Commodore Perry and had personally led the infantry attack. Even as many American generals were discrediting themselves, Scott was gaining the reputation of America's most accomplished soldier. President Madison recognized his personal valor and competence by promoting him to be the youngest general in the army.

In March 1814 Scott rode into Buffalo to establish a basic training program that was both rigorous and exciting. At his Camp of Instruction, Scott acted as drill sergeant, training recruits endlessly in marching and in deploying and using the bayonet. His threadbare regulars drilled up to ten hours a day, six days a week. Hunger, disease and poor pay had led to a high desertion rate in the American forces. When a few of his men took their pay and ran, Scott ordered them hauled back, thus earning a reputation as a severe disciplinarian. A court-martial condemned them to death as deserters. Scott reluctantly gave the order to execute them. By 1813, as conditions in the camps grew worse, more men deserted and more were shot. In all, 136 Americans were executed on a charge of desertion during the war.

Employing French manuals, Scott also organized a general staff, introducing a new level of professionalism. By summer, reinforcements poured into the Buffalo encampment: regulars under Major General Jacob Brown; militia under Brigadier General Peter B. Porter; Iroquois warriors led by Red Jacket. Soon, a well-trained, well-disciplined army of 5,000 men considered themselves ready to fight even Wellington's veterans.[20]

As the summer of 1814 came on, President Madison and his cabinet set to work planning one more all-out attempt to seize Canadian territory before large numbers of British veterans arrived in North America. By midsummer, 6,000 disciplined veterans of Wellington's Invincibles were already debarking on the St. Lawrence. To face them, the Army of the North was commanded by Brown, who, as a militia officer, had repulsed the British attack on Sackets Harbor in 1813. This had earned Brown, once a Quaker schoolteacher, a regular-army generalship from Madison, and with this he superseded the useless Wilkinson. Brown received confusing orders from Armstrong in Washington: believing that he was authorized to invade Canada across the Niagara, he crossed the turbulent river on July 3, 1814, with 3,500 men in three columns, two brigades of regulars under Winfield Scott and Eleazar Ripley and militia under Porter. The Americans fired only a few rounds at Fort Erie before the feeble British garrison surrendered. Leaving a small contingent there, Brown ordered Scott's brigade to march up the Canadian riverbank toward Lake Ontario. He sent a request to Commodore Chauncey to meet him with enough ships to make a joint attack along the lake. But Chauncey had already decided not to act any longer as a servant to the army; he ignored Scott's repeated pleading and failed to rendezvous with Brown.

On July 5 Scott's brigade collided with a heavily strengthened British force marching toward Fort Erie. Thinking he had encountered only a small unit, Scott sent Porter and his militia into the woods to clear them of the few British soldiers and Indians he could see. Porter's troops raced back to inform him that the main British army lay just ahead. The British commander, Riall, had crossed the Chippewa River with 2,100 veterans, and they were quick-marching toward Scott. But now Scott's men, drilled all winter at Buffalo, executed a series of difficult maneuvers and hastily formed neat lines of battle.

Assuming that he faced militia, Riall recklessly ordered his troops to advance toward the Americans in straight lines across an open field. In the past, their glistening bayonets and disciplined maneuvers under fire had cowed the Americans. This time the Americans, outfitted in their new bucket hats and gray uniforms—none of the traditional blue cloth was available—that would become the dress uniform of West Point cadets, engaged the British with musket and cannon fire. The Americans got the better of an artillery duel, their musketry proving even more accurate and deadly. Witnessing the precise American maneuvers, their speed and accuracy of fire, the astonished Riall exclaimed, "Those are Regulars, by

God!" Seeing that his own regulars were taking a severe pounding, Riall ordered his battered force to retreat. At Chippewa Plains, American soldiers were proving their ability to stand up to the British. The first clear-cut infantry victory of the war restored American morale.[21]

When Lieutenant General Gordon Drummond, the overall British commander in Canada, learned of the bruising engagement, he rushed reinforcements to Riall. Even though victorious, Scott, deprived of naval support, had no choice but to retreat to Fort Erie and reorganize his line of supplies and communication or risk being cut off from his base. To delay the pursuing British, Brown sent Scott back to engage their advance units. Scott found Riall entrenched on a sloping field along Lundy's Lane adjacent to the roaring Niagara Falls. Outnumbered, the Americans faced destruction until Scott rushed up to join the savage fighting, which raged on until midnight.

Three hours into a five-hour battle, the Americans could see that they had to silence British artillery raking the battlefield from the crest of a ridge. After several bloody attempts, the Americans finally dislodged them from the hillside and spiked their cannon. Colonel James Miller's troops made bayonet charge after bayonet charge, overwhelming even Wellington's Invincibles. One British observer wrote to a Halifax newspaper a letter reprinted in the Baltimore press: "The Americans charged to the very muzzles of our cannons and actually bayonetted the artillerymen at their guns." His comment was echoed by Colonel Miller himself: the battle was "one of the most desperately fought actions ever experienced in America." By this time, both sides, exhausted and having sustained far worse casualties than at Chippewa Plains, withdrew from the field in the darkness. The Americans managed to capture Riall and his entire staff, but both Scott and Brown were seriously wounded. America's best young general, Scott, was so severely wounded that he was knocked out of the war. Brown, hit by a spent cannonball and shot through the thigh by a musket ball, also had to be carried off the field.[22]

But the bloodiest single day of the war occurred on August 15, 1814, in a failed British attack on Fort Erie, opposite Buffalo. The fortress had already changed hands four times. A British attacking force of 3,000 of Wellington's Invincibles faced 2,000 well-disciplined Americans. Expecting the worst, one of Wellington's veteran officers paused to scratch a farewell note to his wife. The three-pronged attack got off to a sluggish start. An Indian diversionary force arrived too late. The British colonel leading one column was shot in the head. Neither flanking party reached its objective. Soon, withering American cannon and musket fire cut down the exposed British. As the British tried to fight their way into the bastion, one of their own cannonballs struck the fort's main ammunition storage magazine. The remnants of the battered British force fled back to their lines, leaving 2,000 killed or wounded behind.

The Americans had succeeded in repulsing the British attack, but the determined British now launched a formal siege punctuated by daily cannonades from heavy guns they had brought up. Cannonballs bounced off the three-foot-thick walls for ten days before the British commander ordered a frontal attack. On August 29, one of the balls crashed through the room of General Edmund Gaines, Brown's replacement, so severely wounding him that he, too, had to relinquish command. British artillery barrages became intolerable. On the night of September 17, in a severe rainstorm, the wounded Brown stepped back into command and ordered a sortie by two columns of infantry. After intense fighting in the dark, they managed to spike the guns of two of the three British batteries. Four days later, General Drummond called off the siege. Brown's courageous stand on the Niagara again helped to raise Americans' spirits, but after five major battles in one season, it had become a war of attrition on both sides of the eight-hundred-mile Canadian-American front, a stalemate with no clear victor, orchestrated on both sides by politicians seeking territory as bargaining chips to bring to the table in the impending peace negotiations in Ghent.

THE MORNING OF June 24, 1814, was cool as John Quincy Adams and Jonathan Russell waited for a ferry to take them across the Scheldt River from the Netherlands to Antwerp, Belgium. As toll takers and officials argued over who should pocket their coins, they could see a few remnants of Napoleon's navy—eight ships-of-the-line and five frigates—on the stocks, waiting to be dismantled. Riding all day on a road that was "a perfect level, and well-paved," as Adams noted in his diary, they traveled through a thirty-mile corridor of elms, poplars and oaks bordered by rich fields of grain and well-tended flowers, "the country a continual garden."

By late afternoon, they entered Ghent and took lodgings at the Hôtel des Pays-Bas on the Place d'Armes, "the best public house in the city." Russell had been ill all day. "I dined in my chamber alone," Adams wrote. "Towards evening, I took a walk around the city." He admired its block-paved streets lined with fifteenth-century guild halls and mansions, its network of canals, its fourteenth-century cathedral. The day after their arrival, the American delegation was welcomed by the city's mayor, the Count de Lens, and an aide. They were invited to a ball in honor of the czar, who was expected to pass through Ghent on his way to England.[23]

Five days later, still waiting for Gallatin to arrive from Paris, Adams rose early to see troops "under arms in front of [his] chamber-windows." In a steady downpour that would persist all day, a huge crowd was gathering, waiting for a glimpse of Czar Alexander. The bells of the Cathedral of St. Bavo and the carillon in the fourteenth-century Belfort "began soon afterward to ring," and Adams followed the crowd to one of the streets where the czar was expected to pass. The Russian ruler had entered the city in an open calash so "everybody might have an opportunity to see him," but he abandoned this plan as the rains grew steadily heavier: "He passed just at noon, on horseback, with a suite of fifteen or twenty officers. He was distinguished from them only by the simplicity of his dress—a plain green uniform, without any decoration. . . . Very few of the crowd knew him as he passed."

The czar paused twice as first a Prussian and then a French regiment paraded past him to the beating of drums and the blaring of bugles. Adams had not lost any of his admiration for the Russian emperor, who had befriended him in St. Petersburg: his "affability" was, "as usual, conspicuous." When the cathedral bells finally grew silent, Adams, Clay and their attachés rode to the ball at the Hotel de Ville, attended by "two or three hundred" wealthy merchants and dignitaries and their wives.

Back in his hotel room by midnight, Adams confided to his diary, "The ladies not remarkable either for beauty or elegance." The next morning, exasperated as they waited for the British negotiators to make the short journey across the English Channel, the American commissioners held their first meeting in Adams's chamber. He had moved the commissioners out of the hotel and into less expensive and more expansive quarters, arranging a six-month lease for Lovendeghem, an ornate three-story mansion at the corner of Veldstraat and Voldersstraaton. Purchased in 1783 by the lord of Lovendegham and Ten Broecke, its tall casement windows a necessity in frequently overcast Belgium, it boasted a central courtyard and stables. (Marked by a bronze plaque to commemorate the 150th anniversary of the peace negotiations, it now houses fashionable shops.) As the senior diplomat in the American mission, Adams acted as commission chairman, Gallatin as spokesman. Until the British delegation arrived, the Americans could accomplish little more than agree to hold regular meetings, keep a journal and subscribe to two English newspapers.[24]

Before they could hope to achieve peace for America, the American delegates had to make peace among themselves. Living in such close quarters strained relations among such individualistic characters. Brash, dashing, hard-swearing westerner Henry Clay loved whiskey, gambling, snuff and bragging. Jefferson loyalist Russell, the youngest and least accomplished delegate, went along with anything Clay said and plotted among the others. It was the brilliant, soft-spoken monetarist Gallatin, whose "quickness of understanding . . . sagacity of penetration, and the soundness of his judgment" would come to most impress Adams, his sense of humor defusing many confrontations. Bayard, a fierce Federalist and accomplished orator, would find it difficult to control his bards or his taste for wine.

When Gallatin arrived on July 6 from Paris, the delegation dined together for the first time. Afterward, Adams vowed to resume dining alone, complaining to his diary, "They sit after dinner and drink bad wine and smoke cigars, which neither suits my habits nor my health, and absorbs time which I cannot spare." Adams had foregone the expense and convenience of a secretary, so he consumed long hours writing and making copies of documents while his colleagues relaxed and talked informally after dinner. Once it became clear to what an extent he was affronting his colleagues—and after a few choice words of unsolicited advice from the gregarious Henry Clay—Adams consented to rejoin the group, but he refused to share their nightly excursions to the theater or concerts or any other of the city's revelries.

When the puritanical Adams arose at four thirty in the morning to study his Bible, Henry Clay's all-night gambling parties in the next room were just breaking up. Adams put in six-hour stints at his writing table, penning almost daily letters to his wife, Louisa, back in St. Petersburg or to Monroe in Washington, keeping his diary and drafting statements for the delegation to present to the British. After the commission's two- to three-hour afternoon meetings each day, he pointedly took two-hour walks, counting his paces and fretting that he was becoming corpulent. After dinner, he returned to his room to write even more.[25]

On his solitary perambulations during the next thumb-twiddling six weeks of awaiting the British delegation, Adams immersed himself in Ghent's Renaissance culture. In St. Bavo's towering Gothic cathedral he studied the rich works of Flemish art by Peter Paul Rubens. He marveled at the *Adoration of the Mystic Lamb*, the winged altarpiece of Jan van Eyck, its iridescent, naturalistic detail made possible by his early fifteenth-century invention of oil painting.

Still awaiting the British on August 1, Adams joined his colleagues at the annual presentation ceremonies of the Academy of Fine Arts. Seated on the stage together, to the flourish of horns and trumpets, each one rose and presented prizes to young artists for their accomplishments in painting, drawing and architecture. Each prizewinner invited his presenter to his home. Adams accompanied a fifteen-year-old boy through a street festooned with flowers and decorations and crowded with well-wishers. At dinnertime, the Society of St. Cecilia serenaded the commissioners at their Lovendeghem rooms. After dinner, a hospitality-weary Adams joined his colleagues and trooped off to the Society of Fine Arts ball.[26]

IN THE CHESAPEAKE early that summer of 1814, the elderly Admiral Warren, his seven-year tenure as commander of the North Atlantic station ending, struck his pennant and, with his share of the proceeds of prize money from the capture of slaves, ships and assorted booty—British naval historian Brian Arthur estimates his take at £100,000—sailed home to England. The Admiralty replaced him with Alexander Forester Inglis Cochrane, younger son of the eighth earl of Dundonald. Cochrane, who had fought in the Revolution, hated Americans, in part because his older brother, peering over the ramparts at Yorktown in the last days of that war, had been killed by a cannonball.

Cochrane was eager to attack America's Atlantic coast. He especially wished to damage the war effort in the slave states, the source of most of the support for the continuation of the conflict. Scores of runaway slaves had already found sanctuary with the British. Cochrane's proclamation in April 1814 induced hundreds more to follow their lead, many serving as guides or scouts and some three hundred seeing combat as a special corps of blue-uniformed colonial marines based at the main British base on Tangier Island in Chesapeake Bay. While Americans accused Cochrane of fomenting a slave uprising, some British critics alleged that blacks who answered his call were subsequently sold as slaves in the West Indies. He also authorized the arming of Indians in British-occupied West Florida.

Early in June, Cochrane received a letter from Prevost, averring that, in the spring, American forces under Colonel John B. Campbell, while raiding several Canadian towns along the northern shore of Lake Erie on a mission to destroy food stores, distilleries and mills provisioning the British army, had looted homes and burned private property in five towns—Patterson's Creek, Charlotte's Creek, Port Talbot, Log Point and Dover—their vengeful battle cry, "Remember Black Rock and Buffalo." Prevost, livid, asked Cochrane to "assist in inflicting that measure of retaliation which shall deter the enemy from a repetition of similar outrages." Cochrane's reaction was to issue new orders to the captains and commanders of his fleet:

> It appears that the American Troops in upper Canada have committed the most wanton & unjustifiable outrages on the unoffending Inhabitants by burning their Mills & houses & by a general devastation of private property. . . . You are hereby required and directed to destroy & lay waste such Towns and Districts upon the Coast as you may find assailable. . . .

Cochrane's proclamation opened the way for British attacks the length of the Atlantic seaboard, untethering Royal Navy blockade ships and drawing on newly arrived troop reinforcements from the Iberian front. According to a Royal Navy report filed at fleet headquarters in Bermuda, under the new order, between April 1 and May 22, British blockade ships "captured, recaptured, detained or destroyed" twenty-five American ships at sea.[27]

For the first time, inland privateering bases became targets. On the night of April 7 the British squadron on Long Island Sound, which had been blockading New London, carried out a daring raid up the Connecticut River that destroyed twenty-seven privateers anchored at the shipbuilding center of Essex, then known as Pautopang Point. A great sandbar at the river's mouth that prevented large ships from entering had made Essex seem a safe haven for privateers. Captain Richard Coote of the *Borer*, after handpicking 136 sailors and marines and dispersing them among six ship's boats armed with swivel guns and carronades, led the raid. First storming the undefended fort at Saybrook at the river's mouth, they rowed the six miles upriver against the tide, arriving off Essex at three thirty in the morning. Coote would report that

> [w]e found the town alarmed, the militia all on alert and apparently disposed to oppose our landing with one four pound gun. . . . After the discharge of the boats' guns and a volley of musketry from our marines, they prudently ceased firing.

Coote told terrified townspeople that they had come to burn vessels and, unless they were fired upon, he would spare the town's inhabitants and private property.

The royal marines cordoned off the town while sailors torched twenty-five vessels, ranging from twenty-five-ton coastal sloops to the four-hundred-ton ship *Osage*. It was ten in the morning by the time they had loaded the two largest privateers, the schooner *Eagle* and the brig *Young Anaconda*, with naval stores and a large supply of rum from the waterfront warehouses and ships' chandleries and towed them downriver on the falling tide. The *Young Anaconda* promptly ran aground. Coote ordered its purloined cargo transferred to the *Eagle* and, as militia from Lyme and Saybrook gathered along the shore, shifted instead the stolen goods to his boats and set fire to the *Eagle*. Ignoring a demand from a militia officer to surrender, he waited until dark and then, the boats' oars muffled, rowed downriver.

From New London, Captain Stephen Decatur dispatched marines to reinforce local militia and unlimber artillery on both riverbanks. As the British raiders ran a gauntlet of intense fire, every boat sustained damage, two sailors were killed and two wounded before the raiding party regained the protection of the blockade ships at ten that night. Following the most devastating raid and the greatest single loss of American shipping in the entire war, as well as the only battle fought in Connecticut, the economy of Essex and the fortunes of its shipbuilding families lay in smoldering ashes.[28]

As a result of a conveniently timed petition by the provincial government of Nova Scotia to the Prince Regent, the British Ministry made the propitious decision to move quickly to restore the pre-Revolution boundary line between Massachusetts and Canada. In August 1814, the British Cabinet drew up a list of their demands for their peace commissioners. On the pretext that they needed a direct line of communication between the main British naval base in the North Atlantic at Halifax and the Canadian capital at Quebec, Bathurst authorized an invasion of Maine. Nova Scotia governor John C. Sherbrooke assembled an expeditionary force of army and naval units to "occupy the Penobscot with a respectable force, and to take that river . . . as our boundary, running a line from its source in a more westerly direction than that which divides us from the Americans."[29]

On August 26, 1814, a British invasion force of five men-of-war, led by the seventy-four-gun *Dragon* and escorting ten troop transports carrying 3,000 of Wellington's battle-seasoned Invincibles, sailed from Halifax toward Machias, its first target. Learning that the American corvette *Adams* had slipped into the Penobscot and sailed upriver to the privateering base at Hampden, Sherbrooke redirected the expedition. Adding four more ships to his squadron, he sailed upriver and attacked the fort at Castine. The terrified militia fled, leaving the garrison only twenty-eight regulars. Refusing to surrender the fort, its commandant, Lieutenant Andrew Lewis, fired a token salvo toward an approaching British schooner, spiked the fort's four 24-pounders and, before dragging away two fieldpieces, detonated the powder magazine.

When the British came ashore, they took over a second fort, billeting their troops in the customs house and courthouse and the officers in the town's best homes. Sherbrooke issued a proclamation, making it clear that the British were taking "possession of the country lying between the Penobscot River and Passamaquoddy Bay." As a British port of entry, Castine became the British capital of Maine. A bargaining chip in peace negotiations at Ghent, Castine became a magnet for massive smuggling from New England to Canada. In towns bordering the Penobscot from Bangor north, the populace took oaths of neutrality, some even swearing oaths of allegiance to the King.[30]

In Massachusetts and Connecticut, governors continued to stonewall the federal government's requests for militia. Newspaper editors and antiwar politicians proposed that the states sequester their federal taxes and instead pay their own militias whenever needed, but only for defense. President Madison justifiably worried that Federalist New England was about to secede from the Union. To foster disunion had, indeed, become the British strategy. Cochrane and Cockburn were to make diversionary raids that would cause the Americans to abandon their invasion of Canada and pull back troops from their northern border to defend the Middle Atlantic states. To accommodate the new policy, in a replating of its failed Revolutionary War strategy, Prevost received instructions from London to lead a major offensive from Montreal into New York, seize Lake Champlain and position himself to follow the Champlain–Lake George–Hudson River corridor, which would act as a boundary between a seceded New England and a diminished United States.

IN MARCH 1814 Robert Rowley, captain of the thirty-eight-gun British frigate *Melpomene*, had sailed from Chatham, England, his ship crammed with three hundred troops bound to Bermuda to join Cochrane's expedition. To "what part of the Coast of America," he wrote to his cousin Owsley Rowley, lord lieutenant of Huntingdonshire, "I know not—but I hope to God we shall be successful and lessen the dignity, and the pomp, of a misjudged and impolitic people." Rowley specifically hoped to punish the South: "The [words deleted] Virginians are Democrats"—an expletive to him. "It is them we have been opposed to." Like so many Englishmen who believed the declaration of war had been "unwarrantable & unjust in the extreme," he believed that the "Federalists are gaining ground—the Cry for peace is resounded where they dare open their lips. . . . Something 'Ere long must take place, there will be a division in the States no doubt."

By early July, Rowley was in Chesapeake Bay as part of Cockburn's campaign of harassment. Writing about a raid on July 19, Rowley recounted how, at dawn of that day, he had led a division of Cockburn's

1,500-man force of marines and sailors up a creek to take the town of St. Leonard's by surprise. "The inhabitants being peaceable we did not fire any of their houses," Rowley noted. "The Ladies declared we were very civil and vastly polite." By ten that night, Rowley and his raiders "were all on board again"—with eighty hogsheads of tobacco (fetching $500 each on the English market), "some flour, Military Clothing, several stand of Arms."[31]

While it was British policy to harass Atlantic Coast towns and cities to force the Americans to draw off forces from the Canadian theater, Rowley's letter makes it clear that the British were systematically plundering American plantations around Chesapeake Bay and in the Virginia Tidewater for the profit of their navy officers and crewmen. After each raid they carefully enumerated the number of hogsheads of tobacco taken and, in many instances, the number of schooners seized to transport the heavy barrels of tobacco to prize auctions at Halifax. Admiral Cockburn himself, describing a devastating raid on Chaptico, Maryland, on July 30, put it this way: "We marched to [Chaptico] and took possession without opposition. I remained all day quietly in Chaptico whilst the boats shipped off the Tobacco." His report to Admiral Cochrane that he met with no opposition leaves out the salient details of how his raiders passed their day in Chaptico, details that might make it clear that the sole purpose of the raid was to plunder the town and haul away its lucrative tobacco crop.[32]

A newspaper account of the Chaptico raid told a different story:

> They got about 30 hhds. [hogsheads] of tobacco and other plunder, the inhabitants having moved all their property out of their grasp. . . . Yet here they made a most furious attack. . . . They picked their stolen geese in the church, dashed the pipes of the church organ on the pavement, opened a family vault in the churchyard, broke open the coffins, stirred the bones about with their hands in search of hidden treasure.[33]

On June 20 the British met resistance. Rowley reported "two men killed two wounded and an attempt to poison some of us by putting Arsenic in some Whiskey laid out for Jack [the sailors] to take." It was not the only time this had occurred: earlier that month, Captain James Scott and his men had discovered a suspicious table setting at a house that had served as militia headquarters "as if it had been the scene of a carousing party." Among the "glasses, bottles of liquor, &c.," Scott noticed "that the glasses had not been used." Suspecting poison, Scott sent the full bottle's contents to the surgeon aboard Cockburn's flagship *Albion*. The bottles "were found to contain a very large quantity of arsenic."[34]

Wherever Rowley and his raiders even suspected resistance, he wrote home, "we burnt and destroyed Houses, Corn and every thing in our route." Cockburn, testified Rowley, had one "inviolable rule":

> Any person who stays by his property and does not drive his stock away
> he affords protection & purchases from him at the market price—but if
> they run away & stock driven off—then we hunt for stock, drive it down
> to the boats & take it off as plunder & fire their houses.[35]

"The warfare is a strange one," Rowley wrote to his brother, "and a most harassing one to the Enemy as well as to ourselves, for it is intensely Hot." His thermometer sometimes registered "79 to 89 in the shade at intervals—to move in the heat of the day double quick time in chace [*sic*] of an Enemy Carrying a musket, & days provisions is trying to the Constitution. I have had two attacks of Cholera . . . it produces such immediate debility." But when he returned to his ship, Rowley could enjoy his prizes. "I have quite an establishment on board—a very nice little Charger taken at Nomini where they fired at us briskly. A Mule & Cow have I also."[36]

Rowley pilfered the horse from the Westmoreland County, Virginia, stables at Nomini Hall, the vast ancestral plantation of Robert Carter III, whose family had traditionally served by royal appointment on the colony's executive council. Carter had recently died after manumitting all 492 of his slaves, the largest number of slaves freed before the Civil War. Interestingly, there is no mention of slaves in Rowley's account of loot taken in the July raid, nor does he mention that the raiding party burned the Nomini church after stealing the silver. Cockburn's squadron was systematically scouring the Tidewater and scourging tobacco plantations in a war that had been, from its outset, economic as well as political.

By July 1814 the policy of deliberate plundering was being held out as an incentive for British officers. When Admiral Cochrane issued his "destroy and lay waste" order, he appended a secret memo, authorizing his officers at their discretion to spare most kinds of property in return for tribute. Evidently relieved, the admiral's new fleet captain, Edward Codrington, wrote home to his wife, "I hope it will not be the less productive of prize money, of which I begin to expect a bigger share than I had promised myself." By July 18 Cockburn was complaining that the Virginia and Maryland shorelines seemed to have been picked clean. "I have sent 84 more hogsheads of tobacco down to vessels to go to Halifax and under convoy of the Dragon," Cockburn wrote to Captain Watts of the *Jaseur*. "There is now no more tobacco than what you have at Tangier, but I have sent the Swan in search of some I have had information of."[37]

As Cockburn intensified his incessant pillaging from a base of St. George's Island in mid-Chesapeake, Royal Marine raiding parties were augmented by the newly created Corps of Colonial Marines, black marines the British called "Ethiopians." Cockburn chose Tangier Island as their base. With a deepwater harbor in the middle of the lower Chesapeake at its widest point twelve miles from the nearest mainland, his new base was an easy sail from the Patuxent and Potomac Rivers. The island's watermen suddenly found themselves neighbors to two hundred black troops, who were put to work building Fort Albion with barracks to house 1,000 officers and redcoats, a hospital with one hundred beds, a church, twenty dwellings lining streets and large storage sheds for plunder. Surrounding this new base of operations were 250-yard-long timber-and-earth walls and a pair of redoubts with heavy cannon. Eventually the Colonial Marines would be joined by some seven hundred women and children. From this large fort deep within American territory, Cockburn launched attacks in the spring and early summer up Virginia rivers with Indian names—Yeocomico, Annemessex, Rappahannock and Pungoteague—carrying off more slaves, livestock and produce and burning out anyone who resisted, which began to happen with increasing frequency.

At seven o'clock on the morning of May 29, Cockburn anchored his flagship, the seventy-four-gun ship-of-the-line *Albion*, at the mouth of the Pungoteague on Virginia's Eastern Shore. Militia had tried to prepare a defense with a rusty, worn-out Revolutionary War four-pounder. At sunrise, their guns and rockets blazing, five hundred Royal Marines clambered from their barges and drove seventy 2nd Virginia Regiment militiamen into the woods, spiked the small cannon, burned two small barracks and plundered John Smith's home. Suddenly, 1,000 militia charged out of the woods. The British retreated hastily to their boats, leaving six marines dead. In the largest engagement of the war on Virginia's Eastern Shore, the Americans prevailed in a heartening volte-face.

The Battle of Pungoteague also marked the initiation under fire of the black Colonial Marines. Cockburn noted in his report that thirty new marines, trained on Tangier Island, were in the thickest of the fighting. "Though one of them was shot & died instantly in the front of the others . . . it did not daunt or check the others in the least but on the contrary animated them to seek revenge." The Colonial Marines had "behaved to the admiration of Every body." He would write to Admiral Cochrane that black troops "are really very fine fellows," adding "they have induced me to alter the bad opinion I had of the whole race & I now really believe these we are training, will neither shew want of zeal or courage when employed by us in attacking their old masters."[38]

As Cockburn's flotilla systematically ravaged the lower Chesapeake, he encountered new and more determined resistance from Joshua Barney, a Baltimore-born veteran of the American Revolution and the French navy. Barney had served with distinction as a ship's captain in his teens, first as a privateer and then in the Continental Navy. Becoming a commodore in the French navy, he had again fought the British in the Caribbean. When the War of 1812 came, Barney outfitted a privateer operating out of Baltimore. His feared twelve-gun topsail schooner *Rossie* captured eighteen British ships, netting captain and crew $1.5 million in prize money after fierce engagements.

When the British began to terrorize the Chesapeake in the summer of 1813, Barney submitted a detailed plan to Navy secretary Jones. He pointed out that much of the two-hundred-mile-long bay and its tributaries were navigable to shallow-draft oared vessels, which could hunt down British barges when they were away from their warships' protecting guns. Enthusiastic, Jones offered Barney a commission as sailing master commandant to lead an upper Chesapeake flotilla, which would be built and based at Baltimore.

Initially composed of eight row barges, row galleys, city barges and other vessels built for the navy, Barney's flotilla continued to grow to about two dozen lightly armed vessels, purchased with funds provided by the Maryland Assembly and outfitted under Barney's expert eye. Each seventy-five-foot gun barge, designed with high gunwales to prevent taking on water from the "Chesapeake chop," was steered with a yoke rudder that allowed a cannon to be fired over it. Powering the craft were twenty rugged oarsmen and two triangular-shaped lateen sails. Each barge carried a stubby carronade in its bow and a long gun in the stern.

The British took seriously the threat from Barney's flotilla, and they, too, built more barges. On June 1, 1814, Barney for the first time challenged elements of Cockburn's squadron, including the fourteen-gun schooner *St. Lawrence*. But now he faced the seventy-four-gun ship-of-the-line *Dragon*, capable of destroying much of his flotilla with a single broadside. Barney prudently decided to retreat, taking shelter in the shallow Patuxent River, the backdoor water route to Washington, D.C., where the British dared not follow him. Or so he assumed; in fact, some of the smaller British ships followed him up the river, driving his barges farther upstream into the even shallower St. Leonard Creek.

One week later the British appeared, their small barges warily navigating the tortuous tidal creek. Supporting them, miles distant, a frigate, a sloop and a schooner rode at anchor at the Patuxent's mouth. Commodore Robert Barrie, leaving the security of the *Dragon*, personally directed the attack from a barge. Ignoring a raucous cloud of Congreve rockets, Barney's men pulled hard on the oars, aided by a stiff breeze filling their lateen sails. As they raced to engage the British, sailors stood with their port-fires ready to touch the match holes of the eighteen galleys' cannons. The British came about and fled, but that afternoon they returned with more barges. Pulling even closer, they fired their Congreve rockets. One actually found its mark, exploding a barrel of gunpowder that obliterated an American flotillaman and set a boat afire. Barney's son, sailing master of one of the flotilla's squadrons, leaped into the boat and doused the blaze.

In two more forays in two days, Barrie committed twenty-one barges and seven hundred men and towed two schooners into the battle. To galvanize the sweating oarsmen as they hauled the heavy ships over the shoals in searing summer heat, a military band played marches by Mozart and Haydn. The two flotillas squared off in hours-long combat accompanied by shrieking rockets and barking cannon fire. One shot slammed into an

American barge below the waterline and sank it. The schooner *St. Lawrence*, feeling its way into the narrow mouth of the creek, ran aground in the sand. Barney's gunners poured cannonballs into her hull as her crew fled ashore. One salvo struck Barrie's barge, cutting it in two; another made a direct hit on a rocket boat. After a six-hour fight without a single casualty, Barney and his exhausted flotillamen finally retired into the safety of a cove. Nearly defeating a superior British force, Barney had succeeded in buying the government time to prepare adequate defenses.

But when no militia or field artillery rushed to Barney's defense so near to the nation's capital, Cockburn fathomed the full extent of the capital's vulnerability. Keeping Barney's flotilla bottled up in the Patuxent, Cockburn occupied himself with almost daily plundering raids, picking clean the tobacco plantations of the Virginia and Maryland shoreline as he reconnoitered, sounding the rivers around the bay and waiting for Cochrane to arrive from Bermuda with Wellington's promised Invincibles. Along the way, as he regularly applied the torch, Cockburn encountered more and better organized resistance.

On August 4 for instance, Cockburn led five hundred marines in a routine raid ten miles up the Yeocomico River. Captain Rowley reported to his kinsman, "We met the warmest resistance." He went on,

Field pieces opened on us just at day light. . . . They fired some excellent shot. . . . [Our] troops were out in an instant though up to their hips in the water and galling "fire" away we dashed. . . . They fled in all directions. . . . All this done between 6 A.M. & noon. At 1 P.M. we observed a body of Cavalry collected and infantry drawn up on a hill above the town of Kinsale.

We got into our boats again pulled up directly for them, when at two they opened their fire, our boats & schooners with Guns returned a sharp fire and the Marines landed. They fled. Here we killed 8. Saw a quantity of blood evidently from wounded carried off. This village was immediately fired their breastworks & battery destroyed, burnt 3 schooners brought off four.

On the 6th in the [evening] we saw about 1000 Collect at the mouth of the River Coan throwing up breastworks: although the following morning was Sunday the Admiral made a dash. They kept up a brisk fire at our boats but retreated. We destroyed their batteries. . . . [W]e fired their houses brought off 20 Hhds of Tobacco, 3 schooners.[39]

ACCUSTOMED TO LITTLE or no opposition, Cockburn wrote Cochrane that he was worried about Commodore Barney's Chesapeake flotilla: "How sharply and unexpectedly Jonathan has exerted himself in putting forth his marine armaments in this Bay." His gunboats still bottled up, Barney was concerned about Secretary of the Navy Jones. One day, Jones wanted him to free his vessels by hauling them overland to the bay; the next day, Jones told him to strip the vessels and scuttle them. Before Barney could do either, he was surprised to receive reinforcements to augment his one hundred marines and field guns. Colonel Decius Wadsworth arrived on June 24 with elements of the 36th Infantry, two 18-pound cannon, some smaller fieldpieces and a portable furnace to heat shot. The next day the 2nd Battalion of the 38th Infantry arrived, exhausted after a quick march in the broiling summer sun. Now Barney was ready to fight his way out.[40]

Aided by Barney's sailing master John Geoghegan and seventeen sailors, Wadsworth dragged the guns to high ground around the mouth of St. Leonard Creek. He placed them behind the brow of a hill, where they could blast the blockaders while Barney's barges rowed downriver, their cannon blazing. Stripped of their masts and sails, the barges ghosted down the creek. At four in the morning, the guns began firing hot and cold shot at the British blockaders' two frigates, a schooner and barges. Caught sleeping, the British took a pounding until they could bring their guns to bear. Their flagship, the frigate *Loire*, hulled fifteen times, lost rigging from the slow, sometimes high fire.

Suddenly the American guns fell silent. A British flanking party had rowed upriver and begun firing rockets. When the American gunners stopped firing long enough to reposition cannon to meet them, the raw, exhausted militia, thinking the gunners were retreating, fled, leaving Barney's boats exposed to furious grape and canister shot. Believing his chance to escape lost, Barney withdrew his boats back up the creek. To his amazement, at sunrise Barney saw that it was the British who were withdrawing. The *Loire* was sinking. Leaving behind two old and slow gunboats, Barney and his flotilla rowed hard, bursting out of their trap in

St. Leonard Creek and into the broad Patuxent, where they were in a better position to intercept a British naval attack on Washington.

That same day Cockburn fired off a letter to Admiral Cochrane, stress-
ing that the defenses of the region were weak and several major cities were
vulnerable to attack. "The country is in general in a horrible state; it only
requires a little firm and steady conduct to have it completely at our mercy."
Cockburn provided Cochrane with accurate assessments to back up his
assertion that, increasingly, Americans were providing him with everything from livestock to intelligence of enemy troop strength gleaned in
Washington; he was even receiving free copies of the administration's
mouthpiece, the National Intelligencer. With absolute discretion to select
the target of his punitive expedition, Cochrane had been toying with a
variety of schemes: should he take New Orleans with the aid of the Creek,
or should he occupy Block Island as a base for subjugating New England?

It was apparently Captain Joseph Nourse who advised Cockburn that,
by attacking up the Patuxent River, a small army could easily march right
into Washington and burn it.

Cochrane wrote back, suggesting that he was free to attack Baltimore,
Washington and Philadelphia. On July 17 Cockburn again wrote Cochrane,
this time citing the comparative ease of attack and the resultant political
impact, specifically recommending Washington as the target. Cockburn's
suggestion exactly suited Cochrane's altered agenda. On July 21, just before
Cochrane received Cockburn's latest dispatch, the Pactolus arrived at fleet
headquarters in Bermuda with word from London of a setback: only 2,814
of Wellington's Invincibles, not 20,000, drawn from the 4th, 44th and 85th
Foot, would reinforce him. Taken together with Cockburn's forces, Cochrane had a total of 4,000 men for his Chesapeake incursion.[41]

In Bermuda, aboard Cochrane's flagship Tonnant, shirt-sleeved Captain Wainwright logged the temperature at 113 degrees. After five stifling
days in Hamilton Harbor, the sloop-of-war St. Lawrence had come alongside with dispatches from the Chesapeake, including answers to a long
query Cochrane had sent Cockburn seeking his advice on a suitable use
for the expanded invasion fleet.

> I feel no hesitation in stating to you that I consider the town of Benedict
> in the Patuxent, to offer us advantages for this purpose beyond any other

spot within the United States. . . . Within forty-eight hours after the arrival in the Patuxent of such a force as you expect, the City of Washington might be possessed without difficulty or opposition of any kind.

Not only would the operation be swift and easy, but the taking of an
enemy's capital is "always so great a blow to the government of a country."
Attacking Washington would be of greater advantage than attacking Baltimore or Annapolis. Cockburn spelled out his tactical plan:

> If Washington [as I strongly recommend] be deemed worthy of our <u>first</u>
> efforts, although our main force should be landed in the Patuxent, yet a
> tolerably good division should at the same time be sent up the Potowmac
> with bomb ships etc, which will tend to distract and divide the enemy,
> amuse Fort Washington, if it does not reduce it, and will most probably
> offer other advantages. . . .[42]

Cochrane no longer vacillated. His decision leaked belowdecks faster
than the aging troop transport *Diadem*, crammed with the sweltering 85th
Regiment of Foot, wallowed west to join Cochrane's twenty-four ship convoy. On August 1 Major General Robert Ross, a forty-seven-year-old veteran of the Irish Rebellion as well as the 1813 Peninsular campaign, was
still recovering from a sabre wound to his neck. Handpicked by the Duke
of Wellington to lead all British land forces in America, Ross stepped
aboard the *Tonnant* at noon. At last the towering flagship could weigh anchor and set sail for the Chesapeake.

ON AUGUST 7, 1814, as a British armada approached the North Carolina
coast, three British peace negotiators checked in to the Hôtel du Lion d'Or,
a few cobbled blocks from the American delegation. The next morning,
Anthony St. John Baker, secretary to the British mission, exchanged bows
with U.S. commissioner James Bayard and proposed that the Americans
meet at one o'clock the next afternoon at the British delegation's hotel. At
noon Adams summoned his colleagues to his chamber and heatedly argued that the British summons, according to his studies of texts on diplomacy, balked at this "offensive pretension to superiority" because it was
"the usage from Ambassadors to Ministers of an inferior order." Adams's

suggestion that they meet at a neutral location led to their first encounter between the two delegations the next day at the Hôtel des Pays-Bas, a former Carthusian monastery with a vast wing—which was immediately commandeered by the British delegation.[43]

On the afternoon of August 8, the American commissioners met the three fairly undistinguished British emissaries; the first team had been dispatched by Lord Liverpool with the Duke of Wellington to the Congress of Vienna. Appointed head of the British delegation at Ghent, Rear Admiral Lord James Gambier was a former Lord of the Admiralty who had earned the peerage for destroying the neutral Danish fleet and shelling Copenhagen in 1807. The young lord attempted to ingratiate himself with Adams. He confided that he, too, had lived in Boston as a boy: his father had been in command of British ships there in the early 1770s, adding that, during the Revolutionary War, he himself had commanded a frigate based in New York. The second British negotiator, Henry Goulburn, a thirty-year-old member of Parliament and career bureaucrat, had served as undersecretary of state for war and the colonies. He would eventually become a member of the Privy Council and serve as chancellor of the exchequer. Lord Castlereagh had charged Goulburn with protecting increasingly appreciated British interests in Canada while attempting to garner complete control of the Great Lakes. The third delegate, Dr. William Adams, was an Oxford-educated Admiralty lawyer. Quincy Adams, no relation and a lawyer himself, considered him a "blunderbuss of the law"; Bayard, "a man of no breeding."[44]

The peace talks commenced to a drumbeat of dismal American battlefield news for the Americans, from bloody stalemate on the Niagara frontier to British pillaging in the Chesapeake. With Napoleon exiled on Elba, convoys carrying Wellington's Invincibles continually sailed from the vanquished French ports toward undefended American targets. Goulburn confidently announced British demands: American surrender of the Maine district of Massachusetts and creation of a 250,000-square-mile Indian buffer state in the Old Northwest that would encompass present-day Indiana, Illinois, Wisconsin, Michigan and much of Ohio and Minnesota: this was intended to block American settlement in the vast Louisiana Purchase. In addition the British demanded the abrogation of American rights to dry codfish on Canadian shores, a privilege hard-won by John

Adams in the Treaty of Paris of 1783 and considered indispensable to New England's vital cod fisheries.

Between carving out a vast Indian buffer state and dropping the international boundary line by at least one hundred miles, these demands meant that the United States stood to lose about one-third of its land, a territory the size of Great Britain. Moreover, the British refused to discuss their policy of impressment. At their second meeting three days later, the British stipulated that the Indian reserve was a sine qua non in any treaty and insisted that American states were to be open to British traders. At a third session ten days later, they demanded demilitarizing the Great Lakes and gaining access to the Mississippi River.

Indignantly, Adams protested that the American delegation had not been instructed to discuss Indian territorial claims or fishing rights. And an Indian buffer zone, he argued, would impinge on American sovereignty and dispossess 100,000 settlers already living in the Old Northwest. Bayard objected as well, claiming that the British terms sounded like those of a conqueror to a conquered nation.

The negotiations were on the point of collapsing. However, on the evening of August 8, after the British unveiled their harsh terms, Adams, Bayard, Clay and Gallatin were preparing their answer for the next day's confrontation when a courier arrived from Paris with fresh instructions from Monroe. By one o'clock in the morning, they had deciphered the code. In secret communiqués he had received from his emissaries in London and Paris, Monroe had gained advance intelligence of even more extravagant British demands: U.S. renunciation of its fishing rights off Newfoundland, cession of Louisiana to Spain, abandonment of all trade with the British West Indies and exclusion of all American shipping from the Great Lakes.

With the American government strapped for funds, Madison was eager to speed along the peace process by eliminating its thorniest issue: the commissioners had permission to omit any stipulation on impressment if it became absolutely necessary. The gloomy Madison had become convinced that, since Napoleon had capitulated, the Royal Navy would no longer need to impress American seamen to man its European blockading fleet: to him, impressment had become a dead letter. Certain that Napoleon's surrender was final and unconditional, Madison and Monroe had decided to drop the principal American demand. Even before the decisive cabinet meeting of June 27, Madison had made up his mind. Monroe wrote to the American negotiators, "on the subject of impressment, on which it is presumed your negotiations will essentially turn" they were permitted to "concur in an article stipulating that the subject of impressment, together with that of commerce between the two countries, be referred to a separate negotiation." The major cause of the War of 1812 had disappeared![45] On August 9, Adams laid out what remained of the American position: mutually agreed-upon definitions of blockade and neutral rights and compensation to individuals for captures and seizures before and during the war. Gallatin tried to counter the British demand for an Indian buffer zone by arguing that the United States already planned to negotiate treaties with warring Indians. The policy of the United States toward the Indians was "the most liberal of that pursued by any nation." Gallatin argued that the British demand was "not only new it was unexampled. No such treaty had been made by Great Britain, either before or since the American Revolution, and no such treaty had, to his knowledge, ever been made by any other European power." Bayard asked whether the purpose of the provision was "to restrict the Indians from selling their lands?" Goulburn countered that "it was not to restrict the Indians from selling their lands" but "to restrict the United States from purchasing them." Even as the British commissioners transmitted the Americans' answers to London, a fifty-ship British armada was sailing to Chesapeake Bay.[46]

When the Ministry's response to the negotiations came back in ten days, it was obvious the British were becoming more confident that war news from the United States gave them greater leverage for a diplomatic victory. Summoning the Americans, the British insisted that, if the United States did not agree to the Indian reserve and sign a provisional article, subject to ratification by Washington and London, the treaty talks would be suspended. If that occurred, Britain would not be bound "to abide by the terms which she now offers." While the British insisted that they were seeking no conquests, they believed it was obvious that the Americans harbored "the design of conquering Canada." The United States would have to agree to maintain no naval forces on the Great Lakes, and to tear down its forts and build no more. Further, the British reiterated their demand for "a small corner" of Maine for a "mere road" from Halifax to Quebec.

Gallatin demanded confirmation of a report in English newspapers that the British had seized Moose Island in Passamaquoddy Bay. The British commissioners said that it was true, that it was rightfully part of New Brunswick Province and wasn't even a fit subject for discussion. The hour-long conference had already grown tense by the time a stunned Gallatin asked what was to be done with American citizens already living in the Old Northwest. British negotiator Adams retorted that "undoubtedly they must shift for themselves." So much for the cordial British manner of the first round of meetings. At this point Quincy Adams said he wouldn't tolerate another conference until he received from the British commissioners a *written* statement of their demands. It had become obvious that the British were becoming more intractable.[47]

For the column "From Our Ministers in Ghent" that was to appear on October 15 in the weekly newspaper *Niles' Weekly Register*, Gallatin wrote, "We need hardly say that the demands of Great Britain will receive from us an unanimous and decided negative. . . . There is not at present any hope of peace."[48]

FOURTEEN

"Hard War"

At dawn on August 17, 1814, Thomas Swann, the U.S. Navy's forward observer at Point Lookout, squinted through his spyglass toward the heat-hazy horizon. Startled, he peered again. It was no mirage: Swann could clearly make out three ships-of-the-line, several frigates, at least nine troop transports—in all he counted twenty-two British warships. Flying from the lead ship—the eighty-gun ship-of-the-line *Tonnant,* captured by Lord Nelson at the Battle of the Nile—was the blue flag of an admiral. There was no mistaking it: this was clearly an invasion force. Dispatching an express rider to pelt the eighty miles to Secretary of War Armstrong in Washington, Swann confirmed what lookouts all along the Maryland shore could see: an enormous invasion fleet converging in the Chesapeake, fifty-one men-of-war in all, strung out over two miles. They appeared to be bound for Baltimore, home port of 126 privateering ships that had captured some five hundred British merchantmen in the first two years of the war.

As a diversion, Admiral Cochrane in the *Tonnant* dropped anchor off Tangier Island for water, detached two squadrons of frigates, sending one up the Potomac River and the other up Chesapeake Bay to a point above Baltimore. On August 19, he ordered the main attacking force up the Patuxent, chosen because of its relatively deep waters and access to good, direct roads to Washington. With scores of British vessels suddenly beating their way up the river, Commodore Barney's Chesapeake flotilla of armed barges, escorted by the sloop *Scorpion*, was now trapped, with nowhere to go except toward shallower narrows farther upriver.

As the British began landing troops at Benedict, twenty-five miles up the Patuxent, Secretary of the Navy Jones rushed a series of orders to Barney to "destroy the flotilla by fire" and "retire before the enemy toward this place opposing his progress." Admiral Cockburn was personally leading his own flotilla upriver, intent on destroying Barney's barges. As the British entered the port town of Nottingham, Barney reached Pig Point, named for the pigs of iron forged in the Patuxent Iron Works.

Selecting four hundred flotillamen, Barney left one hundred men behind with the sick and wounded, giving instructions that Lieutenant Solomon Frazier was to prepare explosives and blow up the fleet if the British tried to seize them. Then Barney quick-marched his men eight miles to reinforce the thousands of untested American militia gathering at the Wood Yard Plantation, twelve miles east of Washington in Prince George's County. When Cockburn rounded Pig Point on August 22, he saw the elusive flotilla stretched out in a long line behind the *Scorpion*. Her pennant still flying, she was "on fire, and she very soon afterwards blew up." Sixteen vessels "were in quick Succession blown to atoms."[1]

Barney's inexplicable immolation of the Chesapeake's only defensive naval force distracted the terrified citizens of the Maryland Tidewater from the real intent of the British arrival in the Patuxent. Between 3 p.m. on August 19 and the next morning, more than fifty men-of-war unloaded 4,370 veterans, their ammunition, supplies, and three light field cannon, a six-pounder and two threes, at the "small, straggling" port town of Benedict. The British naval invasion of the Cheapeake had met no resistance from the U.S. Navy. By July 1814 the British had bottled up in port, captured or destroyed eighteen of its twenty named warships, leaving to defend the Chesapeake "two gunboats, thirteen barges, a 5-gun cutter, a schooner and a pilot boat," notes British naval historian Brian Arthur.[2]

In Washington on August 19 Monroe was at his desk, looking over a routine request for a British prisoner-of-war agent to come to Washington from nearby Bladensburg, a small village just northeast of the capital, on personal business. Suddenly, a young express rider burst in: the British fleet had arrived. Secretary of War Armstrong shrugged off the possibility of any imminent danger to the capital. As erstwhile minister to France, Armstrong had seen a truly great capital city. The British would not squander their expedition on attacking such a sheep walk, as he liked to describe Washington, D.C. Baltimore was the target, he insisted.

Monroe differed. Washington was the obvious target. Madison agreed. During the Revolution the tall, slender, red-haired and dashing Monroe had been a cavalry colonel, fighting wounded at Washington's side at Trenton. He could not sit by idly while the secretary of war did nothing to defend the nation's capital. Could he now have a few horsemen to ride out to the coast to spy out the British? The president promptly gave permission to his secretary of state to take a company of local dragoons as escort. Shortly after two o'clock on Saturday, August 20, a courier overtook Monroe, informing him that the British were already debarking at Benedict.

From a hilltop at Aquasco, three miles northwest of Benedict, Monroe peered toward the British camp, but he could make out few details. In his haste he had left Washington without a spyglass and could not precisely count the British ships. He could not move any closer without risking capture. When the British failed to move, Monroe became convinced that this was not a feint to distract from an attack on Baltimore farther up the bay. He scribbled a note to Madison: "The general idea . . . is that Washington is their object." He handed the note to a dragoon and rode off to determine whether the British were also attacking up the Potomac.[3]

Riding with his dragoons through the darkening night of Sunday, August 21, Monroe arrived at the Wood Yard, the mustering site for hundreds of exhausted militia who had marched all through the furnace-hot day from Virginia and Washington. Arriving at 11 p.m., Monroe went straight into a meeting with Brigadier General William Winder, belatedly appointed by Madison to command the new Eleventh Military District. The ever politically motivated Madison had given Winder command of all the forces in the Washington-Virginia-Maryland district because his father, Levin Winder, a Federalist outspokenly critical of "Mister Madison's War," was governor of Maryland and, as such, controlled the militia. Monroe informed Winder that the enemy was at Nottingham, a small port on the Patuxent only twelve miles away, and, he guessed, with 6,000 men.

With the enemy so close, Winder faced the stark reality of having virtually no army to protect the nation's capital from the veterans who had defeated Napoleon. He did not have the 1,000 regulars promised him when he accepted command; nor did he have the 15,000 militia Armstrong had begrudgingly authorized. He didn't even have the 3,000 militia promised him immediately. He could see around him 140 cavalrymen from George-town, 330 regulars from the 36th and 38th Regiments, less than a quarter of the 1,400 regulars Armstrong had promised for the entire region's de-fense, plus 240 Maryland militia at Bladensburg.

From Baltimore he had also expected the entire 1,400-man federalized 3rd Division of Maryland militia, but they were still two days' march away. He had summoned 2,000 Virginia militia, but they were 120 miles away. At some time in the unspecified future, he would be reinforced by Commodore Barney and his artillery, by his 400 battle-hardened flotil-lamen and whatever cannon they had salvaged and could drag overland from their boats. At the moment he could count only 1,800 weary troops. As his conference with Monroe broke up, Winder ordered them to be roused by reveille at 2 a.m. in time to strike their tents, load the wagons and be ready to march at sunrise to intercept the enemy.

The British army under General Ross was also on the move toward Up-per Marlboro, away from the protection of Cockburn's squadron. March-ing through thick woods under a merciful canopy of trees, the soldiers sang as the army's drummers and fifers played a chorus from Handel's *Judas Maccabaeus*: "See the conquering hero comes / Sound the trumpet, beat the drums." At 8:30 a.m. on Monday morning, August 22, they reached St. Thomas's Church.

Blind without cavalry, Ross was unaware that the vanguard of the American army was just ahead. From the second-floor window of Benja-min Oden's brick farmhouse nearby, Monroe and Winder could see the British army approaching a strategic junction in the road. Here, if Ross chose to advance along the west fork toward Wood Yard, it meant a cer-tain assault on Washington. If he took the north fork toward Upper Marl-boro, he might be bound toward Baltimore after all.

As the two Americans watched transfixed, British skirmishers clashed with American cavalry and followed the dragoons as they retreated toward the Oden farm. Probing cautiously, they came within a mile and a quarter of Monroe and Winder, who had positioned three hundred of his best troops, Major George Peter's Georgetown artillery, Captain John Davidson's light infantry company and Captain John Stull's riflemen two miles farther down the road. The rest of the tiny American army was marching toward the oncoming British. But Ross refused to engage them: he declined to fight the Americans piecemeal. He would wait until all his forces had caught up with him and were ready for one decisive battle. Withdrawing his skirmishers, he took the north fork toward Upper Marlboro, where he intended to camp for the night and march the last twelve miles to Washington the next day.

Ross's feint toward Washington fooled Monroe. At 9 a.m. Monday, August 22, he sent a note to Madison, not knowing that Ross had veered off toward Upper Marlboro. "The enemy are in full march for Washington. Have the materials prepared to destroy the bridges. You had better remove the records." At the White House, Madison responded pessimistically, "I fear not much can be done more than has been done to strengthen the hands of Genl. W[inder]." Then he circulated orders for the removal of public papers, inadvertently setting off a panic. Women and children poured into streets carrying their bedding, clothes and furniture, hoping to find a wagon, but the military had commandeered virtually every wagon in town. "Hacks, carts or wagons cannot be purchased for love or money," complained a visiting New York merchant who was trying to carry eight children out of town.[4]

On the afternoon of August 22, Madison decided he should, as the commander in chief, review the troops and meet with General Winder. He was worried about leaving Dolley alone in the White House since he would be away at least one night. Dolley assured him she "had no fear but for him, and the success of our army." The president left "beseeching me to take care of myself, and of the cabinet papers, public and private." That the diminutive sixty-two-year-old Madison was riding out to review his troops received a less sympathetic reaction from some in the capital. Martha Peter, wife of the commander of the Georgetown Field Artillery, scoffed at the idea. "Our chief, thinking his presence might occasion them great confidence, buckled on his sword, put his holsters on his saddle (pistols in, of course) and set out at five in the evening to visit the camp."[5]

Riding with Madison to the new American camp at Old Fields, seven miles east of Washington, were Attorney General Richard Rush, Navy secretary Jones and three aides. They stopped at a farmhouse a mile from Old Fields for the night, and Madison sent a message to Winder to join them. Winder declined: worn out by a stream of unsolicited advisers, he went to bed in a camp that invited attack. By now he had mustered 3,200 men, mostly militiamen who had been clerks and laborers the day before and were laughing and quarreling in tents lit up by campfires. Jittery sentinels loudly shouted countersigns that could be heard far away. One would mistake a nearby herd of cattle for the British Army and awaken the entire camp at 2 a.m. The next morning Winder rode over to confer with Madison's party, which now included Armstrong as well as Commodore Barney and senior militia officers.

Still incapable of fathoming the objective of a British army camped a day's march from Washington, Winder outlined a menu of guesses. Alexandria? Baltimore? Annapolis was only fifteen miles by a good road from the British camp. Even more likely was an attack on Fort Washington on the Potomac. The upper and lower bridges? (But not Washington itself.) Armstrong opined that the British had come only to destroy Barney's flotilla and that their army was too weak to attack the capital and their incursion was nothing more than "a mere Cossack hurrah." Never once did Winder consider Bladensburg, the little Maryland town northeast of the district with the only bridge across the Eastern Branch of the Potomac just above the city itself.[6]

Riding into camp as the troops lined up for a 9 a.m. presidential review, Madison saw that half the men were still in civilian clothes; others wore only scraps of uniforms. Standing out from the rabble were Barney's flotillamen, many of them black, and Captain Samuel Miller's marines. Navy secretary Jones remarked that their "appearance and preparation for battle promised all that could be expected from cool intrepidity and a high state of discipline." Madison, a slave owner, asked Barney whether the blacks "would not run on the approach of the British." After four months entrusting his life to them, Barney answered, "No sir. They don't know how to run; they will die by their guns first."[7]

Impressed, Madison sent a note to Dolley: "I have passed the forenoon among the troops who are in good spirits & make a good appearance." He reassured her that, according to the "truest information," the British are "not very strong, and are without cavalry or artillery and of course they are not in a condition to strike at Washington." Madison had resumed conferring with Armstrong and Winder when a patrol that had scouted the British at Upper Marlboro rode in and predicted the British army would reach the American camp before daylight the next morning. "They can have no such intention," Armstrong scoffed. "They are foraging, I suppose; and if an attack is meditated by them upon any place, it is Annapolis."[8]

At his capacious commandeered headquarters in the home of Dr. William Beanes, Upper Marlboro's leading Federalist, the British commander in charge of the expeditionary force, General Ross, convened a council of war to decide his next step. He had not yet decided to attack Washington or to retreat to Cochrane's ships. He was concerned that the Americans were gathering in force and were well positioned to block an attack on the capital. It worried him even more that an attack on Washington "completely overstepped" his instructions from London, which was to create a diversion in favor of the Canadian front and to take no unnecessary risks.[9]

But Cockburn was working on him. He offered Ross his troops and sailors to bolster his strength. Just as Ross decided to adopt Cockburn's plan, a message arrived from Admiral Cochrane congratulating Ross and Cockburn on the destruction of Barney's fleet but insisting that, "as this matter is ended, the sooner the army get back the better."[10] Cockburn replied to Cochrane, asserting it was Ross's decision to march on Washington. "I find he is determined," Cockburn wrote, "to push on towards Washington. . . . I shall accompany him & of course afford him every assistance in my power." Cockburn never mentioned Cochrane's directive to Ross.[11]

At 2 p.m., Ross gave officers their orders. He had decided on a circuitous route through the American camp at Old Fields and then across the northernmost bridge of the Eastern Branch of the Potomac, today known as the Anacostia River, before the Americans could reach Bladensburg and block the main road in Washington. Bugles blared. Drums rattled. The men gave three cheers and then marched off with the light infantry in the lead.

As MORE MILITIA marched into the American camp, Winder became convinced he could defeat the British army. Answering his call for militia,

Brigadier General Tobias E. Stansbury had arrived at Bladensburg from Baltimore County with his 3rd Brigade of 1,350 green militamen; the elite, red-plumed 5th Maryland Regiment, made up of 800 blueblood scions of Baltimore families, was expected momentarily; another 800 with eighty horses were marching from Annapolis. In all, Winder would have 6,000 men. Outlining his plans to Madison and his cabinet, Winder prepared to march to Upper Marlboro to confront the British. He sent 300 men under Major Peter to reconnoiter as he ordered Stansbury at Bladensburg to march toward Upper Marlboro.

Peter's advance party had barely approached the outskirts of Upper Marlboro when his scouts hurried back with large numbers of the British close behind them. Peter ordered a retreat. At the American camp at Old Fields, Brigadier General Walter Smith, warned of the British advance, joined Commodore Barney. They swiftly arranged a strong defensive line, the troops extending in a line a quarter mile on each side of the road— Barney, his flotillamen and marines on the right with his heavy naval guns, Smith and the district militia on the left. Winder was still riding toward Bladensburg to organize his plan of attack when an officer overtook him with news of the enemy's advance. With his plan to strike first shattered, he galloped back to Old Fields. The British were only three miles behind him. His troops were ready to fight. But Winder, having once been captured in a botched night attack, refused to fight again in the dark. To the dismay of officers and men, he ordered retreat, the second in two days, back to Washington. Abandoning their formidable position at Old Fields, the exhausted and dispirited American army broke camp and shuffled off as the sun set.

When Madison returned to the White House that night, he was shocked to learn that Winder was retreating—again. He found Colonel George Minor, who had just arrived with a regiment of seven hundred militia from Northern Virginia but with no weapons—and Armstrong had refused to issue them until the next morning. Winder arrived at 9 p.m., and whatever Madison said to him, he left quickly. Later that night, Margaret Bayard Smith, wife of the editor of the *National Intelligencer* and Dolley Madison's closest friend, awakened to banging on her front door. "The enemy are advancing," a friend blurted. "Our own troops are giving way on all sides and are retreating to the city. Go, for God's sake, go."[12]

Six miles northeast of the White House, 2,100 untrained Maryland militia, sweat stained and exhausted, stumbled into Bladensburg. At midnight Monroe galloped into camp with the news, wholly unfounded, that Winder had been captured by the British. He advised Stansbury to attack the British at once at Upper Marlboro—which they had already left. Stansbury, sure that his men were in no condition for a night attack, demurred. Monroe rode off again, back to Washington. Soon afterward nervous pickets fired several rounds. The long roll of drumbeats called the entire camp to arms. Cavalry patrols could find no enemy; at 2 a.m., the men stumbled back to their tents. It was their fourth night without uninterrupted sleep. Only half an hour later, Stansbury received a message from Winder that, leaving behind the Maryland militia, he had retreated to Washington. Stansbury was to "resist the enemy as long as possible."[13] A longtime militia commander with no combat experience, Stansbury called a council of war with his senior officers. They voted unanimously to ignore Winder's order and retreat toward Washington, leaving behind the earthworks they had been digging for days to avoid being trapped on the wrong side of the bridge. At 3:30 a.m., striking their tents, the groggy troops stumbled off, some dropping in the road for a little sleep.

Winder's retreat had turned into a panicked dash. Crossing the Anacostia Bridge late at night, the soldiers marched back and forth, each carrying Harpers Ferry fourteen-pound muskets and assorted gear. Without food for forty-eight hours, they set up tents on high ground overlooking the crossing. Their commander was faring little better. Winder's horse had dropped dead on the way back from the meeting with Madison at the White House, leaving Winder to walk the last two miles to camp. Nobody would give him a horse. He stayed at the makeshift camp only long enough to order the upper bridge burned. Then he dispatched the Washington artillery with three cannon, the entire defense of the capital city, to the lower bridge to await orders to blow it up. Trudging off in the dark to the navy yard to order the explosives, he fell into a ditch, injuring his right arm and ankle.

Before dawn on August 24, Lieutenant James Scott, Admiral Cockburn's aide-de-camp, carrying an urgent message from Admiral Cochrane, overtook the British army at Melwood Plantation (today's Andrews Air Force Base), the target of Cockburn's intended night attack. Cochrane believed Cockburn and Ross's decision to attack the American capital reckless and, if it weakened his forces, capable of endangering his planned attack on New Orleans. Awakening the commanders in the shepherd's hut where they were sleeping on their cloaks, Scott handed Cockburn a message recommending "in strenuous terms an immediate retreat." Handing the note to Ross, Cockburn argued that they were "too far advanced [from the ships] to think of a retreat. If we return without striking a blow, it will be worse than a defeat—it will bring a stain upon our arms."[14] Cockburn was risking his naval career, but the final decision was up to Ross, commander of land forces. His orders from London were to avoid unnecessary risks. "I felt an apprehension of the consequences of failure," he later confessed to his wife, "which bound me not to attempt anything that <u>might be attended</u> with the want of success." But he did not hesitate further. As a glow from the burning bridge tinged the western sky, Ross turned to Cockburn. Clapping his hand to his forehead, he exclaimed, "Well, be it so, we will proceed."[15]

The capital of the United States in 1814 was an adolescent agglomeration of villages within the District of Columbia, including Washington, population 8,208; Georgetown, 4,900; and, across the Potomac, Alexandria, 7,200—in all, according to the 1810 census, roughly 20,000 people. The district's population included 1,400 slaves and 800 free blacks living in shanties. The city's elite included diplomats, high government officials and a gentry of plantation owners. Its burgeoning middle class included government clerks, shopkeepers and tradesmen, many serving in the militia. Poor whites, many of them laborers and indentured servants who had recently immigrated from Ireland and Germany, constructed government buildings and finer homes while they lived in scattered shantytowns. In fourteen years some nine hundred buildings had sprung up. The whitewashed sandstone White House, as it was called after 1810, and the Capitol stood at the opposite ends of poplar-lined Pennsylvania Avenue, standing in the open like temples surrounded by fields of corn, wheat and tobacco. In meadows bounded by oak trees, livestock grazed. When he had first arrived in the nation's capital, Attorney General Rush had described the overall effect as that of "a straggling village but for the size and beauty of its public buildings." That is, until August 24, 1814.[16]

Early that morning, after a few hours' sleep on a cot, Winder, on hearing conflicting reports from his scouts, dashed off a note to Armstrong: "I should be glad of the assistance of counsel from yourself and the Government." The courier delivered the note to Madison by mistake. He rushed to Winder's headquarters, where Monroe and Jones joined him by seven o'clock. The latest rumor was that the British were heading for Bladensburg. Winder dismissed it, but not Monroe: he asked permission to ride out and make sure Stansbury was ready. Officers, government officials and anonymous strangers flowed in and out of the White House, offering their expert opinions. Suddenly, another messenger burst in: the British were definitely on the march to Bladensburg. For some reason, Winder finally considered the information decisive.[17]

Rushing to get his army—cavalry, artillery, the district militia, Scott's regulars and Stull's still rifleless riflemen—to Bladensburg, Winder forgot only his best troops, Barney's 400 flotillamen and Miller's 126 marines, left behind to guard the Eastern Branch. He was riding off when Armstrong appeared. The secretary of war would later insist that he had skipped the council of war because "I took for granted that he had received the <u>counsel</u> he required: for, to me, he neither stated doubt nor difficulty, nor plan of attack or of defence."[18]

For weeks Armstrong had denied Winder everything he had promised. Madison, upbraiding Armstrong for being late, asked whether he had any advice to offer. He had none, he said, but since the battle would be between regulars and militia, the militia would be defeated. Madison, wheeling his horse, urged Armstrong to go to Bladensburg and give Winder all the assistance he could. If any conflict arose over authority, Madison would be there himself to resolve it. Armstrong rode off toward Bladensburg convinced that Madison had just given him command of the army and that Madison would be on the battlefield to back him up. Apparently, so did Winder. Turning to an aide, he blurted, "I am but a nominal commander. The president and secretary of war have interfered with my intended operations, and I greatly fear for the success of the day."[19]

Before Madison, Armstrong and the cabinet rode off to Bladensburg, they inspected Commodore Barney's assigned post at the lower bridge.

Barney exploded: What did they mean, leaving him there to guard a bridge "with 500 of the precious few fighting men around to do what any damned corporal can better do with five"? Madison concurred and ordered Barney to march at once to Bladensburg with his men and guns. As Madison and his cabinet split up, Madison called out to them that, if the city fell, they would meet again at Frederick, Maryland. Impulsively, Secretary of the Treasury Campbell unstrapped his pair of outsized dueling pistols. The diminutive Madison, wearing a small leather cavalryman's cap with a tall, jaunty feather plume, strapped them on. And then, escorted only by the attorney general and a few aides, President James Madison rode off toward the fragile line of defense of the nation's capital.[20]

At Bladensburg, Stansbury was struggling to form his men into lines. As the temperature neared 100 degrees, the last of his exhausted troops, returning by eleven o'clock from their latest march to Washington, joined the main force in a pie-shaped field just west of the village. On their left was the road to Georgetown; on their right, the turnpike to Washington. The point where the roads converged was a narrow wooden bridge about ninety feet long. To the north and west were woods; the river formed the southern barrier. To everyone but Winder, it was obvious that battle would take place here and that the entire British army would have to cross that bridge. At this strategic strongpoint Stansbury decided to make a stand. Civilian volunteers dug earthworks facing the river along a line 350 yards long from the bridge toward town. Baltimore artillery dug out embrasures for six 6-pounders. To their left, Stansbury placed two companies of militia; to the right, Pinkney's battalion of riflemen. Together, the guns and supporting troops covered the bridge and the crossroads. Fifty yards to the rear, Stansbury stationed his supporting troops, two regiments of drafted militia and the elite 5th Maryland militia regiment.

As Stansbury rode to the earthworks to inspect his artillery, Monroe rode along the line, certain he could make improvements. Without consulting anyone, he ordered the two regiments of reserves out of the shaded orchard to a new exposed position five hundred yards behind the front line, well beyond the range where they could offer any support. The secretary of state was not in any chain of command, but the officers and men knew he was very important, so they followed his orders. Where there had formerly been enough troops to defend the hill, now a gaping hole opened up. To correct that, again without consulting Stansbury, Monroe ordered the 5th Maryland out of the orchard and back to the hill, leaving no one to support the artillery or the entrenched infantry. And when Colonel Beall arrived with eight hundred Annapolis militia, even before Stansbury knew of their arrival, Monroe ordered them to the right, up another isolated hill more than a mile from the first line of defense. Stansbury had expected to position them to the left of his line to cover his flank. At that moment Smith arrived with the district militia and began looking for a place to deposit his men. When Stansbury discovered Monroe's interference, he raced up the hill—just as word came that Winder had arrived. Stansbury decided to appeal to him. But as Winder rode around, Monroe stayed at his side, glibly informing him that he had been "aiding" Stansbury and that Stansbury had asked him to inspect and approve his handiwork.

Winder had only enough time to shift artillery to protect the orchard—now empty—and riflemen to protect the artillery. He knew that more guns were coming from Washington. He gave orders to place them on the far left. He did nothing about the bridge. As more Washington militia poured in, the British were already in sight. Smith quickly decided where to place his troops—on either side of the road. At one point, someone discovered that Scott's regulars were right in the line of fire of Peter's artillery. By now, Beall's Annapolis militia were waiting on their hilltop for orders, and Laval's cavalry was still waiting to learn the plan. Leading his horsemen toward the bridge to find Winder, Laval decided to water his horses in the river. When he saw that the British were too close, he turned back—right into Monroe. Ex-cavalry colonel Monroe assigned Laval to a ravine, far to the left and in a gully so deep that Laval's 380 cavalrymen couldn't see out of it.

Armstrong was the next dignitary to arrive and begin an impromptu inspection. He was so busy appraising the troops' positions that he didn't see Madison's party galloping in, right through the Washington militia, Stansbury's lines, the earthworks and right up to the bridge. They were about to pound right across it and into the center of the British line when a volunteer scout, William Simmons—an accountant recently fired by Armstrong for "rudeness to his superiors"—seeing the advancing British from atop Lowndes Hill, spurred his horse down to the bridge, shouting,

"Mr. Madison! The enemy now are in Bladensburg!" Madison, startled, spun around and led his cabinet back toward the American lines.[21]

AFTER A GRUELING twelve-mile march, George R. Gleig, an eighteen-year-old Scottish subaltern in the British 85th Light Infantry (and future chaplain general of the British Army), was impressed as he scanned the American position. The former Oxford divinity student, who had fought under Wellington in Spain, recorded in his journal that he considered it "one of great strength, and commanding attitude. [The Americans] were drawn up in three lines upon the brow of a hill, having their front and left flank covered by a branch of the Potomac, and their right resting upon a thick wood and a deep ravine." Observing the American lines through a spyglass from the second floor of a house on Lowndes Hill, General Ross thought otherwise: the American lines were too far apart to support one another. Ross decided to launch Gleig and the light infantry at the double-quick across the bridge while the rest of his forces came up.

As the close-packed redcoats rushed across the bridge, two American cannons fired. "At the first discharge almost an entire company was swept down," Gleig recorded. After a momentary pause, Colonel William Thornton Jr. led the rest of the 85th "trampling upon many of their dead and dying comrades" to gain a toehold beyond the bridge.[22] Highly disciplined veterans of Spain and Portugal ignored the sniping of American riflemen and surged ahead, the pink-jacketed 4th and 44th regiments streaming over the bridge right behind them. As Congreve rockets began flying in all directions from launchers near the bridge, the 4th peeled off toward the orchard on Stansbury's left flank. In minutes the outflanked American first line began to crumble and then break, the raw militiamen, unnerved by the screaming rockets, unwilling to face the gleaming bayonets. Private John Pendleton Kennedy of the 5th Maryland admitted that, as the first line collapsed, his elite unit "made a fine scamper of it."[23]

The British pressed the Americans relentlessly until the second line disintegrated, the militia fleeing in all directions. The British rushed uphill to the Bladensburg Road and what seemed a painless victory. They only had to cross another narrow bridge over a ravine. They could see large naval cannon in the road on the high ground ahead. Commodore

Barney, who had just arrived in time to see the American army dissolving all around him, sat on his horse, grimly determined to stop the British attack. Five big guns loaded with grapeshot, 500 flotillamen, 114 Marines and hundreds of militiamen were waiting to make their stand.

When the British advanced, Barney later wrote, "I ordered an 18 pounder to be fired, which completely cleared the road; shortly afterwards a second and third attempt was made . . . but all who made the attempt were destroyed." Attempting to skirt Barney's right flank, redcoats crossed to an open field, only to face

[t]hree 12 pounders, the marines under Captain Miller, and my men acting as infantry. Again, the British attackers were totally cut up. By this time not a vestige of the American army remained, except a body of five or six hundred posted on a height on my right, from whom I expected much support from their fine situation. The enemy from this point never appeared in front of us. He however pushed forward with his sharpshooters, one of whom shot my horse from under me, which fell dead between two of my guns.[24]

At one point, Barney ordered his marines to charge the British. His small rear guard, blocking the road to Washington, had managed to keep the whole British army in check for fully half an hour before it again tried to outflank him, this time pushing up the hill where two or three hundred reserves remained. To his "great mortification" they "made no resistance." They fled after only one or two shots were fired. "We had the whole army of the enemy to contend with; our ammunition was expended, and unfortunately the drivers of my ammunition waggons had gone off in the general panic." At this point, a sharpshooter's bullet crashed into Barney's thigh. "Finding the enemy now completely in our rear and no means of defence, I gave orders to my officers and men to retire." Faint from bleeding profusely, Barney stayed behind to surrender. Ross personally paroled him as a prisoner of war and assigned a British surgeon to treat his deep thigh wound. Barney, his flotillamen and the marines had put up the only gallant defense.[25]

As British Lieutenant Gleig recounted,

With the exception of a party of sailors from the gun boats, under the command of Commodore Barney, no troops could have behaved worse than they did. . . . They were employed as gunners, and not only did they serve their guns with a quickness and precision which astonished their assailants, but they stood till some of them were actually bayoneted, with fuses in their hands; nor was it till their leader was wounded and taken, and they saw themselves deserted on all sides by the soldiers, that they quitted the field.[26]

The battle for the capital of the United States lasted three hours. The British suffered far more casualties than the routed Americans: the official tally Cockburn sent to London stated 64 killed and 185 wounded, but Gleig disputes this. He claimed some 500 British were killed or wounded, which accords with Barney's description of the toll his gunners took. American casualties were light, 26 killed and 51 wounded. Other than ranking as America's most disgraceful defeat, the only other distinction attached to the Battle of Bladensburg may be Madison's. He became the only American president ever to join his troops in battle.

Most Americans at the time, however, shared the sentiment of Maryland congressman Joseph Hopper Nicholson, a militia captain: "Good God, how have we been disgraced!" The Marine quartermaster, Captain Bacon, blamed Winder: "General W ought to be hung & would b[e in] any other country." Writing a letter to the *Philadelphia General Advertiser*, another eyewitness declared that "[o]ur militia were dispersed like a flock of birds assailed by a load of mustard seed shot." One of Barney's flotillamen put it in even more down-to-earth terms: "The militia ran like sheep chased by dogs."[27] An enduring sobriquet for the sorry episode flowed from the pen of an anonymous bard who limned the "Bladensburg Races": "And, Winder, do not fire your guns / Nor let your trumpets play / Till we are out of sight / Forsooth, My horse will run away."[28]

SINCE SUNRISE AND off and on all Wednesday morning, Dolley Madison had stood on the roof of the White House, peering through a spyglass in the direction of Bladensburg at the immense cloud of dust. She wrote to her sister Lucy, "watching with unwearied anxiety hoping to discern the approach of my dear husband and his friends." She had received two penciled notes from Madison the day before, she told her sister. "The last is alarming, because he desires I should be ready at a moment's warning to enter my carriage and leave the city." The enemy "seemed stronger than had been reported, and . . . it might happen that they would reach the city, with intention to destroy it." Dolley informed her sister before the day was over, "I am accordingly ready." She had pressed government documents—including the Declaration of Independence—and cabinet papers into trunks along with books, silver, a small clock and the blazing red curtains that had framed her drawing rooms "as to fill one carriage." She was "determined not to go myself until I see Mr. Madison safe, and he can accompany me, as I hear of much hostility towards him."[29]

All of her friends were gone, even the hundred-man White House guard. The chef, French John Sioussat—"a faithful servant"—had offered "to spike the cannon at the gate and lay a train of powder which would blow up the British should they enter the house," but Dolley had refused the offer. Fifteen-year-old slave Paul Jennings and her body servant, Sukey, had also stayed with her.[30]

At noon on Wednesday Dolley resumed composing her epistle to her sister. Looking through her spyglass again from her bedroom window, Dolley turned it in every direction, "hoping to discern the approach of my dear husband and his friends but, alas, I can descry only groups of military wandering in all directions, as if there was a lack of arms, or of spirit to fight for their own firesides!" At three, she continued, "Will you believe it, my Sister? We have had a battle or skirmish at Bladensburg, and I am still here within sound of the cannon! Mr. Madison comes not; may God protect him! Two messengers covered with dust, come to bid me fly; but I wait for him."[31]

"Our kind friend, Mr. [Charles] Carroll, has come to hasten my departure, and is in a very bad humor with me because I insist on waiting until the large picture of Gen. Washington is secured." Supervising French John and Paul Jennings as they tried to remove the eight-by-five-foot replica of Gilbert Stuart's famous Lansdowne Portrait from the wall, she discovered it was bolted in place. She finally gave the order to break the frame to free the canvas on its stretcher. When "two gentlemen of New York," Robert G. L. De-Peyster and Jacob Barker, whom she knew and trusted, suddenly appeared on the scene, she asked them "to secure it under a humble but safe roof."[32]

Just before three, she instructed Jennings to get dinner ready. The president had left word that most of the cabinet and a few "military gentlemen" would be coming. Jennings set the table for forty, not an unusual number, brought up the ale, wine and cider and put the bottles in coolers. As he finished, Madison's freedman servant, Jim Smith, galloped up, waving his hat and shouting, "Clear out, clear out! General Armstrong has ordered a retreat!"[33]

Madison had finally conceded that, with the army in full retreat, there was no way to stop the invasion of the capital city. Her worst fears realized, Dolley would have to leave the White House and the city two hours before the British army marched in. "And now, dear sister," she concluded her letter, "I must leave this house, or the retreating army will make me a prisoner in it, by filling up the road I am directed to take. When I shall again write to you, or where I shall be tomorrow, I cannot tell!"[34]

A short time later, Madison arrived with Attorney General Rush, General John Mason and the man who had undoubtedly saved him, the still-unemployed accountant William Simmons. Taking some refreshments, Madison sent more notes to Dolley where he knew he would find her, at Bellevue, Carroll's Georgetown home. They should rendezvous the next day at Wiley's Inn, near Great Falls, Virginia. Leaving the White House unscathed for the last time, Madison rode off "proudly" with his friends, instructing Simmons to remain behind and give out brandy to the passing troops. Jennings stayed behind, too, watching with dismay as "a rabble, taking advantage of the confusion, ran all over the White House and stole lots of silver and whatever they could lay their hands on."[35]

AFTER ALLOWING HIS exhausted troops a two-hour respite, General Ross, in the gathering dusk, formed his troops into three 1,500-man brigades and led them on the five-mile march into Washington. Stationing two brigades at what became the Old Circus Grounds (at Fifteenth Street and Bladensburg Road N.E.), Ross and Cockburn rode into the city at the head of the 21st Regiment of Foot. Leaving all but a small advance guard just inside the city gates, the general and the admiral rode in the dark down Maryland Avenue. Climbing Capitol Hill and approaching the Capitol building, the party halted two hundred yards short of the Capitol in front of the large brick house of Robert Sewall, recently rented by Gallatin.

As the general and the admiral discussed their next move, a volley of musketry rang out, hitting two men, killing one and shooting Ross's horse out from under him. Breaking down the front door with axes, redcoats searched the house and found no one. Barney's flotillamen, who had never felt bound by Winder's orders to retreat, escaped. Galloping back to fetch light companies of the 21st, Cockburn ordered Congreve rockets fired into Sewall House (now rebuilt as the Sewall-Belmont House at 144 Constitution Avenue N.E.). It was the only private house destroyed because, as one British officer reported, the general's horse had been shot from it. Soon, splintered beams were flying through the night sky. Ross and Cockburn may have once differed on the purpose of their mission, but by the time they entered the city, they had agreed that all public buildings would be destroyed and private property spared, unless they met resistance. In the report he later sent to London, Ross declared that the object of the expedition was destruction of the public buildings. With the experienced Cockburn at his side, Ross set about his mission of methodically putting to the torch every public building.

Whenever the British encountered resistance, they were prepared to set any building afire. After burning Sewall's mansion, soldiers searched the vacated Tomlinson's Hotel, opposite the Senate wing of the Capitol. Finding guns and ammunition, they burned it down. To carry out the ritualistic torching of a building, Cockburn detailed a company of sailors led by Lieutenant George Pratt, a specialist in arson, who had mastered a variety of pyrotechnical devices. As soon as Admiral Cochrane had learned he was to lead the expedition to "destroy and lay waste" the United States, he had written to ask Lord Melville, First Lord of the Admiralty, for "a quantity of combustible matter made up in packages from 50 to 5 pounds each, not to be extinguished by water." The combustible material, when poured into a papier-mâché globe, touched by a hot coal and flung by a match pole, spewed streams of burning, inextinguishable liquid.[36]

At the moment, a far bigger blaze distracted the British. Captain Tingey, the commandant of the finest navy yard in the country since its creation in 1800, was destroying his beloved charge to keep its ships, guns and munitions out of enemy hands. At 8:20, matches were struck and powder trains lit, the flames racing to storehouses, the sail loft, the sawmills, the paint shops, finally igniting the nearly completed sixty-gun frigate *Columbia*, the sloop-of-war *Argus*—just finished—and several brigs and schooners. As new explosions rocked the city, the sixty-year-old Tingey sailed his gig across the river to Alexandria.

Margaret Bayard Smith, wife of the publisher of the *National Intelligencer*, watched the British approach the Capitol building:

> 50 men, sailors and marines, were marched by an officer, silently thro' the avenue . . . when [they] arrived at the building, each man was station'd at a window, with his pole and machine of wild-fire . . . the windows were broken and this wild-fire thrown in, so that an instantaneous conflagration took place and the whole building was wrapt in flames and smoke.[37]

Lieutenant Gleig, who had witnessed such a fiery spectacle once before after the siege of St. Sebastian in Spain, thought the American Capitol was the only building in the "infant town" worthy of note. "This . . . is, or rather was, an edifice of great beauty."[38]

It was not to prove easily burnt down. The British fired Congreve rockets through the windows, but the massive building's ceilings were sheathed with sheet iron. Pratt's incendiary teams had to enter each chamber, chop up the woodwork for kindling, then stack up pyres of mahogany chairs and tables, baize curtains and books, and finally, after dousing them with rocket powder, fire rockets into them. The 740-volume nucleus of the Library of Congress burned, as did the Supreme Court library, including the secret journals of the House. Red morocco chairs fed the flames along with the great gilt eagle that surmounted the clock above the chair of the Speaker of the House. The hands of the clock pointed to 10:00. So intense was the heat that it melted the thick glass skylights. With a thunderous roar, the flames burst through the Capitol dome. The ascending cloud of embers showered the neighborhood, destroying four other buildings, including two houses on North Capitol Street built by President Washington, one of them concealing the congressional papers moved there for their safekeeping. A southwesterly breeze spread more embers, carrying them north and east.

In the guttering firelight, Cockburn and Ross led 150 men a mile along the broad expanse of Pennsylvania Avenue to pay a visit to the White House. They stopped long enough for a late supper at Mrs. Barbara Suter's boardinghouse. The terrified proprietress warmed up some bread and ran out back to kill some chickens. Her uninvited guests might have waited for richer fare.

At 11 p.m., Cockburn and Ross and their staff officers strode into the Oval Dining Room of the White House, to be stunned by the generous table the First Lady had left set for the president's guests. Captain Harry Smith, after filching one of Madison's clean white shirts to replace his filthy, sweaty tunic, sampled the cold cuts and sipped "super-excellent Madeira." Captain James Scott concurred: "Never was nectar more grateful to the palates of the gods than the crystal goblets of Madeira and water I quaffed off at Mr. Madison's expense." Lieutenant Gleig marveled at "spits loaded with joints of various sorts, turn[ing] before the fire . . . and all the other requisites for an elegant and substantial repast."[39]

Before leaving for a simpler supper at Mrs. Suter's, Cockburn toured the house, helping himself only to an old hat and an account book of the president's and a cushion from Dolley Madison's chair to remind him, he joked, of her seat. Sated, the British officers vacated the executive mansion to make way for Lieutenant Pratt's pyrotechnicians. Getting hot coals from a beer house opposite the Treasury Building, Pratt's sailors ignited their match globes and thrust them through the windows of the White House, the Treasury Building and the Southwest Executive Building, home of the secretaries of state and war. As the flames turned the burning buildings into gigantic bonfires, Cockburn and Ross finished their chicken pies and rode back down Pennsylvania Avenue.

Cockburn had a personal mission in mind. Learning from terrified passersby the whereabouts of the *National Intelligencer*, he led the way to its print shop on Sixth Street N.W. Its English-born editor, Joseph Gales Jr., had penned numerous articles deriding Cockburn and his tactics. Cockburn ordered the building burned, but neighbors, fearing the fire would ignite the entire block, pleaded with Cockburn, pointing out that Gales didn't own the building. Cockburn relented, but promised to come back in the morning—it was now past midnight—with crews to pull down the building. In the meantime, he ordered the presses and all the furniture removed, smashed and burned in the street and the fonts either thrown on the fire or tossed into a nearby canal. All of the letters C he ordered to be destroyed so that Gales could never again print his name.

Cockburn stopped last at the Patent Office and Post Office, housed in Blodgett's Hotel (Eighth and E Streets N.W.). There, the superintendent of patents, Dr. William Thornton, designer of the Capitol, pleaded with the British commanders to spare the building. Thornton had already moved all the patent records to safety, but the patent models were too heavy or fragile to move. Thornton successfully appealed to Ross and Cockburn to spare the building on the grounds that the models were the private property of aspiring patentees and that "to burn what would be useful to all mankind would be as barbarous as formerly to burn the Alexandrian Library for which the Turks have been ever since condemned by all the civilized nations."[40]

Exhausted, the British commanders rode away toward their encampment inside the city gates. As the raging fires forged a brilliant dome of light over the city, visible forty miles away in Baltimore, a hard rain began to fall. At a season in Washington known for violent thunderstorms, a West Indian tropical storm swept the city, lifting Lieutenant Gleig from his horse and throwing him to the ground even as it ripped the roof off the Patent Office and lifted many other buildings off their foundations or flattened them entirely. For two hours the torrential rain poured down, quenching the fires by morning and leaving the capital of the United States a blackened, smoldering ruin. A sodden, exhausted British army started its forty-mile-long march back to its ships amid the maelstrom. Many of the hungry troops had filled their knapsacks with pilfered flour, but, as they trudged along in the humid heat behind a herd of sixty cattle, they shed any weight they could, leaving a white trail in their wake.

In a final raid, seventy-five redcoats ran through the smoking ruins of the navy yard to the federal arsenal at Greenleaf Point. They spiked cannon, firing a smaller cannon into the mouth of a larger one to destroy it. They rolled unmounted cannon barrels into the river along with tons of shot and shells. Retreating Americans had secreted 130 barrels of gunpowder in a deep well. But the water in it didn't completely cover the barrels. According to a London newspaper, a British artilleryman accidentally dropped his lighted port-fire into the well, setting off the contents of a powder magazine twenty yards away. "The most tremendous explosion" blew the roof off of a nearby building and flattened buildings burned earlier in the night. Flying "earth, stones, bricks, shot, shells" killed twelve men, badly injuring forty-four more: "The groans of the people almost buried in the earth, or with legs and arms broke, and the sight of pieces of bodies lying about, was a thousand times more distressing than the loss we met in the field the day before [Bladensburg]." Ross gave the order for the badly burned survivors of the arsenal blast to be left behind to the mercy of the Americans.[41]

The District of Columbia's ordeal did not end with its holocaust. A British navy squadron had inched its way through the treacherous Kettle Bottom Shoals up the Potomac toward Alexandria, Virginia. On August 29 the squadron commander, pointing his cannon toward the town, demanded a ransom and threatened a conflagration if he was refused. He agreed to a truce after the city's committee of vigilance promised that there would be no armed resistance. The committee dashed off a desperate plea for an approaching rescue force of 1,100 Virginia militia to stay away. For three days and nights, before sailing for Bermuda with their booty, British sailors emptied the warehouses of Virginia's largest port, cramming the holds of twenty-one surrendered ships with 13,786 barrels of flour, 757 thousand-pound hogsheads of tobacco and vast quantities of cotton, tar, beef and sugar.

THE SHOCK OF British destruction of their capital city seemed to shake Americans out of their torpor. After the five-day uncontested occupation, as the plunder-laden British squadron picked its way for five more days down the Potomac, America's naval heroes—Oliver Hazard Perry, David Porter and John Rodgers—rushed to Washington to punish the withdrawing British ships. Rodgers threatened to burn Alexandria unless the city let him raise the American flag. Monroe, the new secretary of war (and still secretary of state—Madison had finally fired Armstrong), agreed that they should launch fire ships and torpedoes and erect gun batteries on the lower Potomac. From September 3 to 8, they launched the incendiary ships and armed barges and took potshots with cannon, muskets and rifles at passing warships. At Fort Belvoir, Virginia, under a great white flag proclaiming "Free Trade and Sailors' Rights," their battery exchanged fire with British bomb vessels, but the damage to the British was negligible. After a highly profitable twenty-three-day foray, the loot-laden British squadron rendezvoused with the main fleet.

FIFTEEN

"So Proudly We Hail"

A s express riders sped newspapers north and south with accounts of the
debacle, anger, indignation and shame spread throughout the nation.
In Washington, someone scrawled on the scorched wall of the Capitol,
"George Washington founded this city after a seven years' war with
England—James Madison lost it after a two years' war."[1] After searching
frantically in Virginia for two days to find his wife, a shaken Madison returned to the smoldering city, surrounded for the first time by a body-
guard of dragoons. Within days, in the nation's press, former critics of
"Mister Madison's War" were issuing pleas for solidarity. Federalists
turned out for a mass rally in Philadelphia; thousands of citizens began
digging entrenchments. In New York the Federalists' most strident spokesman, Rufus King, started a loan to fund an all-out defense: "I will subscribe to the amount of my whole fortune." In Vermont the Federalist
governor Chittenden, who had a year earlier tried to prevent his militia
from serving outside the state, called for an end to "all degrading party
distinctions." Every official from Rhode Island to Richmond believed his
city would be the next target.[2]

News accounts triggered a financial panic the length and breadth of the
nation. Beginning in Washington, depositors emptied their accounts of

gold and silver specie. Within a week of the torching of the Capitol, there were runs on the banks in Philadelphia and Baltimore, forcing bankers to announce to chagrined depositors that they were suspending the withdrawal of specie. To protect their dwindling reserves, by September 1, New York banks followed suit.

The crisis deepened with the news that Alexandria had surrendered ships and cargoes to the British to avert an attack. In Boston, dreading that the British would extend their policy of looting or ransom to more port cities, "the panic" was "almost universal," reported commercial agent Charles Greene. "All classes of people have been drawing specie out of the banks today," he wrote on September 6. His partner in New York City, Charles Ives, noted that, because it was "almost impossible to draw funds from New York . . . little or nothing is doing in business."[3]

Privateering ships had ravaged British commerce. It was to Baltimore, the nation's third largest city (population 50,000) that the avenging triumvirate of Cochrane, Cockburn and Ross turned next. Writing to Lord Bathurst to explain his choice of targets, Cochrane called Baltimore "the most democratic town and I believe the richest in the union." While Cochrane had respected private property in Washington, Baltimore's citizens could not expect to be spared. "Baltimore may be destroyed or laid under a severe contribution." Ross, commander of all forces once they were put ashore, at first opposed the attack on Baltimore. He thought it could be a disaster. Cochrane wrote Bathurst that Ross "does not seem inclined to visit the sins committed upon His Majesty's Canadian subjects upon the inhabitants of this state."[4]

For two weeks, the British armada rested off Tangier Island in the Chesapeake as Cochrane argued with Cockburn and Ross over the wisdom of attacking Baltimore. Cochrane advocated sailing north to pluck prizes from Rhode Island's ports. He hesitated to risk his men in the Chesapeake's "sickly season" of stifling heat and malaria. Finally persuaded by his scouts that Baltimore was poorly defended and could be taken by a combined overland attack and naval bombardment, on September 7 Cochrane issued orders to set sail.

Baltimore had been girding for attack for more than a year. From the time Cockburn had begun his hit-and-run plundering raids the length of the Chesapeake in mid-1813, senator and Maryland major general Samuel

Smith was certain the British would eventually attack the city. During the Revolutionary War, Smith had successfully defended Fort Mifflin in the Delaware River, delaying for months the British occupation of Philadelphia. As soon as he heard of the debacle at Bladensburg and saw the fiery halo of Washington burning, Smith and his command were certain Baltimore would be next. At an emergency meeting, the city's de facto government—the Committee of Vigilance with Governor Winder at its head—in a highly unorthodox step, placed militia general Smith in charge of defending the city, superseding the governor's discredited nephew, the regular army general Winder, the federal officer in charge of the Tenth Military District.

Smith ordered the entire port heavily fortified. He put more than 10,000 men, black and white, slave and free, to work side by side digging mile-and-a-half-long trenches and constructing breastworks across Loudenslager, Potter and Hampstead Hills—east of the city, and an area that today encompasses Patterson Park—where he concentrated forty artillery pieces, from four- to eighteen-pounders. Safeguarding against an attack from the rear of Fort McHenry, thousands of citizens were building a heavily fortified mountain, still known today as Federal Hill, to protect the rear of the massive, star-shaped brick fortress. Named for Washington's secretary of war, James McHenry, Fort McHenry, the guardian of the tidal approaches to the city's Inner Harbor and scores of privateering ships, had been built at Washington's insistence at the start of the Napoleonic Wars. It was garrisoned in September 1814 by army regulars and hundreds of local militia, in all 4,000 troops under the command of regular army major George Armistead.

Enlisting the city's brickmakers, Smith ordered the construction of two other batteries, Fort Covington (today's Riverside Park) and Fort Babcock, each armed with six cannon, to protect Fort McHenry from flanking attacks. At the water's edge, to face the harbor in front of the main fort, Smith ordered construction of an extensive brick-and-earth battery, its cannons interspersed with furnaces to prepare hot shot. Around the cove, Smith arranged twelve 18-pounders on field carriages, adding a battery on the other side of the narrow channel at Lazaretto Point that could crossfire with Fort McHenry. He established an elaborate flag-and-lantern signal system with lookouts posted at stations on land and on schooners and gunboats that kept Federal Hill in touch with movements on the water. At the suggestion of Stephen Decatur, hero of the Tripoli Wars, he scuttled thirty hulks of old ships rotting along the riverbanks to block the channel. The networks of enfilading artillery made it impossible for the British navy to penetrate the city's inner harbor. Borrowing thirty-eight-pounder naval long guns from the grounded seventy-gun French frigate *L'Eole*, Smith placed them along the mile-long brow of Federal Hill.

Smith immediately set to work building a creditable army, forming brigades drawn from the five hundred sailors serving under Captain John Rodgers, a squad of marines, a pair of regular regiments and the 13,500 militiamen pouring in from Pennsylvania, Maryland, Delaware, the District of Columbia and Virginia. He named seven generals to lead these brigades as they joined in building defenses.

Haunted by the afterglow of the nation's capital in flames, some 11,000 civilian Baltimoreans—nearly one-fourth the populace—turned out to defend their city, working night and day. Want ads in the *Patriot and Evening Advertiser* pleaded for riflemen and artillerists. One ad summoned "elderly men who are able to carry a firelock and willing to render a last service to their country." Citizens were told to collect all the wheelbarrows, pickaxes and shovels they could find and start digging and piling up breastworks, stripping the heavy cannon from privateers in the inner harbor and dragging them onto gun emplacements. With the U.S. Treasury empty, Baltimore banks shelled out $663,000 to buy guns, tents, provisions and forage. Citizens showered the town with hundreds of donations. One gentleman wrote, "Put me down for $50,000 for the defence of Baltimore." The city comptroller logged donated goods and services: "3,000 bricks . . . 2 bundles of lint . . . 5 barrels of whiskey, 2 barrels of shad . . . 3 tons of hay." Maryland-owned cannon too late to fortify Washington were redirected to Fort McHenry. "The guns belong to the U.S.," declared Major General Smith. Militia pouring into the city drilled incessantly.[5]

Smith divided the city into four wards. All men, boys and old men marched each day to dig the defensive two-mile-long line of breastworks from Harris's Creek north across Hampstead Hill, armed at short intervals with semicircular batteries of cannon on movable field carriages. Rodgers posted 170 handpicked Marines at the top of Hampstead Hill at a bastion armed with sixteen field and naval guns, overlooking the strategic intersection of Philadelphia Road, which led into Baltimore, and the forts on the inner harbor side overlooking Fort McHenry. The Rodgers Bastion protected the fort against a surprise attack from the rear. Interconnected breastworks and rifle pits, lined with inner bastions and batteries, paralleled the northern boundary of the city. A second fallback line took shape on high ground at the site of the present-day Roman Catholic Basilica of the Assumption. On high ground to the rear, at the foot of Light Street on present Battery Square, Smith installed a circular battery of seven guns. Wagon trains came from Delaware, crammed with barrels of gunpowder from the E. I. DuPont de Nemours mills.

On alternating days, the city's "exempts from military and free people of color" were to appear with "provisions for the day"—meals—for the volunteers laboring in the steamy heat. Smith appealed to surrounding states to send food. Slave owners from surrounding plantations sent their wards to pitch in under the watchful gaze of constables. Citizens read the morning *Telegraph* for their instructions: fill buckets with water in case Congreve rockets were fired into the city; quench all lights at nightfall so that the enemy could not find its targets.

WHEN HE TOOK command of Fort McHenry in 1813, Armistead had commissioned a team of seamstresses to make a pair of giant flags to fly above the parade ground. He ordered a garrison flag, thirty-by-forty-two feet, and a smaller, seventeen-by-twenty-five-foot storm flag. A thirty-eight-year-old widow, Mary Young Pickersgill—whose mother had fashioned flags in Philadelphia during the Revolution—set to work with her thirteen-year-old daughter and with Grace Wisher, a free black indentured servant girl, and other members of her household on East Pratt Street. For the massive garrison flag, they meticulously measured and cut four hundred yards of English worsted wool bunting into eight red stripes and seven white, each two feet across, on an indigo field adorned with fifteen white cotton stars, two feet from point to point.[6]

IF COCKBURN AND Ross had attacked immediately after razing Washington, they might have taken Baltimore. As it was, Baltimore's herculean defenses were completed within three weeks and not a day too soon. In the early afternoon of Sunday, September 11, 1814, three alarm guns on the courthouse lawn boomed, announcing the arrival of the British. By sun-set, lookouts on Federal Hill could count thirty British sail, including six-teen frigates, rocket ships, bomb brigs and ten troop transports "within the bar," fifteen miles from the city. Parishioners rushed early from church services, and citizen-soldiers ran through the streets to join their units. The *Baltimore Sun* would report that "all the corps of every description turned out with alacrity." Smith ordered the 3,200-man 3rd Brigade, Baltimore's best militiamen under the command of Brigadier General John Stricker—including the 5th, 27th, 39th and 51st Maryland Regiments, a few companies of Pennsylvanians and Major Pinkney's riflemen—to North Point to divine British intentions.[7]

At 3 p.m. the troops marched east on the Philadelphia Road to North Point Road to a narrow part of the peninsula, bedding down for the night at the Methodist Meeting House. By nightfall, Stricker had arranged his men in a line of battle across Patapsco Point, the narrowest neck of land halfway down the peninsula, between Bread and Cheese Creek to the north and Bear Creek to the south. Captain John Montgomery was cover-ing Long Log Lane, the main road to Baltimore, with a battery of six 4-pounders. Stricker sent riflemen ahead two miles to set up a skirmish line; about 140 dragoons rode a mile farther east to Gorsuch's Farm and set up vedettes, from which they peered nervously into the darkness.

Aboard the sloop-of-war *Fairy*, Cockburn wanted to sail up the Patap-sco River and storm Fort McHenry. Cochrane and Ross overruled him in favor of a pincer attack. The troops would land at North Point and advance up the peninsula to assail the city, while the navy would strike the city by water. This time, the people of Baltimore were to be granted no mercy: a letter from Governor-General Prevost in Canada reciting fresh American atrocities had just arrived. Now more than ever, Admiral Cochrane was determined to retaliate. Beginning at four in the morning on September 12, from their fleet anchored in the Patapsco River, the British infantry strike force of 4,760 rowed ashore in whaleboats and barges. As they were at Bladensburg, their ranks were composed primarily of the battle-seasoned 4th, 44th, 21st and 85th Regiments of Foot, augmented by six hundred of Cockburn's sailors and black Colonial Marines.[8]

Clambering up the low bluffs at North Point, they were supported by only four pieces of field artillery. For the fifteen-mile march to Baltimore, each soldier's knapsack was crammed with three days' rations, eighty rounds of ammunition, a blanket, a clean shirt and an extra pair of shoes. The Regulars' goal: to make short work of the militia and to chastise the piratical city and its unruly citizens.

By late morning Stricker had learned that the British were only a few miles away. Dreading a night attack, he decided to provoke an engagement in the daylight. He sent forward a squad of cavalrymen, two companies of militia and a company of riflemen to draw the enemy's attention. At seven o'clock they opened fire on the British vanguard. At the head of the British advance guard, riding on a black charger, came General Ross. Ordering his regiments to bring on the battle, Ross insisted on leading his light infantry up the North Point Road. His eager junior officers quickly got too far ahead of the main force. Ross rode out to rein them in, then turned back to hurry along the light infantry companies. He was riding alone when shots fired by two of Pinkney's riflemen rang out. Lieutenant Gleig, hurrying to the front, would vividly remember the scene:

> The general's horse, without its rider, and with the saddle and housings stained with blood, came plunging onward. In a few moments we . . . beheld poor Ross laid, by the side of the road, under a canopy of blankets, and apparently in the agonies of death. It is impossible to conceive the effect which this melancholy spectacle produced throughout the army. . . . All eyes were turned upon him as we passed, and a sort of involuntary groan ran from rank to rank, from the front to the rear of the column.[9]

Jounced along on a farm cart toward the rear, Ross lapsed into a coma. He was dead by the time he reached the beachhead.

Colonel Arthur Brooke was two miles behind the front line when he learned he had been thrust into command. Rushing forward, he discovered a solid line of American troops standing firm. Giving his troops a pause to eat and drink while he brought up cannon and rockets, Brooke studied the American line five hundred yards across the Bouldin Farm clearing and decided the enemy's weak spot was its left, anchored on Bread and Cheese Creek. In midafternoon he ordered the 44th Regiment to attack through the woods, keeping undercover from American fire. Setting off an artillery and rocket duel with the six American guns, he arrayed his thousands of soldiers, sailors and marines along the haystack-dotted field. Then he ordered the buglers to sound the signal for a frontal attack on the Americans, who waited silently across the meadow behind a zigzagging rail fence.

Lieutenant Gleig recalled,

> The British soldiers moved forward with their accustomed fearlessness, and the Americans, with much apparent coolness, stood to receive them. . . . Volley upon volley having been given, we were now advanced within less than twenty yards of the American line; yet such was the denseness of the smoke, that it was only when a passing breeze swept away the cloud [of smoke] for a moment that either force became visible to the other. . . . The flashes of the enemy's muskets alone served as an object to aim at.[10]

As the 44th and Gleig's 85th charged the center of the American line, American artillery opened fire with old locks, nails, horseshoes—anything that could be crammed into a cannon. The front British rank crumpled, but the surviving redcoats came on, some quick-time, some on hands and knees. They were only a few yards away from the American line when a single militiaman vaulted over a fence, knelt and fired. Suddenly, with a great yell, the whole American line erupted with musket fire. After a savage twenty-minute firefight, the British 4th Regiment managed to turn the American left flank. The 51st Maryland Regiment, sent to reinforce the left, broke and ran. The 39th Maryland, left exposed along the fence, also withdrew.

His defensive line now outflanked, General Stricker decided to withdraw the 5th and 27th Regiments on the right yet still hold out long enough to allow an orderly retreat back to their main defensive lines on Hampstead Hill. Much to the surprise of the British, while American losses included 213 men killed, wounded or captured along with two cannon, British casualties were far worse: 350 dead, wounded or missing. In the Battle of North Point, the American militia once again had faced down Wellington's Invincibles. The militia no longer ran. And by killing the British commanding general for all North America, the illustrious General Ross, one of Wellington's favorite generals, they had dealt a severe blow to British morale both on the battlefront and in England.

As ADMIRAL COCHRANE methodically led his flotilla—three ships-of-the-line, four frigates, three brigs, two schooners and five bomb vessels—up the Patapsco to within five miles of Fort McHenry, he received the shattering news that General Ross was dead. Yet Cochrane remained determined to chastise Baltimore. In the midst of a violent thunderstorm, at six o'clock on the sodden morning of September 13, state-of-the-art bomb vessel *Volcano* opened fire. Each bomb ship was a floating weapons platform bearing four-ton mortars that lobbed ten- to thirteen-inch exploding shells weighing as much as two hundred pounds. In a high-arching trajectory of up to two miles, the projectiles sputtered and sparked before they exploded, raining down deadly shrapnel. Miles away, Lieutenant Gleig, soaked after a night on the march from North Point, saw the first shot and heard its "solitary report, accompanied by the ascension of a small bright spark into the sky." But the shot fell short. Cochrane, aboard the command ship *Surprize*, ordered the entire fleet to move in closer, within a mile and a half of the fort, and open fire.[11]

On the fort's parapet, the storm flag flapping in the high wind behind him, Major Armistead gave the order to open fire. Brick-oven-heated shells hurtled into the front rank of British frigates, setting them afire. In the moats and water batteries, where thousands of frightened men had been hunkering down and cringing, a cheer went up and the band started to play "Yankee Doodle." Cochrane gave the order for his ships to drop back to two miles, out of range of the heavy French guns.

An estimated 1,500–1,800 times in the next twenty-five hours, the low carrumph of mortars firing, sometimes half a dozen at once, preceded a low-pitched explosion that made houses shake inside Baltimore. Shrieking, terrifying, ineffectual rockets, arcing high above the harbor, eerily illuminated the night sky. The deadly sound-and-light show mesmerized 25,000 sodden, silent Americans watching from the trenches, the battlements on Hampstead Hill and their rooftops. With the British ships out of range, very few more shots came from the fort. Mortars sent from Washington without carriages lay useless, silent. But as long as Fort McHenry did not surrender, Baltimore and its prize-laden inner harbor seemed safe. Amid the crashing flash of bursting bombs, hundreds of wagons and carts crammed with the city's poor and their children and all they could carry fled the city, sure they were anything but safe, the ground beneath them trembling with every bomb blast.

Of all the British missiles launched, only about four hundred fell in or around the fortress, killing four and wounding twenty-four of the 4,000 human targets. A woman carrying supplies was cut in half by a rocket; a runaway slave who had joined the 38th U.S. Infantry was killed by shrapnel. After twenty-five hours of firing shells and rockets, Cochrane again ordered ships to move closer, only to be driven back by heavy American fire. An attempt to outflank the fort by twenty-two armed barges and a schooner up the Ferry Branch of the Patapsco in the darkest hours of a moonless night met with the blind fire of fifty of Captain Barney's flotillamen.

Squinting through the fog and driving rain from the four-foot-high plank-covered earthworks of Fort Babcock, the seasoned sailors could make out the faint splashing sound of muffled oars. Sailing master John Adams Webster ordered his gunners to open fire. As the British returned musket fire, Barney's flotillamen could hear their cannonballs strike the barges and the screams of the wounded. Fort McHenry's gunners finally had a target they could hit. After two hours of fighting in the dense fog, the British rowed back to their ships. At seven in the morning on September 14, after receiving a message from Colonel Brooke that he considered the city's defenses impregnable and the risk of heavy casualties and final failure to take the town too daunting, a deeply disappointed Admiral Cochrane decided to end the bombardment. He turned his attention toward his next target, New Orleans, where American privateering ships laden with cargoes worth an estimated 4 million pounds of loot awaited him.

From the deck of American flag-of-truce ship *Minden* where he was kept under guard, Georgetown Federalist lawyer Francis Scott Key had watched the spectacle all night. He had come to negotiate the release of Dr. William Beanes, an elderly antiwar Federalist physician who had offered hospitality in his Marlborough home to the British commanders before the burning of Washington but who then had arrested several British looters. For his temerity, Dr. Beanes had been taken prisoner. Key had been forced to watch the bombardment, himself a hostage, until the battle was over. He watched anxiously all night as the Congreve rockets glared red and hissed toward the darkened fort while bombshells burst over its silent ramparts, Baltimore's prized privateers still rocking safely at anchor in the inner harbor and the massive earthworks on Federal Hill remaining unbreached.

At 5:30 on the muggy morning of September 14, Key was stunned to see that the storm flag that had been fluttering high above Fort McHenry all night was sliding down and, in its place, the immense new garrison flag was rising and unfurling. Key took out the stub of a pencil he had in his pocket and dashed off a few lines on the back of an envelope, describing what he had seen and heard and felt:

> O say can you see by the dawn's early light, What so proudly we hailed at the twilight's last gleaming, Whose broad stripes and bright stars through the perilous fight, O'er the ramparts we watched, were so gallantly stream-ing? And the rockets' red glare, the bombs bursting in air, Gave proof through the night that our flag was still there; O say does that star-spangled banner yet wave, O'er the land of the free and the home of the brave?

Writing more lines as the *Minden* took its hostages back to Baltimore, Key could not sleep until he had turned his jottings into an opening verse that fitted a popular English drinking song—"To Anacreon in Heaven"—the fourteenth-century official song of an eighteenth-century Society of Amateur Musicians in London and popular in America. Robert Treat Paine had borrowed the tune—an isorhythmic motet of repeating pat-terns—in 1798 for a patriotic air entitled "Adams and Liberty" before Key borrowed it once again in 1805 to honor the heroes of Tripoli. Writing out his latest adaptation on a single sheet of paper, he left it untitled. A friend took it to the print shop of the *Baltimore American* where editor Samuel Kennedy—an exiled leader of the Irish insurrection of 1798—struck it off as a handbill. Copies, unsigned and under the heading, "Defence of Fort M'Henry," soon circulated throughout the city. Weeks later, someone gave Key's effort a new title, "The Star-Spangled Banner." Every soldier in Fort McHenry's garrison received a free copy and crowds in taverns all over Baltimore sang it triumphantly. When the *Baltimore Patriot and Evening Advertiser* resumed publication, it ran the anthem in full. Within weeks, newspapers as far away as Concord, New Hampshire and Savannah,

Georgia, copied the lyrics of the song of American resistance and spread them farther.

America at last had a great, if virtually bloodless, victory to immortalize.

A SINGLE CANNON shot from the *Surprize* signaled the British fleet to haul anchor. The sails of the British armada soon ballooned, filled with a fresh breeze that carried them back down the Patapsco and out onto the broad Chesapeake. Out at North Point, thousands of bedraggled, disheartened redcoats waited their turns to be rowed out to their ships to begin the short voyage to Tangier Island and from there on to Halifax or Bermuda or the Gulf of Mexico. As they sailed away, in incredulous Baltimore, as *Niles' Weekly Register* related, "all was for some time still, and the silence was awful."[12]

ACROSS THE ATLANTIC back on August 21, even as Secretary of State Monroe was riding out with his escort of dragoons to espy the British Army's drive toward Washington, John Quincy Adams, Henry Clay and Albert Gallatin were sitting down at their rented desks in the American mission in Ghent, penning the first American reply to Britain's treaty demands. It would be yet another month before they learned from a London newspaper of the debacle. When they met at two that afternoon, Gallatin, the consummate European diplomat, favored striking out, as Adams disgustedly noted in his diary, "every expression that may be offensive to the feelings of the adverse party." The blunt-spoken Kentuckian Clay criticized Adams's penchant for figurative language as "improper for a state paper." As usual, the other delegates agreed that whatever Adams wrote was too long-winded, especially the verbiage he devoted to the proposed Indian reservation. It took four more days of meetings and rewriting before Adams, as head of the mission, arranged the final document.[13]

By the time they sent off their conjoined answer to the British emissaries across town, expecting it would end the peace talks, the British had burned Washington and the president and his first lady and their parties were frantically searching for each other among the refugees flooding northern Virginia. Navy secretary Jones and his family, with Dolley's entourage, were struggling along the crowded road to Salona, where Madison expected to meet them. Unable to reach the rendezvous point, Dolley's party stopped for the night at Rokeby, the home of a friend; Dolley spent the night sitting silently at a window watching the guttering afterglow of the burning capital.

When the Madisons finally were reunited briefly the next day at Wiley's Tavern on Difficult Run, there was no time to commiserate. The cabinet had dispersed in four different directions, some riding to Frederick, Maryland, for one day the capital of the United States. Monroe had gone north toward Baltimore with General Winder. Madison felt lost without Monroe. Even before he received the president's note, Monroe wrote to urge Madison to return to Washington at once. Madison agreed and sent off a note for Dolley to rejoin him in the ruins.

By 5 p.m. on August 27, with his escort of dragoons, Madison rode down Pennsylvania Avenue for a cabinet meeting at the home of Attorney General Rush. They rode past graffiti on the Capitol's scorched walls: "John Armstrong is a traitor." Exhausted, Madison appeared "shaken and woebegone," William Wirt wrote to his wife. "In short, he looked as if his heart was broken." Adding to his woes, Alexander Hanson, now the editor of the *Georgetown Federal Republican*, arrived at night to warn of a plot to assassinate Madison. While no evidence was ever uncovered, a corporal and six soldiers were assigned to guard the president. Once vehemently anti-Madison, the erstwhile Baltimore editor Hanson now expounded: "The fight will now be for our country, not for a party."[14]

On the afternoon of August 28, Dolley returned to Washington in a borrowed carriage that took her past the smoldering White House to the home of Mrs. Richard Cutts on F Street, where she had first lived in Washington. Madison decided they should stay there. As word spread of their return, old friends dropped by and witnessed a changed Dolley: she was depressed, breaking into tears, raging at the British, wishing for an army "to sink our enemy to the bottomless pit." The man held most responsible for the debacle, Armstrong, was discovering how much he was hated. Hanson warned unforgivingly in the *Federal Republican*, "The movements of this fiend should be narrowly watched."[15] Wherever he went, Armstrong met revulsion: his appearance to inspect district militia at Windmill Point set off a riot. Officers laid down their swords rather than salute him; enlisted men working on fortifications threw down their shovels. Members of the 1st Brigade passed a unanimous resolution that they would no longer serve under the "willing cause" of Washington's capture. They told Madison that they would serve under "any other member of the cabinet." Madison urged Armstrong to take a "temporary retirement," visit his family in New York—and leave the next morning. Armstrong announced his resignation in the September 3 *Baltimore Patriot and Evening Advertiser.* Madison immediately appointed Monroe acting secretary of war.[16]

SIXTEEN

"I Must Not Be Lost"

In his final orders, Armstrong had written on July 27 to General George Izard, commander of the northern army, to move the majority of his 4,000-man force from its base at Plattsburgh on Lake Champlain to reinforce Sackets Harbor. Marching west, Izard left the youthful brigadier general Alexander Macomb at Plattsburgh with 1,900 troops, mostly new recruits or invalids. Armstrong believed there would be no offensive from Canada. He was unaware that, since Napoleon's capitulation in April, British forces had been accumulating in Canada until, by late summer, 30,000 troops there made possible an offensive on both the Niagara and the Lake Champlain fronts. Only as he prepared to march west did Izard learn from his Indian spies that a huge British force was concentrating near the border. In a series of desperate letters, he pleaded with Armstrong to change his orders so that he could counter the British threat. He was certain that "in less than three days after [his] departure," Plattsburgh, the strongest American post in the Northeast, would be "in the possession of the enemy," leaving open the road south to the Hudson. He received no reply; on August 20, as Armstrong galloped around Bladensburg countermanding the orders of his generals, Izard, noting that at least 10,000 British troops had crossed the border and were only forty miles away, wrote again: "I must not be responsible for the consequences of abandoning my present strong position."[1]

When still no message came from Washington, the dispirited Izard, taking with him nine regiments of regulars, light artillery and all of the northern army's surgeons, started a slow, circuitous march west. Still waiting for a change of orders that never came, he paused at Lake George; by September 7 he had only reached Schenectady. By the time his troops shambled into Sackets Harbor, the fighting on the Niagara frontier was over. The wrongheaded secretary of war had sent his replacement, Izard, away at the very moment the British were preparing their greatest invasion attempt of the entire war. Ironically, Armstrong's decision played well with the troops left behind at Izard's departure.

A self-described martinet who disdained militia and was proud to be a heavy-handed disciplinarian, Izard eschewed capital punishment and preferred resorting to public humiliation. One Benjamin Lynde, caught stealing, received "twelve bats on his naked posteriors"—a spanking—in front of the assembled troops. David Dickey, convicted of habitual intoxication, had to "ride a wooden horse one hour two successive mornings on the publik paraid." Asa Hopkins, convicted of sleeping on duty as a sentinel, was discharged from the army, but first he was "to have his head shaved, be marked with the letter R on each cheek and the forehead, with Lunar Costic [silver nitrate]" and "drummed out of camp with a halter round his neck." And Timothy Ashley, convicted of insubordination and mutinous conduct, was sentenced to hard labor with ball and chain for the rest of his enlistment; his liquor ration was stopped, and he had to ride the wooden horse one hour every Sunday wearing a hangman's cap and a four-pound shot tied to each foot.[2]

After Napoleon's surrender, the British Ministry decided to attack in a pincer-like formation from Canada while the Americans were distracted by the slash-and-burn diversionary attacks in the Chesapeake. Encouraged by the refusal of Federalists to support "Mr. Madison's War," Bathurst, Castlereagh and Liverpool, the Tory triumvirate determined to prosecute the American war at all costs, believed that a counterattack on the Niagara–Great Lakes axis timed with a joint army-navy thrust down Lake Champlain would give them control of the entire length of the St. Lawrence River. An unopposed summer attack on the Maine coast, designed to create a direct communication between Halifax and Quebec, had also encouraged the British Ministry's belief in the ultimate secession of New England. Swift conquests of American terrain and waters with major infusions of veterans released from the Napoleonic Wars surely would produce major and permanent territorial gains at the treaty talks in Ghent as well as assuring there would be no more American invasions of Canada.

The few thousand untested American militiamen serving as both army and naval defenders of Lake Champlain were probably shielded from this nightmare scenario only because they didn't have an inkling of it. Prevost maintained strict secrecy as he drew down Wellington's Invincibles, quietly massing 11,000 veterans between Montreal and the border in the summer of 1814. American depredations along the Niagara frontier had united French and English Canadians for the first time against the American invaders, making intelligence gathering more difficult. American commanders in Plattsburgh and at their sister base at Burlington relied almost entirely on the newly minted Corps of Observation.

Made up of Caughnawaga Iroquois from the St. Regis reservation in northwestern Franklin County, New York, the corps' organizer and leader was a young mixed-breed named Eleazer Williams. Twenty years old when war came, he had been studying theology to become a missionary to the Indians. Probably descended from an Indian captured during the Deerfield raid of 1704 and Daniel Williams, progenitor of the Williams family of Massachusetts, he was raised by his father, Thomas, an influential chief, in Indian ways and language. A pacifist, he prayed for peace. He agreed to serve the American army only to acquire army rations for hundreds of his people. Commissioned by Dearborn as superintendent general of the Northern Indian Department, Williams organized a team of Indian and white rangers that served as the eyes and ears of the northern army. Refusing to bear arms until the British attack in late 1814, he was paid $400 a year, two rations a day and a horse to gather intelligence. From his base at Charlotte, Vermont, he traversed the border, recruiting Indians, dispensing largesse—including occasional $50 cash bonuses for the chiefs—and, in the first winter, rations for 434 tribesmen. In exchange for the rations, Indians went to work making snowshoes for the army. When the British violated a prewar agreement by placing an armed band at St. Regis, with Williams's information American militia were able to surround and capture the British force.

In late August 1814 Izard's command was transferred to the thirty-one-year-old general Alexander Macomb, a member of the first graduating class from West Point, an expert in the construction of frontier fortifications and a skilled artillerist. One of a growing number of bright young officers replacing the older generation, Macomb, as inspector general, grew frustrated at the army's inefficiency, in particular its inability to know its own troop strength. He was promoted to general early in 1814, in time to witness the invasion of Canada, where American forces were commanded by the infamous Wilkinson.

Trying to redeem his botched invasion attempt of the year before, Wilkinson failed to secure adequate provisions and munitions. He ignored intelligence gathered by Williams's Corps of Observation about the impregnability of the stone and timber fortifications at Lacolle Mill on the Richelieu River. After a poorly planned and armed attack in deep snow on March 30, 1814, of the small outpost's stone mill and blockhouse, he abandoned the third American invasion attempt only five miles inside Canada. After this latest failure, Armstrong relieved Wilkinson of command.

Taking command of what remained of the northern army, Macomb briefly panicked. He found "everything in a state of disorganization—works unfinished & a garrison of a few efficient men and a sick list of one thousand." Writing to his father, Macomb bemoaned being left "the remnant of Gen. Izard's Army, invalids and convalescents, except about 600 men." Left with 921 men who were either too old, too sick or too terrified to fight, he realized he did not even know the size or makeup of the army of veterans gathering only a few miles to his north. He sent for Eleazer Williams and asked him for intelligence reports every ten hours. When Williams arrived, he found that Macomb had already started building new batteries; the general, working with his troops and carrying logs, was so covered with dirt that Williams nearly overlooked him.[3]

FOR MORE THAN a year, since the capture of the two American sloops, the British had maintained naval superiority from their base at Isle aux Noix, five miles above the border on the Richelieu River. There they assembled a squadron of gunboats augmented by captured and repaired American vessels and crewed by seamen borrowed from troop transports arriving at Quebec. For much of that time, the young American commander, Thomas Macdonough, had relied on one sloop and half a dozen gunboats in largely unsuccessful attempts to repel British raids.

In July 1813 Governor-General Prevost had ordered Commander Daniel Pring, in charge at Isle aux Noix, to take the offensive. Pring crowded 946 officers and men aboard the *Eagle* and the *Growler,* three row galleys and forty-seven bateaux. Under the command of Lieutenant Colonel John Murray, the invasion force attacked the normally fortified town of Plattsburgh, left undefended when its garrison marched off to join the American attack on York. Unopposed, the British moored in the Saranac River and plundered and destroyed the town, arsenal, blockhouse, log barracks and government storehouses, taking away large quantities of pork, beef, flour, hard bread, whiskey, soap and vinegar.

In their overnight occupation, the British also thoroughly looted private homes, carrying off furniture, books, clothing, cooking utensils, groceries and dry goods. Landing again at Cumberland Head, they destroyed a large storehouse; then they sailed to Chazy Landing, destroyed a store and, dropping anchor in Maquam Bay, proceeded to march overland to Swanton, Vermont, where they burned the unoccupied militia barracks, a hospital and all government property. Sworn depositions sent to Washington also alleged several rapes and attempted rapes on both shores.

While the troops carried out these raids, the *Eagle,* the *Growler* and a row galley seized the sloop *Essex* and sailed on to Burlington. There Macdonough had gathered his minuscule flotilla, including the eleven-gun sloop *President*, two gunboats and two unfinished sloops at the foot of a cliff where a battery of long guns stood loaded and ready. From two miles offshore the British blasted away, hoping to destroy Macdonough's ships and three public warehouses, but heavy American fire drove them off after a twenty-minute exchange. Sailing farther south, the British seized another sloop and a schooner before taking two more sloops at Charlotte. Twenty miles farther south still, they scooped up nearly all the merchant vessels on the lake, except those Macdonough had managed to protect at Burlington, before taking their prize fleet back to Isle aux Noix. On the way to their base, the redcoats on the New York side rowed into the Great Chazy River. On August 3, 1813, they marched overland, burning blockhouses, barracks and a warehouse full of hay and capturing a company of sick militiamen.

This devastating raid finally convinced Navy secretary Jones to grant Macdonough's request for authority to commission, arm or acquire a suitable fleet to reclaim the lake. Within the month, Macdonough had outfitted a merchant sloop with eleven cannons, christening it the *Preble* after his former Barbary War commander, and equipped another sloop, the eleven-gun *Montgomery*. When the British attempted a further raid on Plattsburgh in early September, Macdonough chased them back to Canada, their flight formally acknowledging American naval superiority on Lake Champlain.

The U.S. secretary of war John Armstrong, who had failed to fortify either the Chesapeake region or Washington, D.C., had also insisted there would be no enemy offensive against Lake Champlain. He seemed completely oblivious to the implications of Napoleon's capitulation. Since April, as Prevost maintained strict secrecy, the British had been rapidly reinforcing their forces in Canada. By late summer 30,000 veteran redcoats hovered at the border. Simultaneous British attacks on the Niagara and the Lake Champlain fronts seemed almost a certainty.

ALL THROUGH THE winter of 1813–14, a full-fledged arms race had been underway on Lake Champlain. While the British built a new fleet at Isle aux Noix, Macdonough took winter quarters at the Vermont village of Vergennes, population 835, virtually hidden some twenty-three miles south of the 4,000-man army base at Burlington and up narrow, winding Otter Creek, seven miles from the lake. There Macdonough built his shipyard at the foot of a waterfall that generated abundant power. A forest of hardwood timber and nearby deposits of iron ore gave Macdonough the raw materials, and positioned him amid already functioning iron forges, blast furnaces, rolling mills, a wire factory and grist, saw and fulling mills. The Vergennes works would produce 1,000 thirty-two-pound cannonballs in time for the 1814 campaign.

In December Navy secretary Jones gave Macdonough permission to build either fifteen more gunboats or a ship and three or four gunboats. Macdonough opted for the ship; later, he would build the gunboats as well. To Macdonough's great good fortune, America's master shipbuilders, the

Brown Brothers, were once again commissioned to come to Vergennes from New York City. Arriving in March 1814, Noah Brown and his 140-man team laid the keel for the corvette *Saratoga* and began converting the 120-foot steamboat *Ticonderoga* into a seventeen-gun schooner. Brown contracted to finish the twenty-six-gun *Saratoga* in sixty days: it took him forty. When word arrived of the full-blown British invasion on the Chesapeake, shipbuilding on Lake Champlain reached fever pitch. By May, everything needed to fit out the *Saratoga* had reached Vergennes.

Teams of axmen combed the hillsides for white pine, in five and a half days cutting and forwarding enough timber to build three ships. The *Ticonderoga*'s exterior planking averaged three inches thick. Even thicker planks supported the gun ports. Timbers still standing in the forest on March 2 became the *Saratoga*'s keel on the seventh. The 143-foot corvette, a truncated frigate, slid into the water on April 11. Anchors, guns, cables and rigging took longer. Mud season made heavy wagonloads nearly immovable. One consignment of cables required eighty teams of oxen. Shot that couldn't be produced in Vergennes came over the mountains in oxcarts from Boston and up from Troy, New York. In less than a month, Brown's shipwrights built and launched nine row galleys, each seventy-five feet long and fifteen feet wide, armed with a twenty-four-pound long gun and a thirty-two-pound carronade and rowed by twenty-six oarsmen. In less than two months, Brown had built Macdonough's fleet, now powerful enough to reclaim control of Lake Champlain.

The British learned of the shipbuilding enterprise up Otter Creek. Anticipating a British raid to close off the creek by sinking ships laden with rock, Macdonough mounted a battery at its mouth. Garrisoned by engineers and gunners rushed from Burlington, he armed Fort Cassin with seven 12-pounders and mounted them on ship's carriages just in time. In early April Pring sailed from Isle aux Noix on the maiden voyage of the twenty-gun brig *Linnet*, the largest ship on the lake, escorted by six sloops and ten galleys filled with troops. On April 14 he bombarded Fort Cassin, dismounting one American gun and slightly wounding two men. But the American gunners gave the British ships such a pounding for an hour and a half that, unwilling to risk coming any closer, Pring sailed away. Fort Cassin and its gunners saved Macdonough's embryonic navy.

On May 26, 1814, Macdonough sailed the *Saratoga* out onto the broad lake at the lead of a fleet of five ships and six gunboats, intent on breaking up large-scale smuggling on the lake. Macdonough and other American commanders had long expressed frustration in their attempts to interdict blatant, well-organized cross-border smuggling. When Zebulon Pike was in command at Plattsburgh, he described citizens and soldiers along the border as "void of all sense of honor or love of country." Macdonough fulminated at the covert collusion of a people he was attempting to protect from the enemy as they unabashedly provided vital military information: "The turpitude of many of our citizens in this part of the country furnishes the Enemy with every information he wants." As historian Peter Andreas puts it, "Nowhere was [smuggling] more apparent than in the U.S.-Canada borderlands, where Americans proved more enthused about illicitly trading with their northern neighbors than conquering them. This diverted scarce supplies to the enemy, increased the costs of feeding U.S. soldiers, and undermined popular support for the war." With only sixteen customs officials in all of upstate New York, revenue agents faced armed smugglers who either avoided or overpowered them, sometimes even robbing them of duties they had collected.

Even when customs collectors, with the aid of customhouse spies, succeeded in seizing contraband, the smugglers could afford to lose half their shipments and still "make money faster than those who follow the 'dull pursuits' of regular business," as one agent wrote to the Salem Gazette in the autumn of 1814.[4] British purchasing agents paid an above-market ten to twelve dollars per hundredweight for beef on the hoof driven north from downstate New York and from all over Vermont and New Hampshire. Customs collector Sailly at Plattsburgh helplessly observed, "I foresee that all the cattle of Vermont and eastwardly will find their way to Canada, and I fear our own troops hereafter may suffer from want of meat." The extent of the illicit trafficking astounded at least one British officer. "Self, the great ruling principle," Lieutenant Napier wrote in his journal in May 1814, "[is] more powerful with Yankees than any people I ever saw."

An exasperated Izard had complained,

On the eastern side of Lake Champlain, the high roads are found insufficient for the supplies of cattle which are pouring into Canada. Like herds of buffaloes, they press through the forest, making paths for themselves. . . . Nothing but a cordon of troops, from the French Mills [in northern New York] to Lake Memphramagog [straddling the Vermont-Canada border] could effectively check the evil. Were it not for these supplies, the British forces in Canada would soon be suffering from famine, or their government be subjected to enormous expense for their maintenance.[5]

Building on trade routes and networks they had developed during Jefferson's embargo, smugglers on both shores of Lake Champlain came even to influence British policy. Preparing to invade the Champlain valley, Prevost wrote,

Because of Vermont's decided opposition to the war, and very large supplies of the specie daily coming in from thence, as well as the whole of the cattle required for the use of the troops, I mean for the present to confine myself in any offensive operations which may take place to the Western side of Lake Champlain.

Prevost wrote to his superiors in London that he would not need more funding to feed his armies. Abundant wheat was flowing from Maine to New Brunswick, and "two-thirds of the army in Canada are at this moment eating beef provided by the American contractors, drawn principally from the States of Vermont and New York."[6]

IN LATE AUGUST General Macomb learned from Eleazer Williams and his Corps of Observation that the British intended to attack Plattsburgh, not Sackets Harbor, as had been assumed. Macomb buttressed defensive works south of Plattsburgh village on a high bluff where the Saranac River emptied into Lake Champlain. With water protecting three flanks, he laid out three forts (Brown, Moreau and Scott) in a straight line across the narrow peninsula with two blockhouses to protect the open, landward end of their positions. Each strongpoint sat behind high earthen fortifications graded so that the British would have to approach them from the north, up steep ascents protected by thick abatis. Cannon capable of firing forty-two-pound shells, dragged up by teams of oxen, strengthened the strongpoints' approaches. Macomb chose several hundred men to harass the British advance by burning bridges and felling trees. In three rainy days, he moved 720 sick men a mile and a half offshore to Crab Island and posted a six-pounder cannon for their defense.

Answering Macomb's call for volunteers, 2,200 Vermonters and 700 New Yorkers quick-marched to Plattsburgh. All over Vermont, even as, once again, the state's governor refused to give a direct order for the militia to fight outside its borders, men volunteered. At Middlebury, two hundred men stayed up all night in a lawyer's office molding cartridges; in St. Albans, eighty men commandeered small boats to ferry them to the New York shore. The call reached Montpelier, in central Vermont, as news arrived of the burning of Washington. An aged Revolutionary War veteran, Captain Timothy Hubbard, took to the streets, cane in hand. He rounded up a drummer and a fifer to march at his side. They crisscrossed the town, imploring men to march with them to Plattsburgh. By day's end, Hubbard had enlisted two-thirds of the town's eligible men. Stepping off the next morning with their muskets, blankets and cookpots for the forty-mile march to Burlington to be ferried across Lake Champlain, they took their places in the trenches at Plattsburgh just in time for the British onslaught.

ON SEPTEMBER 1, 1814, one week after the torching of the nation's capital and two days after most of the Plattsburgh garrison marched off to Sackets Harbor, the largest British Army to invade the United States since 1776 crossed the New York border. Prevost, in overall command, arrived the next day with the rest of his army of 9,067 veterans. He planned a joint army-navy attack, his immediate objectives being the American base at Plattsburgh and the shipbuilding center at Vergennes. For success, he needed complete control of the lake, and he predicated his ground campaign on a swift naval victory that would guarantee the safety and supply of his land forces. He detached Major General Thomas Macdougall Brisbane and 3,500 regulars to pin down Macomb's force of 1,900 at the Saranac. Major General Frederick Robinson, son of New York Loyalist colonel Beverley Robinson—the go-between in the Benedict Arnold–John André conspiracy in the Revolutionary War—was to cross the Saranac a few miles upstream with 2,500 men, followed by Major General Manley Power's brigade of 3,500 men. As Robinson turned the American left flank and rolled it up, Brisbane was to assail the American center. All three generals had fought under Wellington on the Iberian Peninsula.

Issuing a proclamation to American citizens, Prevost promised to restrain looting and extend "kind usage and generous treatment" to "peaceable and unoffending inhabitants," yet his arrival set off a panic in the Champlain valley. In Plattsburgh, Dr. William Beaumont wrote,

> The people are all frighten'd nearly out—out, did I say? rather into their wits—if they have any—moving everything off—under the expectation that all will be burnt or destroyed—poor souls, many of them, love & uphold the British—censure & condemn our own Government—complaining they have no protection—neither will they take up arms to defend themselves. . . .[7]

In actuality, Macomb had already ordered the elderly, women and children to be evacuated.

On September 6 a British advance guard halted just north of Plattsburgh. Macomb had ordered the planks removed from all bridges across the Saranac. Macdonough's anchored gunboats shelled the British along the shore as Major John Wool and 250 men, including many fifteen-year-olds, ambushed the inland British flanking force, which got lost trying to find a suitable ford. The English suffered two hundred casualties even before the battle began. Pausing for several more days, the cautious Prevost waited for his fleet to arrive from Isle aux Noix.

After years of protesting that he would not take up a "carnal weapon" and fight, Eleazer Williams, leaving his base at Charlotte on the Vermont shore, relented and accepted a musket. In what may have been his most valuable service, he proposed a ruse to Macomb. He crossed to Burlington and obtained a letter from Colonel Elias Fassett declaring that Governor Chittenden was marching toward St. Albans with 10,000 men, while 5,000 more were on the march from the west and another 5,000 from central Vermont. Williams then arranged for the letter to fall into British hands.

But Prevost thought that he had already won the battle for permanent naval superiority of Lake Champlain, thanks to the newly built 1,200-ton,

37-gun British frigate *Confiance*. A square-rigged, three-masted warship with much thicker timbers than Macdonough's *Saratoga*, it was the largest vessel ever to sail on Lake Champlain. But the *Confiance* was not ready: it was still moored at Isle aux Noix, lacking basic equipment. At this unpropitious moment, the Royal Navy commander of the lakes, Commodore Yeo, replaced the experienced Pring with Captain George Downie, who was entirely unfamiliar with Lake Champlain or the ships under construction there.

The substitution of Downie for Pring and the consequent delay infuriated Prevost: though the navy had an entire summer to prepare, Prevost found himself inside the United States without naval support. He bombarded Downie with daily proddings. Downie could only sputter in reply that he couldn't find gunlocks anywhere and that captain and crew, many of them untrained soldiers unfamiliar with the ship, did not know each other or their officers and had no time for gunnery drills.

On September 1, as the British expeditionary force crossed the frontier, Commodore Macdonough guided his squadron into Cumberland Bay near Plattsburgh and anchored his ships two miles from shore, out of range of British artillery. Aboard the *Saratoga*, pilot Joseph Barron Jr. knew that the British would wait to run before the prevailing north wind, against the strong northward current of the lake. He recommended that Macdonough anchor inside the bay where it was two miles wide, midway between the town of Plattsburgh and Cumberland Head. Barron knew that the British ships would have difficulty maneuvering against the wind in such a confined space. Also, by avoiding the open lake where British long guns would have a distinct advantage, Macdonough could exploit his superiority in shorter-range carronades that fired heavier shells.

Macdonough did as Barron recommended. He anchored his ships inside the bay in a line running northeast to southwest, with *Eagle* at the northern end of the line, behind *Saratoga*, then *Ticonderoga* and *Preble*. *Eagle* lined up with the mouth of the Saranac; *Preble* lay a mile and a half north of Crab Island. Forming a double line, Macdonough's six galleys and four gunboats posted in twos and threes, forty yards west of the larger ships. Aboard *Saratoga*, Macdonough's sailing master attached spring cables, hawsers running the length of the ship to the stern, where he dropped smaller, lighter kedge anchors. By cutting the bowline and hauling on the spring anchor line, the vessel could be pivoted to present unused guns to batter an enemy ship with broadsides after the enemy's guns became disabled.

Nearly a week later, on September 7 Downie and the British squadron finally set sail from Canada—and *Confiance* immediately ran aground in the Richelieu River. Freed on the eighth, she entered the broad lake on the ninth. Downie commanded sixteen ships: the thirty-seven-gun *Confiance*, the eleven-gun *Finch*, the sixteen-gun *Linnet*, the eleven-gun *Chubb* and twelve gunboats. That night Downie's gun crews had their first drill—scouring the gun barrels by firing without shot—as British army and navy officers sat down to a sumptuous dinner served on fine linen at Prevost's headquarters at Chazy, New York. At dawn on the eleventh, the British squadron finally rounded Cumberland Head. With more ships, more men and more long-range cannons, Downie had intended to cruise out of American range and splinter their ships, challenging Macdonough to come out and fight in open waters. But Macdonough refused. By remaining at anchor, with his sails reefed, Macdonough claimed another advantage: he stayed immune to the vagaries of the wind.

It was Downie who took Macdonough's challenge. He decided to engage the Americans at close range. With all the confidence of his flagship's name, Downie steered his flotilla into the bay at 9 o'clock the morning of September 11, as Americans crowded the shores to watch and Canadian spectators bobbed nearby in small boats. Stepping off his ship at Cumberland Head, Downie reconnoitered Macdonough's fleet in a small boat. He planned to turn at the head of the American line, raking it with broadsides and sailing *Confiance* between *Saratoga* and *Ticonderoga*. Suddenly, the wind shifted to northeast. Downie found himself unable to maneuver easily. Immediately coming under heavy fire from *Saratoga*, *Confiance* signaled to drop anchors four hundred yards from it and *Ticonderoga*; *Linnet* and *Chubb* fell into line to confront *Eagle*.

Eagle's gunners quickly shredded *Chubb*'s sails and rigging, leaving it badly damaged and drifting through the American line until it surrendered. *Preble* mauled *Finch* so badly that it drifted onto a reef off Crab Island, where Macomb's invalid men, firing their six-pounder, forced it to strike its colors. On the eastern end of the line, *Preble*, badly damaged, left the American line and sailed toward shore, leaving *Ticonderoga* to face four gunboats and ward off their boarding parties. As British marines began clambering aboard, *Ticonderoga* was at a serious disadvantage: it had been fitted with the wrong gunlocks. But sixteen-year-old midshipman Hiram Paulding—whose father had found Benedict Arnold's treason plans in John André's boot—ran from gun to gun, firing his pistol into the priming hole. At the northern end of the line, *Eagle* suffered severe fire from both *Linnet* and *Confiance*. *Eagle*'s commander ordered the anchor cable cut, allowing the ship to drift on the current astern of the *Saratoga*, where it anchored again and poured fire into the *Confiance*.

Only fifteen minutes into the battle, Downie was standing behind one of his guns when it took a direct hit from the *Saratoga*. The heavy gun flew back and killed him. Macdonough, too, was knocked down twice—the first time by a piece of spanker boom while sighting a gun. (That task was ordinarily undertaken by a lieutenant, but *Saratoga*'s had been killed, one of forty men struck down by *Confiance*'s first broadside.) Pilot Barron, standing behind Macdonough, was killed by a cannonball. Macdonough was knocked down a second time by the head of a decapitated soldier.

Hot shot from the *Confiance* twice set *Saratoga* afire before its marines, many of them now replacing dead gunners, could staunch the flames. All but one of *Saratoga*'s starboard guns were knocked out of action, while only four of *Confiance*'s remained intact. Macdonough gave the order to cut the bow anchor cable and man the capstan. Under murderous fire, the few unwounded men hauled on the capstan, taking up the slack of the spring cables to the kedge anchors astern, slowly swinging *Saratoga* around until its undamaged port guns could bear on the crippled *Confiance*. When the British crew attempted to imitate Macdonough's innovative maneuver, *Confiance* became stuck perpendicular to the *Saratoga*, which raked the British ship's gun deck from bow to stern. By now *Confiance* had taken 105 rounds through its hull—nearly double that of *Saratoga*—and was heeling hard to port, fast filling with water that threatened to drown scores of wounded belowdecks.

At 11 o'clock, after two bruising hours of battle, the battered British flagship struck its colors. Aboard *Linnet*, Pring fought through twenty minutes more of broadsides from the *Saratoga* and the *Ticonderoga* until his surviving crewmen refused to man their guns any longer.

In two hours and twenty minutes, the British lost a devastating 194 of their 1,050 officers and crew, the American casualties only 52 killed and another 58 wounded of a force of 850. Julius Hubbell, a magistrate who witnessed the battle from Cumberland Head, remembered that "the firing was terrific, fairly shaking the ground along the shore, and so rapid that it seemed to be one continuous roar, intermingled with spiteful flashing from the mouths of the guns, and dense clouds of smoke soon hung over the two fleets."

When the smoke dissipated, Pring and the captains of the three other British warships came under guard to surrender their swords to Macdonough, who refused them. Before dark, he dashed off a message to Secretary of the Navy Jones: "The Almighty has been pleased to grant us a signal victory on Lake Champlain, in the capture of one frigate, one brig and two sloops of war of the enemy." He was still unaware that he had won a decisive victory.[8]

As soon as the battle on the lake had begun that morning, British land batteries, expecting the order from Prevost for a general assault, unleashed a massive bombardment that knocked out one of the American blockhouses. But Prevost's order didn't come until the next morning. With instructions from London not to overextend or expose his forces, Prevost decided that, without naval support, he was entirely justified in ordering an immediate retreat to Canada.

Two days later, Admiral Cochrane abandoned the British invasion of the Chesapeake after failing to subdue Baltimore and heavily defended Fort McHenry. In the same week, General Drummond left Fort Erie after a six-week siege, proclaiming himself victorious and leaving its battered hulk to the Americans. In just ten days, the entire British offensive in America had collapsed. When the Duke of Wellington learned of the debacle on Lake Champlain, he persuaded the British Ministry to sign a peace treaty. British lieutenant colonel John Murray, who had sacked Plattsburgh a year earlier, wrote in admiration, "This is a proud day for America—the proudest day she ever saw."

Overnight, Macdonough moved "from a poor lieutenant," as he later wrote, to a captain and a rich man, thanks to his $22,000 in prize money from the auctioning of the British fleet. He also earned a congressional gold medal—and a place in history. Over the months and years, appreciation of the significance of his bravery and his ingenuity would continue to grow.

Receiving unaccustomed good news amid Washington's ruins, Navy secretary Jones proclaimed that Macdonough's victory was "not surpassed by any naval victory on record." The naval historian Alfred Thayer Mahan, himself an admiral, in his epic *Sea Power in Its Relations to the War of 1812*, went nearly as far. "The battle of Lake Champlain, more nearly than any other incident of the war of 1812, merits the epithet 'decisive.'" In 1904 Assistant Secretary of the Navy Charles H. Darling noted, "Macdonough alone among all American commanders is distinguished in having commanded the only smaller fleet that ever defeated a larger one." His predecessor in the office, later president Theodore Roosevelt, trimmed Oliver Hazard Perry's sails while topping off Macdonough's: "It will always be a source of surprise that the American public should have so glorified Perry's victory over an inferior force, and have paid comparatively little attention to Macdonough's victory, which really won against decided odds in ships, men, and metal. . . . Down to the time of the Civil War he is the greatest figure in our naval history." Yet the ultimate historical judgment may have been rendered by Sir Winston Churchill. In his magisterial *History of the English-Speaking Peoples*, the former First Lord of the Admiralty unqualifiedly pronounced the Battle of Lake Champlain as "the most decisive engagement of the War of 1812."[9]

When news of the American victory and the British retreat reached Paris, crowds in the gardens of the Palais Royale erupted in cheers. In London, the *Morning Chronicle* greeted the news with "a sense of horror and indignation." In Parliament, opposition leader Samuel Whitbread condemned Cockburn and Ross for an act even "the Goths refused to do at Rome," their conduct "detested and abhorred by all who respected the character of this country and the civil rights of the world." He likened Washington to the imperial capital where the Visigoths had decided "to preserve works of elevated art" as "an act of wisdom" while "to destroy them was to erect a monument to the folly of the destroyer." Apart from "sullying the British name," the British commanders had accomplished nothing.[10]

SLOW COMMUNICATION CONTINUED to dog the peace negotiations. It took five weeks for Adams to learn of the destruction of Washington. In the intervening month, the British were able to send communications to their foreign secretary, convene cabinet meetings and return answers. Adams had become convinced that the British were stalling. After six weeks without a joint meeting, Adams complained to Louisa in St. Petersburg, "It appears to me to be the policy of the British government to keep the war as an object to continue or close, according to the events which may occur in Europe or America. If so they will neither make peace, nor break off the negotiations."[11]

The weeks of waiting for news from America had strained relations among the American emissaries. At 3:45 a.m. on September 8 Adams complained to his diary, "Just before rising, I heard Mr. Clay's company retiring from his chamber. I had left him with Mr. Russell, Mr. Bentzon and Mr. Todd at cards. They parted as I was about to rise." Russell, Adrian Bentzon (son-in-law of John Jacob Astor) and John Todd—extending his stepfather's load of debt—frequently played cards, smoked cigars and drank wine nearly until dawn, adding to the corkage fees that the pinch-penny Adams had negotiated with the landlord. Two weeks later Adams was sufficiently annoyed to log, "Another card party in Mr. Clay's chamber last night, and I heard Mr. Bentzon retiring from it after I had risen this morning." Devastating news from home still had not arrived by September 29 when Todd threw a lavish ball in the mission's courtyard. Invitations had gone out to 150 guests; 130 came, but "none of the British Legation." Adams recorded,

> All the principal noblesse and merchants of the city were here. The company began to assemble between seven and eight o'clock. At eleven we had supper; after which the dancing recommenced, and the party broke up just before three in the morning. I played whist with the Intendant's lady, Madame Borlut de Lens, the Mayor's sister, and Prince d'Aremberg, the Commander-in-chief of all the Belgian troops. I danced part of a Boulangere.
>
> Our garden was illuminated with the variegated colored lamps, and there was an inscription of eight poor French verses over the central gate . . .[12]

Apart from infrequent dispatches from Washington, the legation received its news from the *London Times*. From its pages they learned of the sack of Washington. On October 14 Adams read in the editions for the tenth and eleventh that the British had taken Machias, Maine and other towns around Passamaquoddy Bay and of "the taking of Plattsburg by the British Canadian Army."

It would be weeks more before the American diplomats learned that the news from America was also unsettling the British administration. At first denying the battlefield reports, the Cabinet pointed to the increased effectiveness of the British blockade. Appointing Sir Edward Pakenham, brother-in-law of Wellington, to replace Ross, they pressed ahead with preparations to attack New Orleans. Bathurst, secretary for war and the colonies, wrote to Henry Goulburn in Ghent that there was no change in the Ministry's diplomatic posture. Even though Prevost had failed in his objectives to hold Plattsburgh and wipe out the American naval base at Vergennes, the treaty must be based on the doctrine of *uti possidetis*, keeping territory already taken.

Bathurst was not being completely candid. Public resistance in Britain was mounting over the staggering tax load to cover war expenses. Drawing the sharpest criticism of the Ministry's policy were the special wartime income tax and the hated land tax, which exacted from the landed classes, according to the British social historian Lawrence Stone, one-fourth of the assessed value of land every year that the fighting dragged on. In only two years the navy's payroll had exploded from 145,000 men to 207,000. To the cost of blockading the entire American and European seacoasts had been added the cost of providing escort vessels for merchant ships forced to sail in convoys to ward off attacks by some 1,800 American privateers.

From Paris where he was serving as the British ambassador, Lord Wellington reported crowds cheering American victories while spitting on the restored King Louis XVIII and clamoring for the return of Napoleon from exile on Elba. Lord Liverpool, writing to Wellington and to foreign secretary Lord Castlereagh in Vienna, fretted about the czar, "half an American," openly sympathetic toward them and refusing to remove his armies from Poland. Liverpool feared Alexander would ally himself with the United States and continue the war. After reading dispatches from Lake Champlain and Baltimore at an emergency cabinet meeting on October 1, Liverpool wrote to Castlereagh of the government's "anxious desire to put an end to the war." He felt "too strongly the inconvenience of a continuance not to make me desirous of concluding it at the expense of some popularity."[13]

Liverpool sent off to Ghent a drastically reduced peace proposal. On October 8 the secretary of the British legation interrupted the Americans' dinner. The Privy Council, jettisoning their assurances to safeguard the interest of their Indian allies, had decided to scrap their insistence on a buffer zone between the United States and Canada, on demilitarizing the Great Lakes and on holding occupied Maine: they would settle instead for a corridor to ease communications between Halifax and Quebec Province.

As if from habit, Adams was suspicious. Goulburn had clothed the Ministry's concession in his customary huffy rhetoric. The tone of the British note was "arrogant, overbearing and offensive." All the years of enduring British condescension welled up in him. He raged at accepting the Privy Council's ultimatum on the Indians, insisting on trading insult for insult. He exhumed Monroe's ultimatum that, unless the British ceded all of Canada, the peace commissioners were to break off talks and come home. Gallatin and Clay tried to calm him down, but only when Bayard uncorked a bottle of Chambertin did Adams's temperature abate. He still believed that the British were stalling. Their mention of *uti possidetis* proved that, despite their military failures at Baltimore and Plattsburgh, they still intended to seize more territory to buttress their negotiating position. For five days Adams, Clay and Gallatin worked over an answer. On October 24 they had one, gathering in Clay's room to sign it. They rejected the British call for *uti possidetis*, again stating that they were not authorized to cede any territory.[14]

Incredulous, Goulburn dashed off a letter to the Ministry. Did London want the talks to go on? A courier sped to London, carrying both the American response to the British and Goulburn's query. Studying the documents at Fife House, Liverpool wondered whether the Americans were fully rational. He wrote to Castlereagh in Vienna that the war "will probably now be of some duration." He feared that some of Britain's allies were not "indisposed" to helping the United States. Lord Walpole had warned that "a most powerful party" in Russia would support any intervention by the czar. Liverpool wrote to Wellington in Paris of the Americans'

"extravagant doctrines . . . they would never cede any part of their domin-
ions, even though they should have been conquered."

Liverpool realized that to prolong the American war would necessitate
floating a new loan over the objection in Parliament that the propertied
class was being forced to pay for extending the Canadian frontier. All
he could do was to "hope to gain a little more time" before the negotiations collapsed, he wrote to Goulburn, at least until after the King's Speech
at the opening of Parliament on November 8.[15]

Liverpool was not alone in worrying about the cost of the war dragging
on. Early in November 1814 the United States defaulted on its loans. The
Treasury was empty. Smugglers, after all, didn't pay customs duties, still
the principal source of government revenue. Between April and October,
only eighteen customs-paying ships from neutral nations eluded British
blockaders and reached American customs houses.

The cash-strapped government's critical shortage of cash was proving
embarrassing. Congress refused to compensate Joshua Barney's unpaid
flotilla men for the clothing they lost in action. The secretary of the Navy
told one of his purchasing agents to drag his feet for sixty to ninety days
before paying any bills, and then only to accept U.S. Treasury notes as payment. The Treasury experimented with $100 bonds, but few would invest
in them. With much of the nation's supply of silver and gold smuggled out
of the country to Canadian and English banks, the government even resorted to issuing $3 notes as a substitute for hard money.

In some states these notes would not "pass," as the shipbuilding Brown
brothers, who had employed more than 1,000 men to build the navies
on Lake Ontario and Lake Champlain, complained. Threatening to abandon their contracts unless they received $200,000 in specie, they protested
that they would be ruined if they accepted the heavily discounted U.S.
government notes. But probably the greatest embarrassment occurred in
Maryland. The government's bill of exchange to purchase copper to strike
pennies was "protested and returned unpaid." The U.S. Mint ran out of
copper in 1814 and could mint no more of the most commonly used coin.
There was no 1815 penny.

Despite the good news arriving from Baltimore and Lake Champlain,
the effects of the British blockade caused one Federalist to lament to the
Massachusetts legislature, "We are in a deplorable situation, our com-

merce dead; our revenue Gone; our ships rotting at the wharves. . . . Our Treasury drained—we are Bankrupts."

With America unable to borrow money at home, its emissaries in Europe asked for help. Crawford wrote from Paris that he could not obtain another loan from the French government and, despite Gallatin's strong connections, Willink Brothers in Amsterdam rejected his request for a $10 million loan as well. At this inauspicious moment, Adams received word from London that the legation's account with Baring Brothers & Co. was overdrawn by an astonishing $200,000.[16]

ON THE SAME day that Liverpool had brooded over American intransigence, he received two letters from the Duke of Wellington. "You can get no territory," the duke stated flatly; "indeed the state of your military operations, however creditable, does not entitle you to demand any; and you only afford the Americans a popular and creditable ground which, I believe, their government are looking for, not to break off negotiations but to avoid to make peace." Liverpool had been pressuring Wellington to take over command of British forces in America. If the cabinet insisted, he would go the next year "but I would do you but little good." But then Wellington had reconsidered: he was still needed in Europe. Especially if revolution broke out again or if the Allies divided at Vienna, he had to remain in Europe. And too many good generals had already been killed in the American war, which to him was only a sideshow. "I must not die."[17]

ON OCTOBER 31 Anthony St. John Baker, secretary to the British legation, arrived at the American mission with a packet stating that the British would have nothing more to say. Unless the Americans accepted their terms or proposed terms of their own, the war would continue. For the first time, the Americans could put forth an agenda. Most of the original issues were already off the table: impressment, neutral rights, indemnities for seized ships and cargoes. The negotiations had come down to British refusal to honor American cod-drying rights off the Canadian Maritimes and free passage of British ships on the Mississippi, both assured by the Treaty of Paris of 1783.

Britain sought to barter access to the Mississippi and its markets for the right to dry cod onshore in New Brunswick and Nova Scotia. Adams's father had once deadlocked negotiations for American independence until New England's mainstay fishing industry was protected. Henry Clay, leader of the War Hawks whose constituents had contributed the most troops to the conflict, now fulminated about British ships on western waters, paced and cursed at the notion of swapping the Mississippi for "drying fish." The British also insisted on holding captured Moose Island, between Maine and New Brunswick. Quincy Adams objected to giving up any American territory whatsoever. Bayard favored giving up the island.

"Mr. Bayard," Adams asked, "If it belonged to Delaware, would you?"[18]

Bayard laughed and replied that Delaware could not afford to give up any territory.

Gallatin worried that his fellow commissioners would sacrifice the interests of New England. Already the Massachusetts General Court had called a convention of all the New England states to be held at Hartford on December 15 to consider forming a New England confederacy, seceding from the United States and negotiating a separate peace. He supported Adams's contention that the fisheries were "of great importance in the sentiment of the eastern section of the Union." If they signed a treaty without restoring prewar rights or abandoning any New England territory, Gallatin argued, "It would give a handle to the party there now pushing for a separation from the Union."[19]

There was one treaty clause over which there seemed to be no disagreement. Prisoners of war were to be released and repatriated. More than 21,000 luckless American privateersmen had been captured by the British, more than 5,000 of them incarcerated at Dartmoor Prison in western England in a vast, dank, pestiferous dungeon where hundreds had died of smallpox, pneumonia and floggings.

By November 10, the American delegates, aware that their continued silence could be regarded as tacit acceptance of British terms, were still divided. Adams had just received a dispatch from Monroe authorizing the commission to make the status quo antebellum the basis of the treaty. In an impassioned speech Adams suggested that they set aside their sectional disagreements, ignore British demands and propose a peace treaty based on this principle—to return to an America before there was a war and to resolve all the thorny unsettled questions like boundary lines and fishing rights and sailing privileges by forming separate commissions to negotiate them in a reasonable time after the war ended. Finally Adams declared that he would "cheerfully give [my] life for peace on this basis."

He predicted that the British would reject the proposal, but if they did and the talks collapsed, it would make American demands seem less extravagant. Gallatin cheered Adams on, and, as usual, Bayard followed Gallatin's lead. Russell demanded to know why they should set aside the proposal they had been hammering out piecemeal for weeks. Adams countered that they should set aside all the "knots of the negotiations for solutions now" and "make peace first."[20]

Unmoved, Clay stunned his compatriots by suggesting that the war should go on for another three years. "Three years more of war would make us a warlike people, and that then we should come out of the war with honor." He argued that now the United States had "only a half-formed army"—and a proportionate reputation. He suggested playing "brag" with the British emissaries. They had been playing "brag" throughout the negotiations, "and he thought it was time for us to begin to play 'brag' with them. He said the art of it was to beat your adversary by holding your hand with a solemn and confident [face] and outbragging him."

"Ay," retorted Bayard, "but you may lose the game by bragging until the adversary sees the weakness of your hand. Mr. Clay is for bragging a million against a cent."[21]

Yet Clay finally agreed to decide later whether he would sign the actual treaty. That night, the Americans sent their sixth diplomatic note in two months to the British legation. As they waited for a reply, the cautious Adams confided to Louisa that the British

[h]ave withdrawn just so much of their inadmissible demands as would avoid the immediate rupture of the negotiation. They have varied their terms . . . abandoned the claims which they had declared indispensable preliminaries, only to bring them forward again whenever the circumstances of the war might encourage them to insolence and . . . are now delaying their reply to our last note . . . only to receive accounts of success from America . . . to dictate new terms to us.[22]

The American proposal and the British delegation's answer arrived at Fife House in London just as the local newspapers for November 18 reprinted a shocking article carried in the American press. Against all diplomatic protocol, President Madison had published all of the British delegation's demands and all the documents and exchanges of notes of the peace conference through the end of August. The American newspapers reported that the disclosures had enraged the American people, uniting them more than they had been for many years. The House of Representatives had ordered the printing of 10,000 copies and was circulating them throughout Europe. Liverpool could only sputter that Madison had behaved "most scandalously." While publication in London appalled the English public, the Whig opposition party in Parliament delightedly declared that the cabinet's sub rosa demands were preposterous.

The latest American note arrived in London just as Wellington wrote the Cabinet of continued unrest in France. A peace treaty "might as well be signed now."[23]

After another emergency meeting of the Privy Council, Liverpool dispatched the council's decision to Castlereagh in Vienna:

> We have determined if all other points can be satisfactorily settled, not to continue the war for the purpose of obtaining or securing any acquisition of territory. We have been led to this determination by the consideration of the unsatisfactory state of the negotiations at Vienna, and by that of the alarming situation of the interior of France. We have also been obliged to pay serious attention to the state of our finances. . . . Under such circumstances, it has appeared to us desirable to bring the American war if possible to a conclusion.[24]

At noon on December 1, for the first joint meeting since August 19, the Americans drove to the Hôtel des Pays-Bas. Lord Gambier, the armchair admiral heading the delegation, was resplendent as usual in his gold braid and dress sword. Unusually effusive, he obviously was relieved that the Americans had not broken off the talks.

For three hours the delegates sat across from each other at a great oval table and, as servants stoked the fire, debated the articles one by one, threshing the verbiage until the chaff was gone and the kernels of disputes isolated. Moose Island called for a commission after peace was restored. The commissions would be composed of one representative from each nation with "a friendly sovereign" as a mediator. The length of time to elapse between ratification by each government and the end of hostilities, proposed by the British, received unanimous American consent. But the question of British access to the Mississippi triggered hours of acrimonious debate that left both sides uncertain of the outcome or of the intentions of the British Ministry. Adams left the session frustrated that he had been dueling with "an adversary who, after demanding empires as an indispensable preliminary, falls to playing pushpins to straws."[25]

In London, Bathurst studied the record of the session and wrote back quickly to Goulburn, "You have managed very well to bring the business so near to a conclusion." He instructed the emissary to seek "fair equivalents" for concessions—fishing rights for Mississippi sailing rights, for example. The British delegation was to do its "utmost" on the questions of Passamaquoddy Island and indemnification for seized American property and was to submit an article "for the more effective Abolition of the Slave Trade." But Goulburn must understand that Parliament was about to reconvene. "We are anxious as ever to bring the Treaty to a conclusion." Opposition leaders in Parliament were petitioning against the income tax—"and we have difficulty in keeping the Manufacturers particularly in Birmingham quiet," as they "clamored for a restoration of trade with the United States.[26] One day after their new instructions arrived from London, the British summoned the Americans to a Saturday afternoon meeting. Only after hours of combative debate did Adams reveal that the cabinet considered it hopeless to expect the Americans to yield on either sticking points—Mississippi or fishing rights—but that there must be fair equivalents of exchange. Contrary to Bathurst's expectations, the Americans also balked at a slave trade proposal as an intrusion on their sovereignty.

When they reconvened the next day for two hours, this time the Americans were united. Clay surprised his colleagues by insisting that the refusal of the British to vacate islands they had only recently seized violated the doctrine of status quo pro ante. For two more days the talks remained acrimonious until Admiral Gambier suggested that the Americans prepare an ultimatum that the British could either accept or reject.

The next day, when Adams received the latest written British response, he discovered to his amazement that the British had relented on all the impediments, relegating the remaining points of contention to peacetime commissions. The American version of the treaty had been accepted with few changes.

Ultimately, the treaty stipulated that peace would bring a return to the status quo antebellum if both parties ratified the document within four months. Meanwhile, there would be no armistice, and the fighting could continue. After ratification, all places and property, public and private, would be restored to their prewar status. All POWs would be repatriated as soon as they repaid any debts. All unresolved issues would be mediated by postwar commissions composed of one representative of each nation with a friendly sovereign as mediator. Boundary disputes, including the question of Moose Island, would be mediated. The Canadian-American border would be provisionally extended from the southwest corner of the Lake of the Woods in present-day Western Ontario, along the forty-ninth parallel to the "Stony Mountains"—the Rockies. Both nations were to restrain their Indian populations from further cross-border hostilities. With the treaty, the Indians became the greatest casualties of the war, with any hint of an Indian reserve gone.

Russell immediately proposed that the state of the negotiations be kept secret.

For weeks Bentzon, Astor's son-in-law, with no official function, had hovered around the legation, accompanying delegates to social engagements. Adhering to Gallatin especially, he was trying to glean information that might give his father-in-law some speculative advantage. Before going off to London the day after the agreement, he called on Adams at eight in the morning:

> Bentzon . . . was as inquisitive about the state of the negotiations as he could indirectly be. With Mr. Gallatin he was more direct . . . [Astor] had before the war made a settlement [Astoria] at the mouth of the Columbia River. A British ship of war, the <u>Raccoon</u>, has, during the war, broken it up. Bentzon stated . . . that Astor had a ship [undoubtedly the *Beaver*] at Canton, in China; that if peace should be made, the instant it is signed Astor intends to dispatch an order from England, without waiting for the ratification in America, to the ship at Canton to proceed immediately to Columbia River and renew the settlement there before the British will have time to anticipate him.

Bentzon suggested there was a "public interest" to the project that would justify telling him "the state of the negotiations and the prospects of peace." When neither Adams nor Gallatin would divulge the treaty terms, Bentzon left for London.[27]

ON THURSDAY, DECEMBER 22, as he waited anxiously for the draft treaty to be approved in London, Adams paced the streets of Ghent. Turning the corner toward the Lovendeghem, he saw Bayard rushing toward him, waving his arms. The British had accepted! Adams sent a courier to Bordeaux to delay the dispatch ship *Transit* so that it could carry a copy of the treaty to America. In Adams's chamber that evening Clay still raged against signing the document but when Gallatin called for a vote, Clay was outvoted. Meeting the next day at the American legation, the British produced final instructions for the treaty. On December 23 each side accommodated petty changes in wording proposed by the other. After three hours, the commissions agreed that they should meet the next day, December 24, at the Hôtel des Pays-Bas to sign the treaty.

At four o'clock in the afternoon of Christmas Eve, 1814, the five Americans climbed into their carriages, pulled up their lap robes against the chill of a gathering darkness, and rode off to the Hôtel des Pays-Bas for the last time. In the great oval hall, both delegations made small corrections. At six, as the carillon of St. Bavo's Cathedral tolled the Angelus, the eight diplomats signed the Treaty of Peace and Amity between His Britannic Majesty and the United States of America. After five months of tempestuous negotiations, Gambier and Quincy Adams exchanged the signed copies. Gambier wished that the peace would be permanent; Adams wrote in his diary, "I hoped it would be the last treaty of peace between Great Britain and the United States." At six thirty the peace commissioners of both nations climbed into their carriages and rode to a Te Deum Mass in the Gothic immensity of St. Bavo. There the choir of the St. Cecilia Society sang both nations' anthems, "Rule Brittania" and "Hail Columbia."

That evening, Adams wrote to his wife Louisa in St. Petersburg, where she was attending the birthday ball of the czar in a dress she had retailored to fit their meager budget. In his memoirs, the future president John Quincy Adams wrote, "I consider the day on which I signed [the treaty] as the happiest of my life, because it was the day on which I had my share in restoring peace to the world."[28]

By midafternoon of December 26, British legation secretary Anthony St. John Baker had reached London. Three days later the cabinet and the prince regent—the future King George IV—ratified the treaty. Clay's secretary Henry Carroll sailed for the United States with the treaty in hand aboard the sloop-of-war *Favorite* on January 2, 1815, with Baker accompanying him. They reached New York City after a stormy forty-day winter crossing of the North Atlantic. They arrived in Washington six days later, on February 17; at eleven o'clock that night, the Senate unanimously approved the treaty and Madison signed it. Shortly before midnight, Baker and Monroe exchanged ratified copies.

Madison proclaimed the nation at peace the next day. In London, the *Times* roared its disapproval: "We have retired from the combat with the stripes yet bleeding on our backs." In Vienna, at the peace conference for all Europe, Lord Apsley wrote to Bathurst in jubilation, "The news of the American peace came like a shot here." Castlereagh also was ecstatic: "It has produced the greatest possible sensation here," he wrote Lord Liverpool. "I wish you joy of being released from the millstone of an American war."[29]

As ALL EUROPE celebrated and Adams and his colleagues prepared to leave Ghent to negotiate a trade treaty with Britain in London, in Hartford, Connecticut, disgruntled Federalists would have no idea for weeks that a peace treaty had been successfully negotiated. On December 15, twenty-six delegates from Massachusetts, Connecticut, Rhode Island, New Hampshire and Vermont had assembled to discuss their opposition to the war and other objectionable policies of Madison's administration. Mainly Federalists, they were meeting in secret to protest the ruin of New England's shipping industry by the embargo and Madison's war. Among their grievances was the help given France by fighting its enemy, the British. When they parted on Christmas Day, they issued a report urging that the states be given more control over their military defenses. Among the amendments they proposed were controls on the federal government's ability to declare war or restrict trade.

Parts of New England had already effectively broken away. Historian

Donald R. Hickey found that other exposed towns also came to terms with the British. On Cape Cod, many communities paid tribute to avoid bombardment and plundering. On Block Island (part of Rhode Island) people were "in the daily habit of carrying intelligence and succour to the enemy's squadron," which prompted American officials to cut off all trade with the island.[30]

The convention's report, published as an extra edition of the Hartford *Connecticut Courant* on January 6, would be reprinted throughout the nation. In New England James Otis and Daniel Webster applauded the proceedings, in Webster's words, as "moderate, temperate & judicious." But Andrew Jackson later said that if he'd been stationed in New England, he would have arrested and court-martialed the "monarchists & Traitors."[31] Delegates were on their way to Washington to present their demands to Madison and Congress when they learned of the peace treaty—and of Andrew Jackson's great military victory at New Orleans.

EVEN AS THE peace commissioners celebrated in Ghent on Christmas Day, Lieutenant General Sir Edward Pakenham, brother-in-law of Wellington who had served on his staff in the Peninsular War, landed near New Orleans to take over command of some 7,500 veterans shipped from Bordeaux by way of Jamaica. In mid-December, after Cochrane arrived with his fleet from the Chesapeake, Pakenham decided on a land attack of New Orleans. He faced Jackson, arriving from Pensacola, which he had seized in defiance of an order by Madison. Jackson was preparing to oppose an enemy attack from the Mississippi, but Pakenham and Cochrane had decided to attack Lake Borgne, forty miles east of New Orleans, with fifty vessels carrying troops.

In Washington congressional leaders, still unaware that the peace accord had been settled, were pessimistic about the latest British invasion. New Hampshire congressman Daniel Webster wrote from Washington to his brother Ezekiel: "We hear that the British are near New Orleans. As that place is likely to become the theater of interesting operations I shall try to send you a map—I have no doubt the British will take it. . . ."[32]

Ordering a quick march to New Orleans on December 15, Jackson declared martial law in the city. Meanwhile, appearing to be disembarking his troops at a leisurely pace, Pakenham had the advance guard quick-march to an undefended point seven miles below New Orleans. Jackson countered swiftly with 5,000 troops in a night attack that interdicted the British vanguard. While the British regrouped, Jackson retreated two miles to a dry canal five miles south of the city and constructed a line of breastworks between an impassable cypress swamp and the eastern bank of the Mississippi. In a furious artillery duel on New Year's Day, Jackson outgunned the British. While the cautious Pakenham waited for reinforcements, Jackson attacked with his main force of 5,300 men on January 8.

Jackson positioned 4,500 troops, many of them expert Tennessee and Kentucky riflemen, in the shoulder-deep entrenchments. When the British, with closed ranks, pressed two frontal attacks, Jackson's riflemen and artillery cut them down with incessant, withering fire at close range. Each time the survivors retreated. The slaughter lasted only half an hour, but sharpshooters quickly picked off Pakenham and two of his generals who had insisted on riding on their chargers in their distinctive red uniforms and bicorn hats. In the two assault waves and a collateral action on the west bank of the river, 2,042 British veterans of the Iberian Peninsular campaign against Napoleon were killed, wounded or captured. Jackson lost only thirteen men killed and thirty-nine wounded. Some of the British soldiers survived only because they hid under the bodies of the dead and dying until the shooting stopped. The surviving senior British officer, General John Lambert, ordered his troops to withdraw to Cochrane's ships, which sailed away a few days later. In the greatest land battle of the war, fought sixteen days after the signing of the peace Treaty of Ghent officially ended the War of 1812, Andrew Jackson emerged as the nation's war hero.

THE WAR OF 1812, probably America's most obscure conflict, has been called "unnecessary" by Winston Churchill and "the forgotten war" by numerous historians. The view of contemporaries was quite different. To Madison's administration, bankrupt and homeless, the months preceding the Peace of Christmas Eve were arguably the most desperate time in the young nation's history. Without money, men or ideas to win the struggle, the peacetime victory of Jackson and his makeshift army bathed the nation in an afterglow that became known as the Era of Good Feeling. What had not happened seemed more important than anything achieved by the squandering of millions of dollars, the loss of 20,000 lives from combat or disease or the suffering of 20,961 naval prisoners of war. The United States had not won—nobody had won—but it had not lost, an achievement that would have been envied by Napoleon.

In fact, the War of 1812 can only be accurately described as a costly stalemate.

The monetary expense of the forty-two-month-long war was staggering, bringing the United States to the brink of economic collapse. Two months before the war's end, the United States could no longer pay the interest on its debts and defaulted on them. According to British naval records, Britain captured, burned or sank 1,407 American ships, leaving only 402 afloat by war's end. The Admiralty did not take into its accounting the profits of American privateers—which, according to U.S. Merchant Marine records, netted $45 million from the capture and sale of 1,300 British prizes—nor the 254 British vessels captured and sold by U.S. Navy warships. In the eyes of the world, the United States emerged a naval power.

Ironically, because the British blockade had bottled up almost all of the U.S. Navy's ships in port for most of the war, the American navy emerged virtually intact, capable of sailing to the Mediterranean and cowing the North African states into dropping any further demands for ransom.

Entering the war reliant entirely on undisciplined militia, by war's end the United States army was able to stand and fight the toughest professional killers in the world, Wellington's Invincibles, while being trained and led by a command structure that increasingly exhibited military professionalism. The old officers of the Revolution had been replaced by young, battle-tested leaders who trained their men in the first boot camp and who dressed them in distinctive uniforms that became the dress uniform of their proud, embryonic military academy at West Point. The United States had not succeeded in three invasions of Canada, but neither had the British succeeded in their invasion of the United States.

A new nationalism emerged immediately. "Who would not be an American?" demanded *Niles' Weekly Register*. "Long live the republic! All hail! Last asylum of oppressed humanity!" James Madison, barely escaping with his life from the flames of a burning capital, was able to tell a Senate that unanimously ratified the peace treaty of "a campaign signalized by the most brilliant successes."[33] Even John Adams congratulated Madison on a job well done. The proverbial David had, in the popular consciousness, slain Goliath.

America had a new mythology of heroes: a dying Captain Lawrence uttering, "Don't give up the ship!" and Francis Scott Key penning a national anthem, transforming a night of horror into verses sung to a tune that could best be sung as it had for centuries—after a few stiff drinks. Towering above all in the new pantheon stood Dolley Madison on the roof of the White House, trying to pick out her husband as his mere presence, however brave, undermined his confused battlefield commanders.

Out of the unintended consequences came significant changes. John Jacob Astor's employees, driven out of the first American post on the Pacific, had to find a safe route to bring his trove of pelts back to the East. The route they followed for the first time with wagons became the Oregon Trail. Commodore Macdonough, looking for a new command, became the captain of the world's first steam warship, designed by his friend Robert Fulton. The Indians who had fought and died with promises of their own vast reserve were brushed aside as the British government sought to end the war in a hurry to avoid censure from its opponents in Parliament over the high costs of continuing the war. In a stroke of the pen, the Indians were cleared out of the way for American expansion and massive immigration that would gobble up their lands. And to the north, Canadians, by learning to bury ethnic differences and fight in common to resist the American invaders, emerged as a cohesive nation that, in not too many more years, would declare its independence from the British Empire.

Most of all, the War of 1812 was a defining moment in the economic history of the nation that emerged from a half-century-long trade war as a major maritime power, a sovereign nation with worldwide commercial networks. Decades of embargoes and blockades had encouraged the development of internal industry and transportation so that the United States no longer was dependent on European policies and prices. It was not the Second American Revolution. It was the War of American Economic Independence, the last chapter of the American Revolution.

ACKNOWLEDGMENTS

In 1993, soon after my *Thomas Jefferson, A Life* appeared, I had one month before the paperback edition went to press to find and correct any errors or omissions. Reviewing microfilm generously provided by the Manuscripts Division of the New York Public Library, I discovered a diary of his travels to New England in the summer of 1791.

On a junket with his closest friend, James Madison, first secretary of state Jefferson learned over dinner in Bennington, Vermont, that the British had built a stockade on North Hero Island in Lake Champlain, well within U.S. territory. A British ship was stopping and searching American vessels carrying goods into Canada. One American craft had capsized, its crew drowning. Cutting short his tour, Jefferson dashed off a message to President Washington and hurried back to the capital at Philadelphia.

Under the 1783 Treaty of Paris that supposedly ended the American Revolution, the British had agreed to vacate their forts and trading posts around the Great Lakes and along the Canadian frontier. The building of a new fort on American soil in peacetime was my first hint that the struggle for American independence had not ended. As I researched other books, I began to discern a pattern of British refusal to acknowledge American economic independence and agency.

Reexamining notes from a 1983 visit to the Lilly Library of the University of Indiana during research for *A Little Revenge: Benjamin Franklin and His Son,* I found notes about Franklin's Loyalist son William's exile in Britain. The moment that William learned that Detroit had fallen to the British in the War of 1812, the octogenarian former royal governor dashed to the nearest American consulate to claim his share of a 20 million acre British land grant—today's Midwest—scotched by American independence. Believing he was at last rich, Governor Franklin died happy a week later. From those notes I first learned of the fall of Detroit.

Reviewing research notes from the archives of the Loyalist Museum in St. John, New Brunswick, for *Benedict Arnold, Patriot and Traitor,* I discovered that Arnold received a massive Crown land grant in Upper Canada (Ontario Province), including much of York, its provincial capital (modern-day Toronto). I soon learned of its invasion by American forces in the War of 1812, which provoked the British burning of Washington, D.C. Re-examining cartons of notes for my biographies of George Washington, Alexander Hamilton and Ethan Allen, I accumulated evidence of a continuous drumbeat of British-imposed obstructions to American trade.

I am indebted to the staffs of the Morgan Library, of Mount Vernon, the New York Public Library, the New-York Historical Society, the Rare Books division of the Firestone Library of Princeton University, the Henry Huntington Library and the Fort Ticonderoga Museum for decades of their skilled assistance as I pored over their carefully-guarded treasures. Jefferson once said, "I cannot live without books." I cannot live without librarians.

It became clear that, after drawing on my biographical research, I must attempt to assemble these shards of evidence into a new work and undertake new research into what Winston Churchill characterized as "an unofficial trade war" between Britain and America that lasted from the death of George II until the Treaty of Ghent that ended the War of 1812.

I must acknowledge the support and encouragement I received as I turned from investigative journalism to the study of the past. I especially owe thanks to the late Whitfield J. Bell, Librarian of the American Philosophical Society, to Esmond Wright at the United States Institute of United States Studies at the University of London and to Lawrence Stone, the Shelby Cullom Davis Professor at Princeton University, who encouraged me to study Tudor-Stuart and Georgian England as well as the American Revolution.

Inspired by readings given me by my visionary friend David Weissgold, I began to explore the landmarks of the War of 1812 by travelling first to the medieval Flemish city of Ghent, the unlikely site of protracted peace negotiations. It is still possible to walk in the footsteps of American negotiators John Quincy Adams and Henry Clay. The always-generous staff of the Bailey-

Howe Library at the University of Vermont prepared me by yielding up early editions of Adams's diaries and memoirs. From their pages, I could fathom the principal events of the war from both sides as reflected in the ebb and flow of negotiations.

Wars were seasonal in those days; so was my research. In summers, I retraced the three failed American invasions of Canada and the British seizure of the Penobscot region of Maine. The decisive naval battles of both the Revolutionary War and the War of 1812 took place on Lake Champlain virtually within sight of my study. My research of the war on the mountain lake built on the seminal work of the late Allan Everest of the State University of New York at Plattsburgh and of young Theodore Roosevelt. Art Cohn, founder and director emeritus of the Lake Champlain Maritime Museum, kindly gave me his publications on the construction of Commodore Thomas Macdonough's Lake Champlain flotilla built by Noah and Adam Brown of New York City. Their skilled teams built Macdonough's ships in half the contracted time, just as the same master craftsmen had built the brigs of Oliver Hazard Perry that won the Battle of Lake Erie. The travels of these shipwrights took me to Presque Isle off Erie, Pennsylvania, where I could walk around the protected bay where they laid the keels and set the cannon in a matter of weeks.

An autumn visit to the Chesapeake enabled me to document the British devastation of the region. My good friend and benefactor the late Dr. John W. Heisse Jr. had regaled me with stories of growing up in Baltimore and visiting the massive earthworks on Hampstead Hill, today's Prospect Park, and Federal Hill, the mountain made by 11,000 men and women, slave and free, as a British armada approached. His daughter, Karen Heisse, generously put aside her own research and guided me to the Maryland Historical Society's exhibits commemorating the British attack in 1814 and to the sites of General Samuel Smith's impenetrable defensive network.

In Columbia University's archives I would later find Smith's unpublished autobiography with his day-to-day notations of the city's courageous citizenry as they successfully thwarted the massive British invasion. At Fort McHenry National Historic Park, staff historian Yolanda Brown guided me through magnificent bicentennial exhibits.

At the head of the Chesapeake, I visited Havre de Grace, vengefully sacked and burned by British admiral George Cockburn, the most hated man in America. Cathy L. Visconti of the town's chamber of commerce graciously pointed us toward the town fort and the homes, the tavern and the Anglican church looted and torched by a British raiding party.

I am especially indebted to Jay Satterfield, Peter Carini and the archival staff of Rauner Rare Books Library at Dartmouth University, to the Special Collections staff of the Firestone Library at Princeton University for documents on James Madison, to Jeffrey D. Marshall, research director of the Wilbur Collection at the University of Vermont, to the archivists of the University of New Brunswick at St. John, the New York Public Library and the New-York Historical Society. The digitized archives made possible by the Public Archives of Canada, the Library of Congress, the Maryland Historical Society, the Alderman Library at the University of Virginia, the Vermont Historical Society and, most especially, the indispensable offerings of the Merchant Marine Association, underpinned my research.

Interlibrary loans facilitated timely research. I am grateful to Brenda Racht of Miller Information Commons at Champlain College for retrieving volumes from as near as Middlebury College and Norwich University and as far as England. To Tammy Poquette, head of Champlain's circulation department, I owe special thanks for extending countless return dates. Individual kindnesses included verifications by University of Vermont's retired archivist, Joseph Blow, of the location of John Jacob Astor's rendezvous with smugglers in Burlington and by Jack Swan of Willsboro, New York, of the exact path General John Burgoyne's army followed along Lake Champlain on its way to defeat at Saratoga.

My family has helped me in ways small and great. To my brother, Roger, who taught me about Revolutionary War cannon made from the bog iron of the Pine Barrens of New Jersey; to my son, Christopher, who took photos of Ft. McHenry's cannon as he jogged past during business trips. Most of all, to my ever-patient, inspiriting wife, Nancy Nahra, who knows so much about the language, the literature and the history of the centuries I write about, and to my daughter, Lucy, my publishing guide star, I owe so much.

This book would not have become possible without the masterful advice and representation of my literary agent, Don Fehr of Trident Media. He led me to a great editor and champion, Karen Wolny at St. Martin's Press, who has given me the enthusiastic support and the freedom to develop a new hypothesis on the founding decades of the American experience and the struggle for true independence. I am grateful to copy editor Ryan Mastellor for fine-tuning my sentences and especially thankful to managing editor Alan Bradshaw for his patience and diplomatic as well as editorial skills, and to editorial assistant Laura Apperson for keeping track of it all.

NOTES

PTJ   *Papers of Thomas Jefferson*

TJ   Thomas Jefferson

TJP   *Thomas Jefferson Papers*

WTJ   *Writings of Thomas Jefferson*

1. "A GLOW OF PATRIOTIC FIRE"

1. The famed 7th Regiment, today renamed the 107th New York National Guard, based in its armory at 66th and Park Avenue.
2. S. Budiansky, *Perilous Fight,* 43.
3. I. W. Toll, *Six Frigates,* 279.
4. Dewitt Clinton speech, Jan. 1807, Annals, House of Representatives, Ninth Congress, 2nd session, 386.
5. W. S. Churchill, *The Great Republic,* 109.
6. Madame de Staël to TJ, November 10, 1812, in D. R. Hickey, ed., *War of 1812: Writings,* 228.
7. TJ to Madame de Staël, May 24, 1813, in Hickey, *War of 1812: Writings,* 229–34. Emphasis in original.

2. "SALUTARY NEGLECT"

1. Quoted in T. Fleming, *Liberty,* 11.
2. Quoted in C. D. Bowen, *John Adams and the American Revolution,* 201.
3. New York City WPA Writer's Program, *Maritime History of New York,* 56.
4. L. H. Gipson, *American Loyalist,* 112–13n.
5. A. M. Schlesinger, *The Colonial Merchants and the American Revolution,* 43.
6. *Proceedings of the Rhode Island Historical Society,* as cited in P. Andreas, *Smuggler Nation,* 21.
7. *Maritime History of New York,* 59–60.
8. Quoted in T. C. Barrow, *Trade and Empire,* 162.
9. Ibid., 161–62.
10. *Correspondence of William Pitt when Secretary of State,* 2:351–55, cited in Andreas, 26.
11. Barrow, 177.
12. J. Curry, *American Constitution Experience,* 80.
13. Minutes of Massachusetts Provincial Council, Feb. 6, 1767, T. 29/38, p. 271, as cited in Barrow, 203; quoted in Bowen, 217.

3. "FORCE PREVAILS NOW EVERYWHERE"

1. W. S. Randall, "William Franklin," in R. A. East, *Loyalist Americans,* 61.
2. R. B. Morris, *Encyclopedia of American History,* 71.

3. "Hints Respecting the Settlement of our American Provinces," Add. Mss., 38355, foll. 14–18, cited in T. C. Barrow, *Trade and Empire*, 176.
4. "Report of the Board of Trade, 1772," in Smyth, *Writings of Benjamin Franklin*, 5:468.
5. Ibid., 175.
6. Barrow, 176.
7. Quoted in W. S. Randall, *George Washington*, 218.
8. Barrow, 176–77, 185.
9. *Connecticut Gazette*, Feb. 7, 1766, quoted in W. S. Randall, *Benedict Arnold*, 41.
10. W. S. Randall, *Ethan Allen*, 55.
11. J. Parker to C. Skinner, in D. L. Kemmerer, *Path to Freedom*, 282f.
12. Samuel Adams, May 15, 1764, in "Instructions of the Town of Boston to Its Representatives in the General Court," MS, Boston Public Library.
13. Deborah Franklin to BF, Sept. 22, 1765, *PBF*, 12:270–71.
14. Gage to Conway, Dec. 31, 1765, quoted in D. H. Fischer, *Paul Revere's Ride*, 380.
15. GW to Robert Cary & Co., Sept. 20, 1765, *PGW*, Col. Ser., 7:402.
16. Ezra Stiles to Leverett Hubbard, Sept. 1, 1766, MS, NHCHS.
17. Quoted in C. Collier, *Roger Sherman's Connecticut*, 52.
18. Quoted in *ABF*, 261.
19. Quoted in full in *PBF*, 13:124–59.
20. I. W. Stuart, *Life of Jonathan Trumbull*; D. M. Roth, *Connecticut's War Governor*, 10–11.
21. BF to WF, Mar. 13, 1768, in *PBF*, 15:75–76.
22. Quoted in Barrow, 226.
23. L. K. Wroth and H. Zobel, *Legal Papers of John Adams*, 2:396–98; L. H. Butterfield et al, eds., *Diary and Autobiography of John Adams*, 1:349–50n.
24. Gage to Barrington, Nov. 12, 1770, quoted in Fischer, 38.
25. Gage to Hillsborough, Oct. 31, 1768, quoted in ibid., 40.
26. R. B. Morris, ed. *EAH*, 78–79.
27. Quoted in Middlekauff, *Glorious Cause*, 209–13.
28. Barrow, 246.
29. Ibid., 247.
30. G. B. Warden, *Boston, 1689–1776*, 283–84.
31. E. Burke, *Burke's Speech on Conciliation to America*, 14, 21–23.
32. GW to Bryan Fairfax, July 4, 1774, in *PGW*, Col. Ser. 10: 109–10.
33. GW to BF, August 24, 1774, in *PGW*, Col. Ser. 10: 154–55.
34. J. Warren, "Suffolk Resolves," 54.
35. *New York Journal*, January 10, 1776.

4. "FOR CUTTING OFF OUR TRADE"

1. H. S. Commager and R. B. Morris, *Spirit of Seventy-Six*, 91.
2. Pitcairn, quoted in E. Stiles, *Literary Diary*, 604–65.
3. L. H. Butterfield et al, eds., *Diary and Autobiography of John Adams*, 314.

4. I. W. Stuart, *Life of Jonathan Trumbull,* 179.

5. B. A. Botkin, *Treasury of New England Folklore,* Lt. Jocelyn Feltham to Thomas Gage, June 11, 1775, in Commager and Steele, *Spirit of Seventy-Six,* 101.

6. O. W. Stephenson, "The Supply of Gunpowder in 1776," 271.

7. D. S. Freeman, *George Washington,* 3:427.

8. Stuart, 197.

9. W. S. Randall, *George Washington,* 153.

10. Ibid., 293.

11. Ibid.

12. Ibid., 148.

13. Stephenson, 271.

14. Ibid., 274.

15. JA to James Warren, quoted in Stephenson, 275.

16. *New York Journal,* January 10, 1776.

17. Quoted in N. L. York, "Clandestine Aid," 27.

18. Ibid.

19. P. Andreas, *Smuggler Nation,* 53–54.

20. Ibid., 48.

21. Ibid., 55.

22. J. M. Volo, *Blue Water Patriots,* 42.

23. W. S. Randall and N. Nahra, *American Lives,* 169, 178.

24. Andreas, 51.

25. Ibid., 50–51.

26. Ibid., 54; T. C. Barrow, *Trade and Empire,* 224–25.

27. T. McGrath, *Give Me a Fast Ship,* 21.

28. Andreas, 24.

29. Ibid., 16–17.

30. Volo, 44–49.

31. W. S. Randall, *Thomas Jefferson,* 271–76.

32. T. Fleming, *Liberty,* 186–98.

33. W. S. Randall, *Benedict Arnold,* 317.

34. W. S. Randall, *On Burgoyne's Trail;* Andreas, 49.

35. Andreas, 49.

36. Volo, 64.

37. GW to Joseph Reed, September, 1780, in Randall, *George Washington,* 390.

38. W. S. Randall, *Ethan Allen,* 434.

5. "TO THE SHORES OF TRIPOLI"

1. Hume to Adam Smith, quoted in J. H. Burton, *Life and Correspondence of David Hume,* 2:471.

2. TJ, quoted in D. Mueller, *Constitutional Democracy,* 114.

3. TJ, quoted in N. E. Cunningham, *In Pursuit of Reason,* 39.

4. TJ to William Stephens Smith, Nov. 13, 1787, in *PTJ*, 12:356.

5. GW to TJ, quoted by Ron Chernow in *Wall Street Journal* interview, February 11, 2012.

6. TJ to JM, quoted in S. Lipsky, *Citizens' Constitution*, 148.

7. TJ, in *Memoir, Correspondence, and Miscellany from the Papers of Thomas Jefferson*, 492.

8. M.L.E. Moreau de St. Méry, *Moreau de St. Méry's American Journey*, 125.

9. GW to Henry Lee, quoted in R. N. Smith, *Patriarch*, 229; GW, Annual Message, 1794.

10. TJ to GW, June 5, 1791, National Archives, *Founders Online*, available at http://founders.archives.gov/documents/Washington/05-08002-0171.

11. R. H. Owens, *The Neutrality Imperative*, 58.

12. GW to George Augustine Washington, quoted in M. A. Bourne, *First Family*, 132.

13. GW to Benjamin Walker, January 12, 1797, quoted in R. N. Smith, *Patriarch*, 172; GW to Richard Henry Lee, Mar. 26, 1796, quoted in R. N. Smith, 289; GW to AH, June 26, 1796, quoted in J. D. Barber, *Pulse of Politics*, 229.

14. GW, *Farewell Address*, quoted in W. S. Randall, *George Washington, A Life*, 492.

15. R. C. Davis, *Christian Slaves*, 23.

16. TJ to James Monroe, Nov. 11, 1784, in *PTJ*, 7:511-12; TJ to John Jay, Mar. 28, 1786, in *PTJ*, 9:357-59.

17. I. W. Toll, *Six Frigates*, 40.

18. The Barbary Treaties 1786-1816, Treaty of Peace and Friendship, signed at Tripoli, November 4, 1796, available at: avalon.law.Yale.edu/18th_century/bar1796t.asp.; LOC, *American State Papers: Senate, 5th Congress, vol. 2. 19.*

19. M. Durey, *Transatlantic Radicals*, 82.

20. Ibid., 88.

21. Ibid., 92.

22. Ibid., 105.

23. A. Taylor, *Civil War of 1812*, 79–86.

24. Moreau de St. Méry, 299.

25. A. Taylor, 76.

26. William Cobbett, *Gazette of the United States*, May 16, 1799, quoted in A. Taylor, 84; Tracy to Wolcott, Aug. 7, 1800, quoted in ibid.

27. Ibid., 85.

28. JA, speech to Congress, May 16, 1797, http://avalon.Yale.edu/18th-century/JA97-03.ASP.

29. M. Miner and H. Rawson, eds., *Oxford Dictionary of American Quotations*, 34.

30. TJ to John Taylor, June 4, 1798, in *WTJ*, 1050.

31. AH to Oliver Wolcott, June 29, 1798, in *Papers of Alexander Hamilton*, 21:522.

32. Moreau de St. Méry, 252–53.

33. TJ, quoted in A. S. Trees, *Founding Fathers and the Politics of Character*, 34.

34. H. V. Jaffa, *New Birth of Freedom*, 37.

35. G. J. McRee, *Life and Correspondence of James Iredell*, 2:357.

36. AH to Theodore Sedgwick, May 10, 1800, in *PAH*, 24:475.

37. Toll, 284–87.

38. TJ to Earl of Buchan, July 10, 1803, in *WTJ*, 1134; TJ to Madame de Staël, July 16, 1807, quoted in *WTJ*, "Thoughts on War and Revolution," 216.

39. B. Arthur, *How Britain Won the War of 1812*, 19–20.

40. G. Wood, *Empire of Liberty*, 641.

6. "THE REIGN OF WITCHES"

1. I. W. Toll, *Six Frigates*, 271.

2. Ibid., 272.

3. A. Taylor, *Civil War of 1812*, 104.

4. Barclay, quoted in ibid., 105.

5. Captain Stephen Decatur, quoted in ibid., 105.

6. Toll, 293.

7. Ibid., 293–94.

8. S. C. Tucker and F. T. Reuter, *Injured Honor*, 1–12.

9. Toll, 296–97.

10. Ibid., 297.

11. Joseph Nicholson to A. Gallatin, July 14, 1807, in A. Gallatin, *Writings of Albert Gallatin*, 360.

12. Quoted in B. Mayo, ed., *Jefferson Himself*, 276.

13. Quoted in N. K. Risjord, *Thomas Jefferson*, 166.

14. Quoted in J. Meacham, *Thomas Jefferson*, 669.

15. Smith to TJ, Oct. 19, 1807, in *TJP*, LOC; TJ to Robt. Williams, Nov. 1, 1807, in Lipscomb & Bergh, 11:378–79; TJ to Thomas Mann Randolph, Nov. 30, 1807, in *TJP*.

16. TJ, annual message to Congress, Dec. 18, 1807, Lipscomb & Bergh, 10:530-3116.

17. B. Arthur, *How Britain Won the War of 1812*, 200, 134.

18. J. H. Ellis, *Ruinous and Unhappy War*, 38–39.

19. Benjamin Smith, quoted in J. M. Smith, *Borderland Smuggling*, 10–11.

20. P. Andreas, *Smuggler Nation*, 78.

21. C. Prince and M. Keller, *U.S. Customs Service*, 75.

22. D. D. Hance, "Early Militia in Rutland," *Rutland Historical Society Quarterly*, vol. 14, no. 2 (Spring, 1984): 34.

23. A. Addis and C. P. Van Ness, *Vermont: Records of the Governor and Council*, 5:472.

24. S. Mills, ed. *Trial of Cyrus B. Dean*, 16.

25. R. E. Eshelman and B. K. Kummerow, *In Full Glory Reflected*, 10–12.

26. TJ to William Eustis, Circular Letter of the Secretary of War to the Governors, Jan. 17, 1809, in Addis and Van Ness, 5:477.

7. "FREE TRADE AND SAILORS' RIGHTS"

1. Quoted in C. Allgor, *Perfect Union*, 27.

2. DCPM to Eliza Collins, quoted in ibid., 28.

3. Ibid., 20.

4. JM to TJ, May 5, 1787, quoted in R. S. Alley, *James Madison on Religious Liberty*, 26.

5. Washington Irving to H. Brevoort, Jan. 13, 1811, quoted in Q. S. King, *Henry Clay and the War of 1812*, 378.

6. A. J. Foster, *Jeffersonian America*, 10.

7. DPTM to Anna Coles, April 26, 1804, quoted in Allgor, 61.

8. Foster, 55.

9. Ibid.

10. Quoted in Allgor, 98.

11. R. L. Ketcham, *James Madison*, 496.

12. Quoted in Allgor, 116.

13. Quoted in ibid., 137.

14. A. J. Langguth, *Union 1812*, 144.

15. Margaret Bayard Smith, "Inaugurations," 529.

16. Quoted in F. Kaplan, *John Quincy Adams*, 258–59.

8. "WAR NOW! WAR ALWAYS!"

1. A. S. Withers, ed., *Chronicles of Border Warfare*, 80.

2. A. J. Langguth, *Union 1812*, 166.

3. Ibid., 167.

4. A. Walker, Journal of Two Campaigns of the Fourth Regiment of U.S. Infantry, 102.

5. Langguth, 170.

6. Ibid., 171.

7. Tecumseh, "Message from the Confederate Nations," in D. R. Hickey, ed., *War of 1812: Writings*, 27–29.

8. Eppes to TJ, March 1811, in J. Meacham, *Thomas Jefferson*, 460.

9. Jonathan Roberts to Alexander Dallas, Dec. 19, 1813, in Dallas Papers, HSP.

10. JM, annual message, Nov. 5, 1811, in R. L. Ketcham, *James Madison*, 716.

11. Ketcham, in 510.

12. JM to Barlow, Nov. 7, 1811 ibid.

13. Calhoun, quoted in A. Taylor, *Civil War of 1812*, 132.

14. HC, quoted in W. L. Mackenzie, *Sketches of Canada and the United States*, 467; TJ to JA, Jan. 21, 1812, in B. Mayo, ed., *Jefferson Himself*, 296.

15. A. Taylor, *Civil War of 1812*, 133; HC, quoted in W. James, *A Full and Correct Account of the Military Occurrences of the Late War*, 1:77; J. Broadwater, *James Madison*, 165; TJ to JM, Feb. 19, 1812, quoted in A. J. Mapp Jr., *Thomas Jefferson*, 230.

16. A. Taylor, 132.

17. G. C. Daughan, *1812: The Navy's War*, 29.

18. E. J. Dolin, *Fur, Fortune and Empire*, 190–92.

19. J. E. Seelye and S. A. Littleton, *Voices of the American Indian Experience*, 196.

20. Meacham, 30.

21. JM, annual message, June 1, 1812, quoted in Ketcham, 509.

22. Calhoun, quoted in ibid., 528.

23. Madison, quoted in ibid, 527–28; T. H. Benton, ed., *Abridgment of the Debates of Congress*, 4:554.

24. A. J. Foster, *Jeffersonian America*, 4.

25. Ibid.

26. Ibid.

27. Ibid., 20, 5, 4.

28. Ibid., 102.

29. Rush, quoted in H. Adams, *History of the United States*, 452.

30. Castlereagh, quoted in D. R. Hickey, ed., *War of 1812: Writings*, 282.

31. AJ to Willie Blount, June 5, 1812, in ibid., 25–26.

9. "A MERE MATTER OF MARCHING"

1. P. D. Nelson, "Henry Lee," *ANB*; P. Aron, *We Hold These Truths*, 202.

2. *Baltimore Federal Republican*, June 20, 1812.

3. Philip Lewis, quoted in D. R. Hickey, *War of 1812: A Forgotten Conflict*, 59.

4. P. A. Gilje, *Rioting in America*, 62.

5. Hickey, *War of 1812: A Forgotten Conflict*, 61.

6. Ibid., 61–66.

7. Ibid., 65–67; A. Taylor, *Civil War of 1812*, 177–78.

8. *National Intelligencer*, Nov. 23, 1811.

9. J. C. A. Stagg, *War of 1812*, 54–55.

10. Ibid., 55.

11. J. R. Elting, *Amateurs, to Arms!*, 2.

12. P. Andreas, *Smuggler Nation*, 85.

13. A. S. Everest, *The War of 1812 in the Champlain Valley*, 77–79.

14. A. Taylor, 152, 161.

15. Ibid., 153.

16. Gerry to Dearborn, quoted in Hickey, *War of 1812: A Forgotten Conflict*, 26.

17. A. Taylor, *Civil War of 1812*, 180.

18. R. Leckie, *War Nobody Won*, 30.

19. Hickey, *War of 1812: A Forgotten Conflict*, 86.

20. A. Taylor, 141.

21. Ibid., 162.

22. A. J. Yanik, *Fall and Recapture of Detroit*, 82.

23. A. Taylor, 164; Yanik, 117.

24. Quoted in A. Taylor, 164.

25. Ibid.

26. *National Intelligencer*, Sept. 12, 1812.

27. Daniel Tompkins to William Eustis, Sept. 9, 1812, MS in McClure Collection, Rauner Library, Dartmouth College.

28. Calvin Everest to Daniel Russel, Sept. 13, 1812, in ibid.

29. W. S. Randall, *Little Revenge*, 225, 497.

30. E. Darnell, *Journal Containing an Accurate & Interesting Account*, 51.

31. K. A. Herkalo, *Battles at Plattsburgh*, 36.

32. Hickey, *War of 1812: A Forgotten Conflict*, 89; H. Adams, *History of the United States*, 528.

10. "PURIFIED AS BY FIRE"

1. B. Arthur, *How Britain Won the War of 1812*, 145; D. R. Hickey, *War of 1812: A Forgotten Conflict*, 101.

2. D. M. Roper, "DeWitt Clinton" in *ANB*; E. G. Burrows and M. Wallace, *Gotham*, 424.

3. Elbridge Gerry to JM, quoted in Hickey, *War of 1812: A Forgotten Conflict*, 28.

4. C. Allgor, *Perfect Union*, 276–77.

5. D. Gordon, ed., *Secession, State, and Liberty*, 146; *Niles' Weekly Register* 2 (Aug. 15, 1812): 389; Webster, "Rockingham Memorial," Aug. 5, 1812, quoted in H. Adams, *History of the United States*, 402.

6. I. W. Toll, *Six Frigates*, 332.

7. Ibid.

8. Ibid., 333.

9. Gallatin to JM, quoted in ibid., 335.

10. C. O. Paullin, *Commodore John Rodgers*, 248.

11. Isaac Hull to Hamilton, July 21, 1812, in W. S. Dudley, *Naval War of 1812*, 1:161–63.

12. S. Budiansky, *Perilous Fight*, 120–21.

13. K. D. McCranie, *Utmost Gallantry*, 37.

14. Hull to Hamilton, Aug. 2, 1812, quoted in ibid., 47.

15. Hamilton to Hull, July 28, 1812, quoted in ibid.

16. D. R. Hickey, ed., *War of 1812: Writings*, 122–23.

17. McCranie, 49.

18. Ibid., 49–52.

19. J. H. Ellis, *Ruinous and Unhappy War*, 82.

20. Thomas McClure to Rev. David McClure, Sept. 1812, MS in McClure Collection, Rauner Library, Dartmouth College.

21. JM, annual message, Nov. 4, 1812, available at Miller Center.org/president/speeches/detail/3619; G. C. Daughan, *1812*, 82.

22. Hickey, *War of 1812: A Forgotten Conflict*, 96–97.

23. Budiansky, 158.

24. Hickey, *War of 1812: A Forgotten Conflict*, 96–97; American Merchant Marine at War, "American Merchant Marine and Privateers in the War of 1812," available at http://www.usmm.org/warof1812.html; T. C. Hansard, ed., *Parliamentary Debates*, 29:649–50.

25. J. Laxer, *Tecumseh and Brock*, 183.

26. R. Soodalter, "Master Shipbuilders of 1812," 20.

27. JM, annual message, Nov. 4, 1812.

28. JQA, *Diary*, Sept. 6, 1812.

29. Ibid.

30. Ibid.

31. Ibid., Sept. 7, 1812.

32. A. de Caulaincourt, *With Napoleon in Russia*, 102.

33. M. P. Rey, *Alexander I*, 245.

34. JQA, *Diary*, Sept. 15, 1812.

35. Ibid., Oct. 25, 1812.

36. Ibid., Sept. 21, 1812.

37. Madame de Staël to TJ, November 10, 1812, in Hickey, *War of 1812: Writings*, 228.

38. JQA, *Diary*, May 11, 1813. Emphasis in original.

39. TJ to Madame de Staël, May 24, 1813, in Hickey, *War of 1812: Writings*, 229–34.

40. R. V. Remini, *Henry Clay*, 106.

11. "FATHER, LISTEN TO YOUR CHILDREN"

1. E. Darnell, *Journal Containing an Accurate and Interesting Account*, 28.

2. William Jones to Isaac Chauncey, quoted in G. C. Daughan, *1812*, 157.

3. R. Soodalter, "Master Shipbuilders of 1812," 20–22.

4. S. J. Burr, *Life and Times of William Henry Harrison*, 198.

5. K. A. Herkalo, *Battles at Plattsburgh*, 40.

6. P. D. Nelson, "Zebulon Montgomery Pike," *ANB*; P. Berton, *Flames Across the Border*, 47.

7. The most detailed depiction of the Battle of York can be found in R. Malcomson, *Capital in Flames*, 186–220.

8. D. R. Hickey, ed., *War of 1812: Writings*, 215–16; D. R. Hickey, *War of 1812: A Forgotten Conflict*, 129.

9. A. Taylor, *Civil War of 1812*, 217.

10. Ibid., 215.

11. Ibid., 216.

12. Hickey, *War of 1812: A Forgotten Conflict*, 135.

13. J. Latimer, *1812: War with America*, 142.

14. S. C. Tucker et al., eds., *Encyclopedia of the War of 1812*, 894.

15. Ibid.

16. Ibid., 884.

17. *Cobbett's Weekly Political Register* 26 (July 2, 1814): 563.

18. Broke, quoted in S. Budiansky, *Perilous Fight*, 226.

19. I. W. Toll, *Six Frigates*, 411.

20. Ibid., 414.

21. W. S. Dudley, ed., *Naval War of 1812*, vol. 3, 296.

22. Budiansky, 254.

23. D. C. Skaggs and G. T. Altoff, *Signal Victory,* 148.

24. Hickey, *War of 1812: Writings,* 323.

25. Ibid., 325.

26. Ibid., 326.

27. N. Nahra, "Tecumseh," in W. S. Randall and N. Nahra, *American Lives,* 1:135.

28. Hickey, *War of 1812: Writings,* 327.

29. Horsman, "Tecumseh," in Tucker et al., *Encyclopedia of the War of 1812,* 505.

30. Edward Lyman to John W. Weeks, July 12, 1813, MS, Weeks Family Collection, Rauner Library, Dartmouth College.

12. "YOU SHALL NOW FEEL THE EFFECTS OF WAR"

1. S. C. Tucker, ed. *U.S. Leadership in Wartime,* 177.

2. R. L. Ketcham, *James Madison,* 561.

3. Monroe to TJ, June 28, 1813, in J. Monroe, *Writings of James Monroe,* 5:271–73.

4. *Niles' Weekly Register,* May 8, 1813.

5. D. R. Hickey, *War of 1812: A Forgotten Conflict,* 111.

6. J. I. Little, *Loyalties in Conflict,* 44.

7. A. Everest, *The War of 1812 in the Champlain Valley,* 1108.

8. R. E. Eshelman and B. K. Kummerow, *In Full Glory Reflected,* 20.

9. S. Vogel, *Through the Perilous Fight,* 4.

10. Eshelman and Kummerow, 29.

11. Captain Frederick Chamier, quoted in H. L. Glatfelter, *Havre de Grace in the War of 1812,* 60.

12. B. Arthur, *How Britain Won the War of 1812,* 110; W. S. Dudley, *Naval War of 1812,* vol. 3: 261.

13. Cockburn, quoted in Eshelman and Kummerow, 24.

14. In addition to the militiaman killed at Havre de Grace, another died at the Battle of Bladensburg and a second—an African American freeman—at Fort McHenry; a flotillaman in Commodore Barney's Chesapeake squadron was also killed. A British artilleryman was killed when a rocket exploded during launching.

15. Cockburn, quoted in Eshelman and Kummerow, 24.

16. Ibid., 26; Sir David Milne, Jan. 2, 1814, Royal Commission on Historical Manuscripts, *Reports on the Manuscripts of Col. David Milne Home,* 160.

17. Rodgers, quoted in S. Budiansky, *Perilous Fight,* 281.

18. Dudley, vol. 3: 78.

19. Ibid., vol. 3: 360.

20. Cassin, quoted in Budiansky, 244.

21. Napier, quoted in Hickey, *War of 1812: Writings,* 270.

22. Ibid.

23. Arthur, 148.

24. Ibid., 145–46, 168, 175.

25. Ibid., 176–77.

26. J. B. Warren to J. Croker, Dec. 30, 1813, in ibid., 103; Warren to Melville, Dec. 30, 1813, ibid., 103.

27. Andrew Mack to Samuel Fletcher, Jan. 9, 1814, MS in McClure Collection, Rauner Library, Dartmouth College.

13. "DESTROY AND LAY WASTE"

1. Gallatin to Clay, Apr. 2, 1814, quoted in ibid., 105–6.

2. Cochrane's proclamation, dated Apr. 2, 1814, in D. R. Hickey, ed., *War of 1812: Writings*, 424–25.

3. Thomas McClure to David McClure, Apr. 12, 1813, MS in McClure Collection, Rauner Library, Dartmouth College.

4. *London Times*, May 24, 1814, in Hickey, *War of 1812: Writings*, 429.

5. Bathurst to Prevost, June 3, 1814, in ibid., 429–31.

6. Gallatin to Monroe, June 13, 1814, in ibid., 432–33.

7. I. Hull to Henry A. S. Dearborn, Aug. 20, 1813, MS in McClure Collection, Rauner Library, Dartmouth College.

8. B. Arthur, *How Britain Won the War of 1812*, 159.

9. J. H. Ellis, *Ruinous and Unhappy War*, 112.

10. Ibid., 159–60.

11. R. V. Remini, *Andrew Jackson*, 48.

12. Hickey, *War of 1812: Writings*, 406–07.

13. Andrew Jackson to Rachel Jackson, Apr. 1, 1814, in ibid., 409–10.

14. A. S. Everest, *War of 1812 in the Champlain Valley*, 137–38.

15. Quoted in C. Crain, "Unfortunate Events," *New Yorker*, October 22, 2012.

16. Arthur, 163.

17. Ibid., 114–15.

18. Ibid., 43.

19. S. Vogel, *Through the Perilous Fight*, 51.

20. J. Latimer, *1812*, 285.

21. *Niles' Weekly Register* 7 (Feb. 25, 1815): 410, cited in Hickey, *War of 1812: A Forgotten Conflict*, 188.

22. James Miller, quoted in E. Cruikshank, ed., *Documentary History of the Campaign on the Niagara Frontier*, 1:120.

23. JQA, *Diary*, June 24, 1814, 119.

24. Ibid., June 29, 1814, 120.

25. P. C. Nagel, *John Quincy Adams*, 218; JQA, *Diary*, June 29, 1814, 120.

26. JQA, *Diary*, July 8, 1814.

27. Cochrane, in Hickey, *War of 1812: Writings*, 483–84.

28. Ellis, 163; 193–95; Arthur, 109; J. Roberts, "The British Raid on Essex," available online at http://connecticuthistory.org.the-british-raid-on-essex/

29. Robert Bathurst to Prevost, June 3, 1814, in Hickey, ed., *War of 1812: Writings*, 431.

30. Sherbrooke to Bathurst, Nov. 20, 1814, ibid.

31. Robert Rowley to Owsley Rowley, March(?), 1814 ibid., 485–86.

32. R. E. Eshelman and B. K. Kummerow, *In Full Glory Reflected*, 65.

33. Ibid.

34. Rowley, in Hickey, *War of 1812: Writings*, 486.

35. Ibid.

36. Ibid., 488.

37. Cockburn, quoted in W. Lord, *Dawn's Early Light*, 46, 52.

38. Vogel, 34.

39. Rowley in Hickey, *War of 1812: Writings*, 487.

40. M. J. Crawford, ed., *Naval War of 1812*, 115.

41. R. Morriss, *Cockburn and the British Navy in Transition*, 100.

42. Lord, 47–48; P. Snow, *When Britain Burned the White House*, 29.

43. Lord, 48–49.

44. JQA, *Diary*, Aug. 7, 1814, 122.

45. Monroe quoted in ibid., Aug. 9, 1814, 124.

46. Quoted in Arthur, 191.

47. JQA, *Diary*, Aug. 19, 1814, 126–27.

48. *Niles' Weekly Register* 7 (Oct. 15, 1814): 75.

14. "HARD WAR"

1. R. E. Eshelman and B. K. Kummerow, *In Full Glory Reflected*, 69, 72.

2. Arthur, 117.

3. Monroe to Madison, Aug. 20, 1814, in *Capture of the City of Washington*, 539.

4. JM to Monroe, Aug. 22, 1814, in J. Madison, *Writings of James Madison*, 8:292; Monroe to JM, Aug. 22, 1814, in S. Vogel, *Through the Perilous Fight*, 97.

5. R. N. Côté, *Strength and Honor*, 4; Vogel, 102.

6. Vogel, 104.

7. M. Greenblatt, *War of 1812*, 10.

8. Madison, *Writings of James Madison*, 293; Vogel, 104–5.

9. Vogel, 106; G. D. Evans, *Facts Relating to the Capture of Washington*, 11.

10. Cochrane to Cockburn, Aug. 22, 1814, in *G. C. Cockburn Memoir of Service*, MS, National Maritime Museum, 134, cited in Vogel, 107.

11. Cockburn to Cochrane, Aug. 23, 1814, in R. Morriss, *Cockburn and the British Navy in Transition*, 106; Vogel, 107–8.

12. M. B. Smith, *First Forty Years*, 99.

13. Vogel, 115.

14. J. Scott, *Recollections of a Naval Life*, quoted in D. R. Hickey, ed., *War of 1812: Writings*, 494.

15. Ibid., 496.

16. J. S. Williams, *History of the Invasion and Capture of Washington*, 277.

17. H. Adams, *War of 1812*, 222.

18. Armstrong, quoted in *Capture of the City of Washington*, 539.
19. P. Snow, *When Britain Burned the White House*, 74; Vogel, 123.
20. W. Lord, *Dawn's Early Light*, 107.
21. William Simmons, *National Intelligencer,* July 7, 1814; Vogel, 131.
22. Gleig, in Hickey, *War of 1812: Writings*, 511.
23. Ibid., 513.
24. *Niles' Weekly Register* 7 (Sept. 10, 1814): 7.
25. Ibid., 7–8.
26. Gleig, in Hickey, *War of 1812: Writings*, 515.
27. Vogel, 358; R. E. Eshelman, *Travel Guide to the War of 1812*, 44.
28. William Abbat, "The Bladensburg Races," *Magazine of History* 19 (1914): 209.
29. C. Allgor, *Perfect Union*, 312; D. Young, *Dear First Lady*, 193.
30. Allgor, 312–13.
31. Young, *Dear First Lady*, 193.
32. Ibid.; Allgor, 313.
33. Allgor, 314.
34. Young, *Dear First Lady*, 193.
35. Allgor, 314–15; P. A. Jennings, *Coloured Man's Reminiscences*, 10.
36. Lord, 46.
37. M. B. Smith, *First Forty Years*, 111.
38. G. R. Gleig, *Narrative of the Campaigns*, 133–34.
39. Eshelman and Kummerow, 102.
40. Ibid., 105.
41. Vogel, 200.

15. "SO PROUDLY WE HAIL"

1. W. Lord, *Dawn's Early Light*, 216.
2. Ibid., 217.
3. B. Arthur, *How the British Won the War of 1812*, 178.
4. Lord, 223.
5. J. T. Scharf, *History of Baltimore*, 89–90.
6. *Baltimore Telegraph*, Sept. 13, 1814; the garrison flag is in the collection of the Smithsonian Institution.
7. Frederick N. Rasmussen, *Baltimore Sun*, Sept. 12, 2014.
8. Scott S. Sheads, *The Chesapeake Campaigns 1813–15*, 75.
9. G. R. Gleig, *Narrative of the Campaigns,* 173–75.
10. G. R. Gleig, *Subaltern in America*, 133.
11. Ibid., 157.
12. Vogel, 334.
13. JQA, *Diary,* 129.
14. Lord, 216–17.

15. Hanson, *Federal Republican*, Aug. 29, 1814.

16. *Baltimore Patriot and Evening Advertiser*, Sept. 3, 1814.

16. "I MUST NOT BE LOST"

1. G. Izard, *Official Correspondence*, 65–72.

2. A. S. Everest, *War of 1812 in the Champlain Valley*, 114.

3. K. A. Herkalo, *Battles at Plattsburgh*, 73.

4. P. Andreas, *Smuggler Nation*, 85.

5. Izard to secretary of war, July 31, 1814, in Izard, 57.

6. Andreas, 86.

7. Everest, 162; D. G. Fitz-Enz, *Hacks, Sycophants, Adventurers, and Heroes*, 197.

8. D. E. Graves, *And All Their Glory Past*, 190; J. Ryun and Sons, *Heroes Among Us*, 271.

9. Ibid.; Mahan, *Sea Power in Its Relation to the War of 1812*, 381; C. H. Darling, "Commodore Macdonough," 81; T. Roosevelt, *Naval War of 1812*, 274, 398; W. Churchill, quoted in J. H. Schroeder, *Battle of Lake Champlain*, preface.

10. I. W. Toll, *Six Frigates*, 439.

11. JQA, *Diary*, Sept. 8 and 21, 1814; JQA, quoted in H. G. Unger, *John Quincy Adams*, 173.

12. JQA, *Diary*, Oct. 14, 1814, 139.

13. F. L. Engleman, *Peace of Christmas Eve*, 205; Liverpool, quoted in A. T. Mahan, "Negotiations at Ghent," 78.

14. JQA, *Diary*, Oct. 24, 1814, 138.

15. Goulburn to Bathurst, in A. W. Wellington, *Supplementary Despatches and Memoranda*, 190; Liverpool to Castlereagh, Oct. 28, 1814, in Yonge, *Life and Administration of Robert Banks*, 2:47, 72.

16. B. Arthur, *How Britain Won the War of 1812*, 189; 187.

17. Wellington to Liverpool, Nov. 9, 1814, in Wellington, 426, 425.

18. Clay, *Papers of Henry Clay*, 3:225.

19. Ibid.

20. JQA, *Diary*, Nov. 28, 1814, 138.

21. Ibid., Nov. 10, 1814, 143.

22. JQA, quoted in Engleman, 245.

23. JQA to Louisa Adams, Nov. 25, 1814, quoted in Unger, 173, 38; Liverpool, quoted in Engleman, 252; Wellington to Liverpool, Nov. 9, 1814, in Wellington, 425–26.

24. Liverpool to Castlereagh, Nov. 18, 1814, quoted in Engleman, 253.

25. JQA, *Writings of John Quincy Adams*, 5:226.

26. Bathurst to Goulburn, Nov. 19, 1814, in B. Jenkins, *Henry Goulburn*, 87–88.

27. Engleman, 275.

28. JQA, *Diary*, Dec. 2, 1814, 147 and Dec. 24, 1814, 151; JQA, *Writings*, 5:256.

29. *London Times*, Feb. 18, 1815; Apsley to Bathurst, Jan. (?) 1815, *Report of the Manuscripts of Earl Bathurst*, 319; Castlereagh to Liverpool, Jan 2, 1815, quoted in Wellington, *Supplementary Despatches and Memoranda*, 9: 523.

30. D. R. Hickey, *War of 1812: A Forgotten Conflict,* 201.

31. Quoted in ibid., 278–79.

32. Daniel Webster to Ezekiel Webster, January 9, 1815, MS in Webster Collection, Rauner Library, Dartmouth College.

33. *Niles' Weekly Register* 7 (Feb. 15, 1815): 385; JM, "Special Message," Feb. 20, 1815, *Addresses and Messages of the Presidents of the United States,* Feb. 20, 1815, 191.

BIBLIOGRAPHY

Adams, Henry. *The War of 1812*. Edited by H. A. DeWeerd. New York: Cooper Square Press, 1999.

———. *History of the United States of America during the Administrations of James Madison*. New York: Library of America, 1986.

Adams, John. *Letters of JA Addressed to His Wife*. Edited by Charles Francis Adams. Boston: Charles C. Little and James Brown, 1829.

Adams, John Quincy. *The Diary of John Quincy Adams, 1794–1845*. London: Longmans, Green, 1928.

———. *Writings of John Quincy Adams*. Edited by Worthington Chauncey Ford. 7 vols. New York: MacMillan, 1913–17.

Addis, A. and Cornelius P. Van Ness. *Vermont: Records of the Governor and Council*. 8 vols. Montpelier, VT: J. and J. M. Poland, 1873–80.

Addresses and Messages of the Presidents of the United States from 1789 to 1839. New York: McLean & Taylor, 1839.

Albion, Robert G., and Jennie Barnes Pope. *Sea Lanes in Wartime: The American Experience*. New York: W. W. Norton, 1968.

Allen, Gardner W. *Our Naval War with France*. Hamden, CT: Archon, 1967.

———. *Our Navy and the Barbary Corsairs*. Hamden, CT: Archon, 1965.

———. *Naval History of the American Revolution*. New York: Russell & Russell, 1962.

Allen. Thomas B. *Tories: Fighting for the King in America's First Civil War*. New York: HarperCollins, 2010.

Alley, Robert S. *James Madison on Religious Liberty*. Amherst, NY: Prometheus, 1985.

Allgor, Catherine. *A Perfect Union: Dolley Madison and the Creation of the American Nation*. New York: Henry Holt, 2006.

Allison, Robert J. *Crescent Obscured: The United States and the Muslim World*. New York: Oxford University Press, 1995.

Althoff, Gerald T. *Amongst My Best Men: African-Americans and the War of 1812*. Put-in-Bay, OH: Perry Group, 1996.

American National Biography. Edited by John A. Garraty, et al. 21 vols. New York: Oxford University Press, 1999.

Andreas, Peter. *Smuggler Nation: How Illicit Trade Made America*. New York: Oxford University Press, 2013.

Ansley, Norman. *The Brief Battle of Fort Cassin, Vermont in May 14, 1814*. Severna Park, MD: Forensic Research, 2003.

——. *Vergennes, Vermont and the War of 1812*. Severna Park, MD: Brooke Keefer, 1999.

Aron, Paul. *We Hold These Truths: And Other Words That Made America*. Lanham, MD: Rowman and Littlefield, 2008.

Arthur, Brian. *How Britain Won the War of 1812: The Royal Navy's Blockades of the United States, 1812–1815*. Woodbridge: Boydell Press, 2011.

Bailey, Thomas A. *A Diplomatic History of the American People*. 6th ed. New York: Appleton Century Crofts, 1958.

Bailyn, Bernard. *Atlantic History*. Cambridge, MA: Harvard University Press, 2005.

——. *Ideological Origins of the American Revolution*. Cambridge, MA: Belknap Press of Harvard University Press, 1967.

Barbuto, Richard V. *Niagara, 1814: America Invades Canada*. Lawrence: University Press of Kansas, 2000.

Barnet, Richard J. *The Rockets' Red Glare: When America Goes to War; The Presidents and the People*. New York: Simon and Schuster, 1990.

Barrow, Thomas C. *Trade and Empire: The British Customs Service in Colonial America, 1660–1775*. Cambridge, MA: Harvard University Press, 1967.

Bellico, Russell P. *Sails and Steam in the Mountains: A Maritime and Military History of Lake George and Lake Champlain*. Fleischmanns, NY: Purple Mountain Press, 2001.

Bemis, Samuel Flagg. *John Quincy Adams and the Foundations of American Foreign Policy*. New York: Knopf, 1949.

Benn, Carl. *The Iroquois in the War of 1812*. Toronto: University of Toronto Press, 1998.

Benton, Thomas Hart, ed. *Abridgment of the Debates of Congress, from 1789 to 1856*. 16 vols. New York: D. Appleton, 1857–61.

Berton, Pierre. *The Invasion of Canada*. New York: Penguin, 1988.

——. *Flames Across the Border: The Canadian-American Tragedy, 1813–1814*. Boston: Atlantic/Little Brown, 1981.

Bickman, Troy. *The Weight of Vengeance: The United States, the British Empire and the War of 1812*. New York: Oxford University Press, 2012.

Bird, Harrison. *Navies in the Mountains: The Battles on the Waters of Lake Champlain and Lake George, 1609–1814*. New York: Oxford University Press, 1962.

Blow, David. *Historic Guide to Burlington Neighborhoods*. 2 vols. Burlington, VT: Chittenden County Historical Society, 1991–97.

———. "Lake Champlain's First Steamboat." *Vermont History* 34 (April 1966): 2–119.

Boatner, Mark Mayo. *Encyclopedia of the American Revolution*. New York: David McKay, 1966.

Boller, Paul F. Jr. *Presidential Wives: An Anecdotal History*. New York: Oxford University Press, 1988.

Botkin, B. A. *Treasury of New England Folklore*. New York: Crown, 1947.

Bourne, Miriam Anne. *First Family: George Washington and His Intimate Relations*. New York: W. W. Norton, 1982.

Bourne, Russell. *Cradle of Violence: How Boston's Waterfront Mobs Invented the American Revolution*. New York: John Wiley, 2006.

Bowen, Catherine Drinker. *John Adams and the American Revolution*. Boston: Little, Brown, 1949.

Bowler, Arthur. *Logistics and the Failure of the British Army in America*. Princeton, NJ: Princeton University Press, 1975.

Broadwater, Jeff. *James Madison: A Son of Virginia and a Founder of the Nation*. Chapel Hill: University of North Carolina Press, 2012.

Brown, Wallace. *The Good Americans: The Loyalists in the American Revolution*. New York: William Morrow, 1969.

Budiansky, Stephen. *Perilous Fight: America's Intrepid War with Britain on the High Seas, 1812–1815*. New York: Knopf, 2010.

Buel, Richard Jr. *In Irons: Britain's Naval Supremacy and the American Revolutionary Economy*. New Haven: Yale University Press, 1998.

Burke, Edmund. *Burke's Speech on Conciliation to America*. Ed. Charles Morris. New York: Harper and Row, 1945.

Burr, Samuel Jones. *The Life and Times of William Henry Harrison*. New York: L. W. Ransom, 1840.

Burrows, Edwin G. "Albert Gallatin." In *ANB*.

———. and Mike Wallace. *Gotham: A History of New York City to 1898*. New York: Oxford University Press, 1999.

Burt, A. L. *The United States, Great Britain and British North America from the Revolution to the Establishment of Peace After the War of 1812*. New Haven, CT: Yale University Press, 1940.

Burton, John Hill. *Life and Correspondence of David Hume*. 2 vols. Edinburgh: Tait, 1846.

Butterfield, Lyman H. et al, eds. *Diary and Autobiography of John Adams*. Vol. 1. Cambridge, MA: Harvard University Press, 1964.

Capture of the City of Washington. In *American State Papers: Documents, Legislative and Executive, of the Congress of the United States*. Class 5, 1:524–98. Washington, DC: Gales and Seaton, 1832.

Carp, Benjamin L. *Defiance of the Patriots: The Boston Tea Party and the Making of America*. New Haven: Yale University Press, 2010.

Carse, Robert. *The Seafarers: A History of Maritime America, 1620–1820.* New York: Harper & Row, 1964.

Casey, Richard F. "North Country Nemesis: The Potash Rebellion and the Embargo of 1807–09." *New-York Historical Society Quarterly* 64 (1980): 31–49.

Caulaincourt, Armand de. *With Napoleon in Russia: The Memoirs of General de Caulaincourt, Duke of Vicenza.* Edited by George Libaire. New York: William Morrow, 1935.

Chapelle, Howard Irving. *The History of the American Sailing Navy: The Ships and Their Development.* New York: Bonanza, 1949.

Charney, Noah. *Stealing the Mystic Lamb: The True Story of the World's Most Coveted Masterpiece.* New York: Public Affairs, 2010.

Churchill, Winston. *History of the English-Speaking Peoples.* 4 vols. New York: Dodd Mead, 1956–58.

Clark, William Bell. *Ben Franklin's Privateers: A Naval Epic of the American Revolution.* Baton Rouge: Louisiana State University Press, 1956.

Clark, William Horace. *Ships and Sailors: The Story of Our Merchant Marine.* Boston: L. C. Page, 1938.

Clay, Henry. *Letters, Correspondence and Speeches.* Ed. by Calvin Colton. 6 vols. New York: G. P. Putnam, 1904.

———. *The Papers of Henry Clay.* 10 vols. to date. Edited by James F. Hopkins and Mary W. M. Hargreaves. Lexington: University of Kentucky Press, 1959–.

Cogliano, France D. *Emperor of Liberty: Thomas Jefferson's Foreign Policy.* New Haven: Yale University Press, 2014.

Collier, Christopher. *Roger Sherman's Connecticut.* Middletown, CT: Wesleyan University Press, 1971.

Collins, Gail. *William Henry Harrison.* New York: Times Books, 2012.

Commager, Henry Steele and Richard B. Morris. *The Spirit of 'Seventy-Six: The Story of the American Revolution as Told by the Participants.* New York: DaCapo, 1968.

Congreve, William. *Details of the Rocket System.* London: J. Whiting, 1814.

Cook, Fred J. *Privateers of '76.* Indianapolis: Bobbs-Merrill, 1976.

Côté, Richard N. *Strength and Honor: The Life of Dolley Madison.* Mt. Pleasant, SC: Corinthian Books, 2005.

Crawford, Michael J., ed. *Naval War of 1812: A Documentary History, 1814–1815.* Washington, DC: Naval Historical Center, 2002.

Crisman, Kevin J. *The Eagle: An American Brig on Lake Champlain during the War of 1812.* Shelburne, VT: New England Press, 1987.

———. *The History and Construction of the United States Schooner* Ticonderoga. Alexandria, VA: Eyrie, 1982.

Cruikshank, Ernest, ed. *Documentary History of the Campaign on the Niagara Frontier,* 4 vols. New York: Arno, 1971.

Cunningham, Noble E. *In Pursuit of Reason: The Life of Thomas Jefferson.* Baton Rouge: Louisiana State University Press, 1987.

———., ed. *Circular Letters of Congressmen to Their Constituents, 1789–1829.* Chapel Hill, NC: Institute of Early American History and Culture, 1978.

Darling, Charles H. "Commodore Macdonough." *Proceedings of the Vermont Historical Society, 1903–1904*. Burlington, VT: Free Press Association, 1905, 59–89.

Darnell, Elias. *A Journal Containing an Accurate & Interesting Account of the Hardships, Sufferings, Battles, Defeat & Captivity of the Kentucky Volunteers and Regulars, Commanded by General Winchester, in the Years 1812–13*. 1854. Reprint. *Magazine of History* 8, extra no. 31 (1914): 1–53.

Daughan, George C. *1812: The Navy's War*. New York: Basic Books, 2011.

Davis, Robert C. *Christian Slaves, Muslim Masters: White Slavery in the Mediterranean, the Barbary Coast, and Italy, 1500–1800*. New York: Palgrave Macmillan, 2003.

Dickerson, O. M. *The Navigation Acts and the American Revolution*. New York: Octagon, 1974.

Dolin, Eric Jay. *Fur, Fortune and Empire: The Epic History of the Fur Trade in America*. New York: W. W. Norton, 2010.

———. *Leviathan: The History of Whaling in America*. New York: W. W. Norton, 2007.

Doyle, William. *The Vermont Political Tradition: And Those Who Helped Make It*. Montpelier, VT: W. Doyle, 1992.

Dudley, William S., ed. *The Naval War of 1812: A Documentary History*. 3 vols. Washington, DC: Naval History Center, 1985–2002.

Dull, Jonathan R. *The Age of the Ship of the Line: The British and French Navies, 1650–1815*. Lincoln: University of Nebraska Press, 2009.

———. *American Naval History, 1607–1865*. Lincoln: University of Nebraska Press, 2002.

———. *The French Navy and American Independence*. Princeton, NJ: Princeton University Press, 1975.

Durey, Michael. *Transatlantic Radicals and the Early American Republic*. Lawrence: University Press of Kansas, 1997.

East, Robert A. *Business Enterprise in the American Revolutionary Era*. Gloucester, MA: P. Smith, 1964.

———. and Jacob Judd, eds. *Loyalist Americans: A Focus on Greater New York*. Tarrytown, NY: Sleepy Hollow Press, 1975.

Eckert, Edward K. "Thomas Macdonough: Architect of a Wilderness Navy." In James C. Bradford, ed. *Command Under Sail: Makers of the American Naval Tradition*. Annapolis, MD: Naval Institute Press, 1985.

Eisenhower, John S. D. *Agent of Destiny: The Life and Times of Winfield Scott*. New York: Free Press, 1997.

Ellis, James H. *A Ruinous and Unhappy War*. New York: Algora, 2009.

Elting, John R. *Amateurs, to Arms! A Military History of the War of 1812*. New York: DaCapo, 1995.

Engleman, Fred L. *The Peace of Christmas Eve*. New York: Harcourt, Brace & World, 1962.

English, Richard. *Irish Freedmen: The History of Nationalism in Ireland*. London: Macmillan, 2008.

Esdaile, Charles. *Napoleon's Wars: An International History, 1803–1815*. New York: Viking, 2007.

Eshelman, Ralph E. *A Travel Guide to the War of 1812 in the Chesapeake: Eighteen Tours in Maryland, Virginia, and the District of Columbia.* Baltimore: Johns Hopkins University Press, 2011.

———., and Burton K. Kummerow. *In Full Glory Reflected: Discovering the War of 1812 in the Chesapeake.* Baltimore: Maryland Historical Society Press, 2012.

Evans, George DeLacy. *Facts Relating to the Capture of Washington.* London: H. Colburn, 1829.

Everest, Allan S. *The Military Career of Alexander Macomb.* Plattsburgh, NY: Clinton County Historical Association, 1989.

———. *The War of 1812 in the Champlain Valley.* Syracuse, NY: Syracuse University Press, 1981.

———. *Recollections of Clinton County and the Battle of Plattsburgh 1800–1840: Memoirs of Early Residents from the Notebooks of Dr. D. S. Kellogg.* Plattsburgh, NY: Clinton County Historical Association, 1964.

Feldman, Jay. *When the Mississippi River Ran Backward.* New York: Simon & Schuster, 2007.

Felknor, Bruce L., ed. *The United States Merchant Marine at War, 1775–1945.* Annapolis, MD: Naval Institute Press, 1998.

Fischer, David Hackett. *Paul Revere's Ride.* New York: Oxford University Press, 1995.

Fitz-Enz, David G. *Hacks, Sycophants, Adventurers, and Heroes: Madison's Commanders in the War of 1812.* Lanham, MD: Taylor Trade Publishing, 2012.

———. *Redcoats' Revenge: An Alternate History of the War of 1812.* Washington, DC: Potomac Books, 2008.

———, and John R. Elting. *The Final Invasion: Plattsburgh, the War of 1812's Most Decisive Battle.* New York: Cooper Square Press, 2001.

Fleming, Thomas. *Liberty: The Revolution.* New York: Viking, 1997.

Forester, C. S. *The Age of Fighting Sail: The Story of the Naval War of 1812.* Edited by Lewis Gennett. Garden City, NY: Doubleday, 1956.

Foster, Augustus John. *Jeffersonian America: Notes on the United States of America Collected in the Years 1805-6-7 and 11–12.* Edited by Richard Beale Davis. San Marino, CA: Huntington Library, 1954.

Franklin, Benjamin. *Papers.* Edited by Leonard W. Labaree et al. 42 vols. to date. New Haven, CT: Yale University Press, 1959–.

———. *The Autobiography of Benjamin Franklin.* Edited by Leonard W. Labaree. New Haven, CT: Yale University Press, 1965.

Freeman, Douglas Southall. *George Washington, A Biography.* 6 vols. New York: Scribner, 1948–57.

Gallatin, Albert. *The Writings of Albert Gallatin.* Edited by Henry Adams. Philadelphia: J. B. Lippincott, 1879.

Garritee, Jerome R. *The Republic's Private Navy: The American Privateering Business as Practiced by Baltimore during the War of 1812.* Mystic, CT: Mystic Seaport, 1977.

Gipson, Lawrence Henry. *American Loyalist: Jared Ingersoll.* New Haven, CT: Yale University Press, 1971.

Gilje, Paul A. *Rioting in America.* Indianapolis: Indiana University Press, 1996.

Glatfelter, Heidi L. *Havre de Grace in the War of 1812: Fire on the Chesapeake.* Charleston, SC: History Press, 2013.

Gleig, George Robert. *A Subaltern in America: Comprising His Narrative of the Campaigns of the British Army, at Baltimore, Washington, &c &c during the Late War.* Philadelphia: Carey and Hart, 1833.

———. *A Narrative of the Campaigns of the British Army at Washington and New Orleans, under Generals Ross, Pakenham, and Lambert, in the Years 1814 and 1815; with Some Account of the Countries Visited.* London: John Murray, 1821.

Gomes, Laurentino. *1808: The Flight of the Emperor.* Guilford, CT: Lyons Press, 2013.

Goodden, Angelica. *Madame de Staël: The Dangerous Exile.* Oxford: Oxford University Press, 2008.

Gordon, David, ed. *Secession, State, and Liberty.* New Brunswick: Transaction, 1998.

Graham, Gerald S. *British Policy and Canada, 1774–1791: A Study in 18th Century Trade Policy.* Westport, CT: Greenwood Press, 1974.

Grant, John, and Ray Jones. *The War of 1812: A Guide to the Battlefields and Historic Sites.* Buffalo: Western New York Public Broadcasting Association, 2011.

Graves, Donald E. *And All Their Glory Past: Fort Erie, Plattsburgh and the Final Battles in the North.* Toronto: Robin Brass Studio, 2013.

———. "The Redcoats Are Coming: British Troop Movements to North America in 1814." The War of 1812 Website. http://www.warof1812.ca/redcoats.htm.

———. *The Rocket's Red Glare.* Toronto: Museum Restoration Service, 1989.

Grays, Edward G., and Jane Kamensky, eds. *The Oxford Handbook of the American Revolution.* New York: Oxford University Press, 2013.

Greenblatt, Miriam. *War of 1812.* New York: Facts on File, 2003.

Greene, Robert E. *Black Defenders of America, 1775–1973.* Chicago: Johnson Publishers, Inc. 1974.

Guttman, Jon. "Detroit Showdown." *MHQ: The Quarterly Journal of Military History* 25 (Autumn 2012): 64–69.

Hagon, Kenneth J. *This People's Navy: Making American Seapower.* New York: Free Press, 1991.

Hamilton, Alexander. *Papers of Alexander Hamilton.* 27 vols. to date. New York: Columbia University Press, 1961–.

Hansard, Thomas Curson, ed. *Parliamentary Debates.* 621 vols. London: Hansard, 1803–1908.

Hanson, John H. *The Lost Prince: Facts Tending to Prove the Identity of Louis the Seventeenth of France and The Rev. Eleazar Williams Missionary Among the Indians of North America.* New York: G. P. Putnam, 1854.

Hedges, J. B. *The Browns of Providence Plantation.* Boston: Boston University Press, 1968.

Heinrichs, Waldo H. Jr. "The Battle of Plattsburgh, 1814." PhD diss., Harvard University, 1949.

Hemenway, Abby Maria. *The Vermont Historical Gazeteer.* 5 vols. Burlington, VT: privately printed, 1867–91.

Herkalo, Keith A. *The Battles at Plattsburgh: September 11, 1814*. Charleston: History Press, 2012.

Hickey, Donald R. *The War of 1812: A Forgotten Conflict*. Chicago: University of Chicago Press, 1989.

———, ed. *The War of 1812: Writings from America's Second War of Independence*. New York: Library of America, 2013.

Hitsman, J. Mackay. *The Incredible War of 1812: A Military History*. Edited by Donald E. Graves. Toronto: Robin Brass Studio, 1999.

Holden, James A. *The Centenary of the Battle of Plattsburg*. Albany: University of the State of New York, 1914.

Holmberg, Thomas. *British Orders in Council, 1800–1810*. Government and Politics: The Napoleon Series, 2007.

Howe, John. "Diary." *Vermont History* 40, no. 4 (Autumn 1972): 262–70.

Izard, George. "Official Correspondence with the Department of War." Philadelphia: Thomas Dobson, 1816.

Jaffa, Harry V. *A New Birth of Freedom: Abraham Lincoln and the Coming of the Civil War*. Lanham, MD: Rowman and Littlefield, 2000.

James, William. *A Full and Complete Account of the Military Occurences of the Late War between Great Britain and the United States*. 2 vols. London: privately printed, 1818.

Jasanoff, Maya. *Liberty's Exiles: American Loyalists in the Revolutionary World*. New York: Knopf, 2015.

Jefferson, Thomas. *The Anas of Thomas Jefferson*. New York: DaCapo, 1970.

———. *Jefferson, Writings*. New York: Library of America, 1984.

———. *Memoir, Correspondence, and Miscellanies, from the Papers of Thomas Jefferson*. Edited by Thomas Jefferson Randolph. Vol. 4. Charlottesville, VA: F. Carr, 1829.

———. *The Papers of Thomas Jefferson*. 39 vols. to date. Princeton, NJ: Princeton University Press, 1950–.

———. *Thomas Jefferson, Annotated Correspondence*. Edited by Brett E. Woods. New York: Algora, 2009.

———. *Thomas Jefferson Papers*. Washington, DC: Library of Congress.

———. *The Works of Thomas Jefferson*. Edited by Paul Worthington Ford. 12 vols. New York: G. P. Putnam's, 1904–5.

———. *The Writings of Thomas Jefferson*. Edited by Andrew A. Lipscomb and Albert E. Bergh. Washington, DC: Library of Congress, 1903–4.

Jenkins, Brian. *Henry Goulburn, 1784–1856: A Political Biography*. Montreal: McGill-Queen's University Press, 1996.

Jennings, Paul A. *A Coloured Man's Reminiscences of James Madison*. Brooklyn, NY: G. C. Beadle, 1865.

Jones, Brian Jay. *Washington Irving: An American Original*. New York: Arcade, 2008.

Kaplan, Fred. *John Quincy Adams: American Visionary*. New York: HarperCollins, 2014.

Keegan, John. *Fields of Battle: The Wars for North America*. London: Hodder and Stoughton, 1995.

Kemmerer, Donald L. *Path to Freedom: The Struggle for Self-Government in Colonial New Jersey, 1703–1776*. Princeton University Press, 1940.

Kent-DeLord Collection. Feinberg Library Special Collections. Plattsburgh State University of New York, Plattsburgh, New York.

Ketcham, Ralph L. *Selected Writings of James Monroe*. Indianapolis: Hackett, 2006.

———. *James Madison: A Biography*. Charlottesville: University of Virginia Press, 1990.

King, Quentin Scott. *Henry Clay and the War of 1812*. Jefferson, NC: McFarland, 2014.

Knox, Oliver. *Rebels and Informers: Stirrings of Irish Independence*. New York: St. Martin's Press, 1997.

Labaree, Benjamin, et al. *America and the Sea: A Maritime History*. Mystic, CT: Mystic Seaport Museum, 1998.

Lambert, Frank. *The Barbary Wars: American Independence in the Atlantic World*. New York: Hill and Wang, 2005.

Langguth, A. J. *Union 1812: The Americans Who Fought the Second War of Independence*. New York: Simon & Schuster, 2006.

Latimer, Jon. *1812: War with America*. Cambridge, MA: Harvard University Press, 2007.

Laxer, James. *Tecumseh and Brock: The War of 1812*. Toronto: House of Anansi Press, 2012.

Leckie, Robert. *The War Nobody Won, 1812*. New York: Putnam, 1974.

Levy, Jack S., and Katherine Barbieri. "Trading with the Enemy during Wartime." *Security Studies* 13, no. 3 (Spring 2004): 1–47.

Lewis, Dennis M. *British Naval Activity on Lake Champlain During the War of 1812*. Plattsburgh, NY: Clinton County Historical Association, 1994.

Lind, Michael. *Land of Promise: An Economic History of the United States*. New York: HarperCollins, 2012.

Linklater, Andro. *Why Spencer Perceval Had to Die: The Assassination of a British Prime Minister*. New York: Walker, 2012.

Lipsky, Seth. *The Citizens' Constitution: An Annotated Guide*. New York: Basic Books, 2009.

Little, J. I. *Loyalties in Conflict: A Canadian Borderland in War and Rebellion, 1812–1840*. Toronto: University of Toronto Press, 2008.

London, Joshua E. *Victory in Tripoli: How America's War with the Barbary Pirates Established a United States Navy and Built a Nation*. New York: John Wiley, 2005.

Lord, Walter. *The Dawn's Early Light*. Baltimore: Johns Hopkins U. Press, 2012 [1972].

Lossing, Benson J. *Pictorial Field-Book of the War of 1812*. New York: Harper & Bros., 1868.

Louisiana State University. "Statistical Summary: America's Major Wars." Edited by Al Nofi. http.//www.cwc.lsu.edu/cwc/other/stats/warcost.htm.

Macdonough, Rodney. *The Life of Commodore Thomas Macdonough*. Boston: Fort Hill Press, 1909.

Macdonough, Thomas. *Letter from the Secretary of the Navy to the Chairman of the Naval Committee Transmitting Documents from Captain Macdonough.* Washington City: Roger Chew Weightman, 1814.

Mackenzie, William L. *Sketches of Canada and the United States.* London: E. Wilson, 1833.

Madison, James. *The Writings of James Madison.* 9 vols. New York: G. P. Putnam's Sons, 1900–1910.

Mahan, Alfred Thayer. *Commodore Macdonough at Plattsburg, 1814.* New York: North American Review Publishing Co., 1914.

———. "The Negotiations at Ghent in 1814." *American Historical Review* 11 (1905–6): 68–87.

———. *Sea Power in Its Relations to the War of 1812.* 2 vols. Boston: Little, Brown, 1905.

Mahon, John K. *The War of 1812.* Gainesville: University of Florida Press, 1972.

Malcomson, Robert. *Capital in Flames: The American Attack on York, 1813.* Montreal: Robin Brass Studio, 2008.

Mann, Robert. *Wartime Dissent in America: A History and Anthology.* New York: Palgrave Macmillan, 2010.

Manucy, Albert. *Artillery Through the Ages: A Short History of Cannon, Emphasizing Types Used in America.* Washington, DC: United States Government Printing Office, 1962.

Mapp, Alf J. Jr. *Thomas Jefferson: Passionate Pilgrim; The Presidency, the Founding of the University, and the Private Battle.* Lanham, MD: Madison Books, 1991.

Matson, Cathy. *Merchants & Empire: Trading in Colonial New York.* Baltimore: Johns Hopkins University Press, 1994.

Mayo, Bernard. *Henry Clay, Spokesman of the New West.* New York: Archon Books, 1968.

———, ed. *Jefferson Himself: The Personal Narrative of a Many-Sided American.* Charlottesville: University of Virginia Press, 1970.

———, ed. *Instructions to British Ministers by the United States.* American Historical Association Annual Report, 1936.

McCranie, Kevin D. *Utmost Gallantry: The U.S. and Royal Navies at Sea in the War of 1812.* Annapolis, MD: Naval Institute Press, 2011.

McCullough, David. *John Adams.* New York: Simon & Schuster, 2001.

McCusker, John J. *Essays in the Economic History of the New World.* London: Routledge, 2014.

McGrath, Tim. *Give Me a Fast Ship: The Continental Navy and America's Revolution at Sea.* New York: Penguin, 2014.

McRee, Griffith John. *Life and Correspondence of James Iredell.* 2 vols. New York: Peter Smith, 1949.

Meacham, Jon. *Thomas Jefferson: The Art of Power.* New York: Random House, 2012.

———. *American Lion: Andrew Jackson in the White House.* New York: Random House, 2008.

Menard, Russell R. *The Economy of British America, 1607–1789.* Chapel Hill: University of North Carolina Press, 1991.

Middlekauff, Robert. *The Glorious Cause: The American Revolution, 1763–1789*. New York: Oxford University Press, 2005.

Miller, John C. *Triumph of Freedom, 1775–1783*. Boston: Little, Brown, 1948.

Miller, Nathan. *Sea of Glory: Naval History of the American Revolution*. New York: David McKay, 1974.

Mills, Samuel, ed. *The Trial of Cyrus R. Dean*. Burlington, VT: Samuel Mills Printer, 1808.

Miner, Margaret, and Hugh Rawson. *Oxford Dictionary of American Quotations*. 2nd ed. New York: Oxford University Press, 2006.

Monroe, James. *The Writings of James Monroe: Including a Collection of His Public and Private Papers and Correspondence*. Edited by Stanislaus Murray Hamilton. 7 vols. New York: G. P. Putnam's, 1893–1903.

Moreau de St. Méry, M. L. E. *Moreau de St. Méry's American Journey [1793–1798]*. Translated and edited by Kenneth Roberts and Anna M. Roberts. Garden City, NY: Doubleday, 1947.

Morgan, Edmund S., and Helen M. Morgan. *Stamp Act Crisis: Prologue to Revolution*. Chapel Hill, NC: Institute of Early American History and Culture, 1953.

Morris, Richard B., ed. *Encyclopedia of the American History*. 6th edition. New York: HarperCollins, 1996.

Morriss, Roger. *Cockburn and the British Navy in Transition: Admiral Sir George Cockburn, 1772–1853*. Exeter: University of Exeter Press, 1997.

Mostert, Noel. *The Line upon a Wind: The Great War at Sea, 1793–1815*. New York: Norton, 2007.

Moultrie, William. *Memoirs of the American Revolution*. 2 vols in 1. New York: *New York Times*, 1968.

Mueller, Dennis. *Constitutional Democracy*. New York: Oxford University Press, 1996.

Muller, Charles G. *The Proudest Day: Macdonough on Lake Champlain*. New York: John Day, 1960.

Murat, Ines. *Napoléon et le rêve Américain*. Paris: Fayard, 1976.

Nagel, Paul C. *John Quincy Adams: A Public Life, a Private Life*. New York: Knopf, 1997.

Nelson, James L. *George Washington's Secret Navy: How the American Revolution Went to Sea*. New York: McGraw Hill, 2008.

Nelson, Paul David, "Zebulon Montgomery Pike," *ANB*.

Nevins, Allan. *Sail On: The Story of the American Merchant Navy*. New York: United States Lines, 1946.

Niles' Weekly Register. Baltimore: H. Niles, 1814–1837.

Owens, Richard H. *The Neutrality Imperative*. Lanham, MD: University Press of America, 2009.

Pakenham, Thomas. *The Year of Liberty: The Story of the Great Irish Rebellion of 1798*. Englewood Cliffs, NJ: Prentice-Hall, 1969.

Palmer, Peter S. *Historical Sketch of Plattsburgh: From Its First Settlement to Jan. 1, 1893*. Plattsburgh, NY: Plattsburg Republican, 1893.

———. *History of Lake Champlain: From Its First Exploration by the French in 1609 to the Close of the Year 1814*. 4th ed. Harrison, NY: Harbor Hill, 1983.

Patton, R. H. *Patriot Pirates.* New York: Pantheon, 2008.

Paullin, Charles Oscar. *Commodore John Rodgers: Captain, Commodore, and Senior Officer of the American Navy, 1773–1838.* Reprint. New York: Arno, 1980.

Peck, Taylor. *Round-Shot to Rocket: A History of the Washington Navy Yard and U.S. Naval Gun Factory.* Annapolis, MD: U.S. Naval Institute Press, 1949.

Perkins, Bradford. *Castlereagh and Adams: England and the United States, 1812–1823.* Berkeley: University of California Press, 1964.

Perkins, Edwin J. *Economy of Colonial America.* New York: Columbia University Press, 1988.

Peskin, Allan. *Winfield Scott and the Profession of Arms.* Kent, OH: Kent State University Press, 2003.

Pitt, William, Lord Chatham. *Correspondence of William Pitt when Secretary of State with Colonial Governors and Military and Naval Commissioners in America, Edited under the Auspices of the National Society of Colonial Dames of America.* Edited by Gertrude Kimball Selwyn. New York: Macmillan, 1906.

Prince, Carl, and Mollie Keller. *The U.S. Customs Service: A Bicentennial History.* Washington, DC: United States Department of the Treasury, 1989.

Proceedings of the Rhode Island Historical Society, 1877–88. Providence, RI: Printed for the Society, 1888.

Quisenberry, Chenault Anderson. *Kentucky in the War of 1812.* Baltimore: Genealogical Publishing Co., 1969.

Rakove, Jack N. *James Madison and the Creation of the American Republic.* Glenview, IL: Scott, Foresman/Little, Brown, 1990.

Randall, Willard Sterne. *A Little Revenge: Benjamin Franklin and His Son.* Boston: Little, Brown, 1984.

———. *Alexander Hamilton: A Life.* New York: HarperCollins, 2002.

———. *Benedict Arnold: Patriot and Traitor.* New York: William Morrow, 1990.

———. *Ethan Allen: His Life and Times.* New York: W. W. Norton, 2011.

———. *George Washington: A Life.* New York: Henry Holt, 1998.

———. *On Burgoyne's Trail to Saratoga.* Burlington, VT: 2013.

———. *Thomas Jefferson: A Life.* New York: Henry Holt, 1993.

Randall, Willard Sterne, and Nancy Nahra. *American Lives.* Vol. 1, *To 1876.* New York: HarperCollins, 1996.

Rao, Gautham. "The Creation of the American State: Customhouses, Law and Commerce in the Age of Revolution." Ph.D. diss., University of Chicago, 2008.

Rappleye, Charles. *Robert Morris: Financier of the American Revolution.* New York: Simon and Schuster, 2010.

———. *Sons of Providence: The Brown Brothers, the Slave Trade, and the American Revolution.* New York: Simon and Schuster, 2006.

Remini, Robert Vincent. *Andrew Jackson.* New York: Palgrave Macmillan, 2008.

———. *The Battle of New Orleans.* New York: Viking, 1999.

———. *Henry Clay: Statesman for the Union.* New York: W. W. Norton, 1991.

———. "Andrew Jackson" in *ANB.*

———. "Henry Clay" in *ANB*.

Report of the Manuscripts of Earl Bathurst. London: His Majesty's Stationery Office, 1923.

Rey, Marie-Pierre. *Alexander I: The Tsar Who Defeated Napoleon*. Translated by Susan Emmanuel. DeKalb, IL: NIU Press, 2012.

Richardson, James D., ed. *A Compilation of the Messages and Papers of the Presidents, 1789–1902*. Washington, DC: Bureau of National Literature and Art, 1902.

Risjord, Norman K. *Thomas Jefferson*. Madison, WI: Madison House, 1994.

Ritcheson, Charles R. *Aftermath of Revolution: British Policy Toward the United States, 1783–1795*. Dallas: Southern Methodist University Press, 1979.

Roland, Alex, W. Jeffrey Bolster, and Alexander Keyssar. *The Way of the Ship: America's Maritime History Reenvisioned, 1600–2000*. New York: John Wiley, 2007.

Roosevelt, Theodore. *The Naval War of 1812*. 3rd ed. New York: Modern Library, 1999.

Roper, D. M. "DeWitt Clinton" in *ANB*.

Roth, David Morris. *Connecticut's War Governor, Jonathan Trumbull*. Guilford, CT: Pequot Press, 1974.

Royal Commission on Historical Manuscripts. *Report on the Manuscripts of Colonel David Milne Home of Wedderburn Castle, N.B.* London: His Majesty's Stationery Office, 1902.

Rutstein, Michael. *The Privateering Stroke: Salem's Privateers in the War of 1812*. Salem, MA: Rutstein, 2012.

Ryun, Jim, and Sons. *Heroes Among Us: Deep Within Each of Us Dwells the Heart of a Hero*. Shippensburg, PA: Treasure House, 2002.

Scharf, J. Thomas. *History of Baltimore City and County, from the Earliest Period to the Present Day*. Philadelphia: Louis H. Everts, 1881.

Schlesinger, Arthur Meier. *The Colonial Merchants and the American Revolution, 1763–1776*. New York: Facsimile Library, 1939.

Schroeder, Charles. *Commodore John Rodgers: Paragon of the Early American Navy*. Gainesville: University of Florida Press, 2006.

Schroeder, John H. *Battle of Lake Champlain: "A Brilliant and Extraordinary Victory."* Norman, OK: University of Oklahoma Press, 2015.

Scott, James. *Recollections of a Naval Life*. 3 vols. London: R. Bentley, 1834.

Scott, Winfield S. *Memoirs of Lieut. Gen. Scott*. New York: Sheldon, 1864.

Seelye, J. E. and S. A. Littleton, *Voices of the American Indian Experience*. Westport, CT: Greenwood, 2012.

Sheads, Scott S. *The Chesapeake Campaigns 1813–15*. Oxford: Osprey, 1814.

Skaggs, David C., and Gerard T. Althof. *A Signal Victory: The Lake Erie Campaign, 1812–1813*. Annapolis, MD: Naval Institute Press, 2003.

Smith, Joshua M. *Borderland Smuggling: Patriots, Loyalists and Illicit Trade in the Northeast, 1783–1820*. Gainesville: University Press of Florida, 2006.

Smith, Margaret Bayard. *First Forty Years of Washington Society: Portrayed by the Family Letters of Mrs. Samuel Harrison Smith*. Edited by Gaillard Hunt. New York: C. Scribner's Sons, 1906.

———. "Inaugurations." *Ladies Magazine and Literary Gazette*. Vol. 4, No. 12 (Dec. 1831).

Smith, Paul. *Letters of Delegates to the Continental Congress*. 16 vols. Washington, DC: Library of Congress, 1976–1990.

Smith, Richard Norton. *Patriarch: George Washington and the New American Nation*. Boston: Houghton Mifflin, 1993.

Smyth, Albert Henry. *Writings of Benjamin Franklin*. 10 vols. New York: Macmillan, 1906–7.

Snow, Peter. *When Britain Burned the White House*. London: John Murray, 2013.

Soodalter, Ron. "Master Shipbuilders of 1812." *MHQ, The Quarterly Journal of Military History* 28, no. 4 (Summer 2016): 20–22.

Spivak, Burton. *Jefferson's English Crisis: Commerce, Embargo, and the Republican Revolution*. Charlottesville: University of Virginia Press, 1979.

Stagg, J.C.A. *The War of 1812: Conflict for a Continent*. New York: Cambridge University Press, 2012.

Stanley, George F. G. *The War of 1812 Land Operations*. Toronto: Macmillan, 1983.

Stephenson, O. W. "The Supply of Gunpowder in 1776." *AHR* 30, no. 2 (Jan. 1925): 276.

Stiles, Ezra. *Literary Diary*. New Haven: Yale University Press, 1901.

Stivers, Reuben Elmore. *Privateers and Volunteers: The Men and Women of Our Reserve Naval Force, 1766–1866*. Annapolis, MD: Naval Institute Press, 1975.

Stuart, Isaac William. *Life of Jonathan Trumbull, Sen., Governor of Connecticut*. Boston: Crocker and Brewster, 1859.

Sugden, John. *Tecumseh: A Life*. New York: Henry Holt, 1997.

Sylvester, Nathaniel Bartlett. *History of Saratoga County, New York*. Philadelphia: Everts and Ensign, 1878.

Syrett, David. *The Royal Navy in European Waters during the American Revolutionary War*. Columbia: University of South Carolina Press, 1998.

Taylor, Alan. *The Civil War of 1812: American Citizens, British Subjects, Irish Rebels & Indian Allies*. New York: Vintage, 2010.

Taylor, Elizabeth D. *A Slave in the White House: Paul Jennings and the Madisons*. New York: Palgrave Macmillan, 2012.

Teeling, Charles Hamilton. *History of the Irish Rebellion of 1798*. Shannon: Irish University Press, 1972.

Toll, Ian W. *Six Frigates: The Epic History of the Founding of the U.S. Navy*. New York: W. W. Norton, 2006.

Tombs, Robert. *The English and Their History*. New York: Alfred A. Knopf, 2015.

Trees, Andrew S. *The Founding Fathers and the Politics of Character*. Princeton, NJ: Princeton University Press, 2004.

Truxes, T. M. *Defying Empire: Trading with the Enemy*. New Haven, CT: Yale University Press, 1993.

Tucker, Glenn. *Tecumseh: A Vision of Glory*. Indianapolis: Bobbs-Merrill, 1956.

Tucker, Spencer C., ed. *U.S. Leadership in Wartime: Clashes, Controversy, and Compromise*. Santa Barbara, CA: ABC-CLIO, 2009.

Tucker, Spencer C., et al., eds. *The Encyclopedia of the War of 1812: A Political, Social and Military History*. Santa Barbara, CA: ABC-CLIO, 2012.

Tucker, Spencer C., and Frank T. Reuter. *Injured Honor: The Chesapeake-Leopard Affair, June 22, 1807*. Annapolis, MD: Naval Institute Press, 1996.

Turner, Wesley B. *British Generals in the War of 1812: High Command in the Canadas*, Montreal: McGill, 1999.

Unger, Harlow Giles. *Henry Clay*. New York: DaCapo, 2015.

———. *John Quincy Adams*. New York: DaCapo, 2012.

United States Navy. RG 24. Navy Deck Logs. USS *Surprise* (*Eagle*) 8-21-1814 to 9-29-1814. Penned by Daniel Records, acting sailing master.

Utt, Ronald. *Ships of Oak, Guns of Iron: The War of 1812 and the Forging of the American Navy*. Washington, DC: Regnery, 2013.

Van Vlack. *Silas Deane: Revolutionary War Diplomat and Politician*. Jefferson, NC: McFarland, 2013.

Vermont. *Records of the Governor and Council of the State of Vermont*. Edited by E. P. Walton. 8 vols. Montpelier, VT: J. and J. M. Poland, 1873.

Vogel, Steve. *Through the Perilous Fight: Six Weeks That Saved the Nation*. New York: Random House, 2013.

Volo, James M. *Blue Water Patriots: The American Revolution Afloat*. Lanham, MD: Rowman and Littlefield, 2006.

Walker, Adam. *Journal of the Two Campaigns of the Fourth Regiment of U. S. Infantry*. Keene, NH: Sentinel Press, 1816.

Warden, G. B. *Boston, 1689–1776*. Boston: Little, Brown, 1970.

Washington, George. *Papers*. Revolutionary War Series, edited by Philander G. Chase et al, 24 vols. to date, 1985–; Presidential Series, edited by Edward G. Lengel et al, 17 vols. to date. Charlottesville, Va.: University of Virginia Press, 1983–.

Wellington, Arthur Wesley, Duke of. *Supplementary Dispatches and Memoranda*. Vol. 9. *South of France, Embassy to Paris and Congress of Vienna*. London: John Murray, 1862.

West, Wallace. *Down to the Sea in Ships: The Story of the United States Merchant Marine*. New York: Noble and Noble, 1947.

Wharton, Francis. *Revolutionary Diplomatic Correspondence of the United States*. 6 vols. Washington, DC: Government Printing Office, 1889.

Whipple, A.B.C. *To the Shores of Tripoli: The Birth of the United States Navy and Marines*. New York: William Morrow, 1991.

Wickwire, Franklin, and Mary. *Cornwallis: The Imperial Years*. Chapel Hill: University of North Carolina Press, 1980.

Williams, John S. *History of the Invasion and Capture of Washington, and of the Event Which Preceded and Followed*. New York: Harper and Brothers, 1857.

Willis, Sam. *The Struggle for Sea Power: A Naval History of the American Revolution*. New York: W. W. Norton, 2015.

Wills, Garry. *James Madison*. New York: Times Books, 2002.

Wilson, David A. *United Irishmen, United States: Immigrant Radicals in the Early Republic.* Ithaca, NY: Cornell University Press, 1998.

Withers, Alexander Scott, ed. *Chronicles of Border Warfare, or, A History of the Settlement by the Whites of North-Western Virginia, and of the Indian Wars and Massacres.* Reprint. New York: Arno Press, 1971.

Wood, Gordon. *Empire of Liberty: A History of the Early Republic, 1789–1819.* New York: Oxford University Press, 2009.

WPA Writers Program, New York City. *A Maritime History of New York.* New York: Works Projects Administration, 1941. Repr. New York: Haskell House Publishers, 1973.

Wroth, L. Kinvin and Hiller Zobel. *Legal Papers of JA.* 3 vols. Cambridge, MA: Harvard University Press, 1965.

Yanik, Anthony J. *The Fall and Recapture of Detroit in the War of 1812: In Defense of William Hull.* Detroit: Wayne State University Press, 2012.

Yonge, Charles Duke. *The Life and Administration of Robert Banks, Second Earl of Liverpool.* 3 vols. London: Macmillan, 1868.

York, Neil L. "Clandestine Aid and the American Revolutionary War Effort: A Reexamination." *Military Affairs* 43, no. 1 (February 1979): 26–30.

Young, Dwight and Margaret Johnson. *Dear First Lady: Letters to the White House.* Washington, DC: National Geographic Society, 2008.

Young, James S. *Washington Community, 1800–1828.* New York: Columbia University Press, 1966.

INDEX